THE EASY EIGHTIES FAKE BOOK

100 Songs in  the Key of C

THE EASY EIGHTIES FAKE BOOK

ISBN 978-1-4234-6941-4

7777 W. BLUEMOUND RD. P.O. BOX 13819 MILWAUKEE, WI 53213

For all works contained herein:
Unauthorized copying, arranging, adapting, recording, Internet posting, public performance,
or other distribution of the printed music in this publication is an infringement of copyright.
Infringers are liable under the law.

Visit Hal Leonard Online at
www.halleonard.com

THE EASY EIGHTIES FAKE BOOK

CONTENTS

4	INTRODUCTION
5	Abracadabra
8	Against All Odds (Take a Look at Me Now)
14	Against the Wind
11	Alone
16	Another One Bites the Dust
18	Baby, Come to Me
20	The Best of Times
22	Brass in Pocket
24	Call Me
26	Candle in the Wind
29	Cars
30	Centerfold
34	Come On Eileen
33	Crimson and Clover
36	Cruel Summer
38	(I Just) Died in Your Arms
44	Doin' It (All for My Baby)
46	Don't Know Much
41	Don't You (Forget About Me)
48	Don't You Want Me
50	Down Under
52	Easy Lover
54	Ebony and Ivory
56	Endless Love
58	Every Breath You Take
64	The Flame
66	Footloose
68	Free Fallin'
70	Girls Just Want to Have Fun
61	Gloria
72	Glory of Love
75	Hard Habit to Break
78	The Heat Is On
80	Heaven
86	Hello
88	Here Comes My Girl
83	Higher Love
90	Hold On Loosely
92	Home Sweet Home
94	Hot Hot Hot
96	How Will I Know
98	Hurts So Good
100	I Just Called to Say I Love You
103	I Love Rock 'n Roll
106	I'll Be There for You
108	If You Love Somebody Set Them Free
111	In a Big Country
114	Jack and Diane
118	Jessie's Girl
121	Jump
124	Just Can't Get Enough

126	Keep On Loving You	192	Stages
128	Lady in Red	193	(Just Like) Starting Over
130	Longer	196	Straight Up
132	Love Shack	198	Stray Cat Strut
134	Lovergirl	200	Sweet Dreams (Are Made of This)
140	Maneater	202	Take My Breath Away (Love Theme)
137	Material Girl	208	Take On Me
142	Mickey	210	This Could Be the Night
145	Missing You	205	Thriller
148	Nine to Five	214	Time After Time
150	Oh Sherrie	216	(I've Had) The Time of My Life
158	On My Own	219	Total Eclipse of the Heart
153	Once in a Lifetime	224	Two Hearts
160	One Thing Leads to Another	230	Up Where We Belong
162	Owner of a Lonely Heart	227	Video Killed the Radio Star
168	Physical	232	Walk Like an Egyptian
165	Pour Some Sugar on Me	234	Walking on Sunshine
170	Private Eyes	238	The Warrior
172	Rebel Yell	241	We Are the World
176	Red, Red Wine	244	What I Like About You
177	Rock the Casbah	246	When I Think of You
180	Sailing	248	Who Can It Be Now?
184	Sister Christian	250	You Give Love a Bad Name
186	Smooth Operator	253	CHORD SPELLER
188	Somewhere Out There		
189	Southern Cross		

INTRODUCTION

What Is a Fake Book?

A fake book has one-line music notation consisting of melody, lyrics and chord symbols. This lead sheet format is a "musical shorthand" that is an invaluable resource for all musicians—hobbyists to professionals.
Here's how *The Easy Eighties Fake Book* differs from most standard fake books:

- All songs are in the key of C.

- Many of the melodies have been simplified.

- Only five basic chord types are used—major, minor, seventh, diminished and augmented.

- The music notation is larger for ease of reading.

In the event that you haven't used chord symbols to create accompaniment, or your experience is limited, a chord speller chart is included at the back of the book to help you get started.

Have fun!

ABRACADABRA

Words and Music by
STEVE MILLER

Copyright © 1982 by Sailor Music

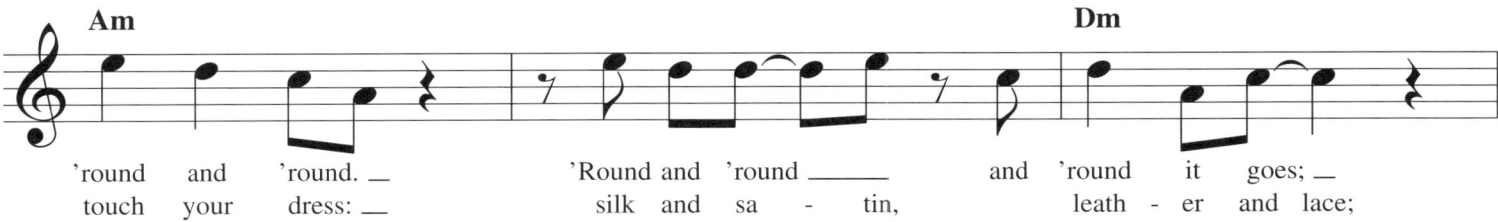
I heat up, I can't cool down. You got me spinnin'
I feel the mag-ic in your ca-ress; I feel mag-ic when I

'round and 'round. 'Round and 'round and 'round it goes;
touch your dress: silk and sa-tin, leath-er and lace;

where it stops, no-bod-y knows. Ev-'ry time you
black pant-ies with an an-gel's face. I see mag-ic

call my name, I heat up like a burn-in' flame,
in your eyes, I hear the mag-ic in your sighs.

burn-in' flame, full of de-sire.
Just when I think I'm gon-na get a-way,

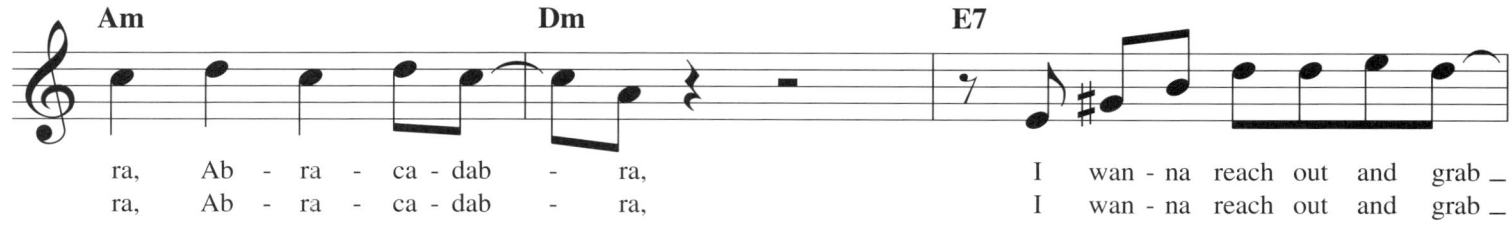
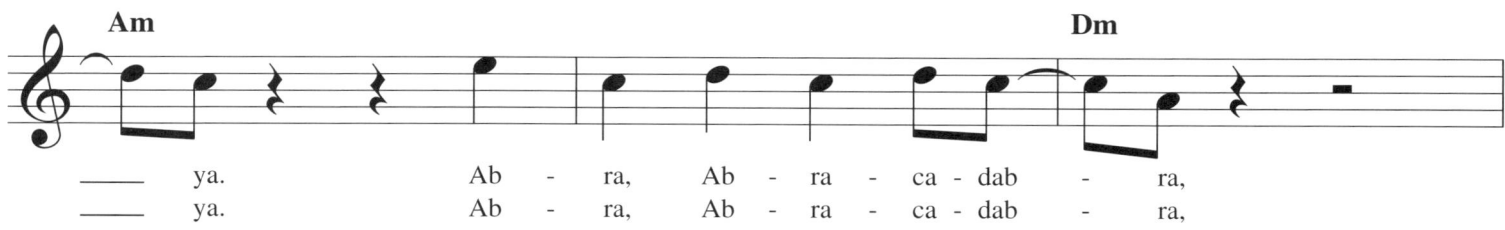

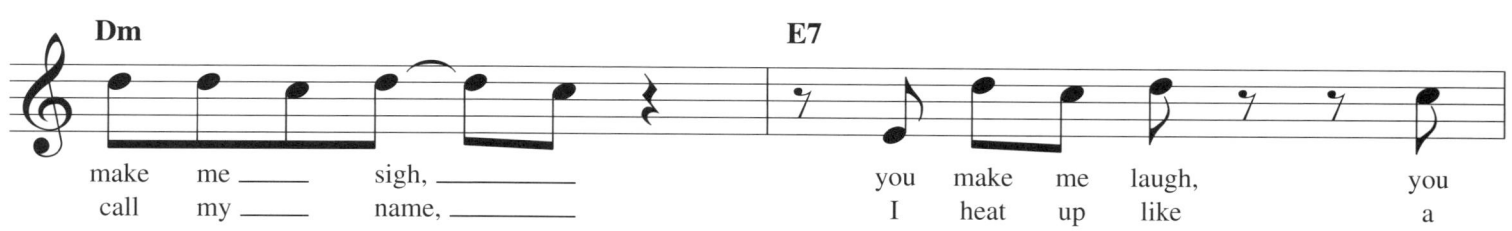

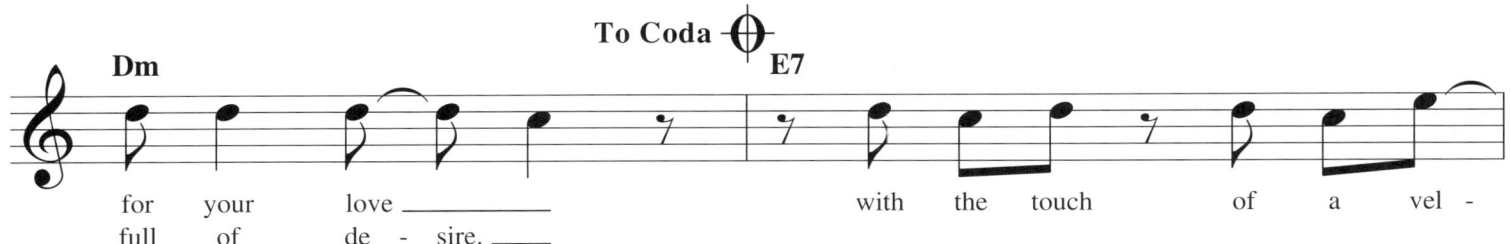
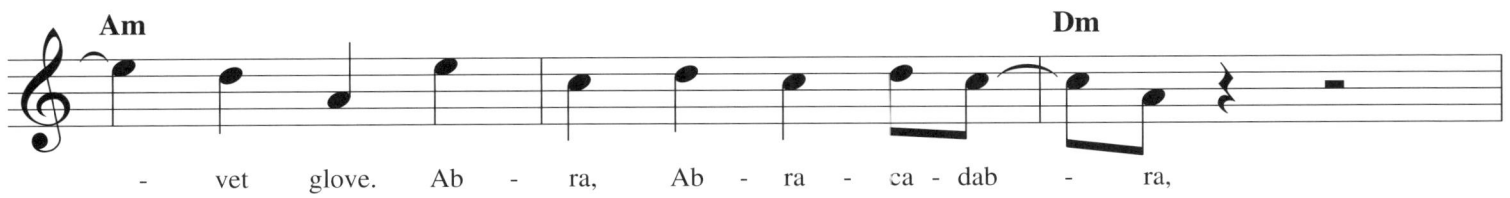

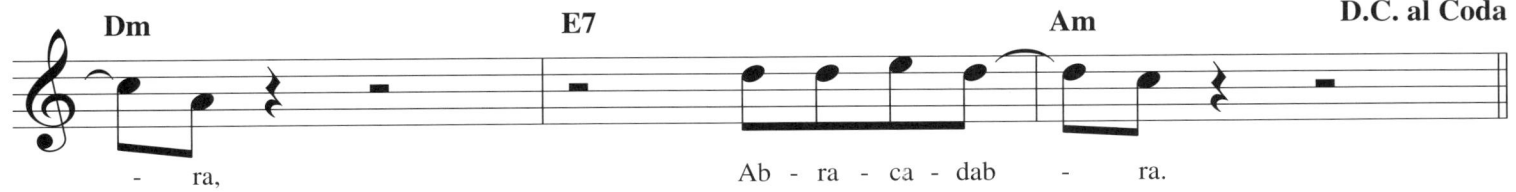
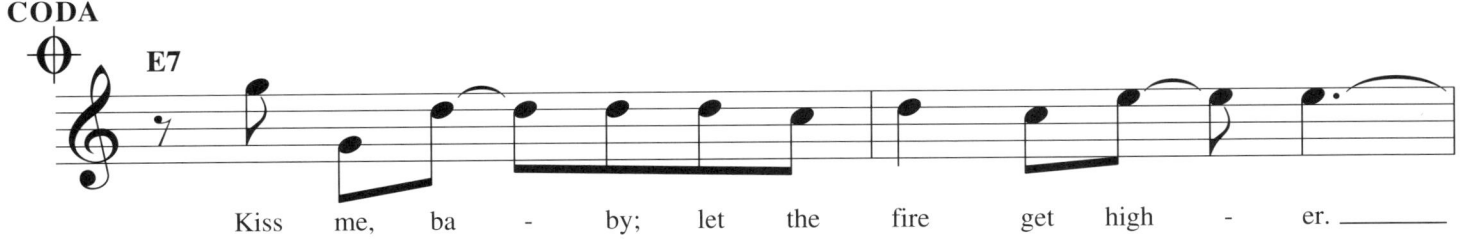
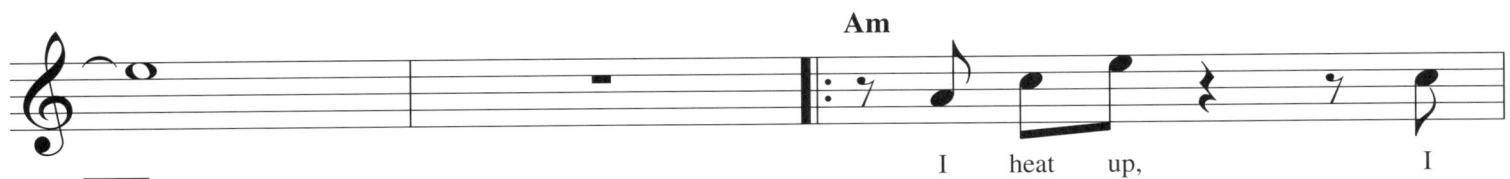

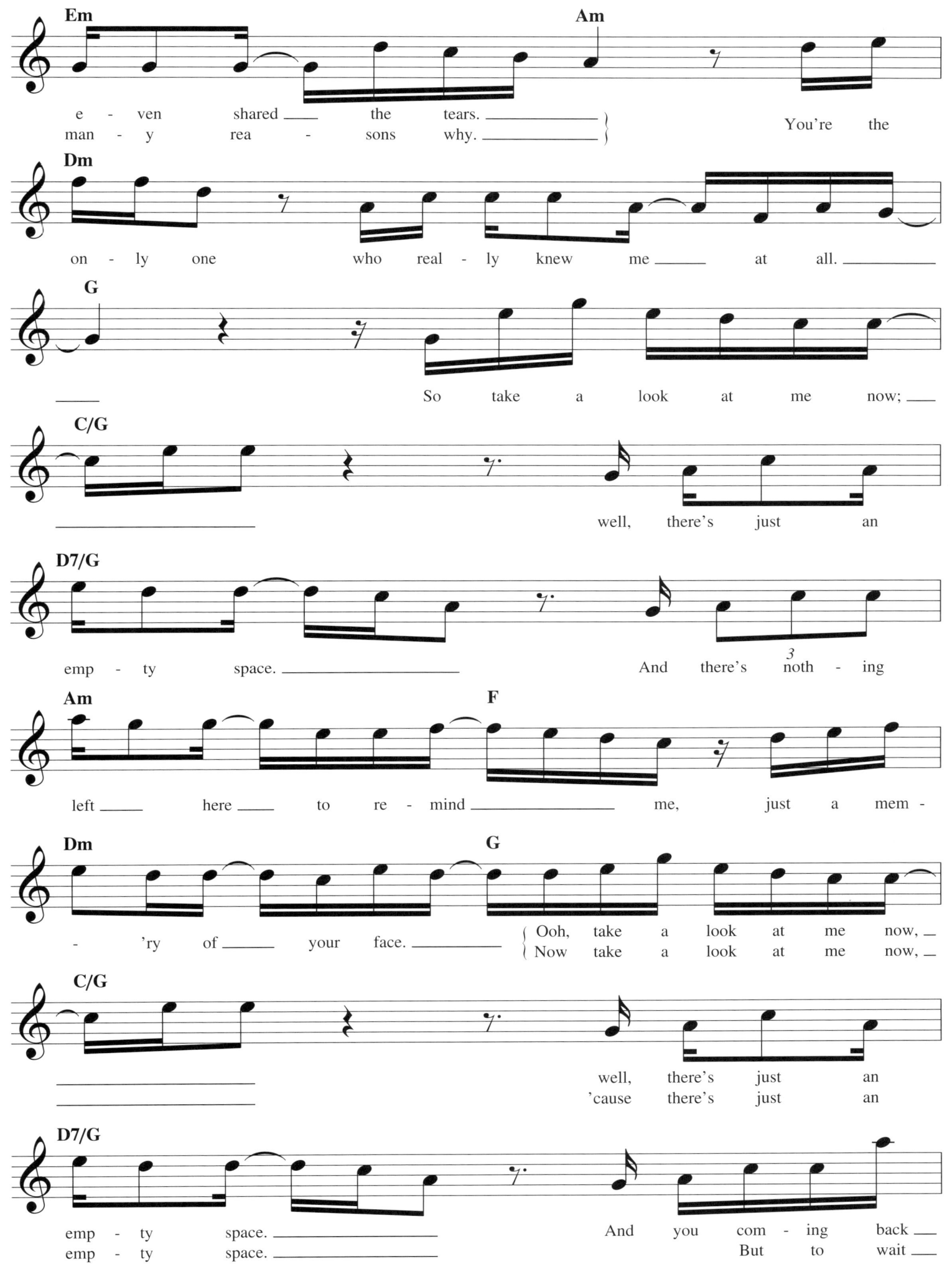

ALONE

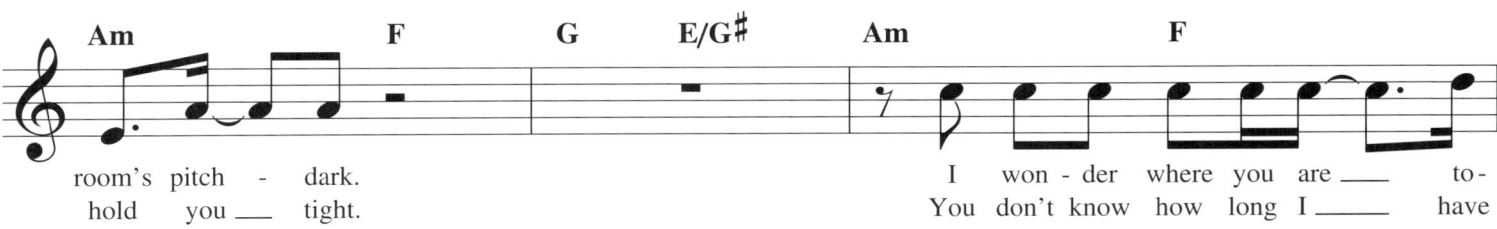

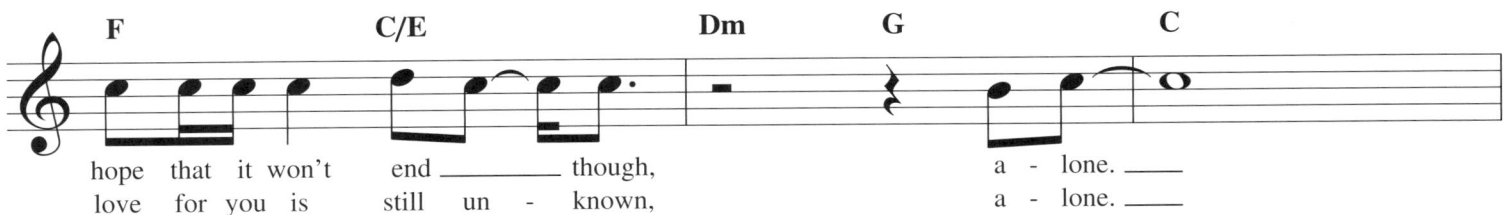

12

'Til now, I always got by on my own.

I never really cared until I met you, and now it

chills me to the bone. How do I get you alone?

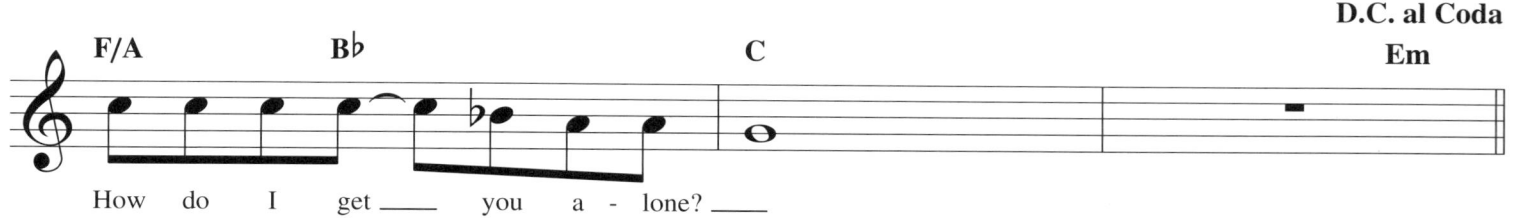
How do I get you alone?

D.C. al Coda

CODA

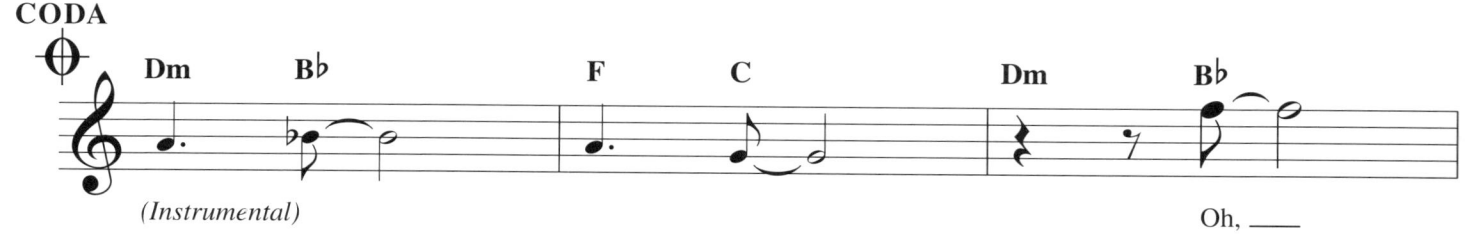
(Instrumental) Oh,

oh, oh. 'Til now, I always got by on my own.

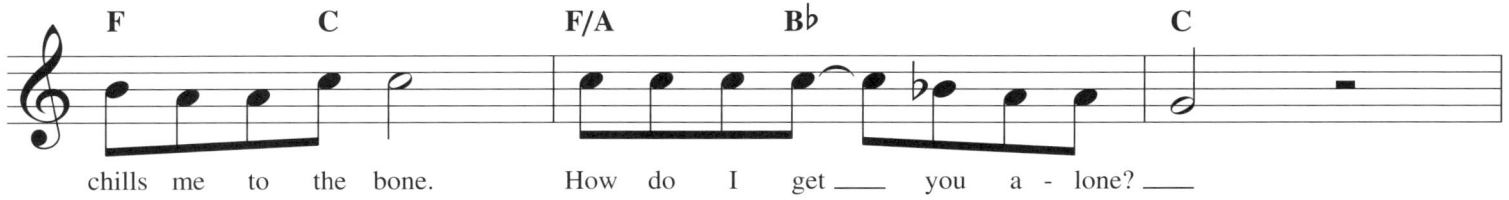
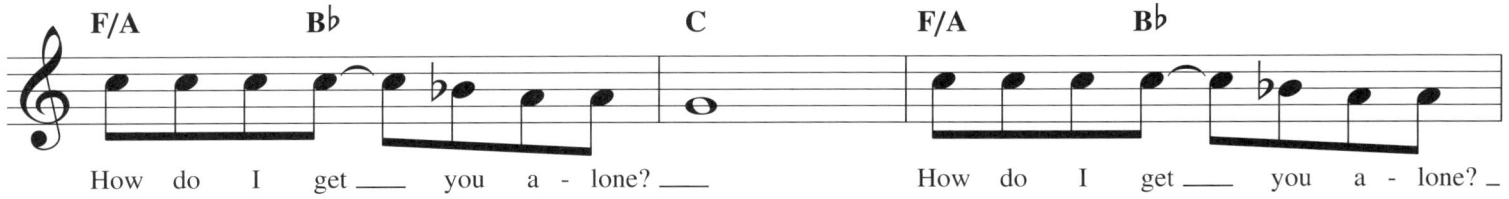
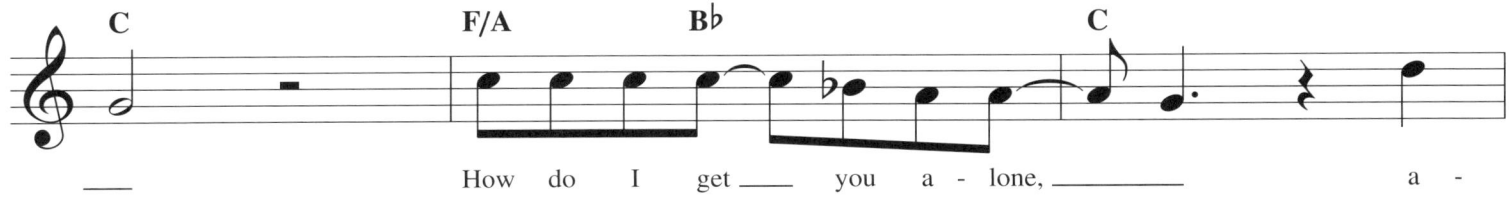
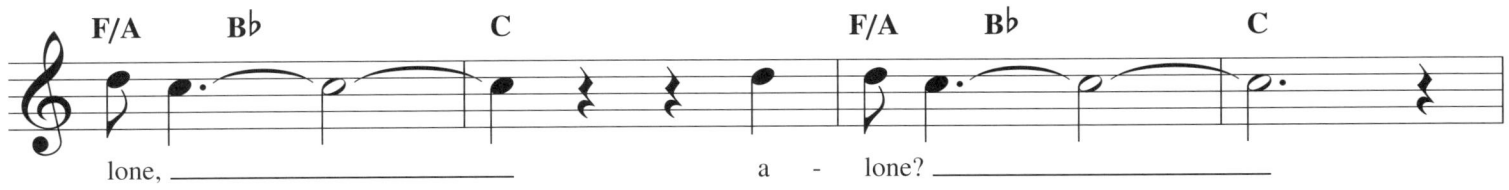
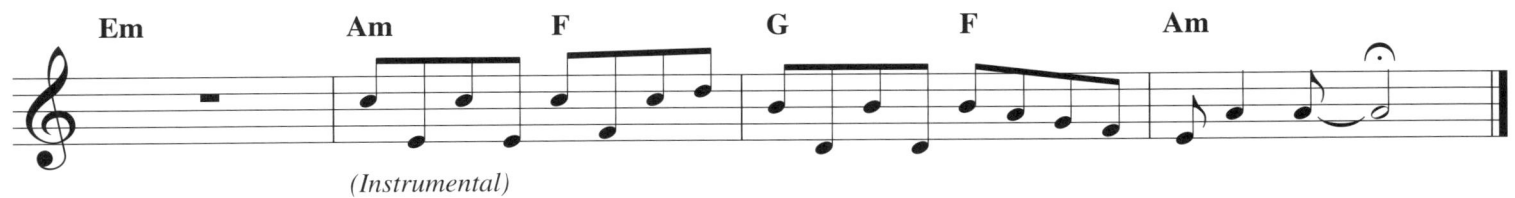

AGAINST THE WIND

Copyright © 1980 Gear Publishing Co.

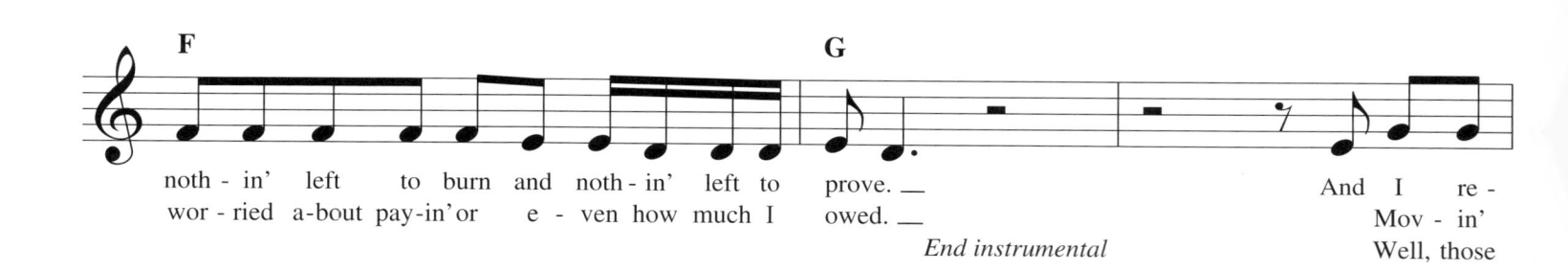

Words and Music by
BOB SEGER

Medium Rock beat

It seems like yes - ter - day, but it was long a -
And the years rolled slow - ly past. And I found my - self a -
Instrumental

go. ___ Ja - ney was love - ly. She was the queen of my nights,
lone, ___ sur - round - ed by stran - gers I thought were my friends.

there in the dark - ness with the ra - di - o play - in' low, ___ and
I found my - self ___ fur - ther and fur - ther from my ___ home, ___ and

the se - crets that we shared. the moun - tains that we moved, ___
I guess I lost my way. There were oh so man - y roads. ___

I was caught like a wild fire out of con - trol ___ till there was
liv - in' to run and run - nin' to live. ___ Nev - er

noth - in' left to burn and noth - in' left to prove. ___ And I re -
wor - ried a - bout pay - in' or e - ven how much I owed. ___ Mov - in'
End instrumental Well, those

ANOTHER ONE BITES THE DUST

© 1980 QUEEN MUSIC LTD.
All Rights for the U.S. and Canada
Controlled and Administered by BEECHWOOD MUSIC CORP.
All Rights for the world excluding the U.S. and Canada
Controlled and Administered by EMI MUSIC PUBLISHING LTD.

Words and Music by
JOHN DEACON

Steady Rock

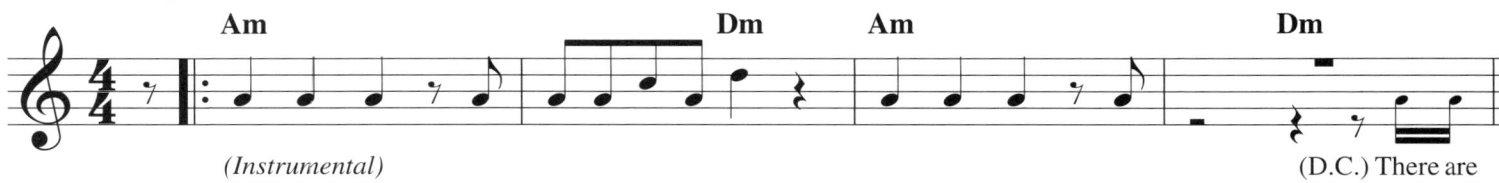
(Instrumental)   (D.C.) There are

Steve walks war-i-ly down the street with the brim pulled way down low.
How do you think I'm going to get a-long with-out you, when you're gone? You
plen-ty of ways you can hurt a man, and bring him to the ground. You can

Ain't no sound but the sound of his feet; ma-chine guns read-y to go. Are you
took me for ev-'ry-thing that I had and kicked me out on my own. Are you
beat him, you can cheat him, you can treat him bad and leave him when he's down. But I'm

read-y, hey! Are you read-y for this? Are you hang-ing on the edge of your seat?
hap-py? Are you sat - is - fied? How long can you stand the heat?
read-y, yes I'm read-y for you. I'm stand-ing on my own two feet.

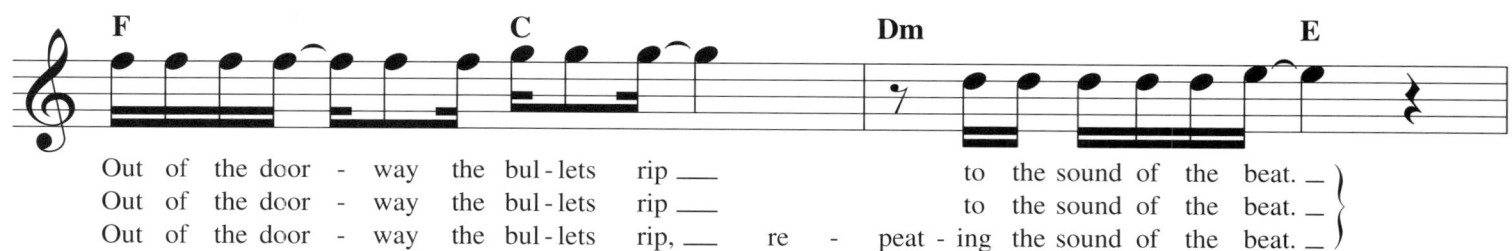
Out of the door - way the bul-lets rip to the sound of the beat.
Out of the door - way the bul-lets rip to the sound of the beat.
Out of the door - way the bul-lets rip, re - peat-ing the sound of the beat.

An - oth-er one bites the dust. An -

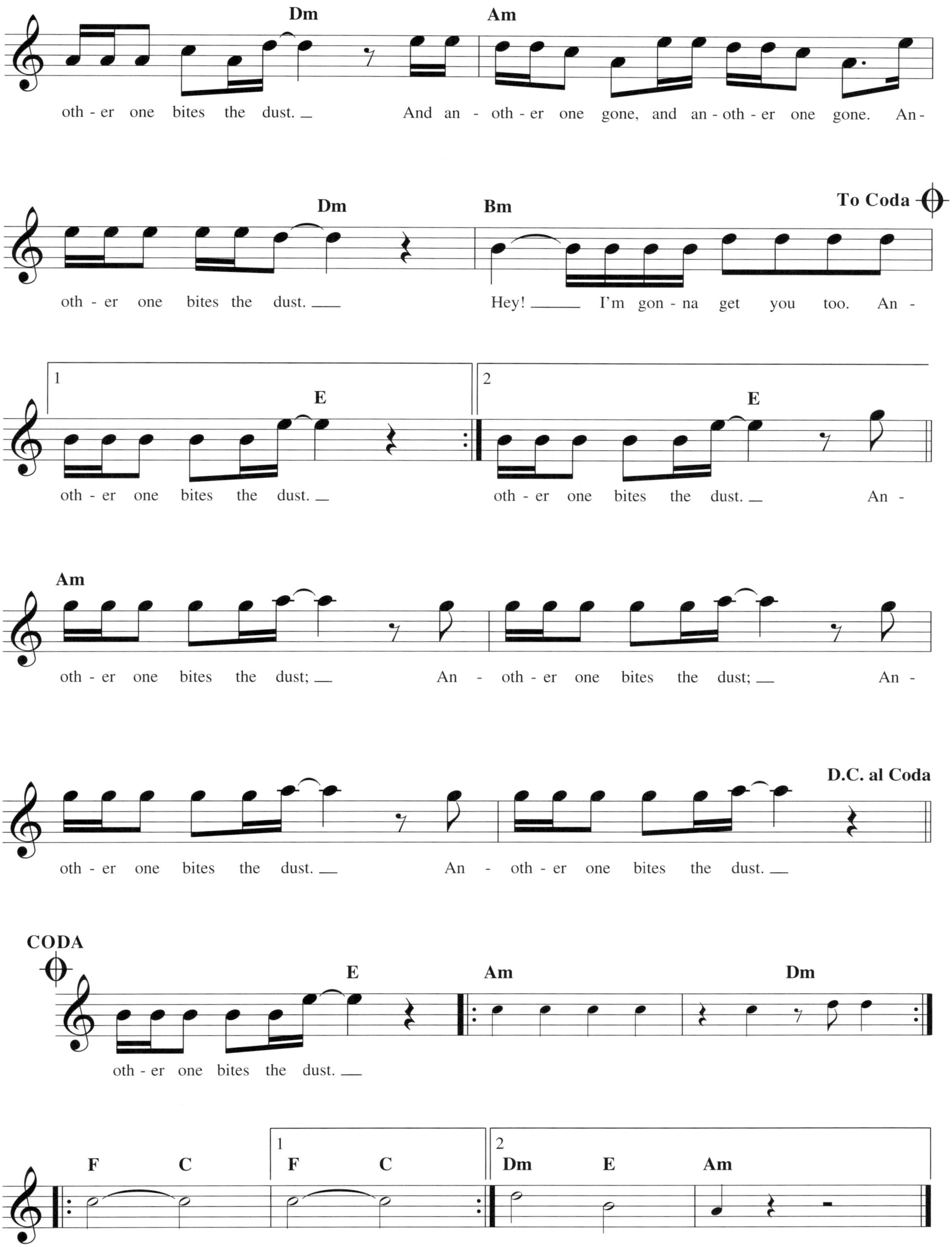

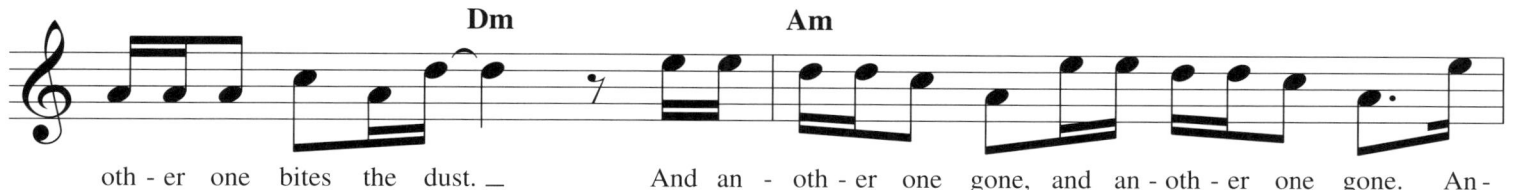
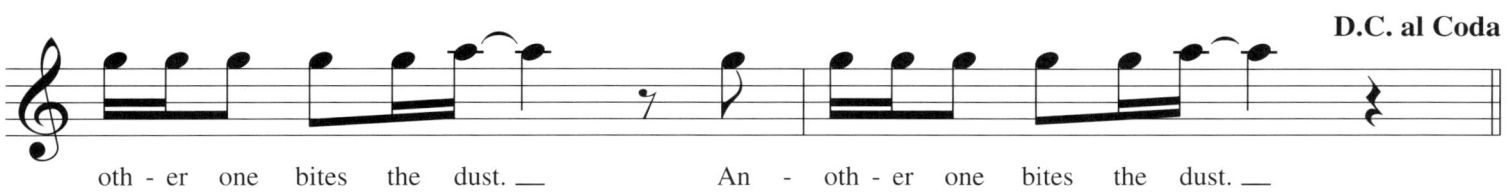
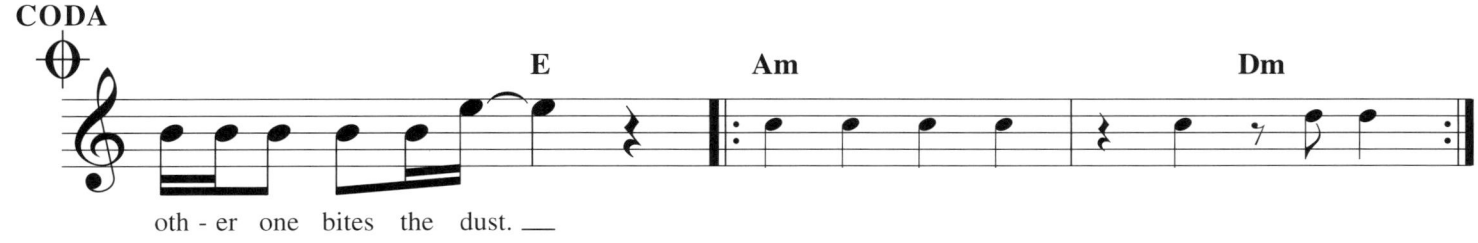
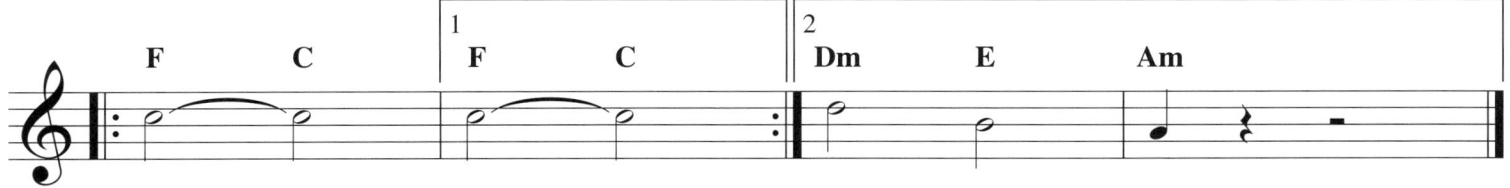

BABY, COME TO ME

Words and Music by
ROD TEMPERTON

Copyright © 1981 RODSONGS
All Rights Administered by ALMO MUSIC CORP.

Think-in' back in time, when love was on-ly in the mind, I re-a-
Spend-in' ev-'ry dime to keep you talk-in' on the line, that's how it

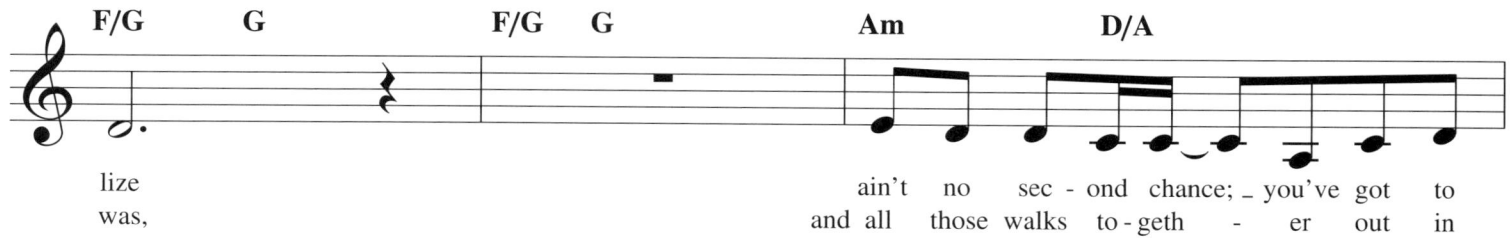
lize
was, ain't no sec-ond chance; you've got to
and all those walks to-geth-er out in

hold on to ro-mance, Don't let it slide. There's a
an-y kind of weath-er, just be-cause. There's a

spe-cial kind of mag-ic in the air when you
brand new way of look-ing at your life, when you

find an-oth-er heart that needs to share.
know that love is stand-ing by your side. Ba-by

come to me; let me put my arms a-round you. This was

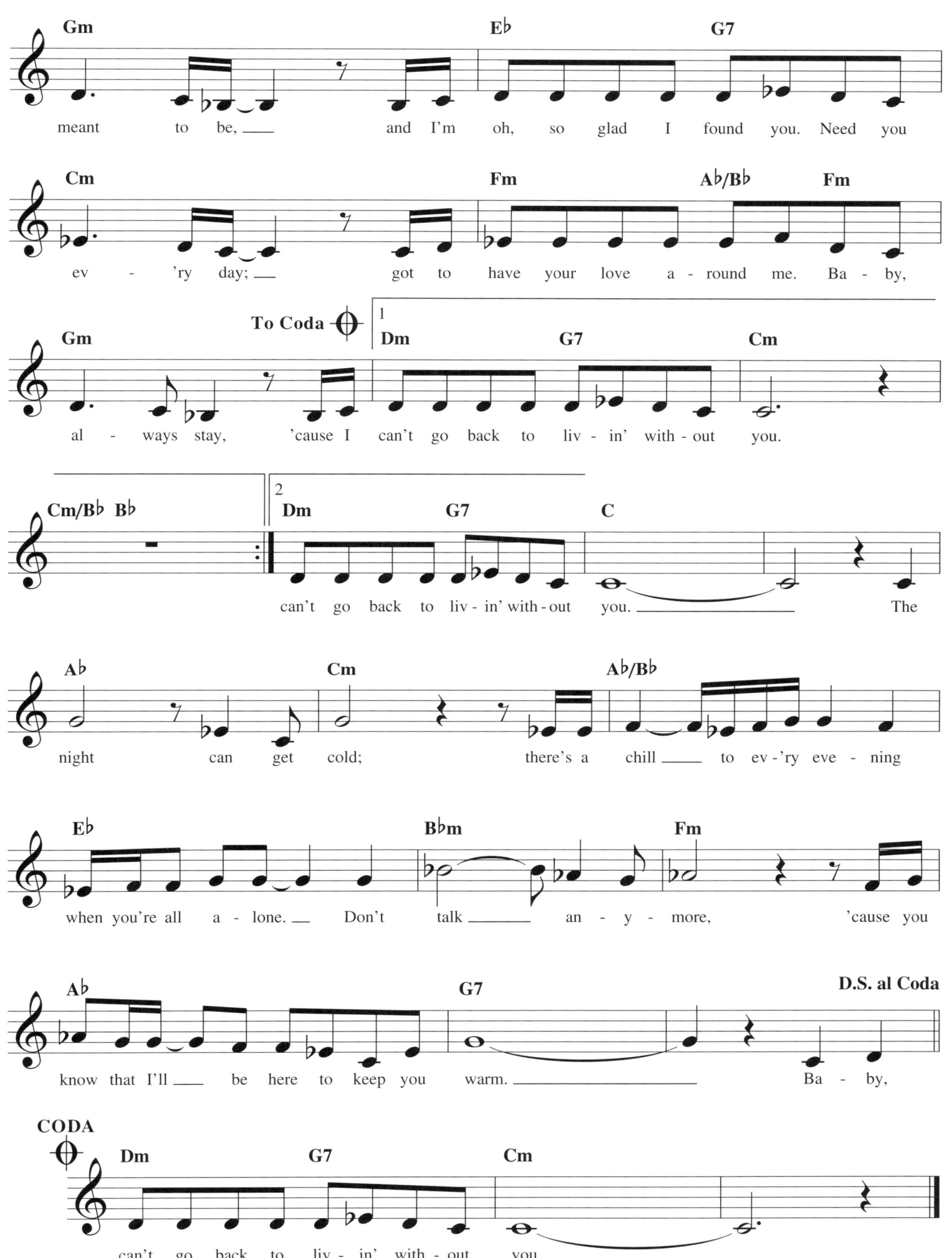

THE BEST OF TIMES

Copyright © 1981 by Stygian Songs

Words and Music by
DENNIS DeYOUNG

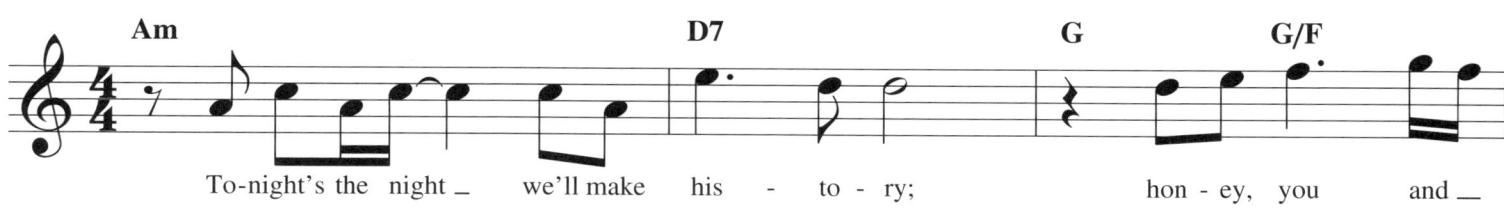

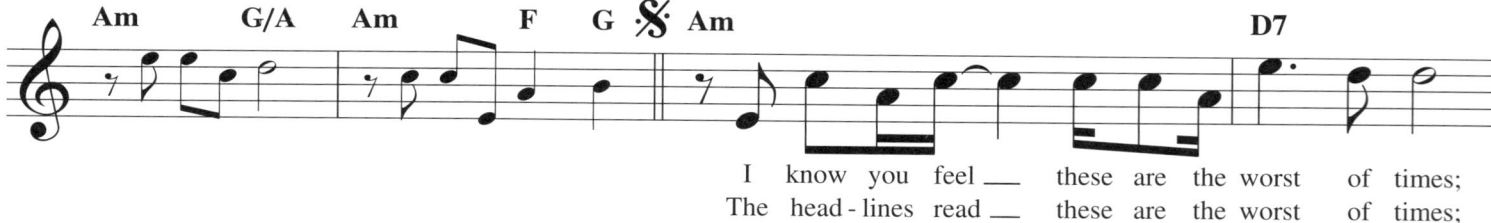
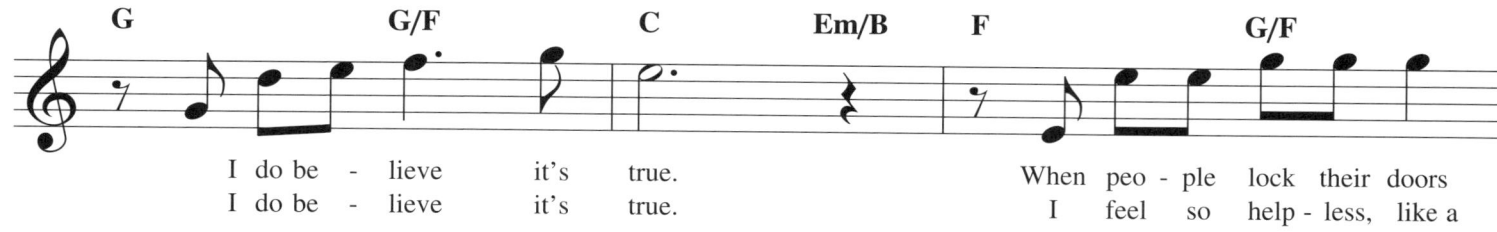

BRASS IN POCKET

© 1979 EMI MUSIC PUBLISHING LTD. trading as CLIVE BANKS SONGS
All Rights for the United States and Canada
 Controlled and Administered by EMI APRIL MUSIC INC.
All Rights for the World excluding the United States and Canada
 Controlled and Administered by EMI MUSIC PUBLISHING LTD.

Words and Music by CHRISSIE HYNDE
and JAMES HONEYMAN-SCOTT

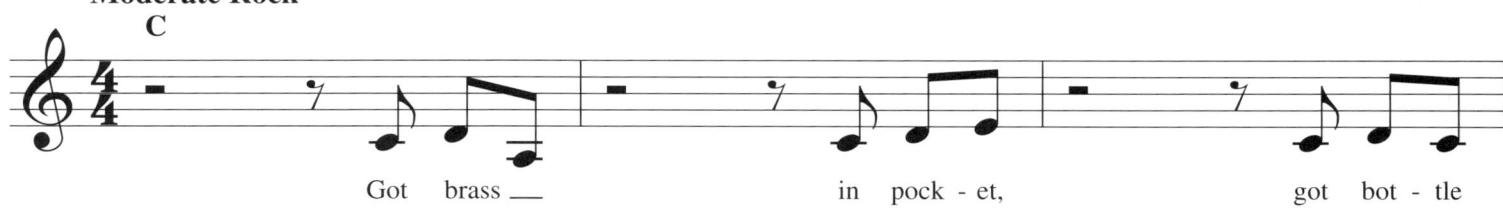
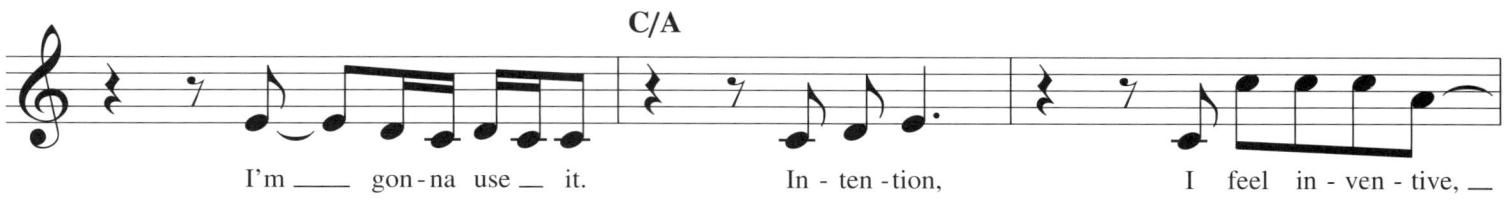

legs; gon-na use my style, gon-na use my side-step, gon-na use my
fin-gers, gon-na use my, my, my i-mag-i-na-tion, 'cause
C
C/A
I gon-na make you see there's no-bod-y else here no one like
F
G
To Coda
me. I'm spe-cial, so spe-cial, I got-ta have some of your at-
1
2
D.S. al Coda
ten-tion, give it to me. ten-tion, give it to me, 'cause
CODA
C
ten-tion, give it to me.
Oh oh oh and when you walk.

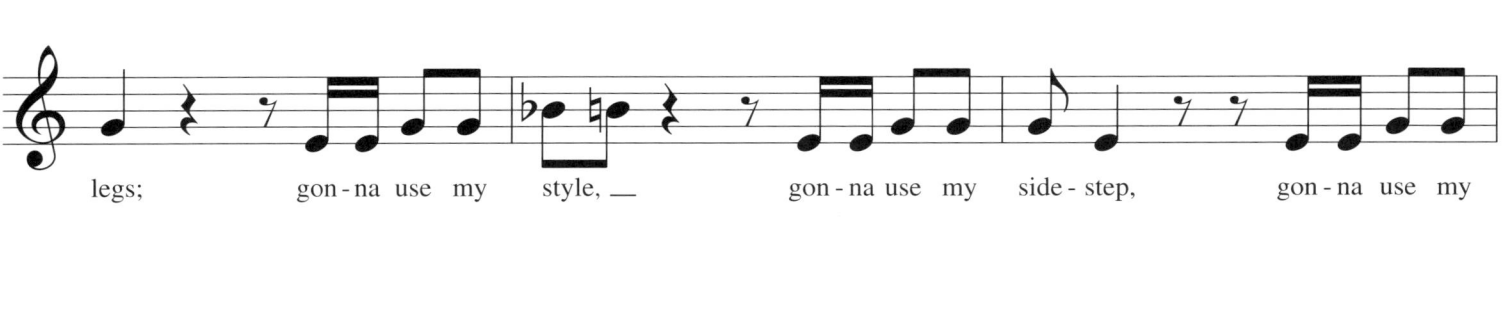

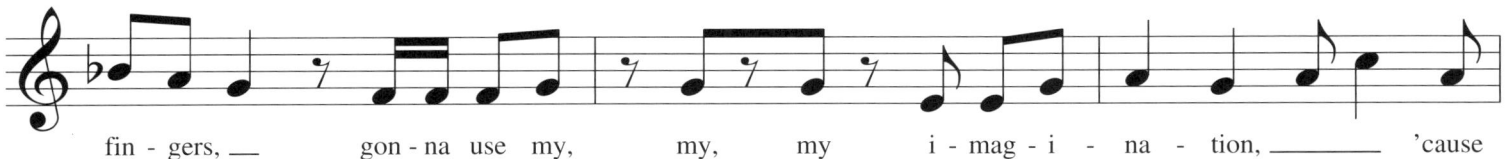

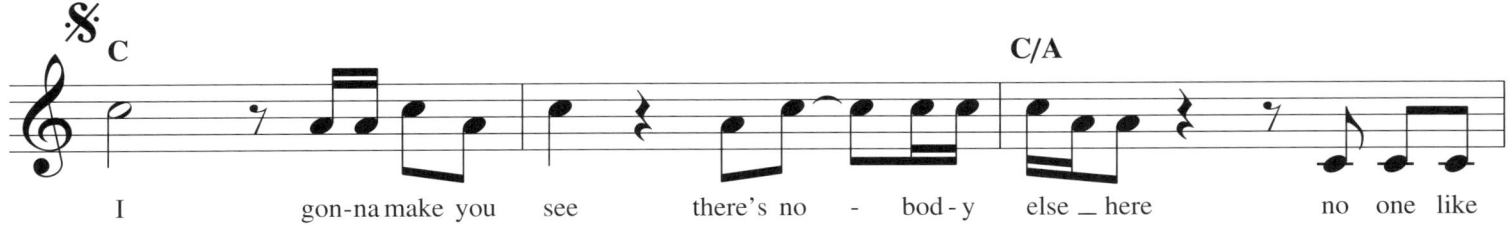

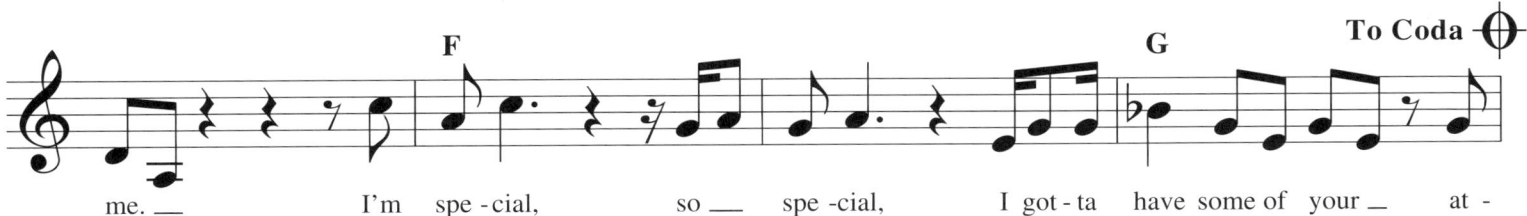

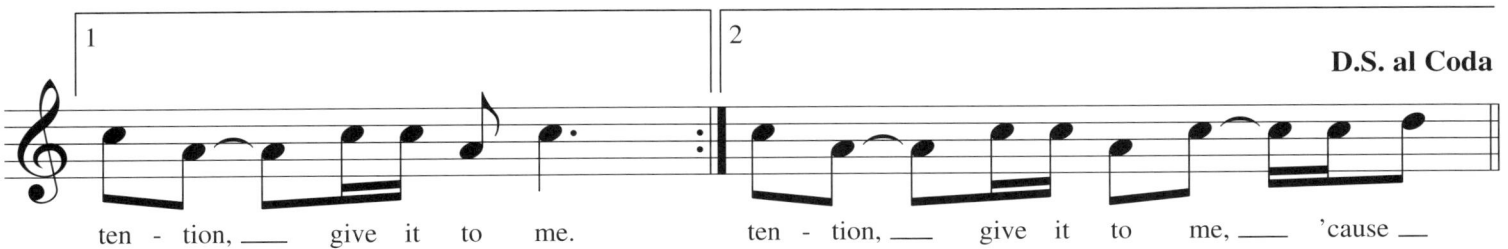

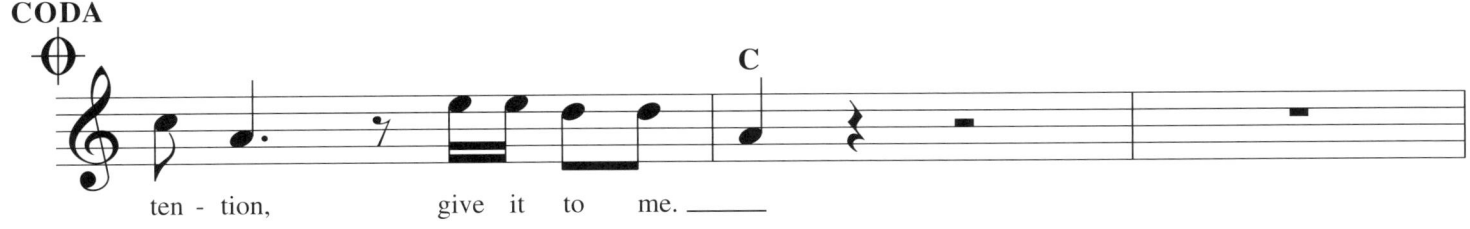

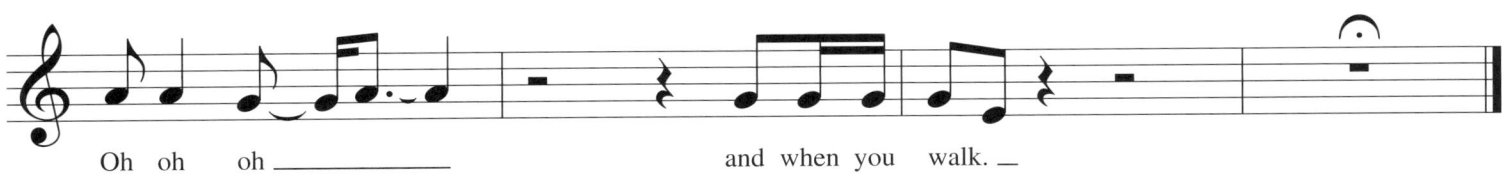

CALL ME
from the Paramount Motion Picture AMERICAN GIGOLO

Copyright © 1980 Sony/ATV Music Publishing LLC, Chrysalis Music and Monster Island Music
All Rights on behalf of Sony/ATV Music Publishing LLC
  Administered by Sony/ATV Music Publishing LLC, 8 Music Square West, Nashville, TN 37203
All Rights on behalf of Monster Island Music Administered by Chrysalis Music

Words by DEBORAH HARRY
Music by GIORGIO MORODER

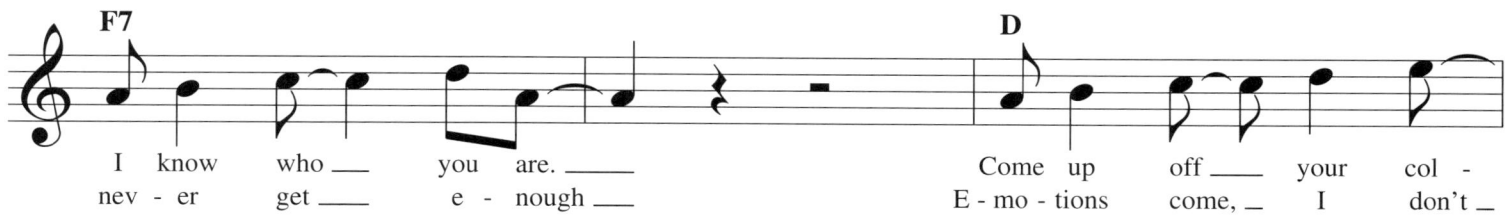

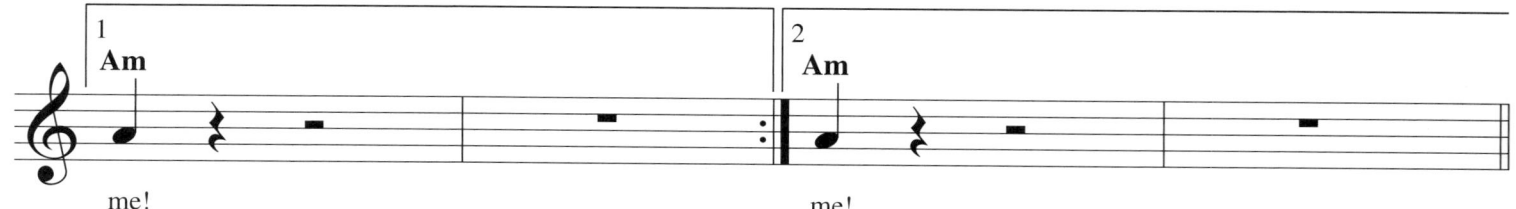

CANDLE IN THE WIND

Words and Music by ELTON JOHN and BERNIE TAUPIN

Copyright © 1973 UNIVERSAL/DICK JAMES MUSIC LTD.
Copyright Renewed
All Rights in the United States and Canada Controlled and Administered by
UNIVERSAL - SONGS OF POLYGRAM INTERNATIONAL, INC.

In a slow 2

Good-bye, Nor-ma Jean. Though I nev-er knew you at all,
Lone-li-ness was tough, the tough-est role you ev-er played.

you had the grace to hold your-self while those a-round you crawled.
Holly-wood cre-at-ed a su - per-star and pain was the price you paid.

They crawled out of the wood-work and they whis-pered
And e - ven when you died, oh, the press

in - to your brain. They sent you on a tread - mill and they
still hound - ed you. All the pa - pers had to say was that

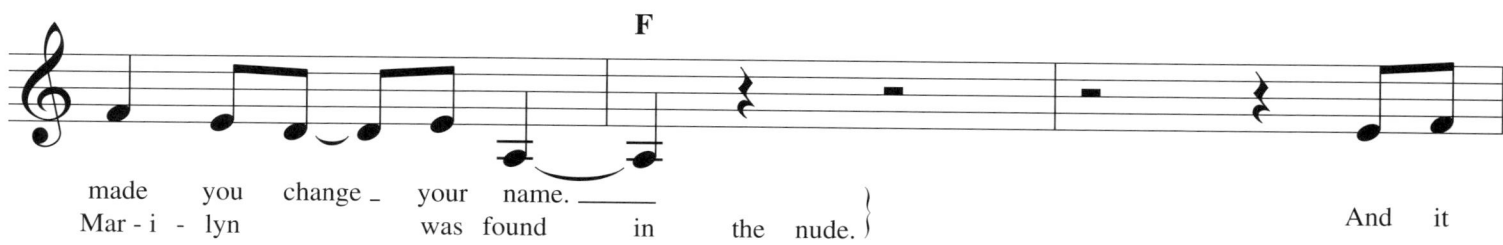

made you change your name.
Mar - i - lyn was found in the nude. And it

seems to me you lived your life like a can - dle in the wind,

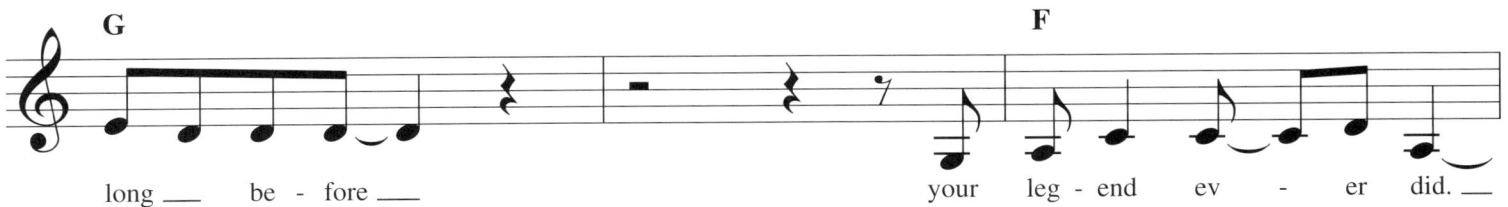

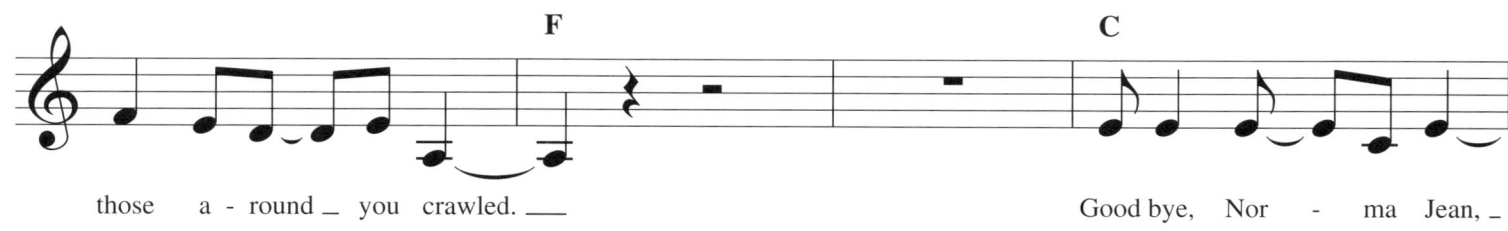

CARS

Words and Music by GARY NUMAN

Copyright © 1979 UNIVERSAL/MOMENTUM MUSIC 3 LTD.
All Rights in the U.S. and Canada Controlled and Administered by
UNIVERSAL - SONGS OF POLYGRAM INTERNATIONAL, INC.

Synth Pop

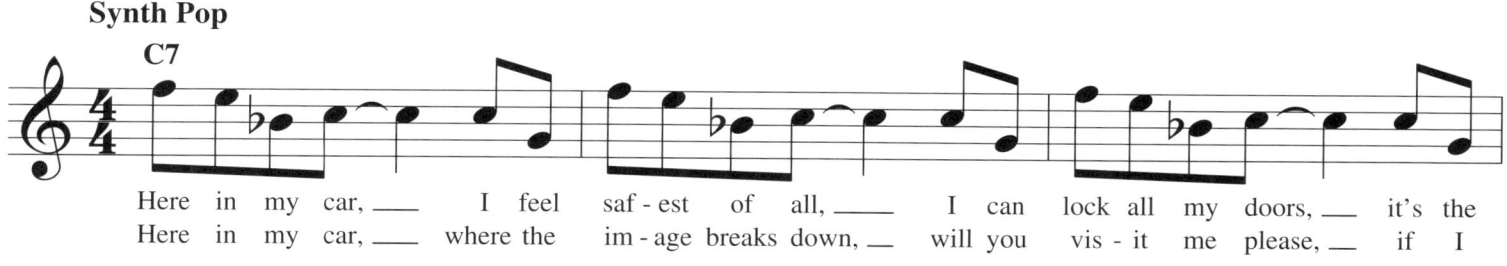

Here in my car, ___ I feel saf-est of all, ___ I can lock all my doors, ___ it's the
Here in my car, ___ where the im-age breaks down, ___ will you vis-it me please, ___ if I

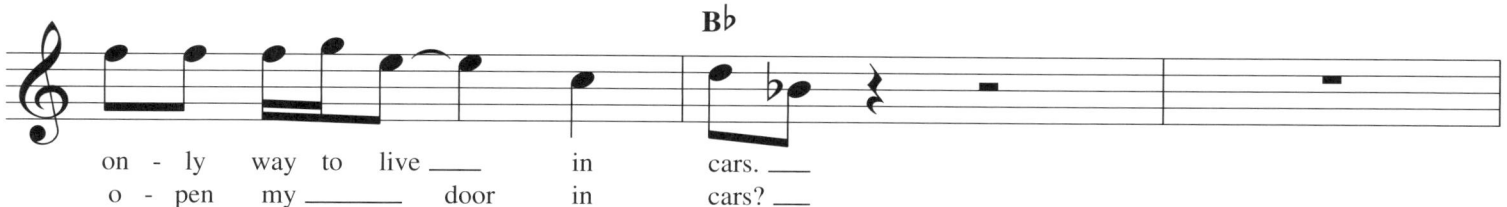

on - ly way to live ___ in cars. ___
o - pen my ___ door in cars? ___

Here in my car, ___ I can on-ly re-ceive, ___ I can lis-ten to you, ___ it keeps me
Here in my car, ___ I know I've start-ed to think ___ a-bout leav-ing to-night, ___ al-though ___

sta - ble for days in cars. ___
noth - ing seems right in cars. ___

(Instrumental)

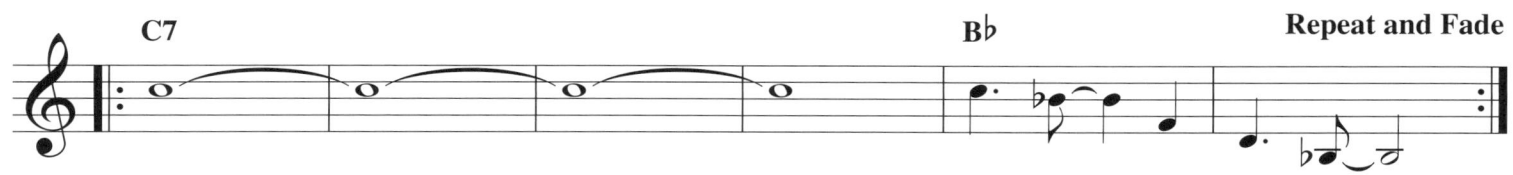

Repeat and Fade

CENTERFOLD

© 1981 CENTER CITY MUSIC (ASCAP)/Administered by
BUG MUSIC and PAL-PARK MUSIC
All Rights for PAL-PARK MUSIC Administered by ALMO MUSIC CORP.

Written by SETH JUSTMAN

Moderately fast

Does she walk? Does she talk? Does she come com-plete? My
It's o-kay, I un-der-stand, this ain't no nev-er nev-er land. I

home-room, home-room an-gel al-ways pulled me from my seat.
hope that when this is-sue's gone, I'll see you when your clothes are on.

She was pure like snow flakes; no one could ev-er stain the
Take your car, yes, we will, we'll take your car and drive it. We'll

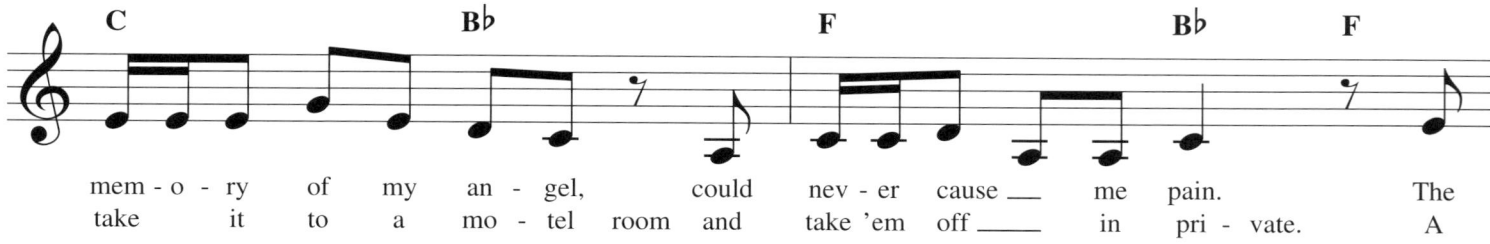
mem-o-ry of my an-gel, could nev-er cause me pain. The
take it to a mo-tel room and take 'em off in pri-vate. A

years go by, I'm look-in' through a girl-ie mag-a-zine, and
part of me has just been ripped, the pag-es from my mind are stripped.

there's my home-room an-gel on the pag-es in be-tween.
Ah no! I can't de-ny it. Oh yeah, I guess I got-ta buy it. } My

COME ON EILEEN

© 1982 EMI MUSIC PUBLISHING LTD. and KEVIN ADAMS MUSIC LTD.
All Rights for EMI MUSIC PUBLISHING LTD. Controlled and Administered by COLGEMS-EMI MUSIC INC.

Words and Music by KEVIN ROWLAND,
JAMES PATTERSON and KEVIN ADAMS

Moderately

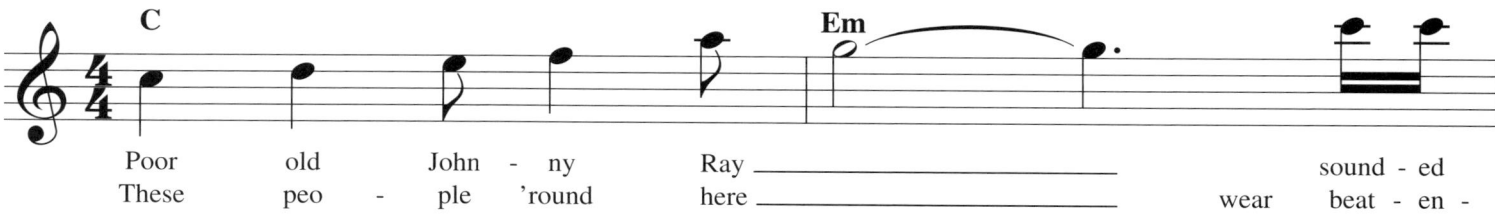

Poor old John - ny Ray _____ sound - ed
These peo - ple 'round here _____ wear beat - en -

sad up - on the ra - di - o; he moved a mil - lion hearts in mon - o.
down eyes sunk in smoke dried fac - es, re - signed to what their fate is, but

1st time only

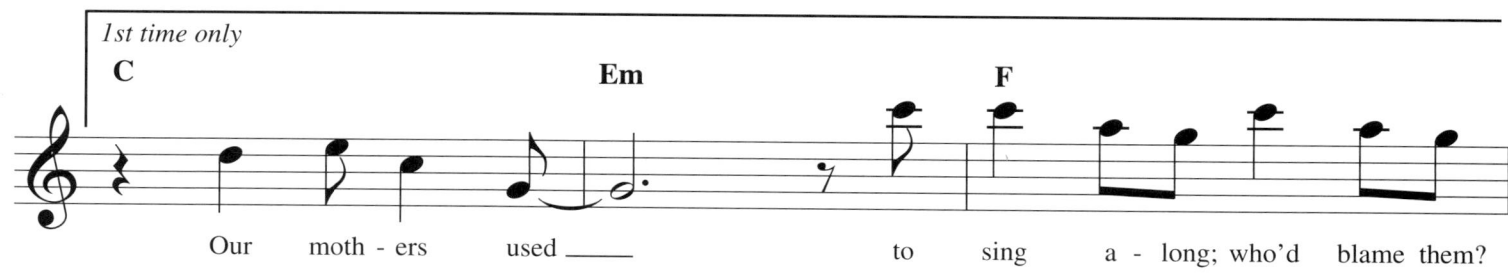

Our moth - ers used _____ to sing a - long; who'd blame them?

You're grown. _____ (You're grown up.) So grown. _____ (So grown up.)
not us, no not us.

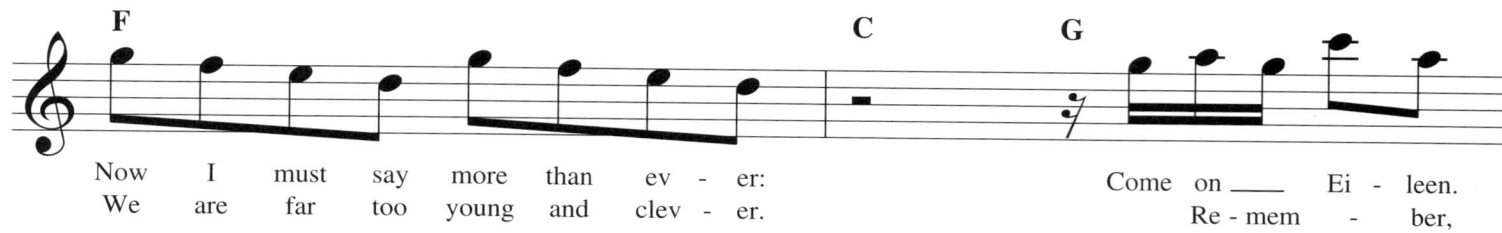

Now I must say more than ev - er: Come on _____ Ei - leen.
We are far too young and clev - er. Re - mem - ber,

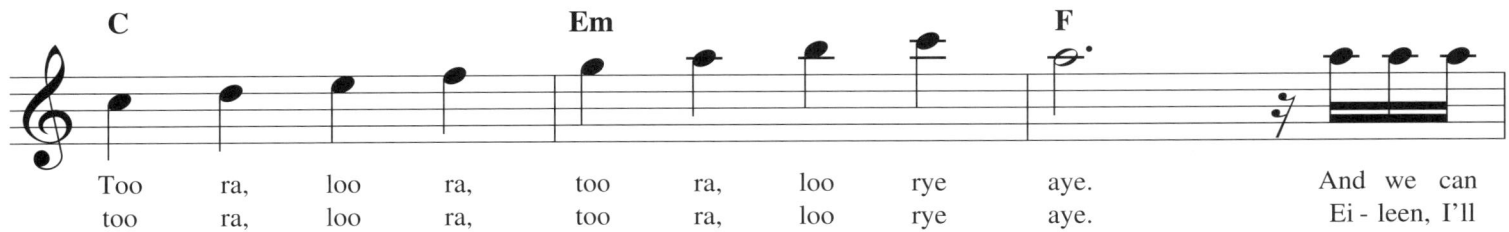
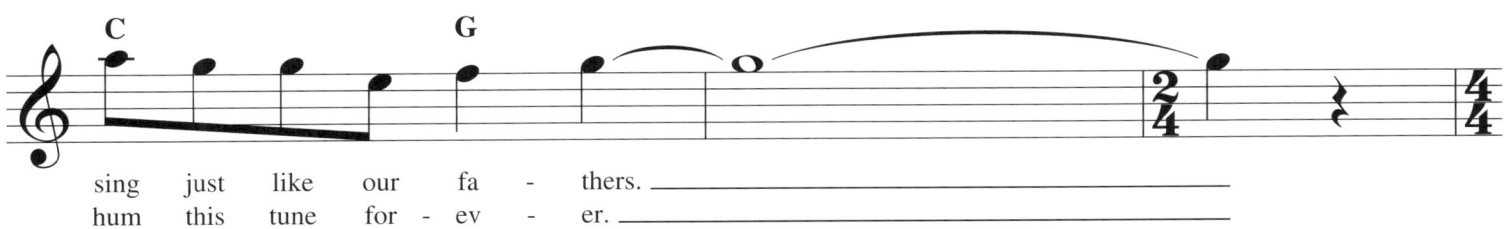

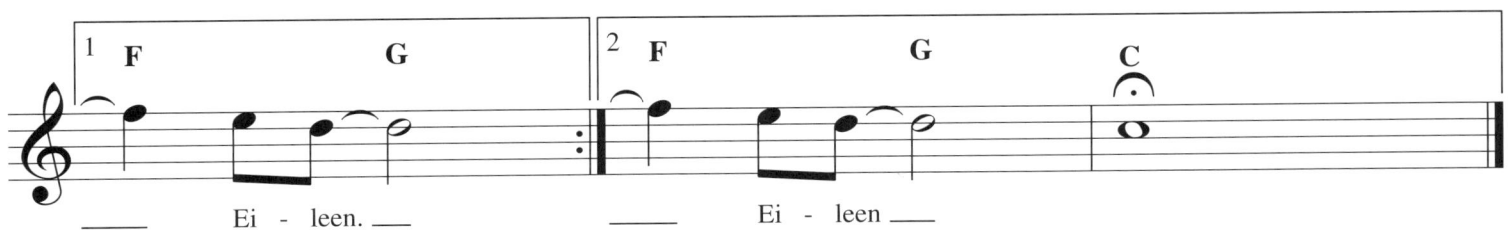

G F Am F G F
on my own. It's a cruel, cruel sum - mer. Now you're gone.
Am F G F Am
You're not the on - ly one. It's a cruel...
(Instrumental)
F Am F
D.C. al Coda
The
CODA
Am F G F Am F
cruel sum - mer,
leav - ing me here
G F Am F G F
on my own. It's a cruel, cruel sum - mer. Now, you're gone.
1
Am F G F
You're not the on - ly one. It's a cruel,
2
Am F G F Am
It's a cruel sum - mer.

(I JUST) DIED IN YOUR ARMS

Words and Music by
NICHOLAS EEDE

Copyright © 1986 Sony/ATV Music Publishing UK Ltd.
All Rights Administered by Sony/ATV Music Publishing LLC,
8 Music Square West, Nashville, TN 37203

Moderate Rock

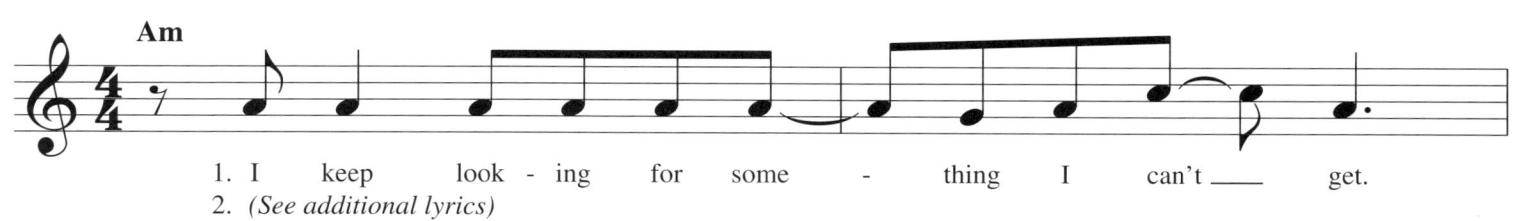

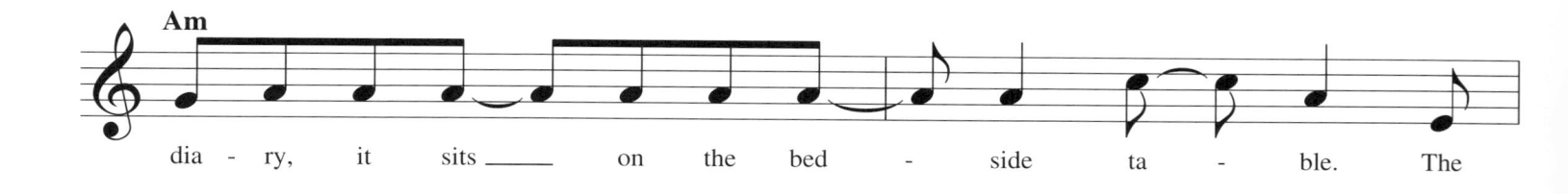

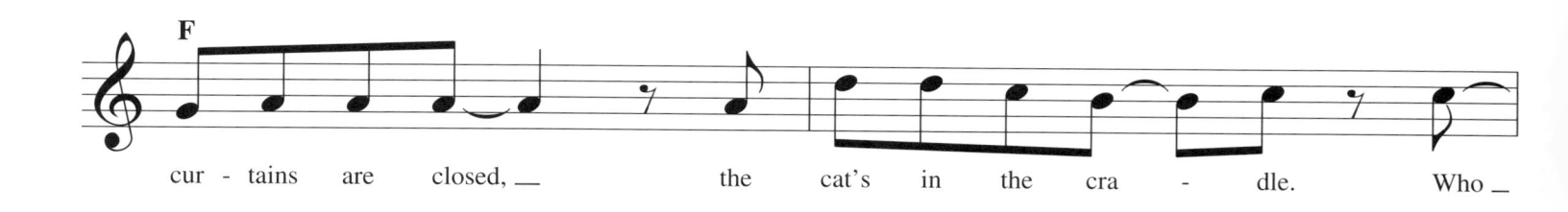

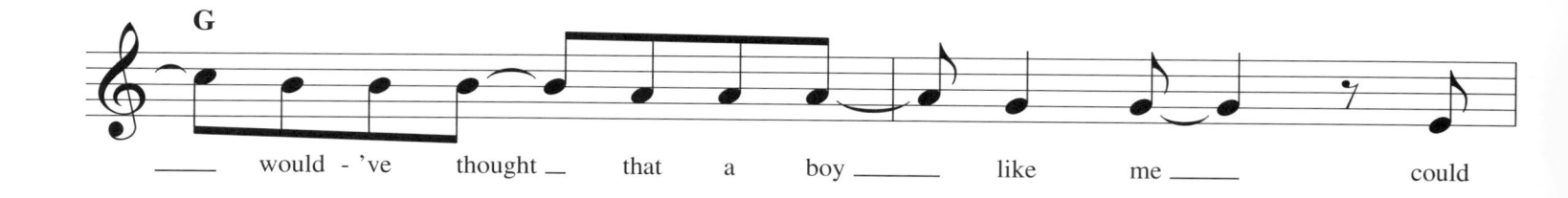

1. I keep look-ing for some-thing I can't get.
2. *(See additional lyrics)*

Bro-ken hearts lie all a-round me, and I don't see an eas-y way to get out of this. Her diary, it sits on the bed-side ta-ble. The cur-tains are closed, the cat's in the cra-dle. Who would-'ve thought that a boy like me could

E
come to this.
Oh,
Chorus
Am
I, I just died
Dm
in your arms
G
to - night.
Em
It must - 've been some-thing you said;
Am
I just died
Dm
in your arms to - night.
G
Em
Oh,
'cause
Am
I, I just died
Dm
in your arms
G
to - night.
Em
It must - 've been some kind of kiss;
Am
I should - 've
Dm
walked a - way,
G
To Coda
1
Em
I should - 've walked a - way.
F
Am
Is there

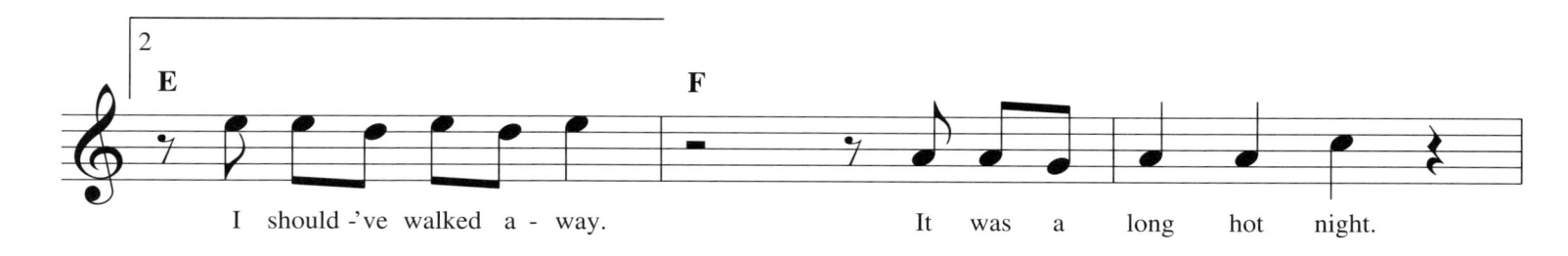

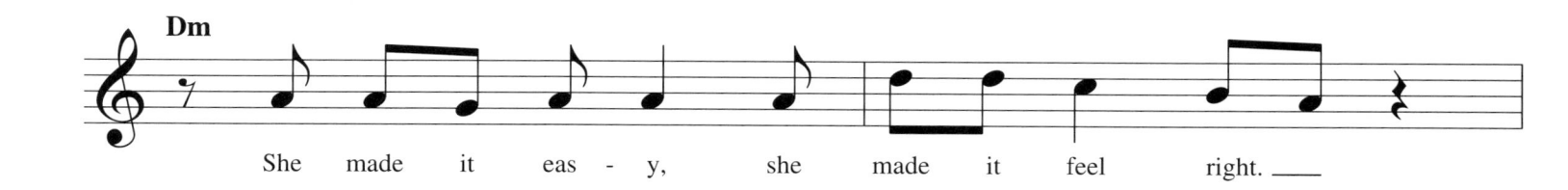

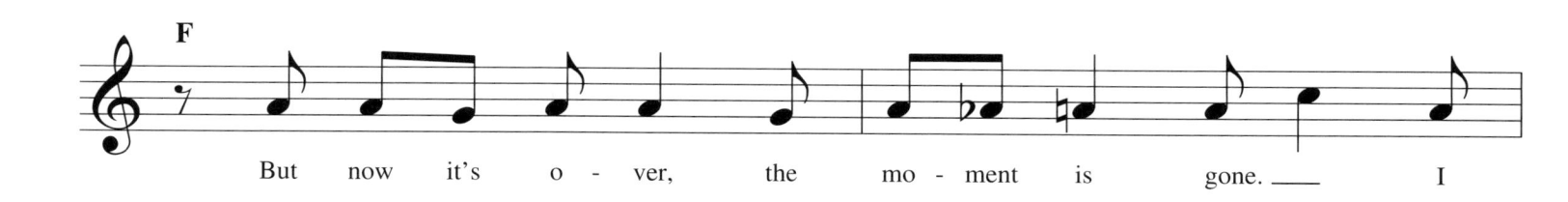

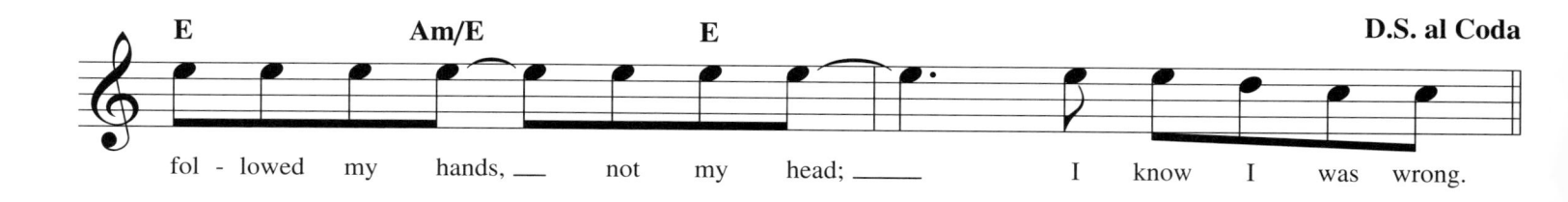

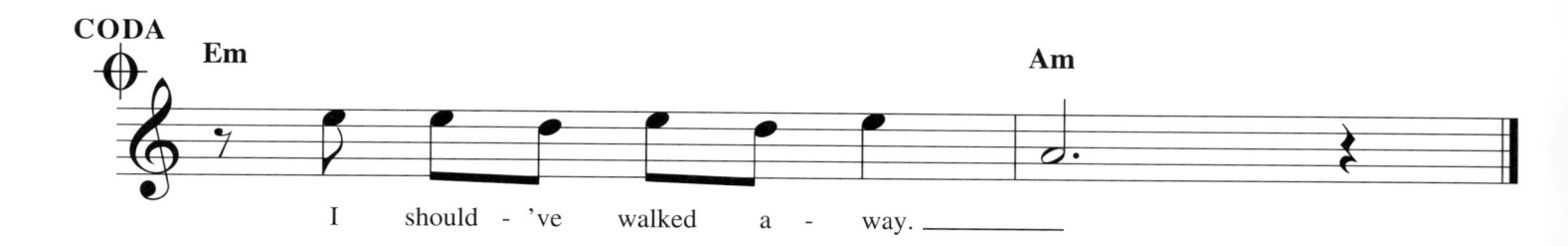

Additional Lyrics

2. Is there any just cause for feeling like this?
   On the surface I'm a name on a list.
   I try to be discreet, but then blow it again.
   I've lost and found, it's my final mistake,
   She's loving by proxy, no give and all take.
   'Cause I've been thrilled to fantasy one too many times.
   Chorus

DON'T YOU (FORGET ABOUT ME)
from the Universal Picture THE BREAKFAST CLUB

Copyright © 1985 USI A MUSIC PUBLISHING and USI B MUSIC PUBLISHING
All Rights Controlled and Administered by UNIVERSAL MUSIC CORP. and SONGS OF UNIVERSAL, INC.

Words and Music by KEITH FORSEY
and STEVE SCHIFF

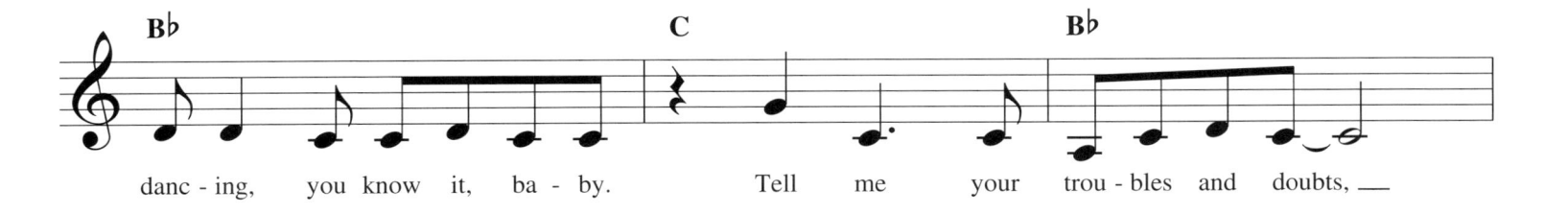

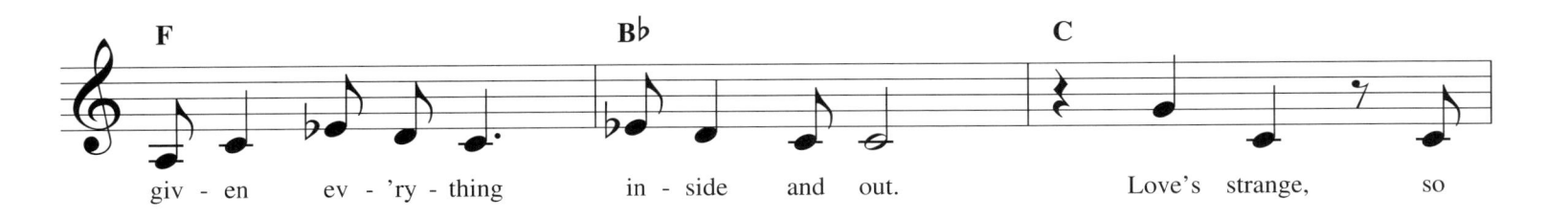

Moderately, with a steady beat

1. Won't you come see a-bout me, ___ I'll be a-lone ___ danc-ing, you know it, ba-by. Tell me your trou-bles and doubts, ___ giv-en ev-'ry-thing in-side and out. Love's strange, so real in the dark, ___ Think of the ten-der things that we were work-ing on. Slow chains may pull us a-part _____ when our life ___ gets in-

2. *(See additional lyrics)*

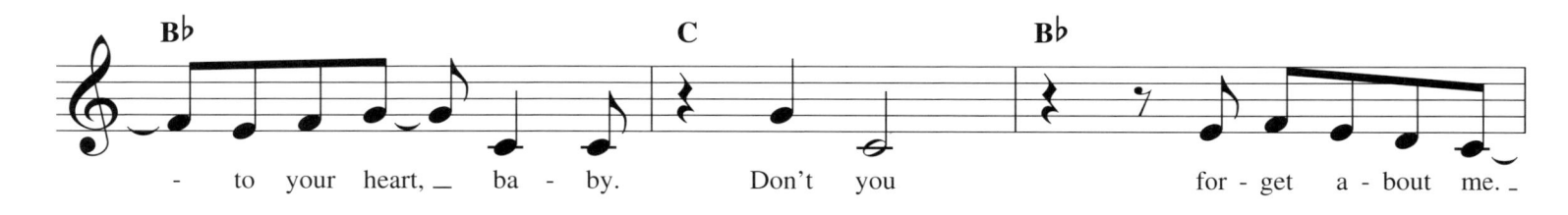

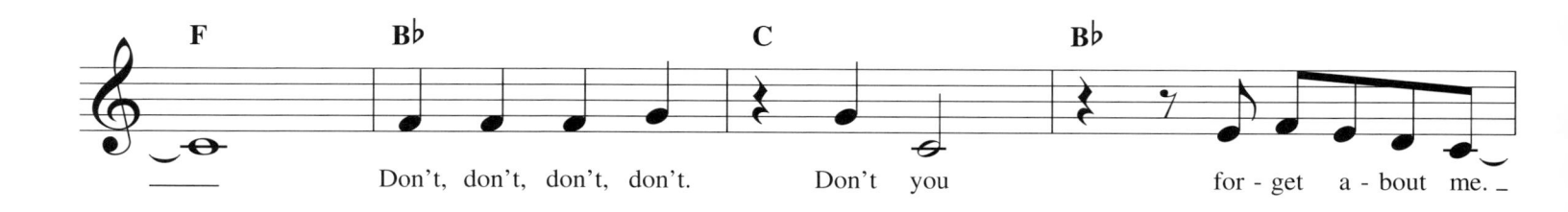

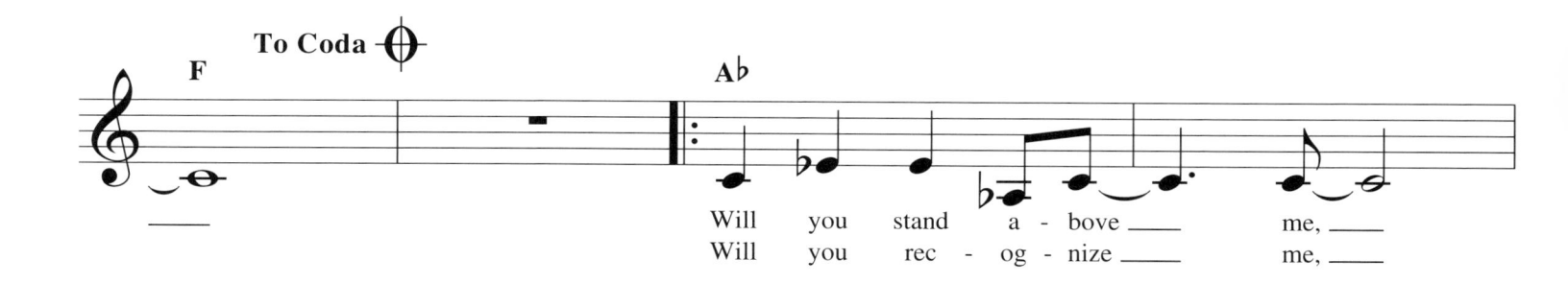

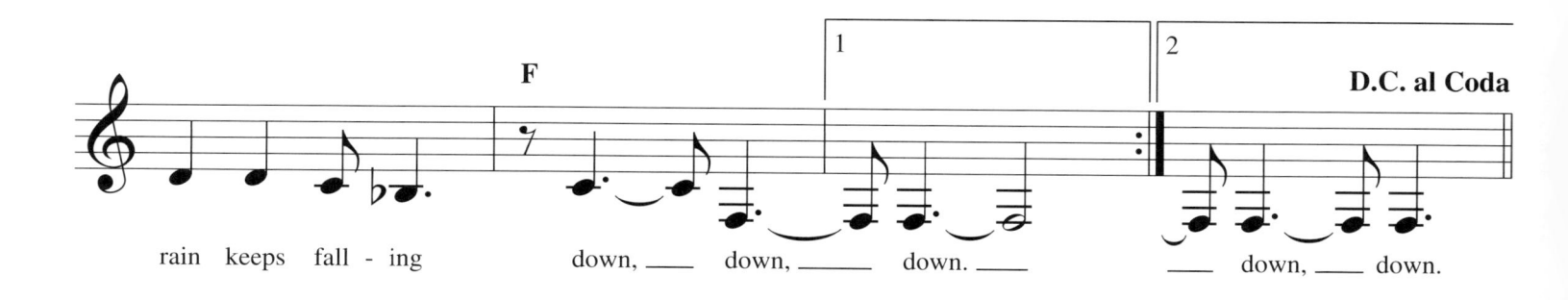

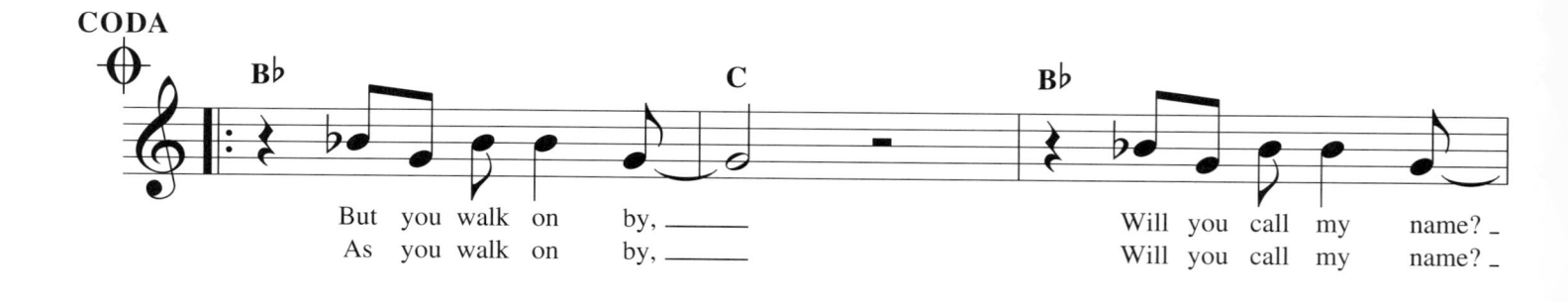

- to your heart, _ ba - by. Don't you for - get a - bout me. _

Don't, don't, don't, don't. Don't you for - get a - bout me. _

To Coda ⊕

Will you stand a - bove __ me, __
Will you rec - og - nize ___ me, __

Look my way, __ nev - er love __ me. ⎫ Rain keeps fall - ing,
Call my name __ or walk on by? _____ ⎭

D.C. al Coda

rain keeps fall - ing down, __ down, __ down. __ down, __ down.

CODA ⊕

But you walk on by, _____ Will you call my name?
As you walk on by, _____ Will you call my name?

When you walk a - way, ___
Or will you walk a - way? ___

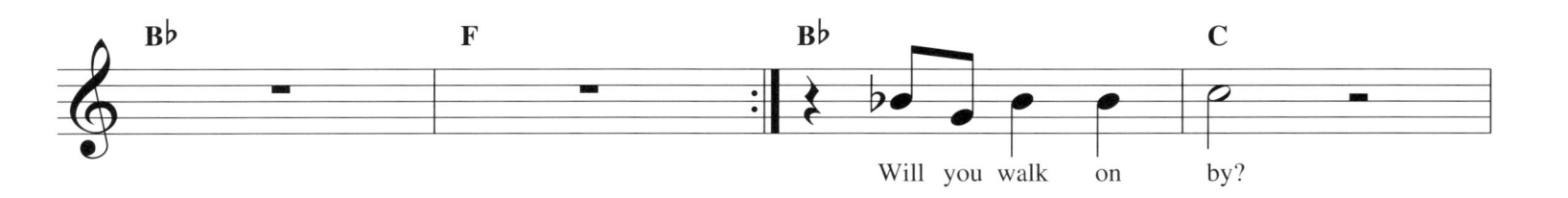

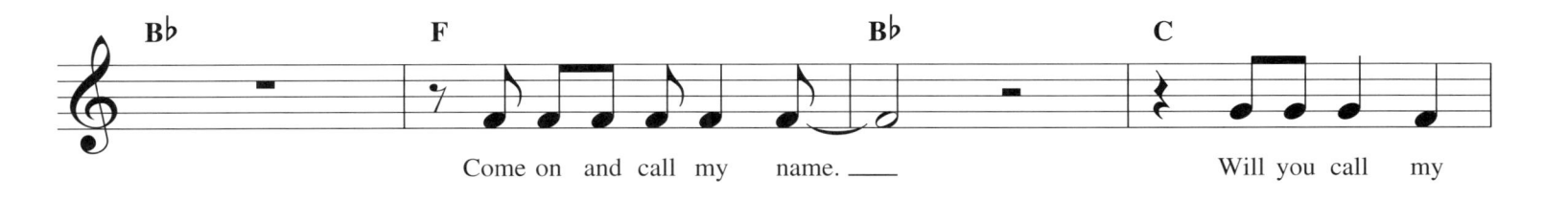

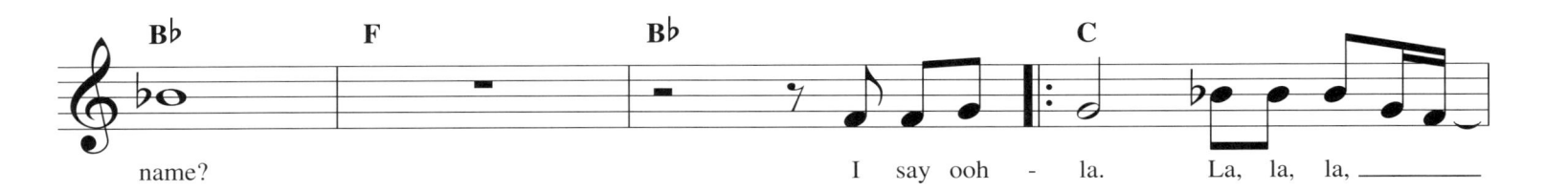

Will you walk on by?

Come on and call my name. ___ Will you call my

name? I say ooh - la. La, la, la, ___

___ la, la, la, ___ la, la, la, la, la, la, la, la, la,

Additional Lyrics

2. Don't you try and pretend,
   It's my feeling, we'll win in the end.
   I won't harm you, or touch your defenses,
   Vanity, insecurity.
   Don't you forget about me,
   I'll be alone dancing, you know it, baby.
   Going to take you apart,
   I'll put us back together at heart, baby.

   Don't you forget about me,
   Don't, don't, don't, don't.
   Don't you forget about me. *(To Coda)*

DOIN' IT
(All for My Baby)

Words and Music by PHIL CODY
and MIKE DUKE

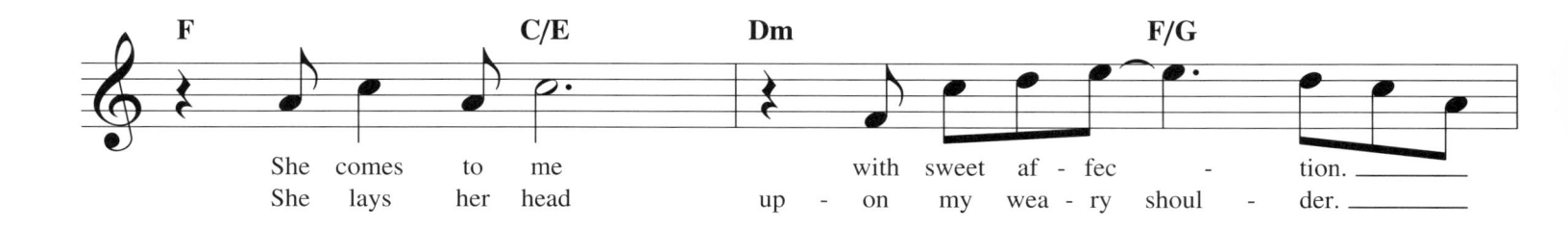

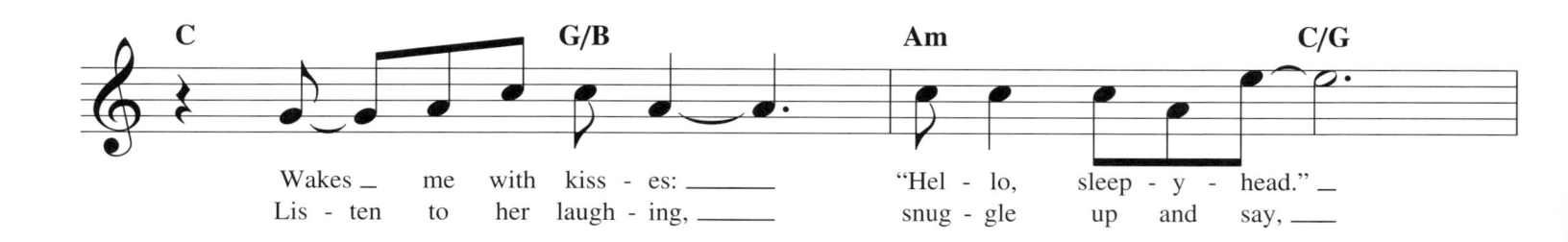

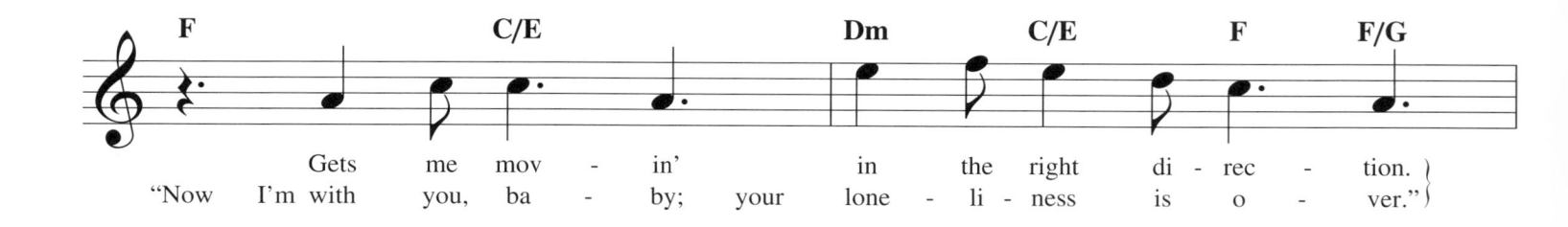

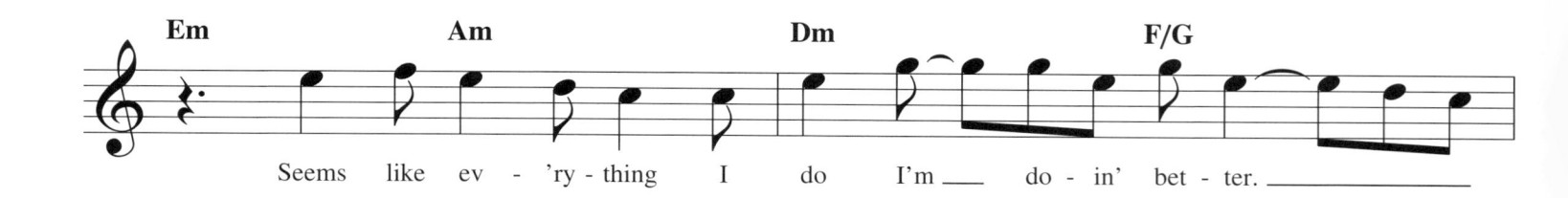

Moderately

12/8

| C | G/B | Am | C/G |

Ear - ly in the morn - in' ____ I'm still in bed. ____
Lat - er in the eve - nin' it's been a bus - y day.

| F | C/E | Dm | F/G |

She comes to me with sweet af - fec - tion. ____
She lays her head up - on my wea - ry shoul - der. ____

| C | G/B | Am | C/G |

Wakes __ me with kiss - es: ____ "Hel - lo, sleep - y - head." ____
Lis - ten to her laugh - ing, ____ snug - gle up and say, ____

| F | C/E | Dm | C/E | F | F/G |

Gets me mov - in' in the right di - rec - tion.
"Now I'm with you, ba - by; your lone - li - ness is o - ver."

| Em | Am | Dm | F/G |

I do my best to give her love that lasts for - ev - er. ____

| Em | Am | Dm | F/G |

Seems like ev - 'ry - thing I do I'm ____ do - in' bet - ter. ____

45

DON'T KNOW MUCH

Words and Music by BARRY MANN,
CYNTHIA WEIL and TOM SNOW

Copyright © 1980 SONY/ATV Music Publishing LLC, Mann & Weil Songs, Inc.,
EMI Blackwood Music Inc. and Snow Music
All Rights on behalf of SONY/ATV Music Publishing LLC and Mann & Weil Songs, Inc. Administered by
Sony/ATV Music Publishing LLC, 8 Music Square West, Nashville, TN 37203

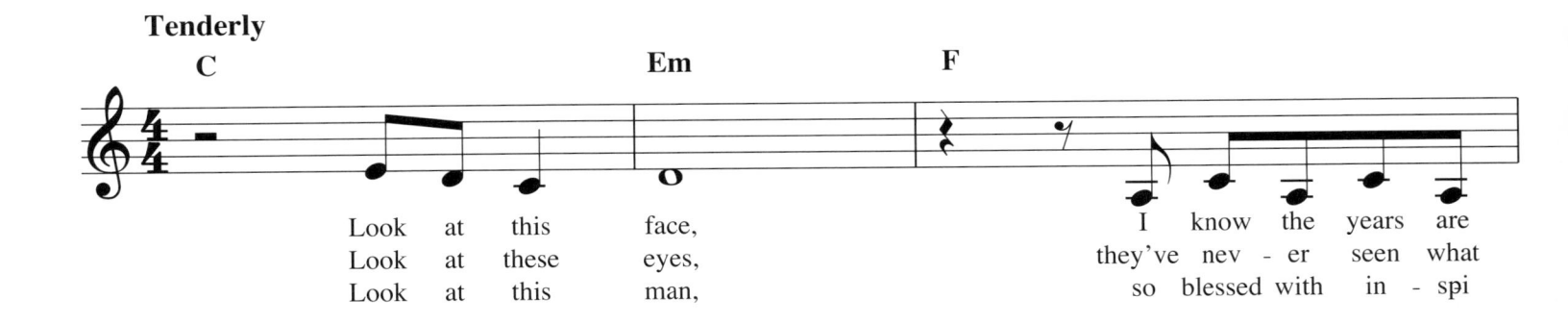

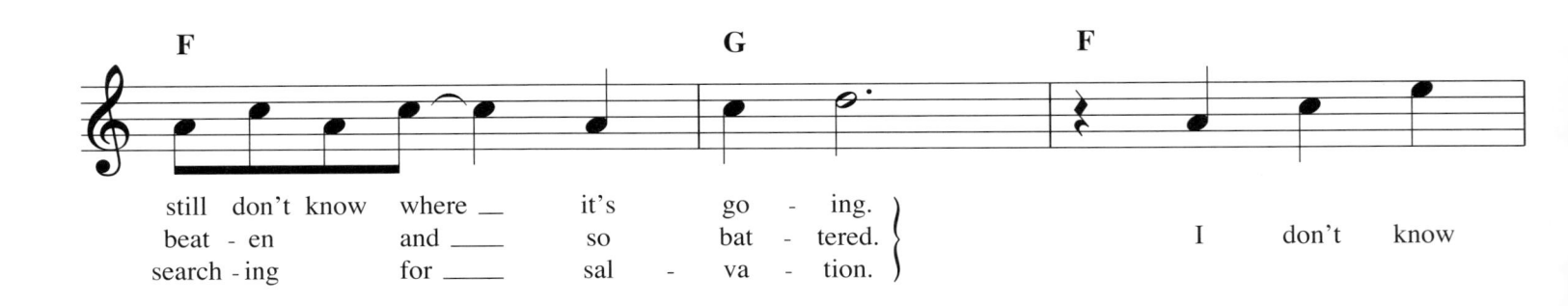

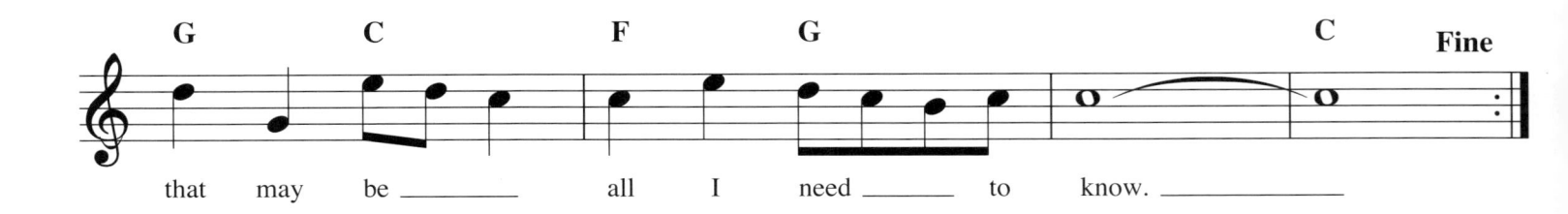

Tenderly

Look at this face, I know the years are show - ing.
Look at these eyes, they've nev - er seen what mat - ters.
Look at this man, so blessed with in - spi - ra - tion.

Look at this life, I still don't know where it's go - ing.
Look at these dreams, so beat - en and so bat - tered.
Look at this soul, still search - ing for sal - va - tion.

I don't know much, but I know I love you, and that may be all I need to know.

Fine

47

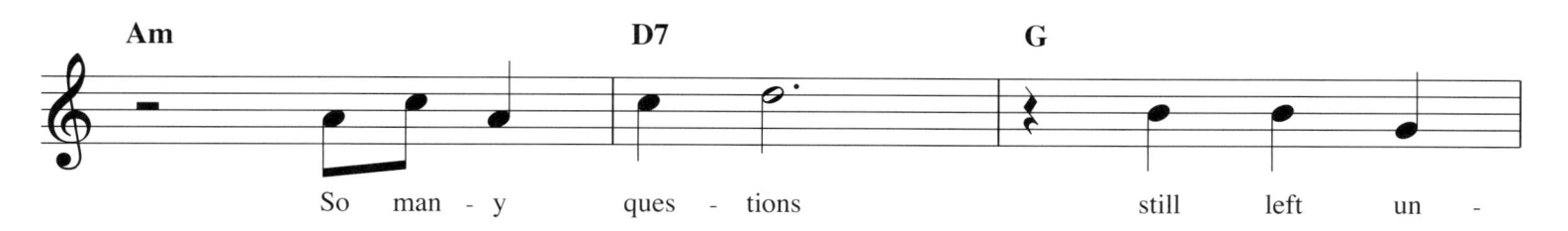

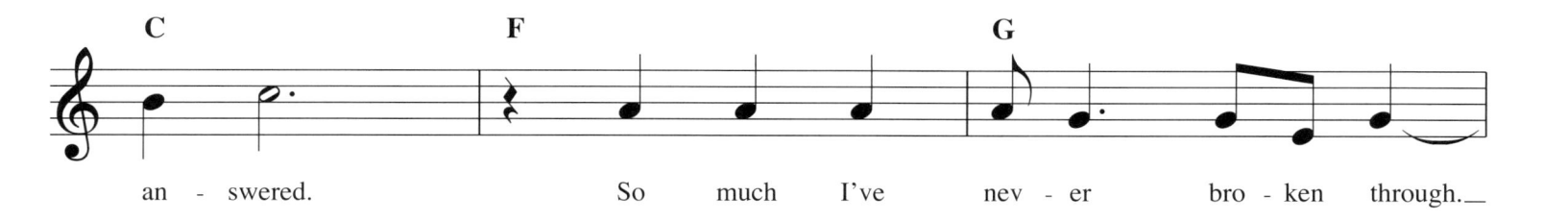

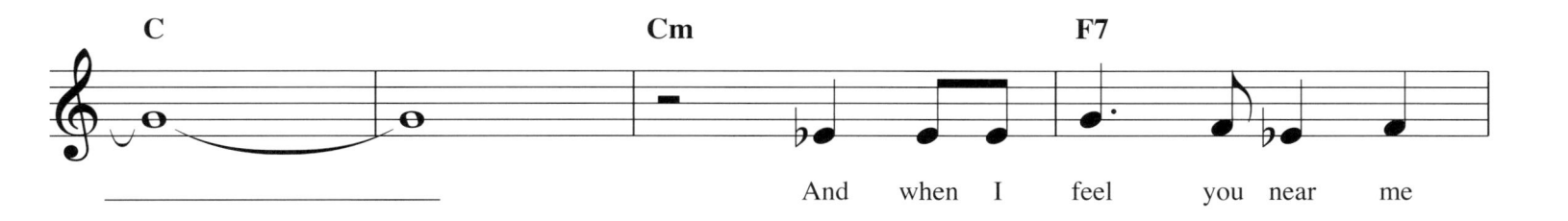

So man-y ques-tions still left un-an-swered. So much I've nev-er bro-ken through.

And when I feel you near me some-times I see so clear-ly the on-ly truth I've ev-er known is me and you.

D.C. al Fine

DON'T YOU WANT ME

Words and Music by PHIL OAKEY, ADRIAN WRIGHT and JO CALLIS

© 1982 EMI VIRGIN MUSIC LTD., SOUND DIAGRAMS LTD. and DINSONG LTD.
All Rights for EMI VIRGIN MUSIC LTD. Controlled and Administered in the U.S. and Canada by EMI VIRGIN MUSIC, INC.
All Rights for SOUND DIAGRAMS LTD. Controlled by WARNER BROS. MUSIC LTD. for the world
All Rights for WARNER BROS. MUSIC LTD. Administered by WB MUSIC CORP.

Moderately fast

1. You were working as a waitress in a cocktail bar when I met you. I picked you out, I shook you up and turned you around, turned you into someone new. Now
2. five years later on you've got the world at your feet. Success has been so easy for you. But don't forget it's me who put you where you are now, and I can put you back there, too.
3., 4. *(See additional lyrics)*

Bridge

Don't, don't you want me? You know I can't believe it when I hear that you won't see me. Don't, don't you want me? You know I don't believe you when you say that you don't need me. It's much too late to find when you

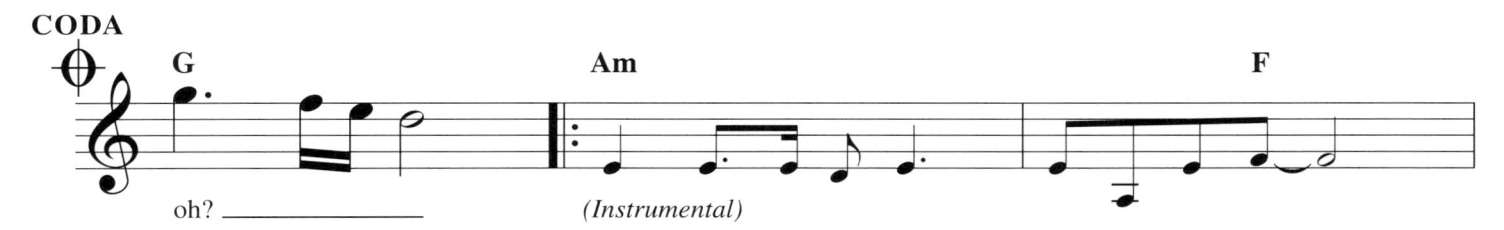

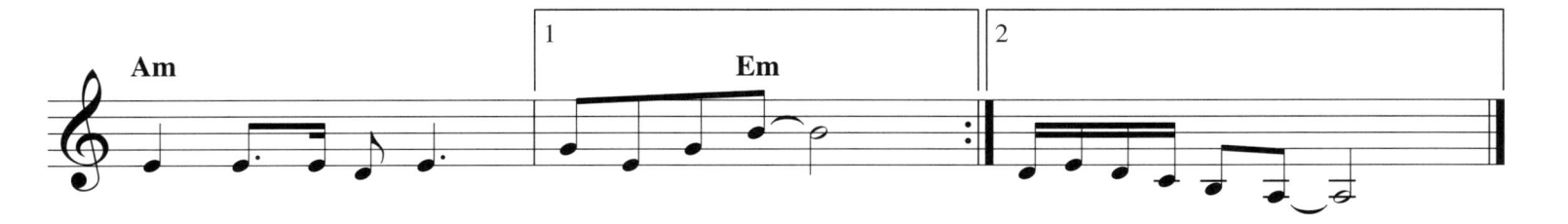

Additional Lyrics

3. I was working as a waitress in a cocktail bar,
   That much is true.
   But even then I knew I'd find a much better place
   Either with or without you.

4. The five years we have had have been such good times,
   I still love you.
   But now I think it's time I live my life on my own.
   I guess it's just what I must do.
   Bridge

DOWN UNDER

© 1982 EMI SONGS AUSTRALIA PTY. LIMITED
All Rights in the United States Controlled and Administered by EMI BLACKWOOD MUSIC INC.

Words and Music by COLIN HAY
and RON STRYKERT

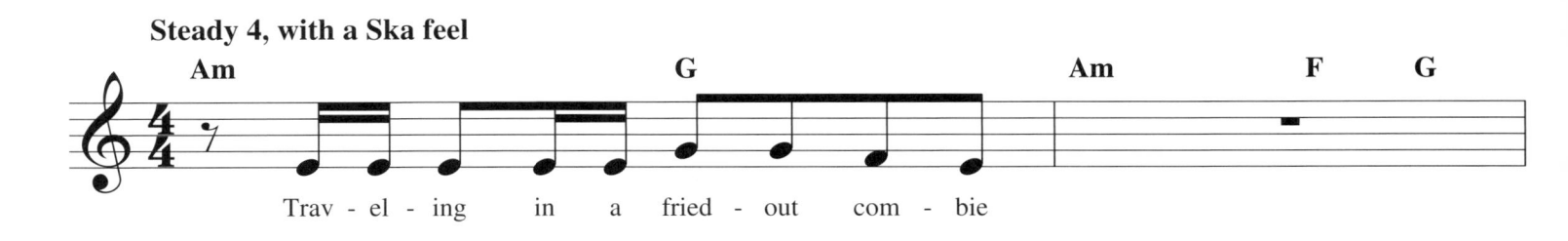

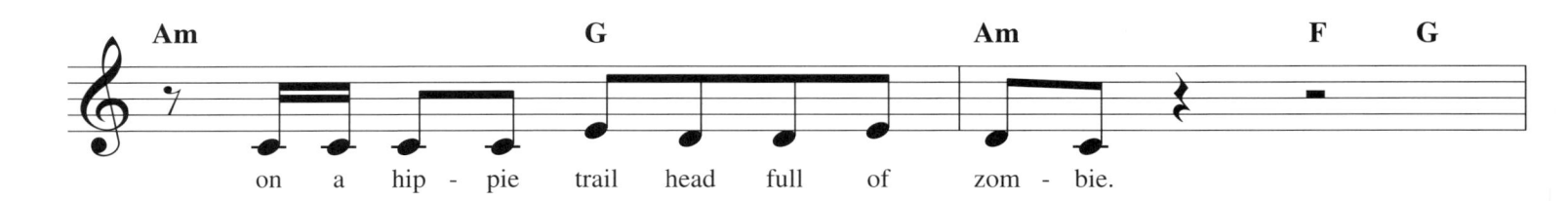

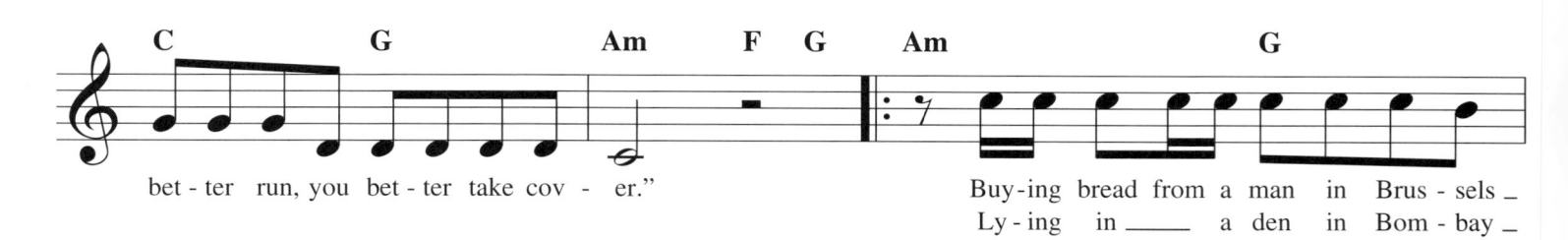

Steady 4, with a Ska feel

Trav-el-ing in a fried-out com-bie

on a hip-pie trail head full of zom-bie.

I met a strange la-dy. She made me ner-vous.

She took me in and gave me break-fast and she said,

"Do you come from a land down un-der? Where wom-en glow and men plun-

der? Can't you hear, can't you hear the thun-der? You

bet-ter run, you bet-ter take cov-er." Buy-ing bread from a man in Brus-sels
Ly-ing in a den in Bom-bay

Am F G Am G
He was six - foot four and full of
with a slack jaw and not much
Am F G Am G
mus - cles I said, "Do you speak - a my lan - guage?"
to say. I said to the man, "Are you try'n to
Am F G Am G
He just smiled and gave me a veg - e - mite
tempt me be - cause I come from the land of
Am F G C G
sand - wich, and he said, "I come from a land down un - der
plen - ty?" He said, "Oh Do you come from a land down un - der
Am F G C G
where beer does flow and men chun -
where wom - en glow and men plun -
Am F G C G
der
der?
Can't you hear, can't you hear the thun - der?
Am F G 1 C G
You bet - ter run, you bet - ter take cov -
Am F G 2 C G Am
er."
bet - ter run, you bet - ter take cov - er."

EASY LOVER

© 1984 PHILIP COLLINS LTD., HIT & RUN MUSIC (PUBLISHING) LTD.,
SIR & TRINI MUSIC and NEW EAST MUSIC
All Rights for PHILIP COLLINS LTD. and HIT & RUN MUSIC (PUBLISHING) LTD.
Controlled and Administered by EMI APRIL MUSIC INC.

Words and Music by PHIL COLLINS
PHILIP BAILEY and NATHAN EAST

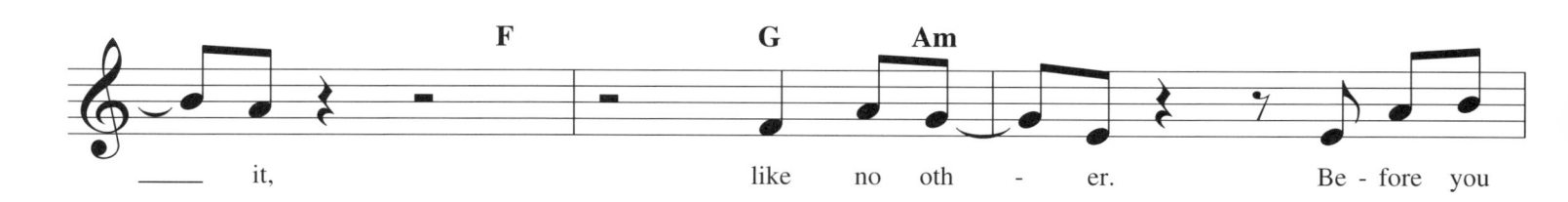

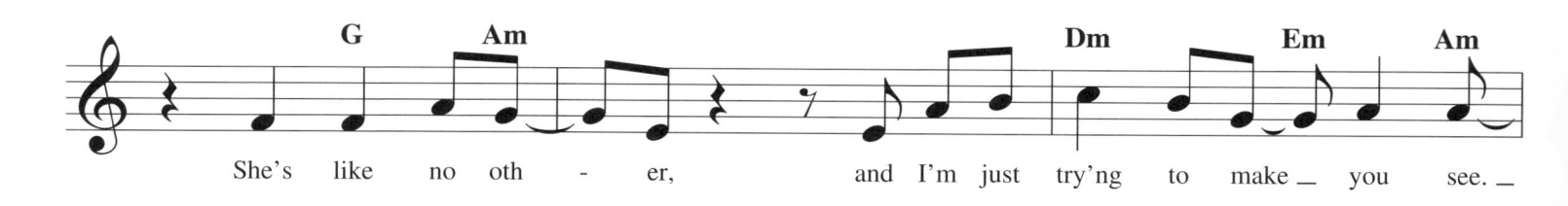

Gentle Rock

Eas - y lov - er. She'll get a hold on you, be - lieve it, like no oth - er. Be - fore you know it, you'll be on your knees. She's an eas - y lov - er. She'll take your heart, but you won't feel it. She's like no oth - er, and I'm just try'ng to make you see.

{ She's the kind of girl you dream of, dream of keep - ing hold of. Bet - ter for - get it.
{ You're the one that wants to hold her, hold her and con - trol her. Bet - ter for - get it.

You'll _ nev - er get it. _____ She will play _
You'll _ nev - er get it. _____ 'Cause she'll say _

_____ a - round and leave you, leave _ you and de - ceive you.
_____ that there's no oth - er till _____ she finds an - oth - er.

Bet - ter for - get _____ it. Oh, _ you'll re -
Bet - ter for - get _____ it. Oh, _ you'll re -

gret it. _____ No, you'll nev - er change her, so
gret it. _____ And don't try to change her. Just

leave her, leave her. Get out quick 'cause see - ing is be - liev - ing. It's the
leave her, leave her. You're not the on - ly one, and see - ing is be - liev - ing.

on - ly way _____ you'll ev - er know _____

she's _____ an eas - y lov - an eas - y lov -

EBONY AND IVORY

© 1982 MPL COMMUNICATIONS, INC.

Words and Music by
PAUL McCARTNEY

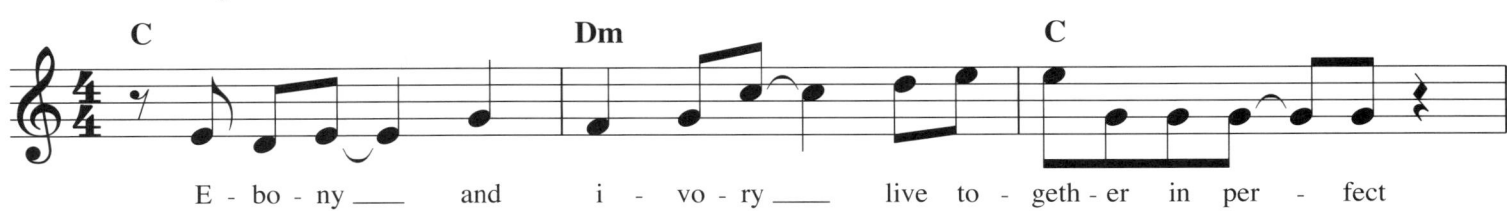

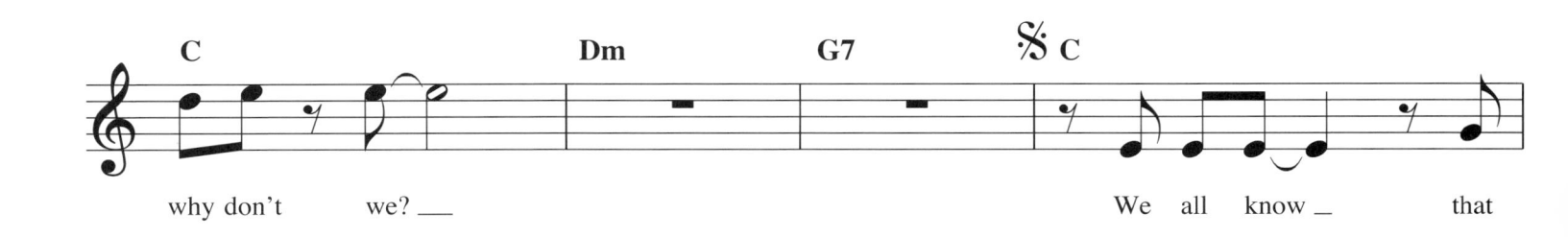

Moderately

E-bo-ny ___ and i-vo-ry ___ live to-geth-er in per-fect har-mo-ny, ___ side by side on my pian-o key-board, oh Lord, why don't we? ___ We all know ___ that peo-ple are the same wher-ev-er you go. ___ There is good and bad in ev-'ry-one, we learn to live, we learn to give each oth-er what we need to sur-vive ___ to-geth-er a-live. ___ E-bo-ny ___ and i - vo - ry, live to-geth-er in per - fect har - mo - ny, side by side on my pian - o key-board, oh Lord, why don't we?

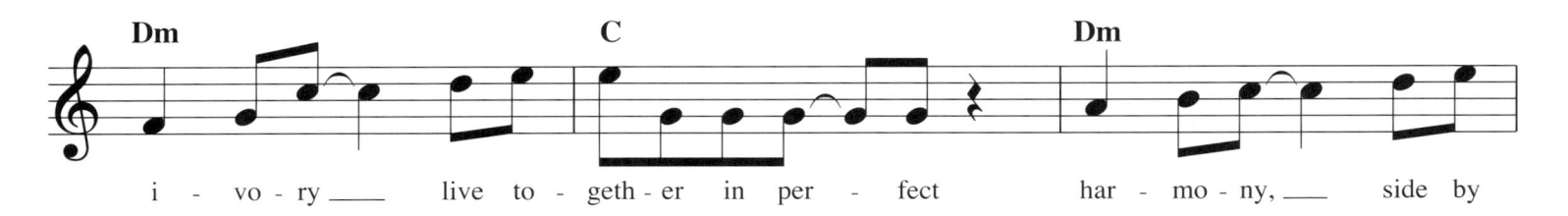

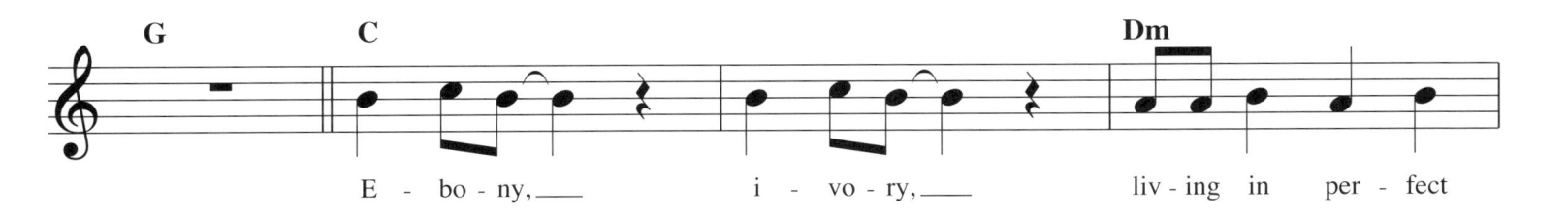

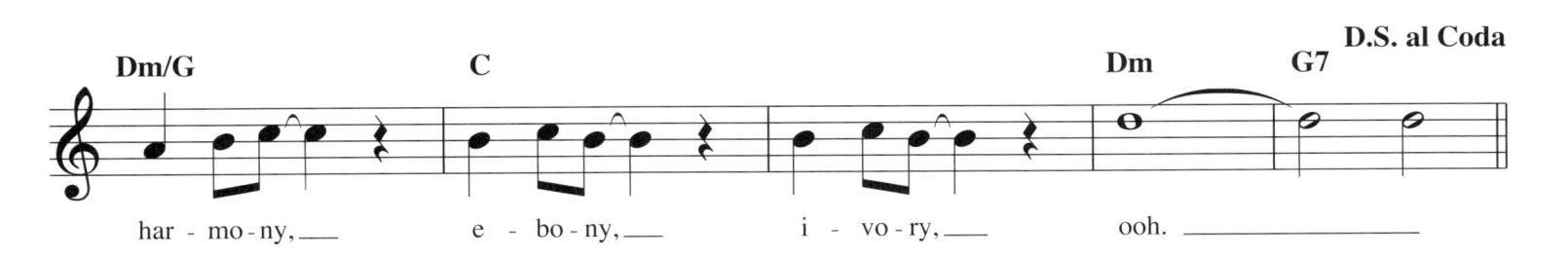

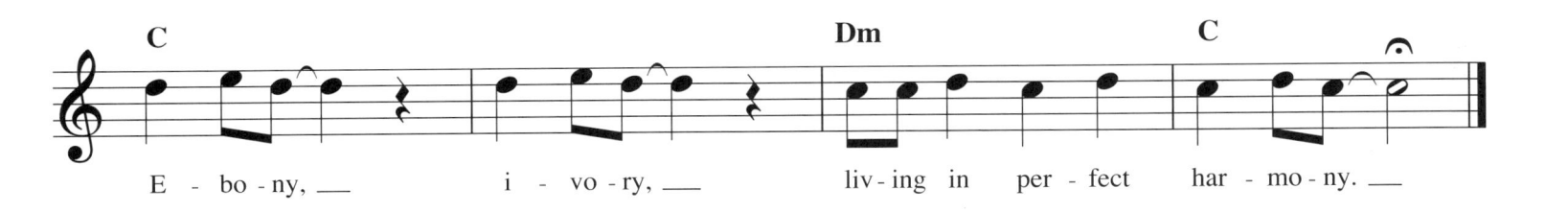

E - bo - ny, i - vo - ry, liv-ing in per - fect har - mo - ny, e - bo - ny, i - vo - ry, ooh.

CODA

Side by side on my pian - o key-board, oh Lord, why don't we?

E - bo - ny, i - vo - ry, liv-ing in per - fect har - mo - ny.

ENDLESS LOVE
from ENDLESS LOVE

Copyright © 1981 by PGP Music, Brockman Music and Brenda Richie Publishing
All Rights for PGP Music Administered by Intersong U.S.A., Inc.

Words and Music by
LIONEL RICHIE

Moderately

My love, — there's on-ly you in my life — the on-ly
Two hearts, — two hearts that beat as — one — our lives have

thing that's right. — My first — love, — you're ev-'ry
just be-gun. — For-ev-er — I hold you

breath — that I take, — you're ev-'ry step I make. — And
close — in my arms, — I can't re-sist your charms. — And

I, — I — want to share all my love
(D.S.) love, — I'd — be a fool for — you, — I'm

with you; — no one else will do. — And your eyes, —
sure. You — know I don't mind, — 'cause

they tell me how much you care. — Oh
you, — you mean the

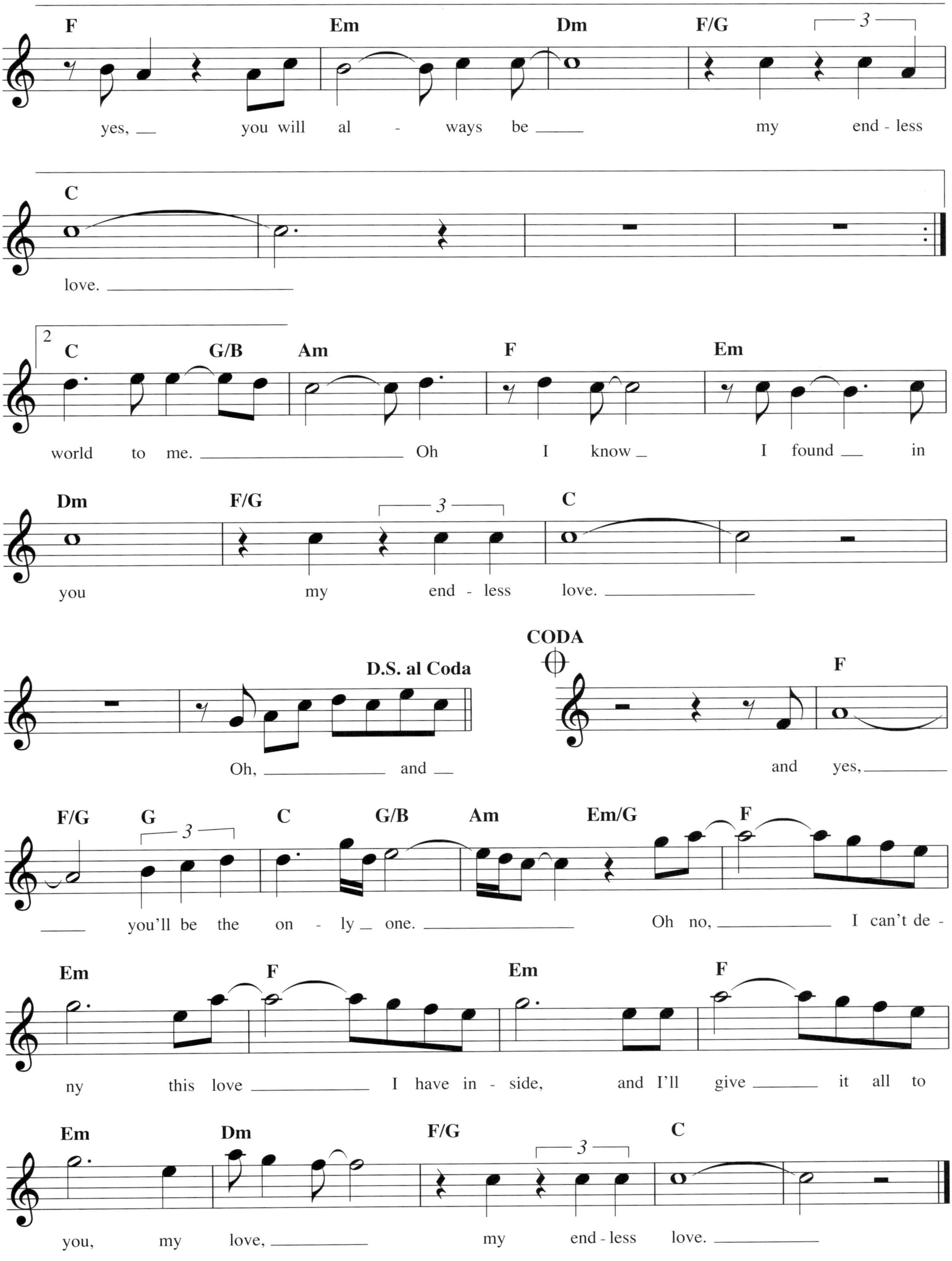
F Em Dm F/G
3
yes, you will al - ways be my end - less
C
love.
2
C G/B Am F Em
world to me. Oh I know I found in
Dm F/G C
3
you my end - less love.
D.S. al Coda
Oh, and
CODA
F
and yes,
F/G G C G/B Am Em/G F
3
you'll be the on - ly one. Oh no, I can't de -
Em F Em F
ny this love I have in - side, and I'll give it all to
Em Dm F/G C
3
you, my love, my end - less love.

EVERY BREATH YOU TAKE

© 1983 G.M. SUMNER
Administered by EMI MUSIC PUBLISHING LIMITED

Words and Music by
STING

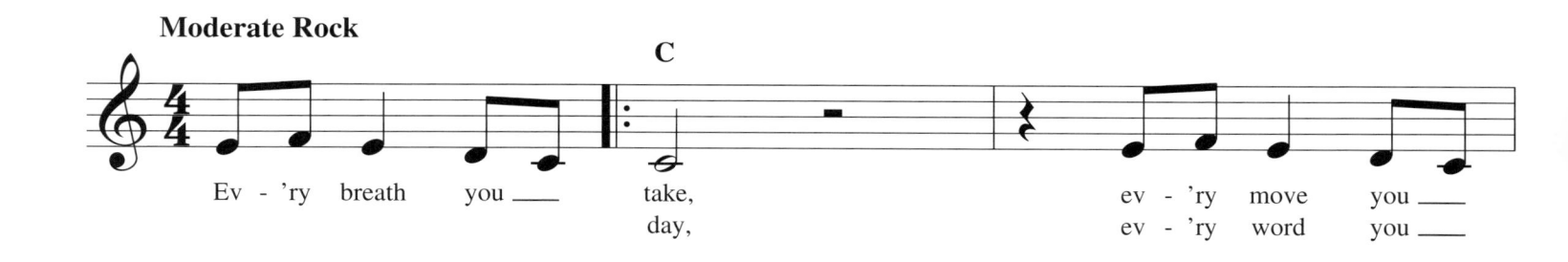

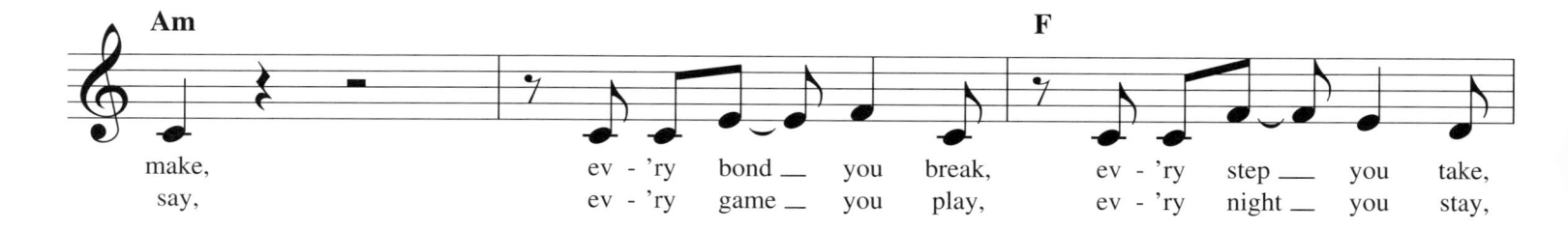

Moderate Rock

C
Ev - 'ry breath you take,
day,

ev - 'ry move you
ev - 'ry word you

Am   **F**
make,   ev - 'ry bond you break,   ev - 'ry step you take,
say,   ev - 'ry game you play,   ev - 'ry night you stay,

G   *1.* **Am**   **G7**
I'll be watch-ing you.   Ev - 'ry sin - gle
I'll be watch-ing you.

2. **C**   **𝄋 F**   **Dm**
                Oh, can't you see   you be-long to

C   **D7**
me.   How my poor heart   aches

G   **G7**
with ev - 'ry step you take.   Ev - 'ry move you

C
Am
make, ev - 'ry vow you break,
F
G
ev - 'ry smile you fake, ev - 'ry claim you stake, I'll be watch - ing you.
Am
To Coda
A♭
Since you've gone, I been lost
B♭
with - out a trace. I dream at night I can on -
A♭
- ly see your face. I look a - round but it's
B♭
you I can't re - place, I feel so cold and I
A♭
long for your em - brace. I keep cry - ing ba -

- by ba - by please. _____ (Instrumental)

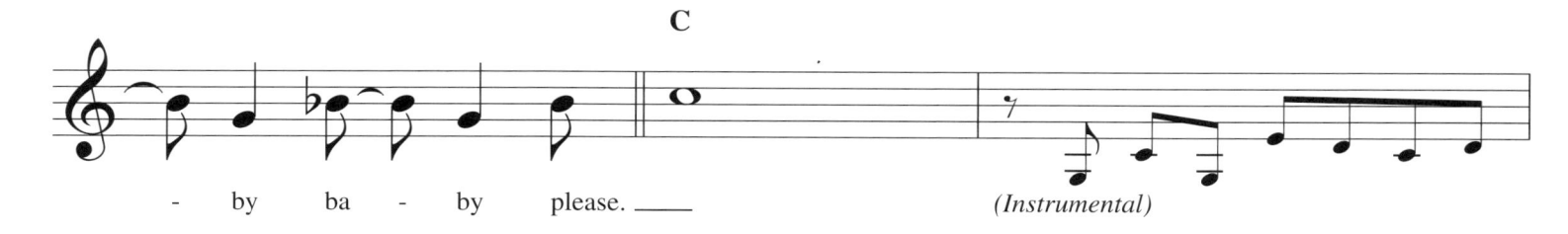

D.S. al Coda
Oh, can't you _____

CODA
Ev - 'ry move _____ you make, ev - 'ry step _____ you take,

I'll be watch - ing you.

I'll be watch - ing you. _____

GLORIA

Original Words and Music by
GIANCARLO BIGAZZI and UMBERTO TOZZI
English Lyrics by TREVOR VEITCH

© 1981 MELODI SPA CASA EDITRICE
All Rights for the United States Controlled and Administered by
EMI BLACKWOOD MUSIC INC. and SONGS OF UNIVERSAL, INC.

Moderately, with a beat

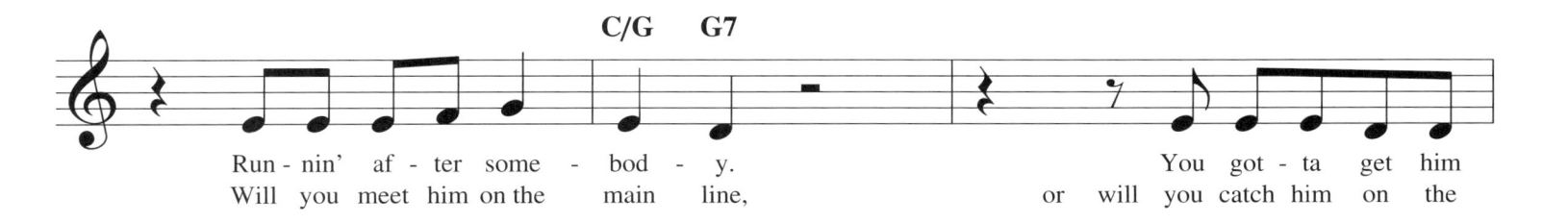

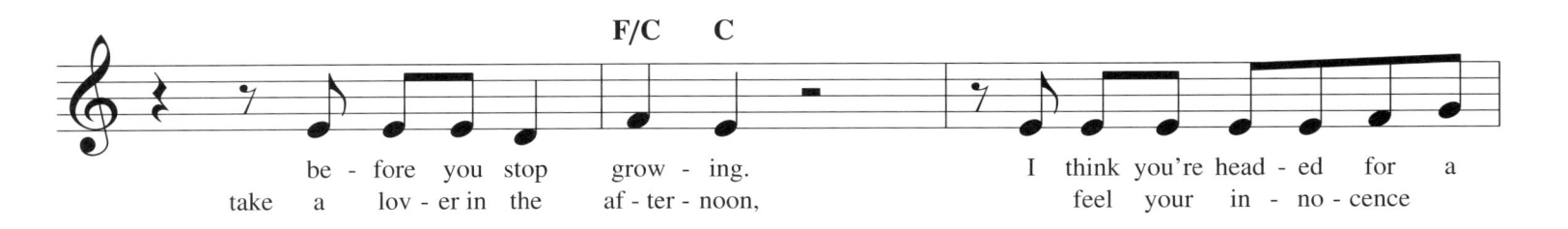

Glo - ri - a, you're al - ways on the run now.
Glo - ri - a, how's it gon - na go down?
Run - nin' af - ter some - bod - y. You got - ta get him
Will you meet him on the main line, or will you catch him on the
some - how. I think you've got - ta slow down
re - bound? Will you mar - ry for the mon - ey,
be - fore you stop grow - ing. I think you're head - ed for a
take a lov - er in the af - ter - noon, feel your in - no - cence
break - down; you're care - ful not to show it.
slip - ping a - way? Don't be - lieve it's com - ing back soon.

(sheet music, page 62)

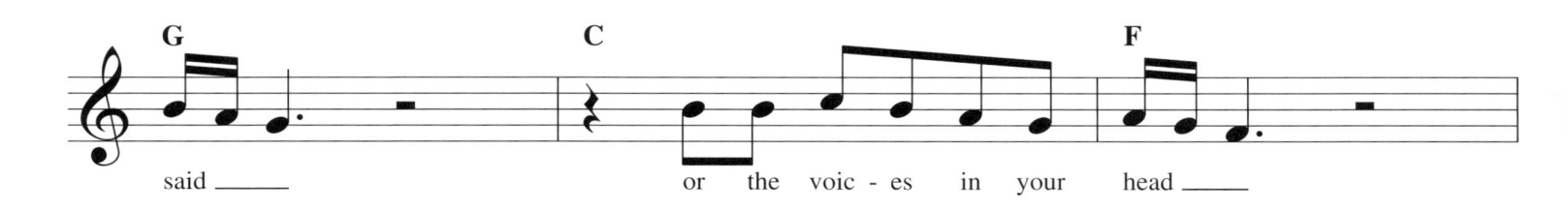

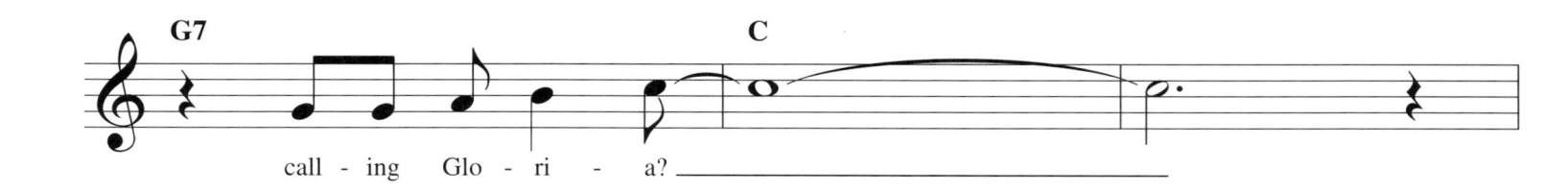

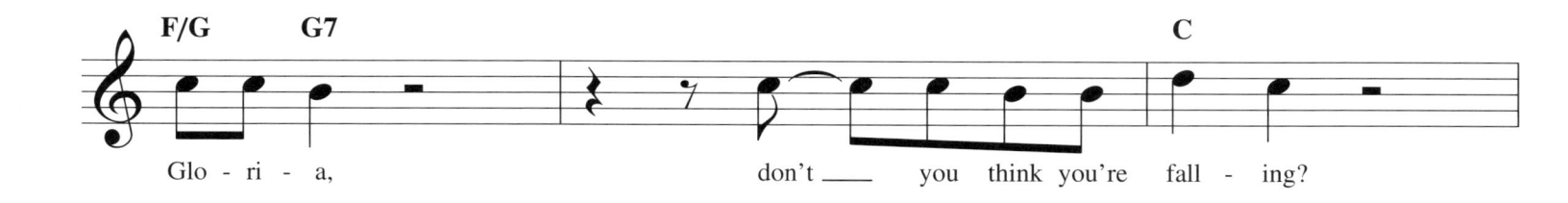

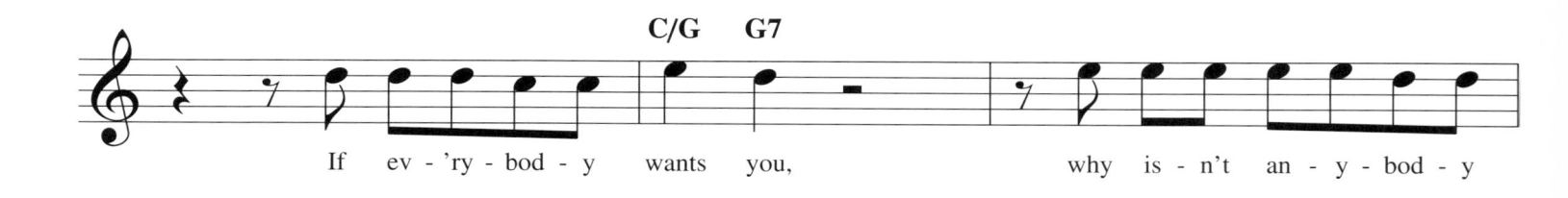

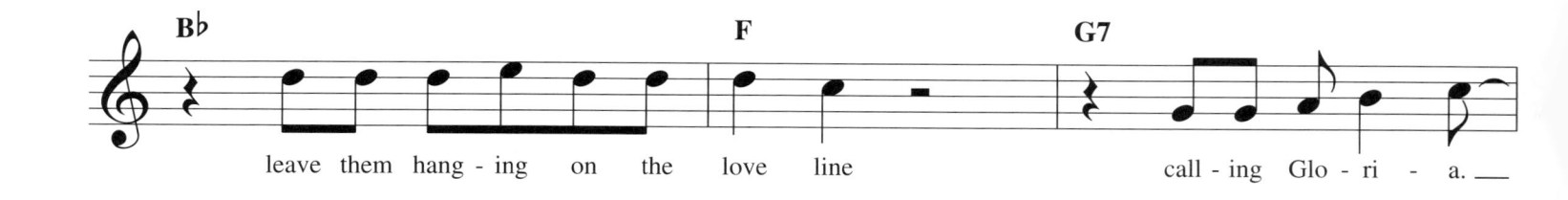

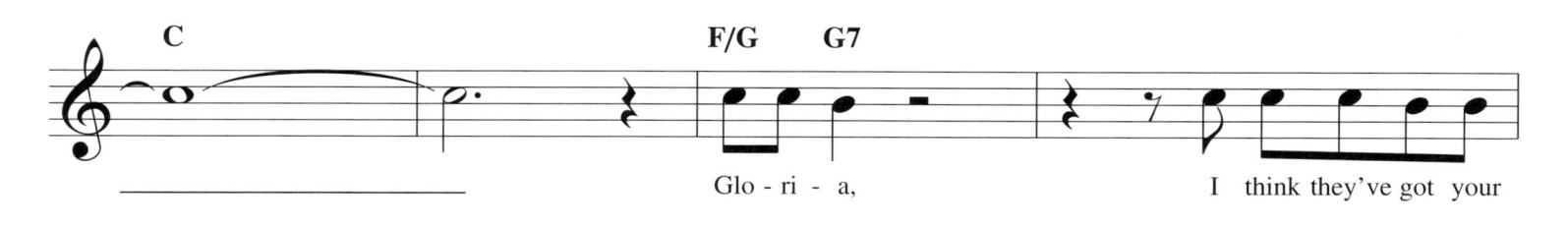

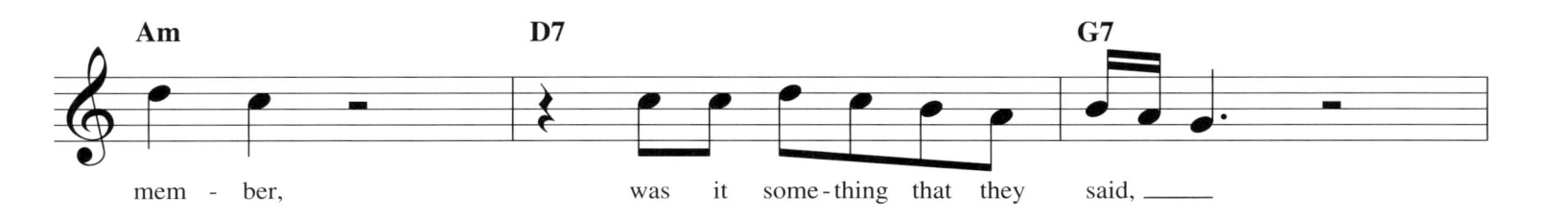

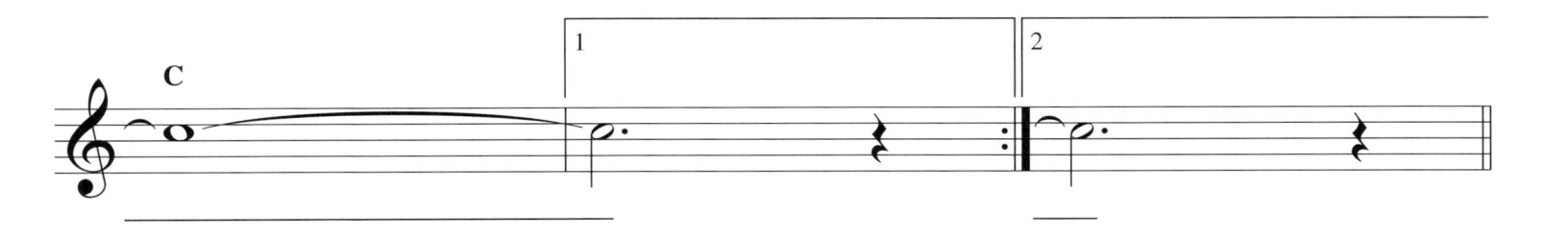

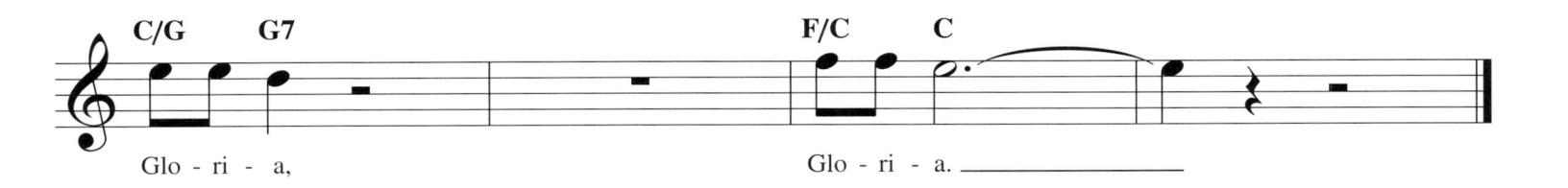

Glo - ri - a, I think they've got your num - ber. I think they've got the a - li - as that you've been liv - ing un - der. But you real - ly don't re - mem - ber, was it some - thing that they said, or the voic - es in your head call - ing Glo - ri - a? Glo - ri - a, Glo - ri - a.

THE FLAME

Words and Music by NICK GRAHAM
and BOB MITCHELL

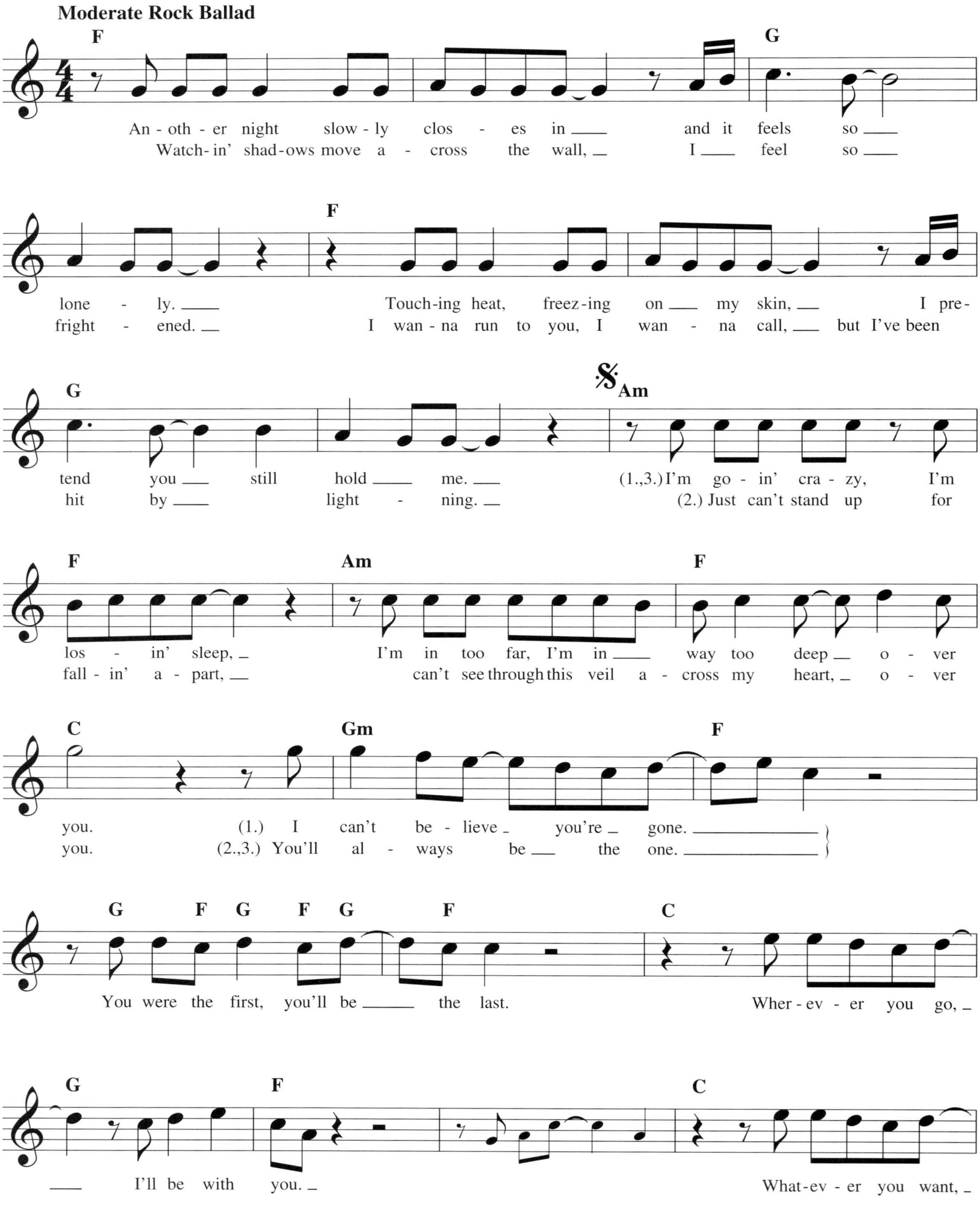

G F C
I'll give it to you.
When-ev-er you need
G C F
some-one to lay your heart and head up-on, re-mem-ber:
To Coda
C F/A B♭
Af-ter the fire, af-ter all the rain, I will be the flame.
1
F
I will be the flame.
G
2
B♭
D.S. al Coda
F
I will be the flame.
CODA
F B♭ C
I will be the flame. I will be the flame.
G F C
I'll be with you.
What-ev-er you want,
G F C
I'll give it to you.

FOOTLOOSE
Theme from the Paramount Motion Picture FOOTLOOSE

Copyright © 1984 Sony/ATV Music Publishing LLC
All Rights Administered by Sony/ATV Music Publishing LLC,
8 Music Square West, Nashville, TN 37203

Words by DEAN PITCHFORD and KENNY LOGGINS
Music by KENNY LOGGINS

Fast Rock and Roll

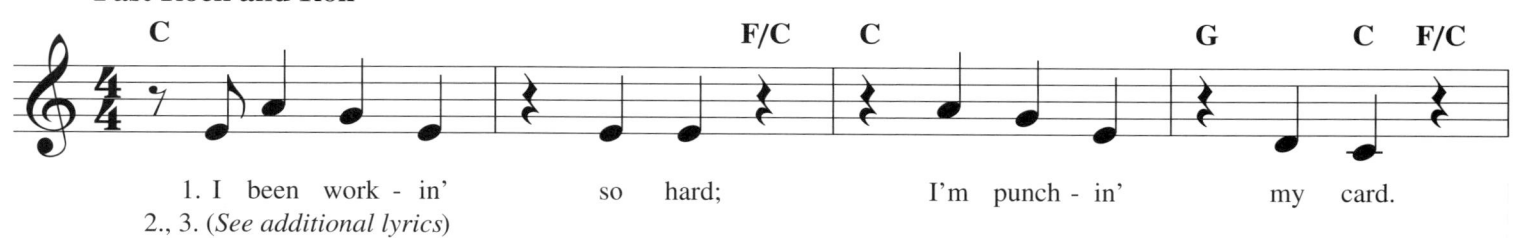

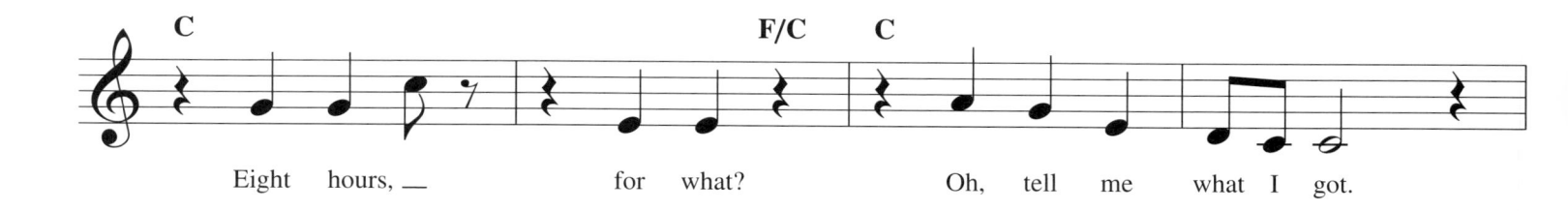

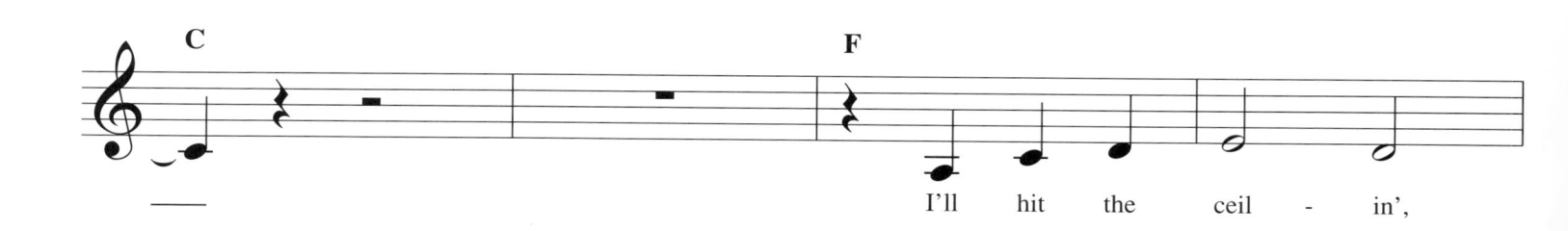

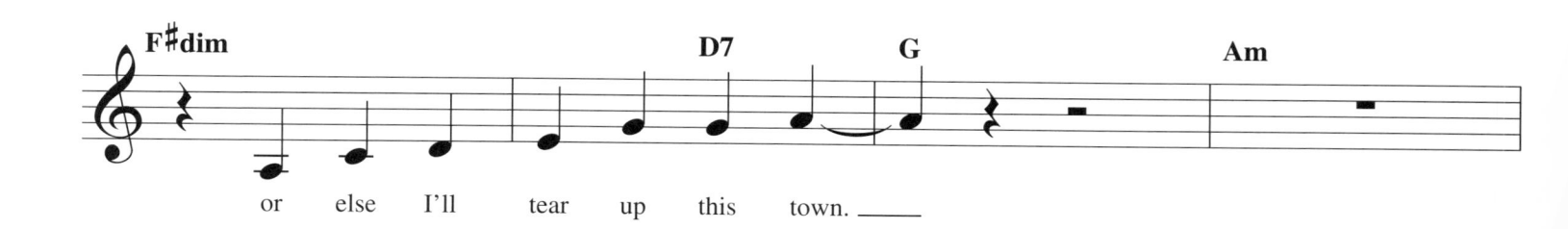

1. I been work-in' so hard; I'm punch-in' my card.
2., 3. *(See additional lyrics)*

Eight hours, for what? Oh, tell me what I got.

I've got this feel-in', that time's just hold-in' me down.

I'll hit the ceil-in',

or else I'll tear up this town.

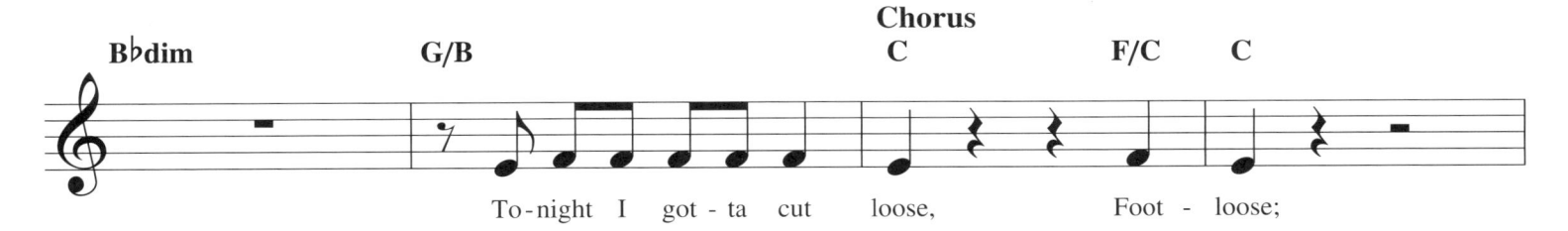

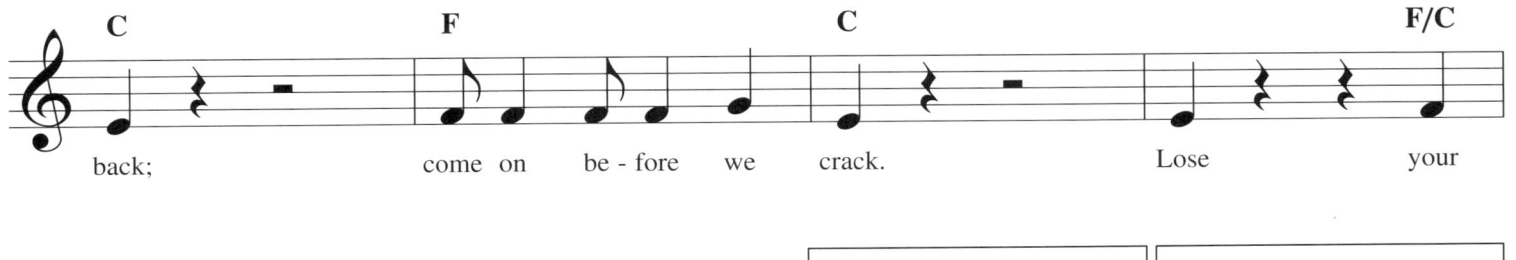

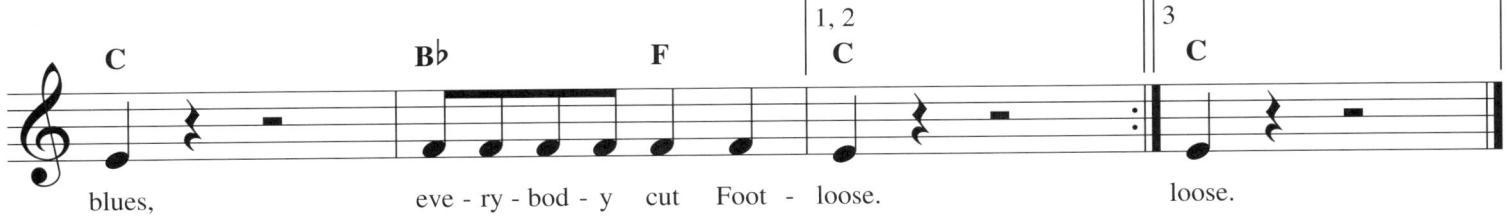

Additional Lyrics

2. You're playin' so cool
   Obeying every rule
   Dig way down in your heart
   You're burnin', yearnin' for some…
   Somebody to tell you
   That life ain't a-passin' you by.
   I'm tryin' to tell you
   It will if you don't even try;
   You can fly if you'd only cut…
   Chorus

3. Loose, Footloose
   Kick off your Sunday shoes.
   Ooh-ee, Marie,
   Shake it, shake it for me.
   Whoa, Milo.
   Come on, come on let's go.
   Lose your blues,
   Everybody cut Footloose.
   Chorus

FREE FALLIN'

Words and Music by TOM PETTY
and JEFF LYNNE

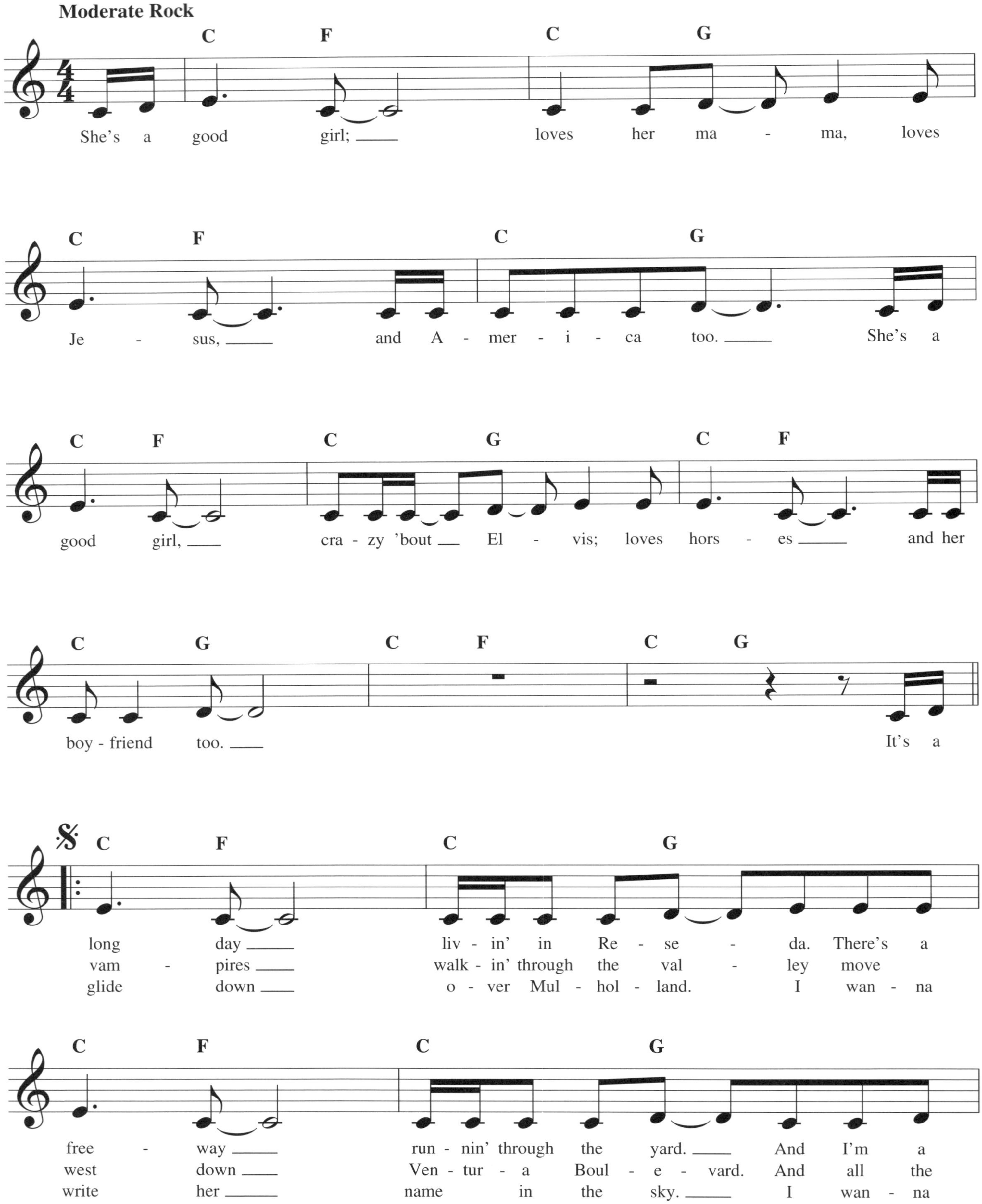

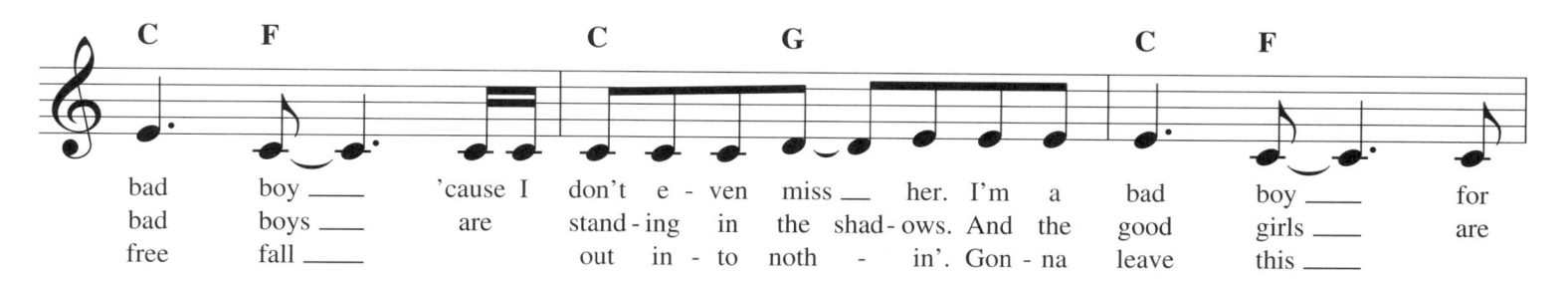

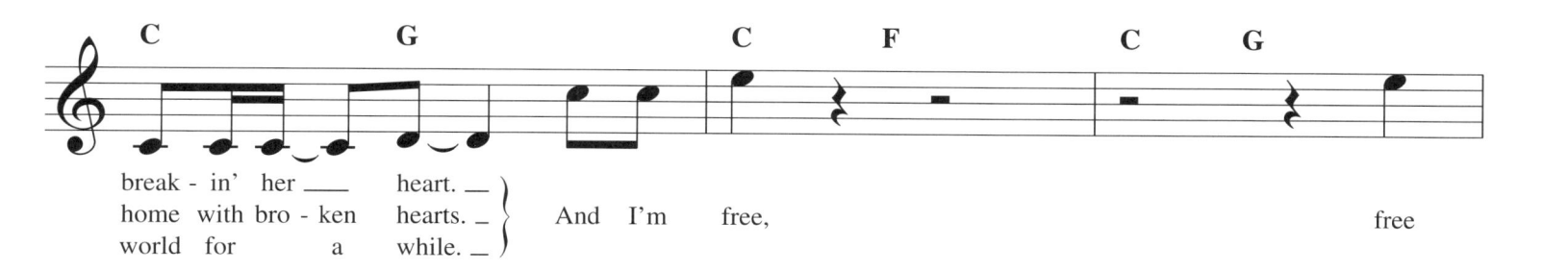

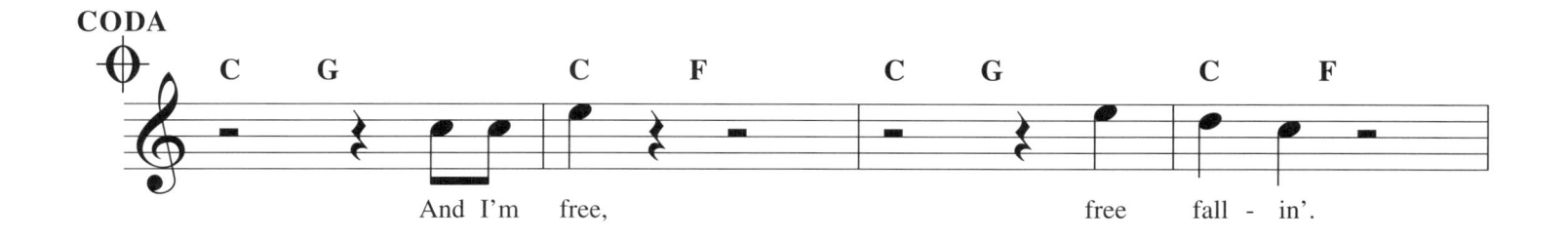

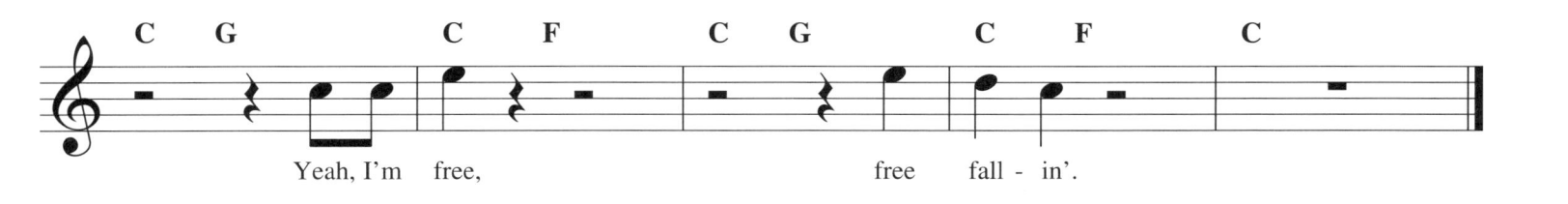

bad boy 'cause I don't even miss her. I'm a bad boy for
bad boys are standing in the shadows. And the good girls are
free fall out into nothin'. Gonna leave this

breakin' her heart. And I'm free, free
home with broken hearts.
world for a while.

fall - in'. Yeah, I'm free, free

fall - in'. All the Wanna

CODA

And I'm free, free fall - in'.

Yeah, I'm free, free fall - in'.

GIRLS JUST WANT TO HAVE FUN

Words and Music by
ROBERT HAZARD

Copyright © 1979 Sony/ATV Music Publishing LLC
All Rights Administered by Sony/ATV Music Publishing LLC,
8 Music Square West, Nashville, TN 37203

Bright Rock beat

I come home in the morn-ing light. My moth-
The phone rings in the mid-dle of the night. My fa-
Some boys take a beau-ti-ful girl and hide

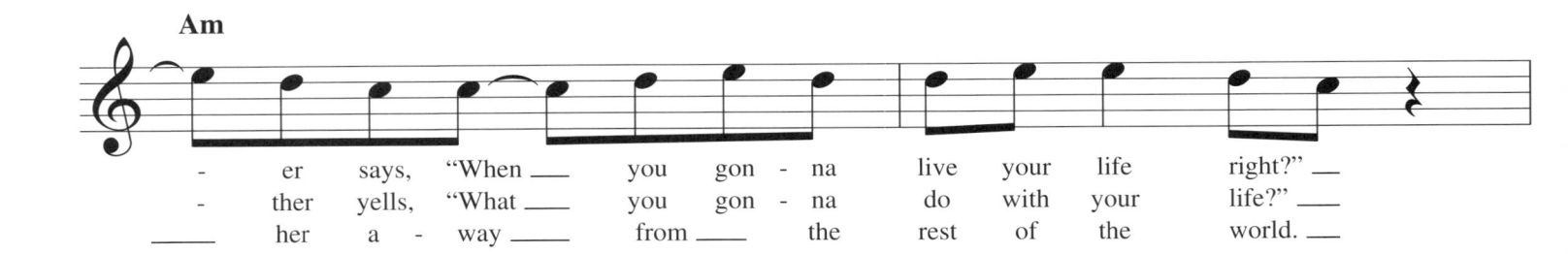

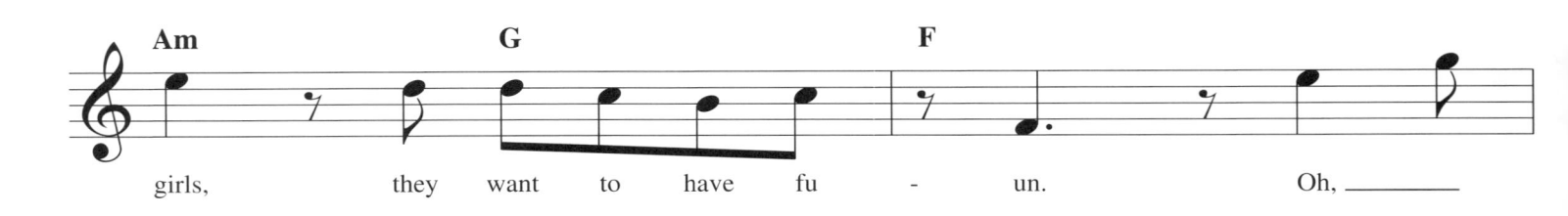

-er says, "When you gon-na live your life right?"
-ther yells, "What you gon-na do with your life?"
her a-way from the rest of the world.

Oh, Moth-er dear, we're not the for-tu-nate ones. And
Oh, Dad-dy dear, you know you're still num-ber one. But
I want to be the one to walk in the sun. Oh,

girls, they want to have fu-un. Oh,

1.
girls just want to have fun. (Instrumental)

2, 3.
girls just want to have...

C
That's all they real - ly want:
Am
some fun.
C
When the work - ing day
is done, oh, girls,
Am
G
they want to have fu -
F
un.
Oh,
Am
girls just
G
want to have
C
fun.
(Instrumental)
Am
To Coda
D.C. al Coda
F
G
CODA
F
G
C
They just wan - na they
Am
F
G
just wan - na.
C
They just wan - na, they just
Am
F
G
wan - na,
C
Girls,
Am
girls just
F
want to
G
have fu -
C
un.

GLORY OF LOVE
Theme from KARATE KID PART II

Words and Music by DAVID FOSTER,
PETER CETERA and DIANE NINI

| C | F | C/E | G7 |

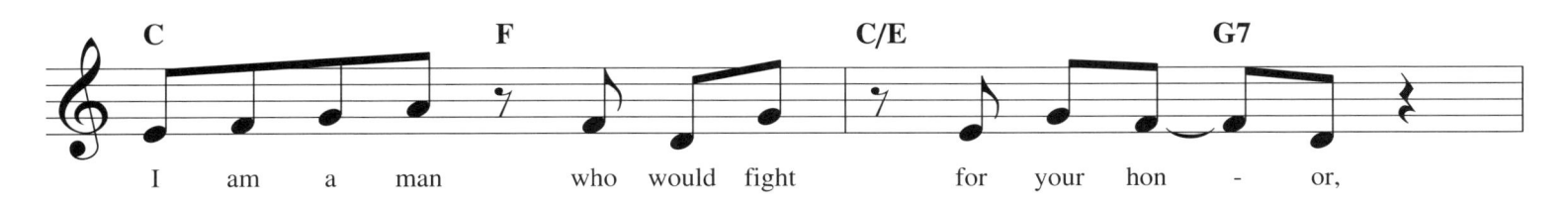

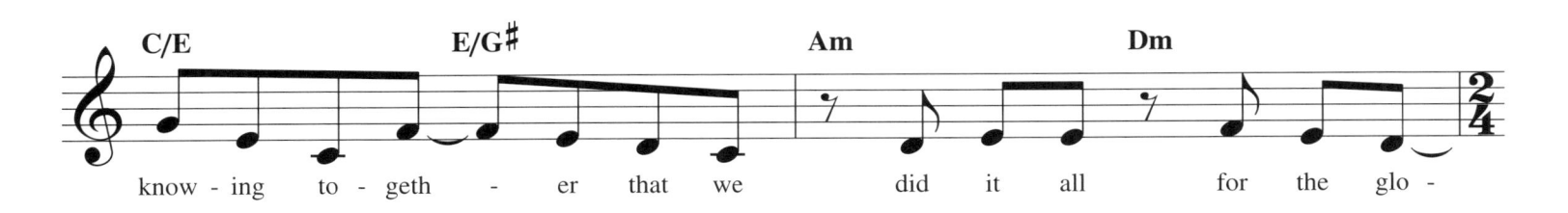

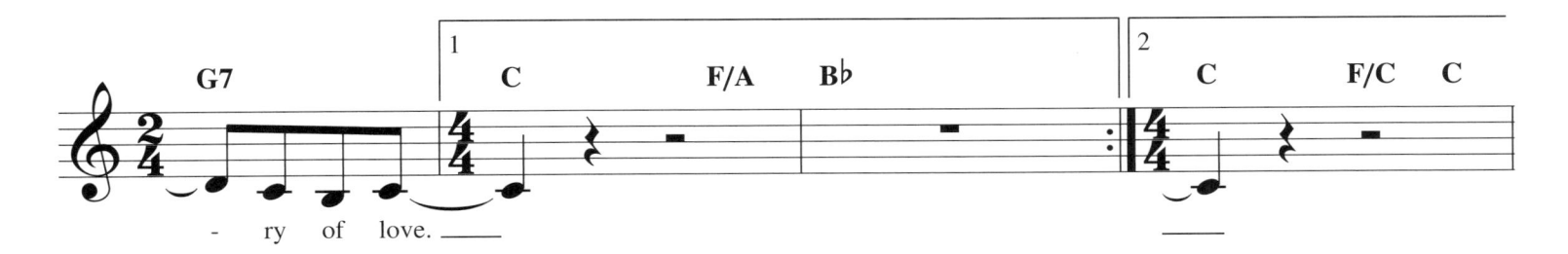

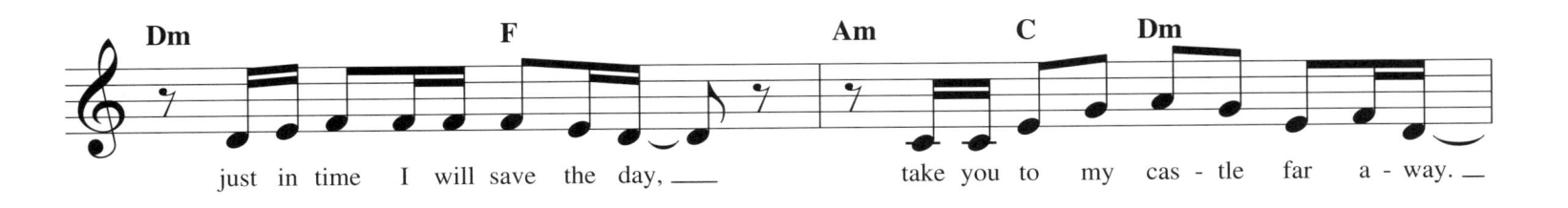

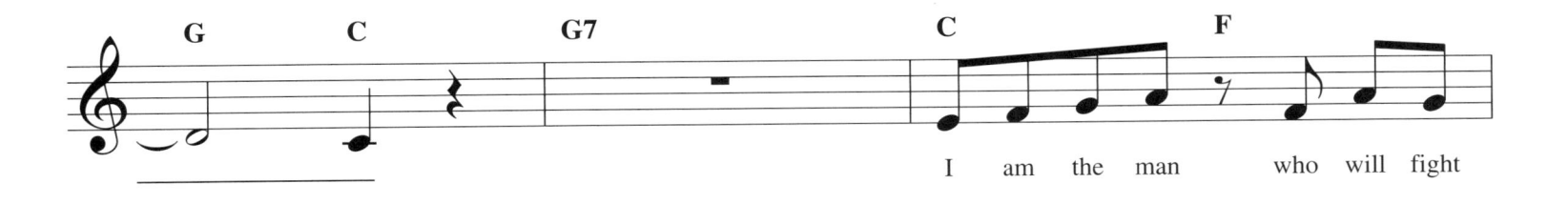

I am a man who would fight for your hon - or,

| C | F/A | Dm | G7 | Am | Dm |

I'll be the he - ro you're ___ dream-ing of. ___ We'll live for-ev - er,

| C/E | E/G# | Am | Dm |

know - ing to - geth - er that we did it all for the glo -

1. | G7 | C | F/A | B♭ |

- ry of love. ___

2. | C | F/C | C |

| Dm | F | G/B | G | C |

Just like a knight in shin - ing ar - mor, from a long time a - go,

| Dm | F | Am | C | Dm |

just in time I will save the day, ___ take you to my cas - tle far a - way. ___

| G | C | G7 | C | F |

I am the man who will fight

C/E G7 C Am Dm G7
for your hon - or, I'll be the he - ro that you're dreaming of. We're
Am Dm C/E E/G♯
gon - na live for - ev - er, know - ing to - geth - er that we
Am Dm G7 C F
did it all for the glo - ry of love.
C/E G Am Dm C/E E/G♯
We'll live for - ev - er, know - ing to - geth - er that we
Am Dm G7 Am
did it all for the glo - ry of love.
F G Am
We did it all for love.
F G Am F G
Repeat and Fade
We did it all for love. We did it all for love.

HARD HABIT TO BREAK

Words and Music by STEPHEN KIPNER
and JOHN LEWIS PARKER

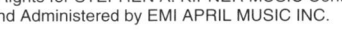

Am			Am/G	

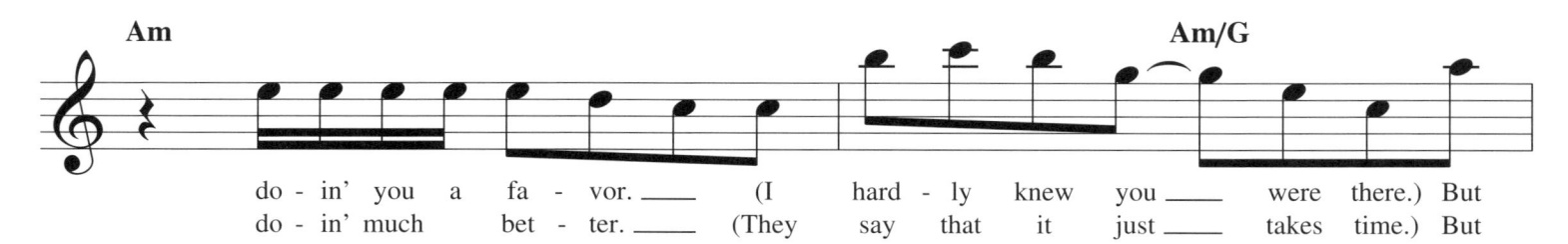

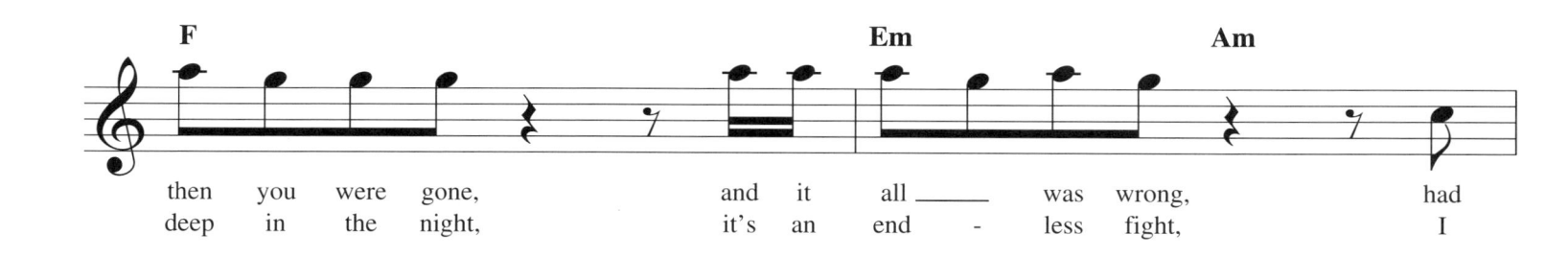

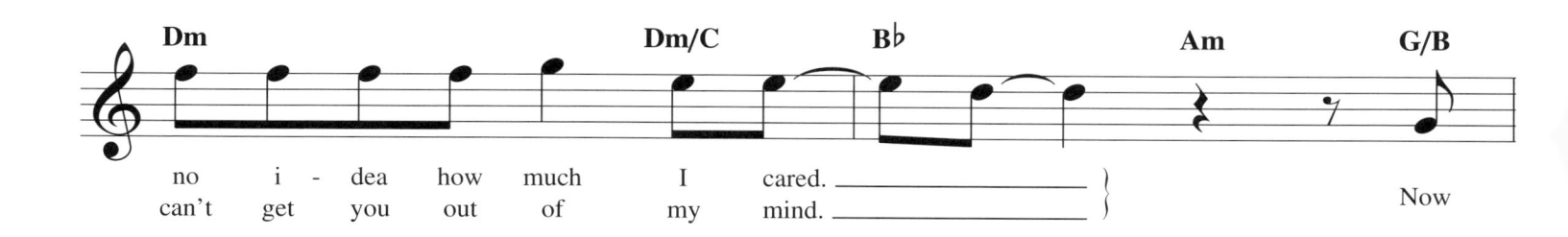

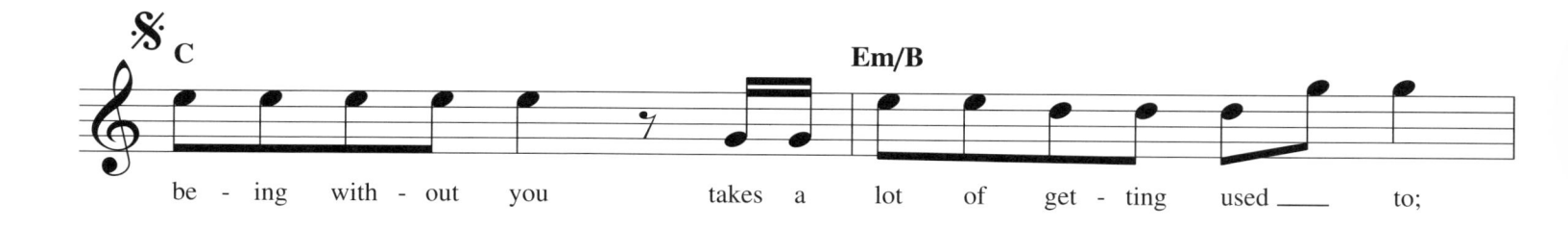

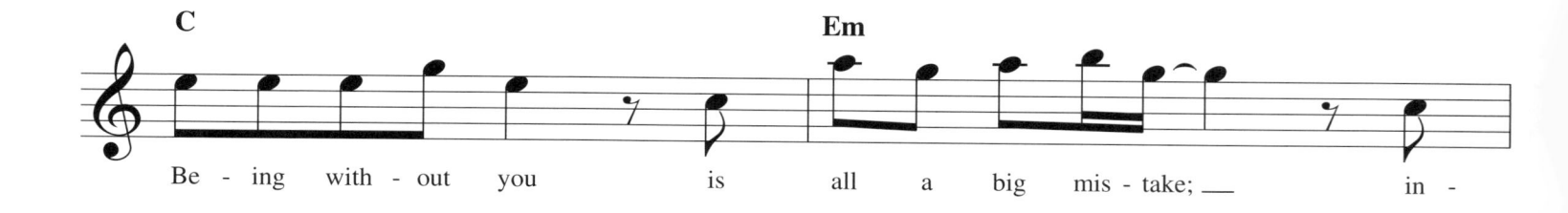

do - in' you a fa - vor. (I hard - ly knew you were there.) But
do - in' much bet - ter. (They say that it just takes time.) But

F		Em	Am

then you were gone, and it all was wrong, had
deep in the night, it's an end - less fight, I

Dm	Dm/C	B♭	Am	G/B

no i - dea how much I cared.
can't get you out of my mind. Now

𝄋 C | | Em/B |

be - ing with - out you takes a lot of get - ting used to;

F/A		Fm/A♭

should learn to live with it, but I don't want to.

C		Em

Be - ing with - out you is all a big mis - take; in -

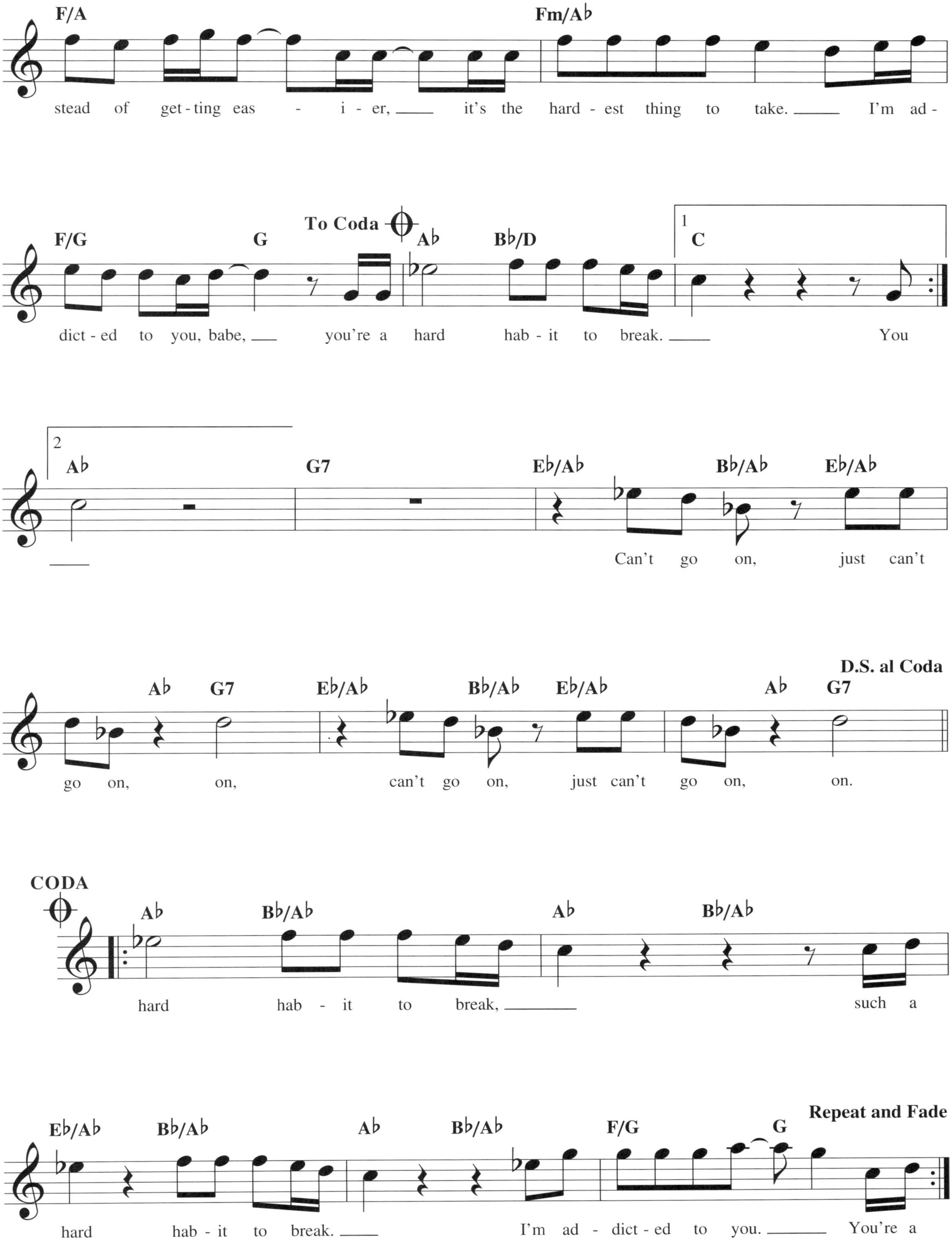
F/A
Fm/Ab
stead of get-ting eas - i - er, it's the hard - est thing to take. I'm ad -
To Coda
F/G G Ab Bb/D
1 C
dict - ed to you, babe, you're a hard hab - it to break. You
2 Ab G7 Eb/Ab Bb/Ab Eb/Ab
Can't go on, just can't
D.S. al Coda
Ab G7 Eb/Ab Bb/Ab Eb/Ab Ab G7
go on, on, can't go on, just can't go on, on.
CODA
Ab Bb/Ab Ab Bb/Ab
hard hab - it to break, such a
Repeat and Fade
Eb/Ab Bb/Ab Ab Bb/Ab F/G G
hard hab - it to break. I'm ad - dict - ed to you. You're a

78

THE HEAT IS ON
from the Paramount Picture BEVERLY HILLS COP

Copyright © 1984, 1985 Sony/ATV Music Publishing LLC
All Rights Administered by Sony/ATV Music Publishing LLC,
8 Music Square West, Nashville, TN 37203

Words by KEITH FORSEY
Music by HAROLD FALTERMEYER

Fast Rock 'n' Roll

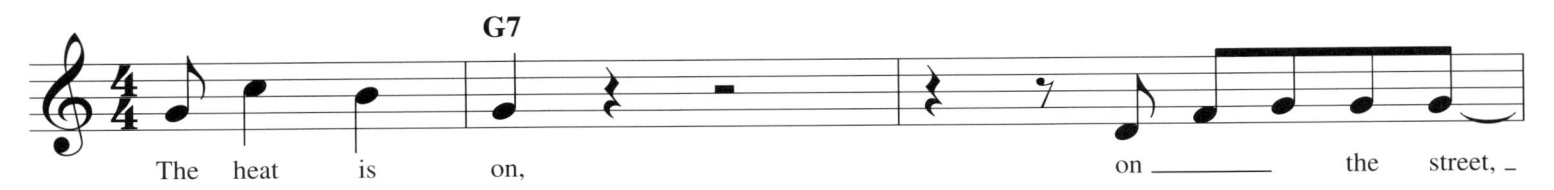

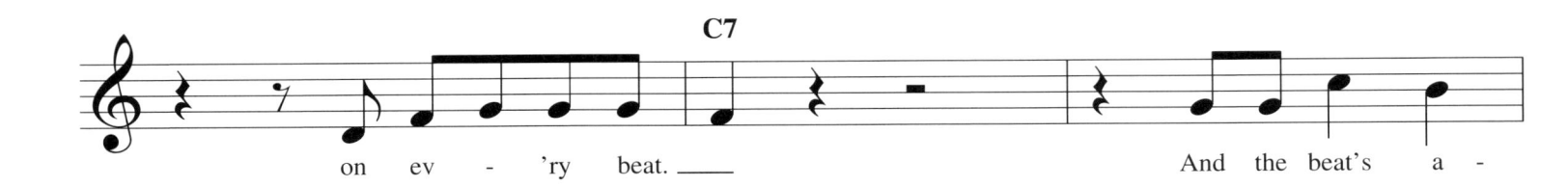

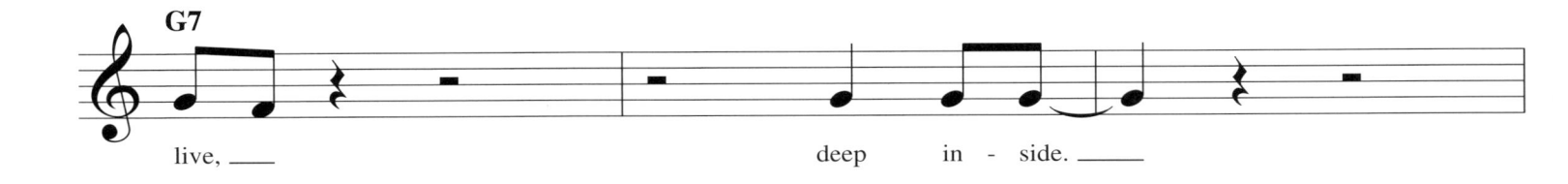

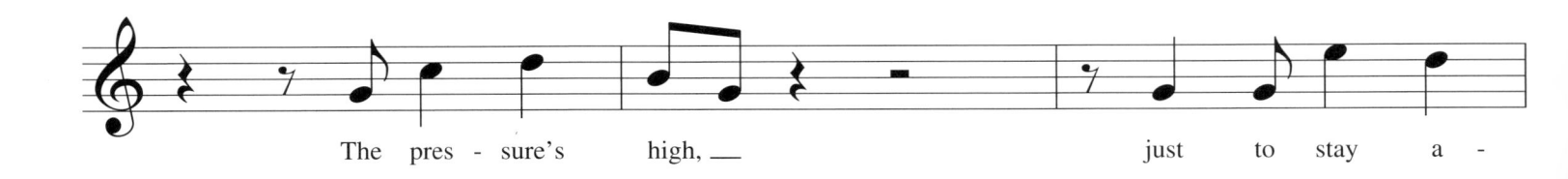

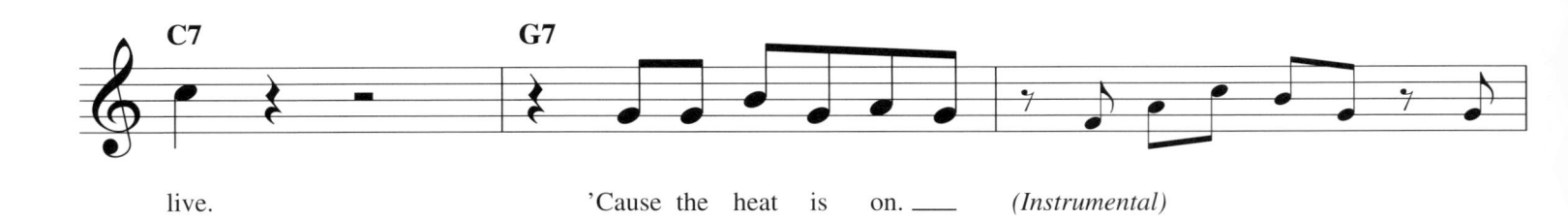

The heat is on, on ____ the street, ____ in-side your head, on ev-'ry beat. ____ And the beat's a-live, ____ deep in-side. ____ The pres-sure's high, ____ just to stay a-live. 'Cause the heat is on. ____ *(Instrumental)*

G C/E F
Oh oh oh oh, oh oh oh oh, caught up in the ac - tion, I'll
F/A B♭ C G
be look-ing out for you. Oh oh oh oh, oh oh oh oh, tell
Dm
me you can feel it; tell me you can feel it. Tell me do you feel it?
N.C. G7
The heat is on, on the street. The heat is
on, the heat is on. The heat is
on, in - side your head. The heat is on; on ev - 'ry beat.
on; the pres - sure's high. The heat is on; the pres - sure's high.
1 C7
The heat is on. The heat is
2 C
The heat is on. The heat is... on!

HEAVEN

Words and Music by
JANI LANE

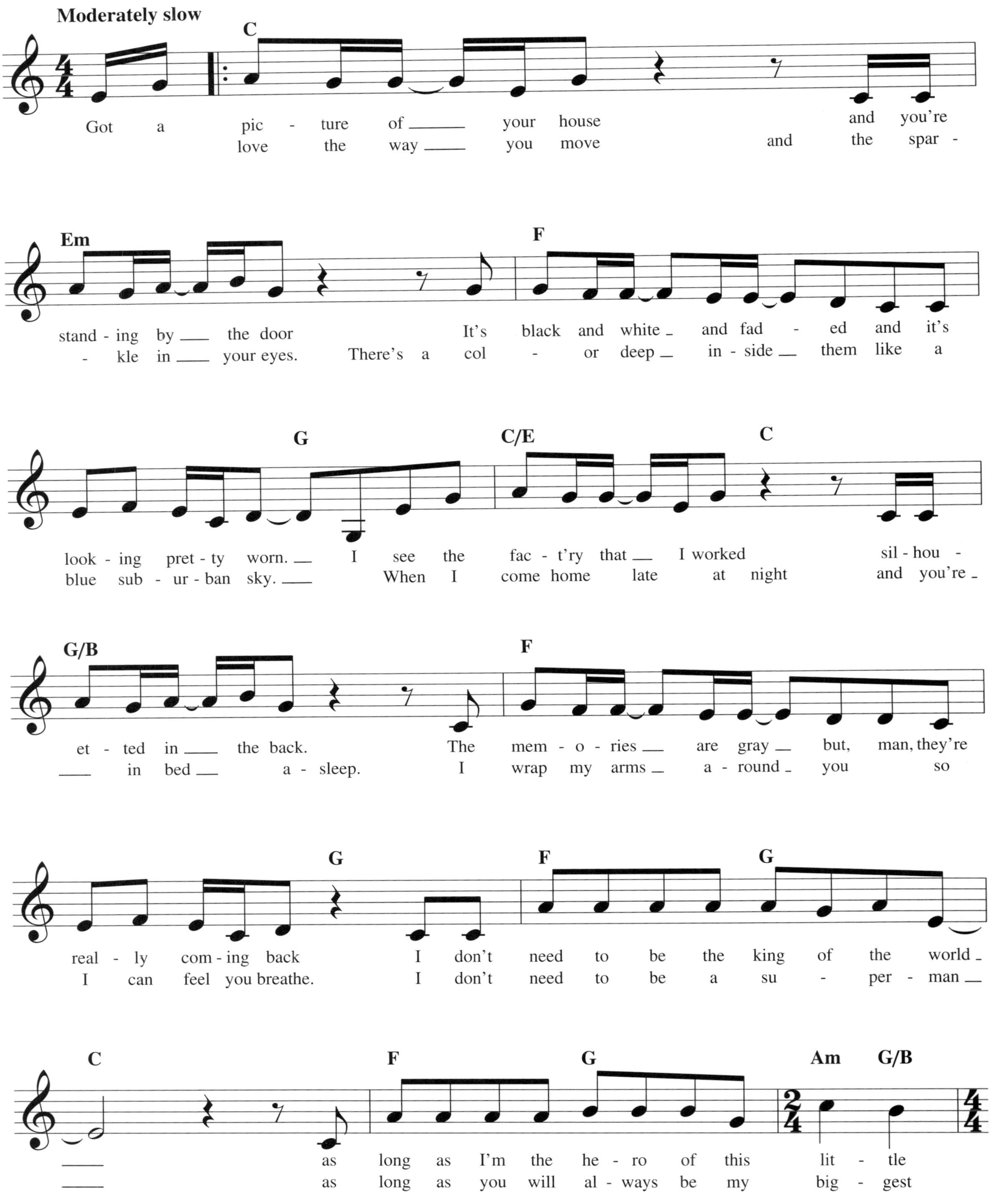

girl. / fan. Heav-en isn't too far a-way. Clos-er to it ev-er-y day. No mat-ter what your friends might say. How I We'll find our way. Yeah. Now the lights are go-ing out a-long the boul-e-vard. Mem-o-ries come rush-ing back and makes it pret-ty hard. I've got no-where left to go, no one real-ly cares. I don't know what to do but I'm

G C G F
nev - er giv - ing up on you. Heav - en is - n't too far a - way,
C G F
clos - er to it ev - er - y day.
C G
No mat - ter what your friends say I
F C G/B F
know we're gon - na find a way. Heav - en, whoa whoa.
G/B C G/B F G/B
Heav - en, whoa whoa.
C G/B F G/B C G/B F
Heav - en is not too far a - way oh oh. Whoa whoa.
3
G/B F
Yeah.

HIGHER LOVE

Words and Music by WILL JENNINGS
and STEVE WINWOOD

Copyright © 1986 BLUE SKY RIDER SONGS and F.S. MUSIC LTD.
All Rights for BLUE SKY RIDER SONGS Administered by IRVING MUSIC, INC.
All Rights for F.S. MUSIC LTD. Administered by WARNER-TAMERLANE PUBLISHING CORP.

Moderate Rock

Think about it! There must be higher love,
-ing and we're just hanging on,

down in the heart or hidden in the stars above. Without it, life is
facing our fear and standing out there alone. A yearning, and it's

wasted time. Look inside your heart; I'll look inside mine.
real to me; there must be someone who's feeling for me.

Things look so bad ev-'ry-where. In this whole world,

what is fair? We walk blind and we try to see,

falling behind in what could be. Bring me a higher love.

84

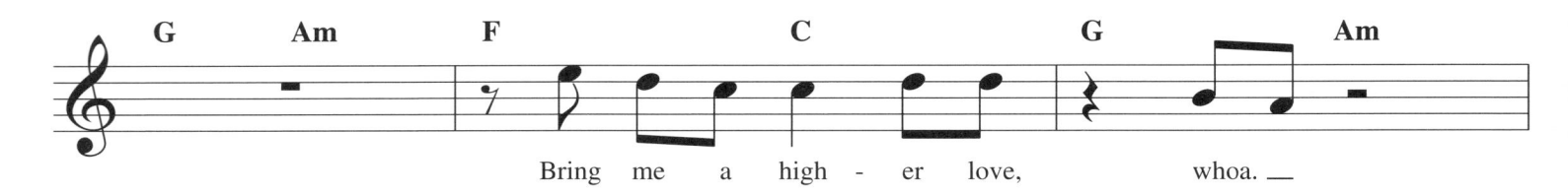

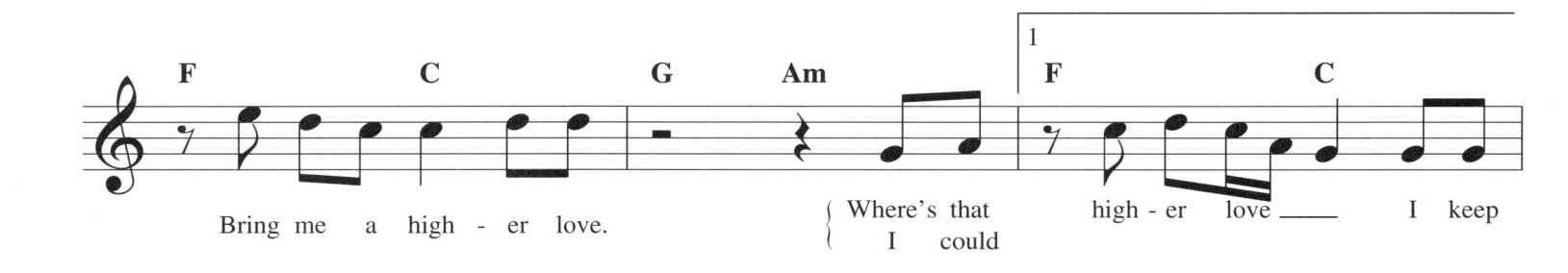

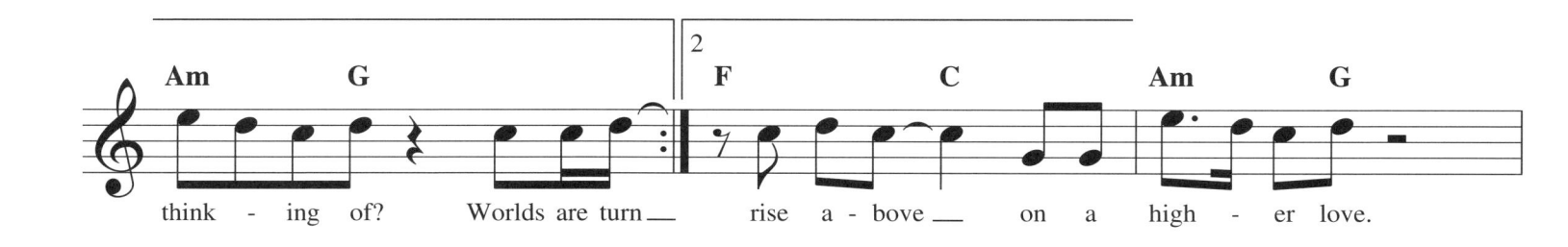

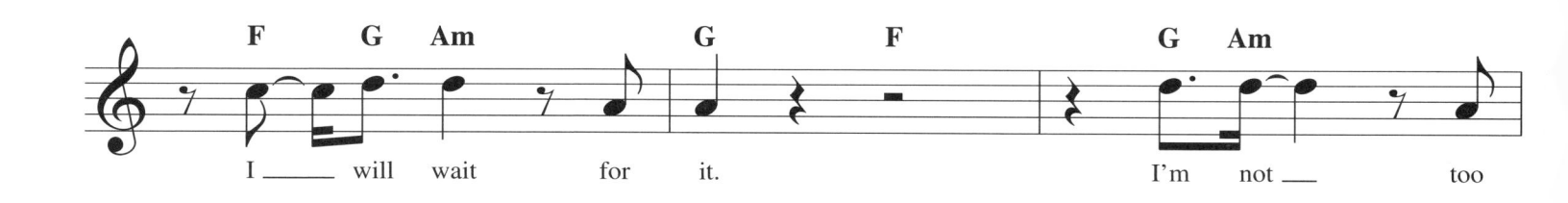

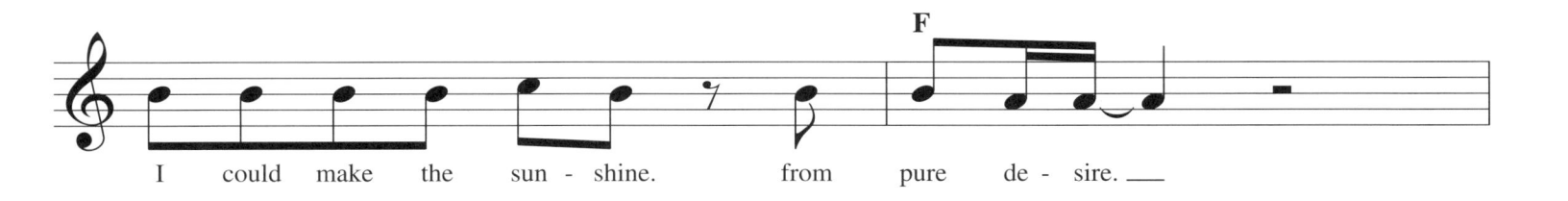

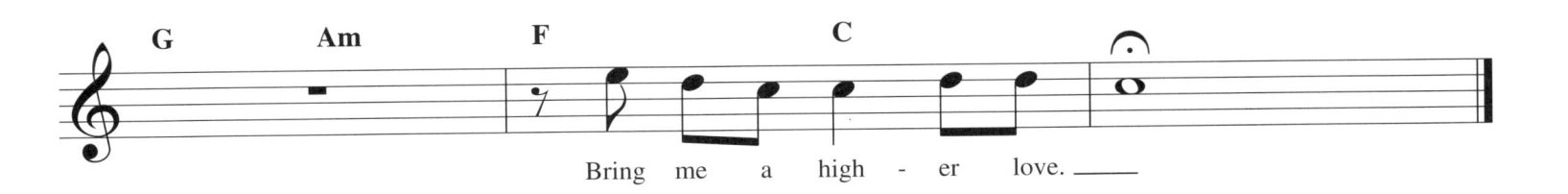

I could light the night up with my soul on fire. I could make the sunshine. from pure desire.

Let me feel that love come o-ver me. Let me feel how strong it could be. Bring me a high-er love. Bring me a high-er love, whoa. Bring me a high-er love. Bring me a high-er love.

HELLO

Copyright © 1983 by Brockman Music and Brenda Richie Publishing

Words and Music by
LIONEL RICHIE

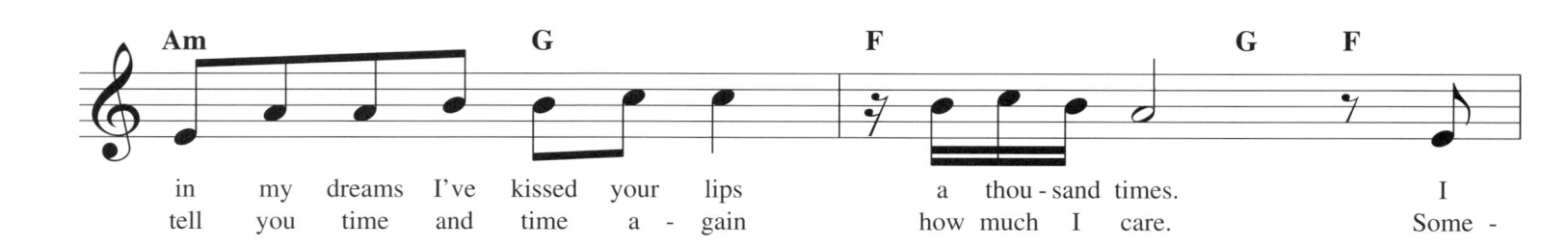

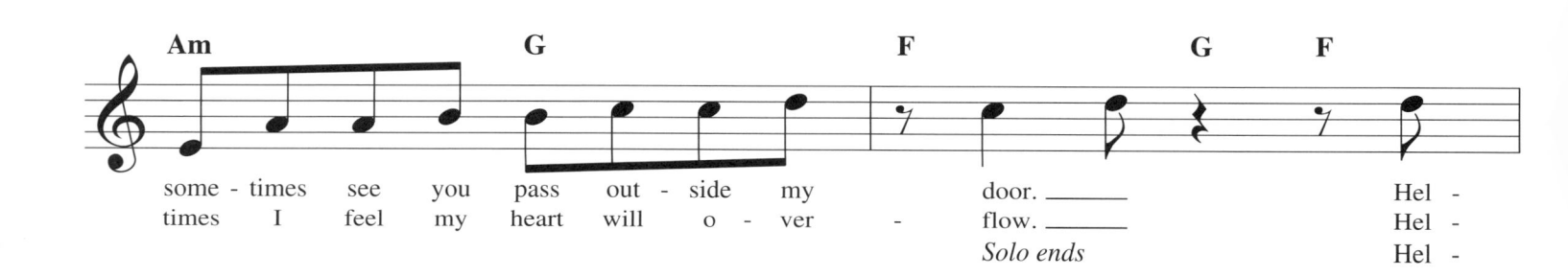

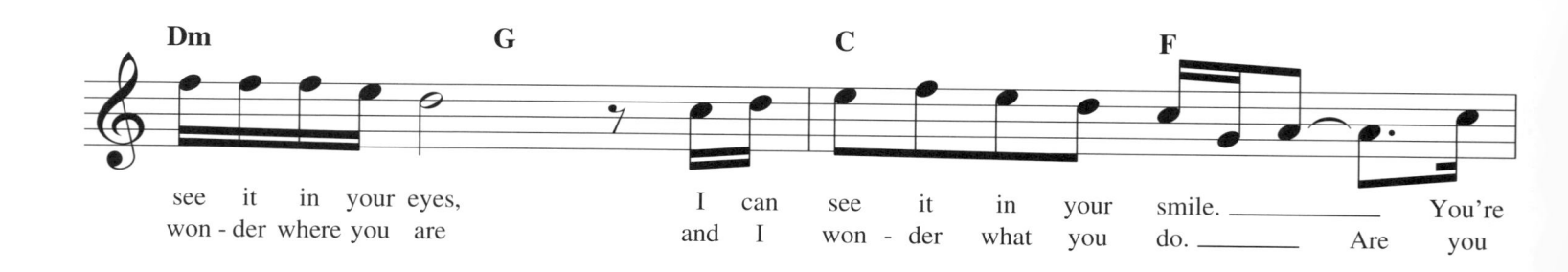

Slow Ballad

I've been a-lone with you in-side my mind and
long to see the sun-light in your hair and
Instrumental solo

in my dreams I've kissed your lips a thou-sand times. I
tell you time and time a - gain how much I care. Some-

some-times see you pass out-side my door. Hel -
times I feel my heart will o-ver-flow. Hel -
Solo ends Hel -

lo, is it me you're look-ing for? I can
lo, I've just got to let you know.
lo, is it me you're look-ing for? 'Cause I

see it in your eyes, I can see it in your smile. You're
won-der where you are and I won-der what you do. Are you

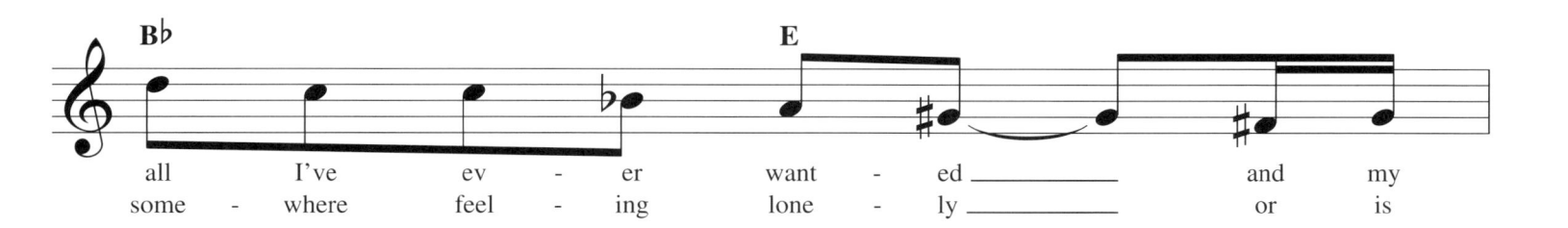

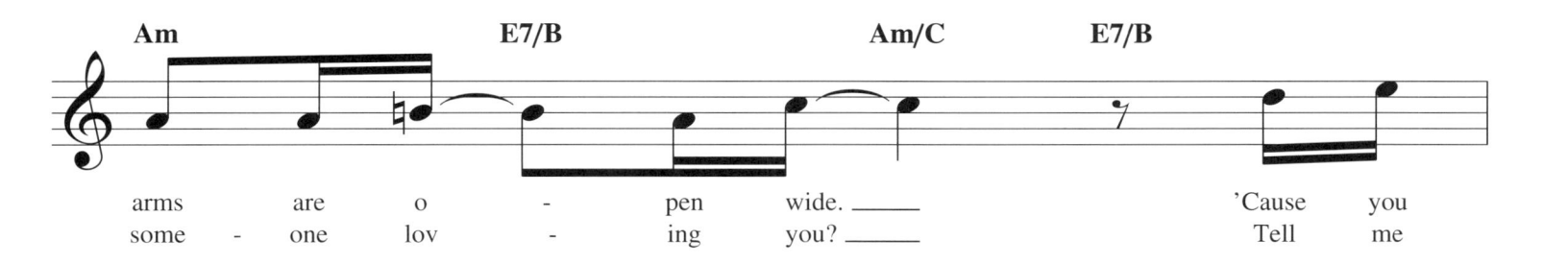

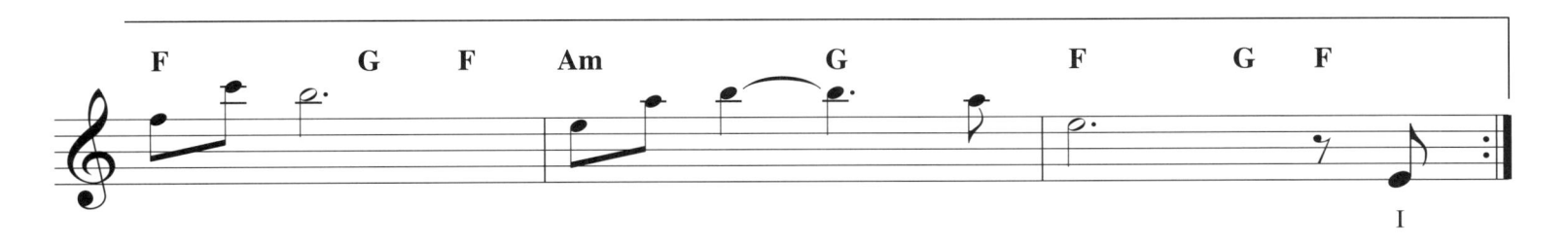

all I've ev-er want-ed and my
some-where feel-ing lone-ly or is

arms are o-pen wide. 'Cause you
some-one lov-ing you? Tell me

know just what to say and you know just what to do and I
how to win your heart for I have-n't got a clue. But,

want to tell you so much, I love you. *(Instrumental)*
let me start by say-ing, I love you.

I

you. *(Instrumental)*

HERE COMES MY GIRL

Copyright © 1979 ALMO MUSIC CORP.

Words and Music by TOM PETTY and MIKE CAMPBELL

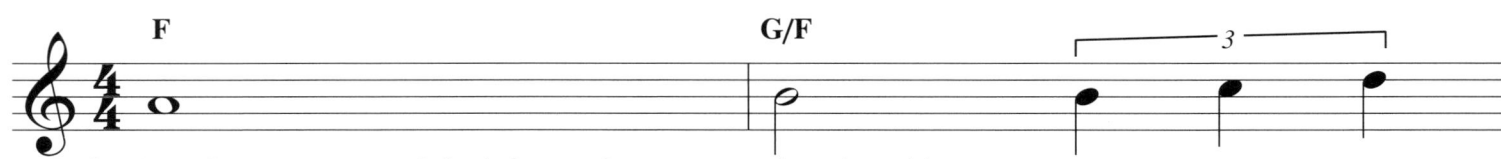

Moderate Rock

(Spoken:) You know, sometimes, I don't know why, but this old town just seems so hopeless.
(Spoken:) Every now and then I get down to the end of the day, I have to stop. ask myself why I've done it.
(Spoken:) Yeah, every time it seems like ain't nothin' left no more, I find myself havin' to reach out and grab hold of somethin'.

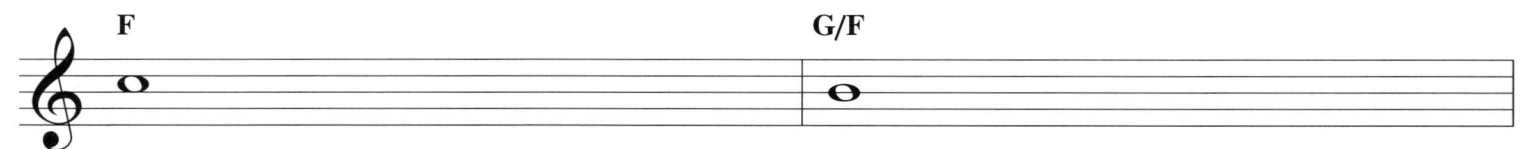

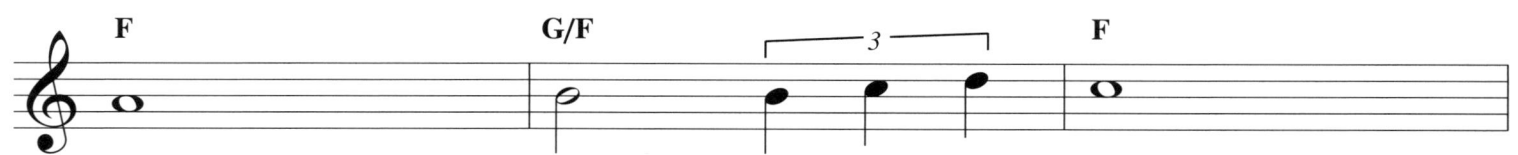

I ain't really sure, but it seems I remember the good times were just a little bit more in focus.
It just seems so useless to have to work so hard, and nothing ever really seemed to come from it.
Yeah, I just catch myself wonderin', waitin', worryin', about some silly little things that don't add up to nothin'.

1. (Sung:) But when she puts her arms a-round me,
2.,3. (Sung:) And then she looks me in the eye

and says, "We're gon-na last for-ev-er," and I can
some-how rise a-bove it.
man, you know, I can't be-gin to doubt it, no,

Yeah, man, when I got that lit-tle girl stand-in' right by my side, you know, I can
tell the whole wide world: shove it. Hey! Here comes my
'cause it just feels so good and so free and so right. I know we ain't
nev-er gon-na change our minds a-bout it.

girl, here comes my girl.

And she looks so right,

she is all I need to-night.

D.C. al Coda
(Spoken:) Oh, watch her walk.

CODA
to-night. (Instrumental)

HOLD ON LOOSELY

Words and Music by JEFF CARLISI,
DON BARNES and JIM PETERIK

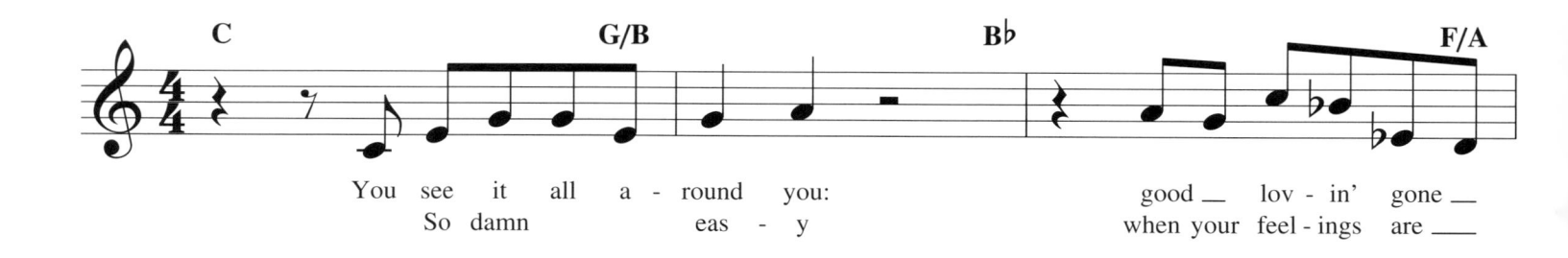

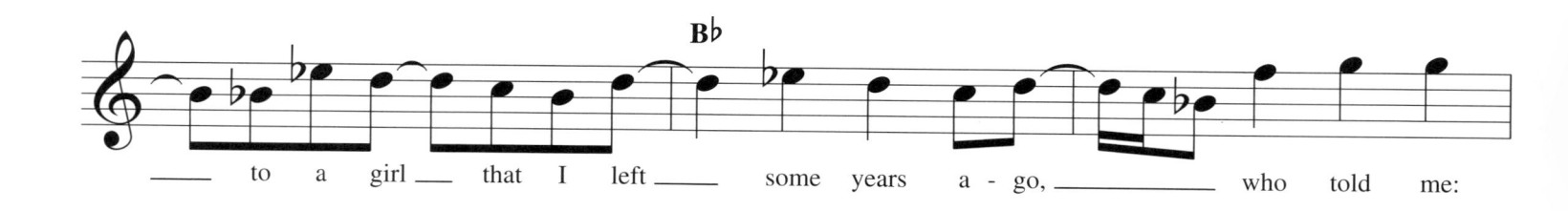

Copyright © 1981 by Universal Music - MGB Songs, WB Music Corp. and Easy Action Music
All Rights for Easy Action Music Administered by WB Music Corp.

You see it all a-round you: good lov-in' gone
So damn eas - y when your feel-ings are

bad. And you be-lieve it's too late when you
such, to o-ver-pro-tect her,

re-al-ize what you had.
to love her too much.
And my mind goes back

to a girl that I left some years a-go, who told me:

Just hold on loose-ly, but don't let go.

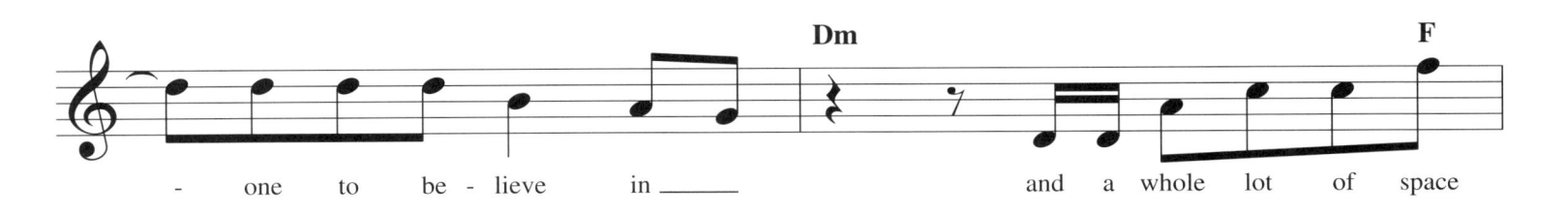

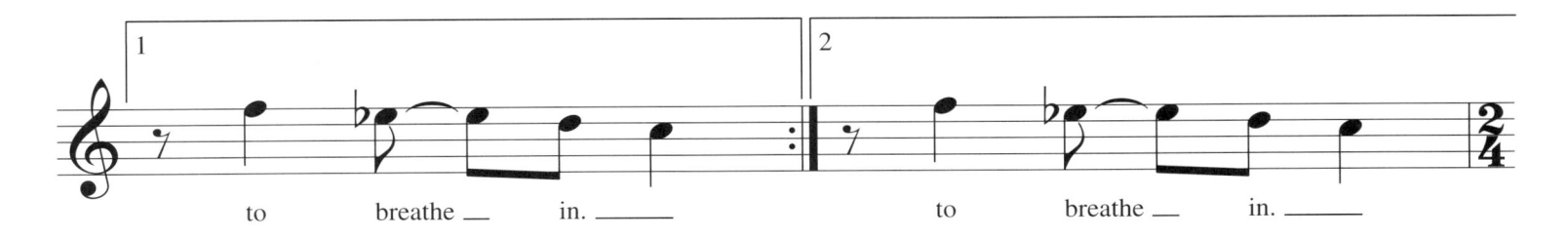

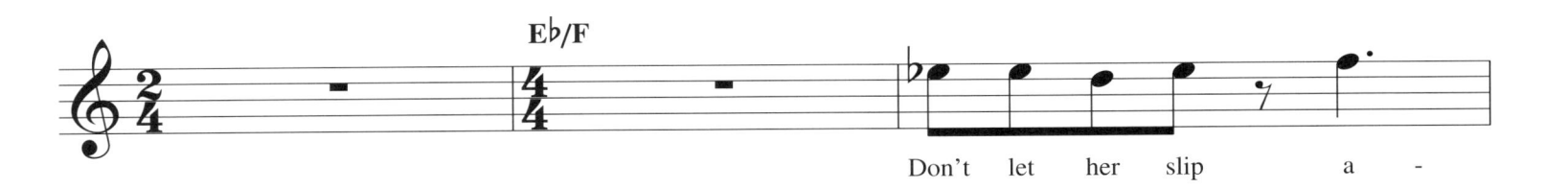

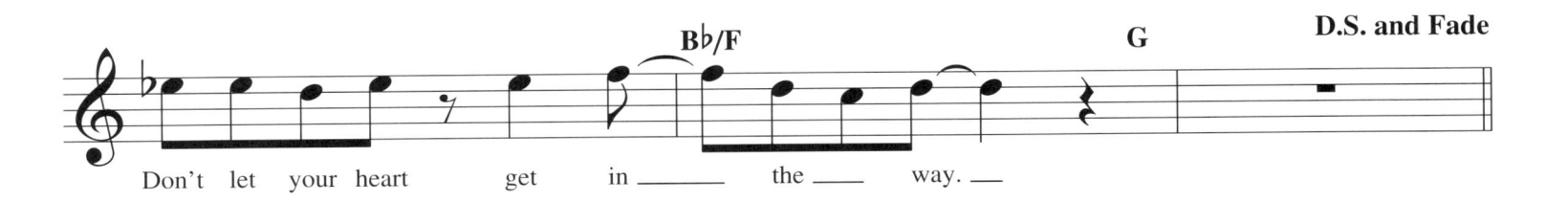

If you cling too tight - ly, you're gon - na lose con - trol. Your ba - by needs some - one to be - lieve in and a whole lot of space to breathe in. to breathe in.

Don't let her slip a - way. Sen - ti - men - tal fool. Don't let your heart get in the way.

D.S. and Fade

HOME SWEET HOME

Words and Music by TOMMY LEE and NIKKI SIXX

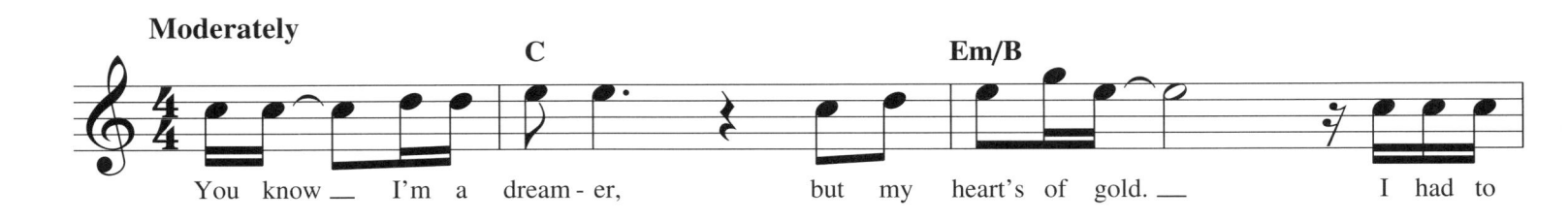

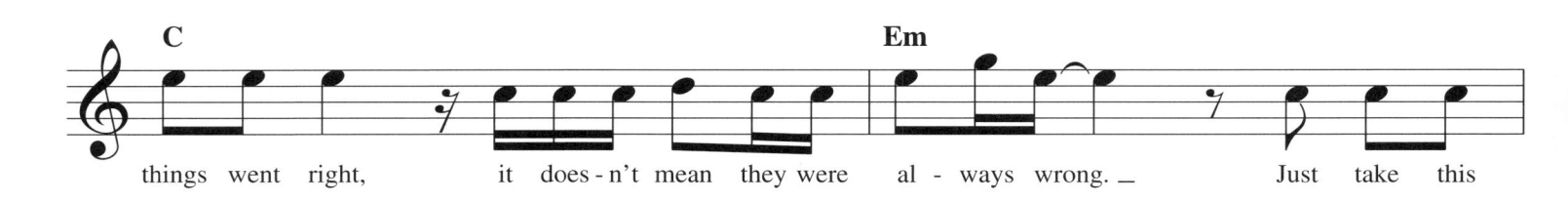

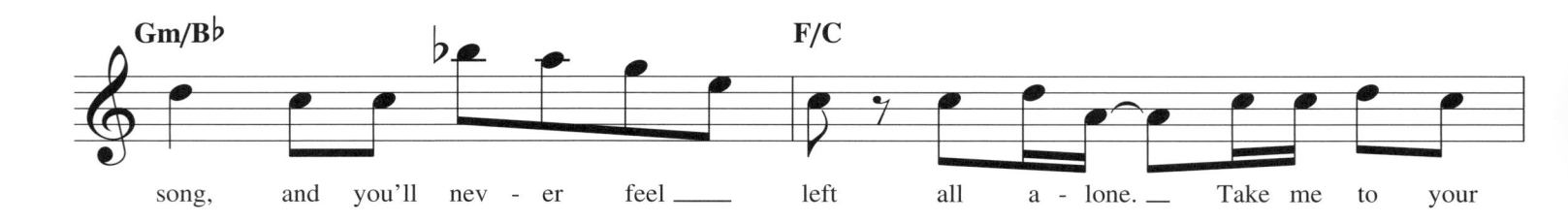

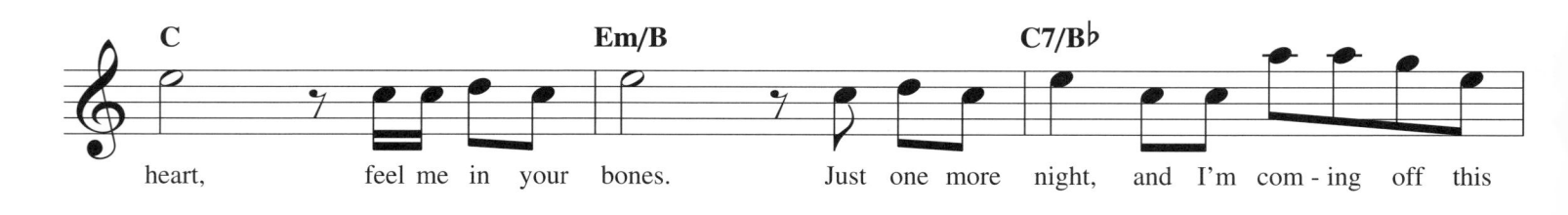

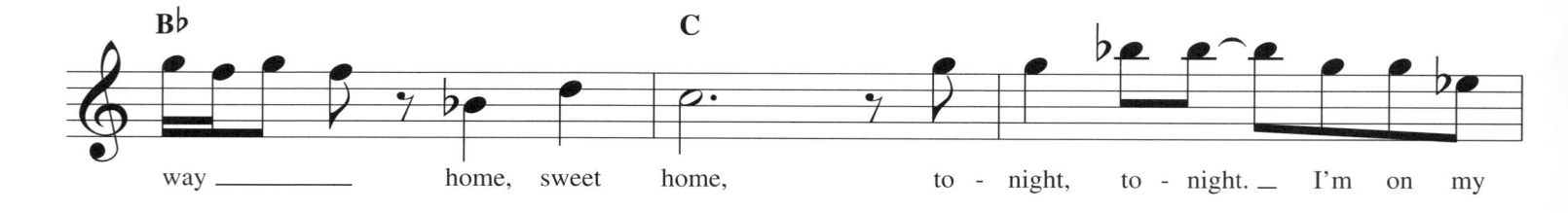

Copyright © 1985 Mars Mountain Music (ASCAP), WB Music Corp. (ASCAP),
Sixx Gunner Music (ASCAP) and Tommyland Music (ASCAP)
Worldwide Rights for Mars Mountain Music Administered by Cherry Lane Music Publishing Company, Inc.

Moderately

You know — I'm a dream-er, but my heart's of gold. — I had to run a-way — high — so I would-n't come home low. Just when — things went right, it does-n't mean they were al-ways wrong. — Just take this song, and you'll nev-er feel — left all a-lone. — Take me to your heart, feel me in your bones. Just one more night, and I'm com-ing off this long and wind-ing road. I'm on my way, — I'm on my way — home, sweet home, to-night, to-night. — I'm on my

A♭ B♭ C
way, I'm on my way home, sweet home.
Em/B
You know that I've seen too man - y ro - man - tic dreams up in
Gm/B♭ F
lights, fall - ing off the sil - ver screen. My heart's like an
C Em/B
o - pen book for the whole world to read. Some - times
Gm/B♭
noth - ing keeps me to - geth - er at the seams. I'm on my
A♭ B♭
way, well, I'm on my way home, sweet
C
home, to - night, to - night. I'm on my
A♭ B♭ C
way; just set me free, home, sweet home.

HOT HOT HOT

Words and Music by
ALPHONSUS CASSELL

Copyright © 1983, 1987 Chrysalis Music Ltd.
All Rights in the U.S. and Canada Administered by Chrysalis Music

Moderate Latin Dance

Me mind on fi - re, me soul on fi - re, feel - ing
See peo - ple rock - ing, hear peo - ple chant - ing, feel - ing

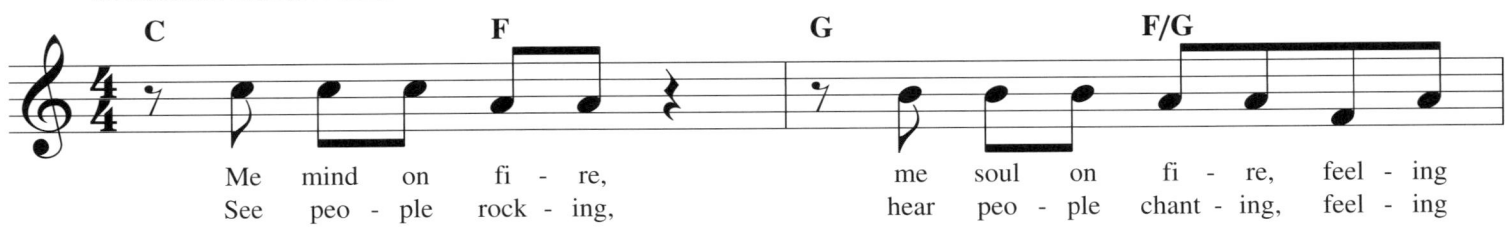

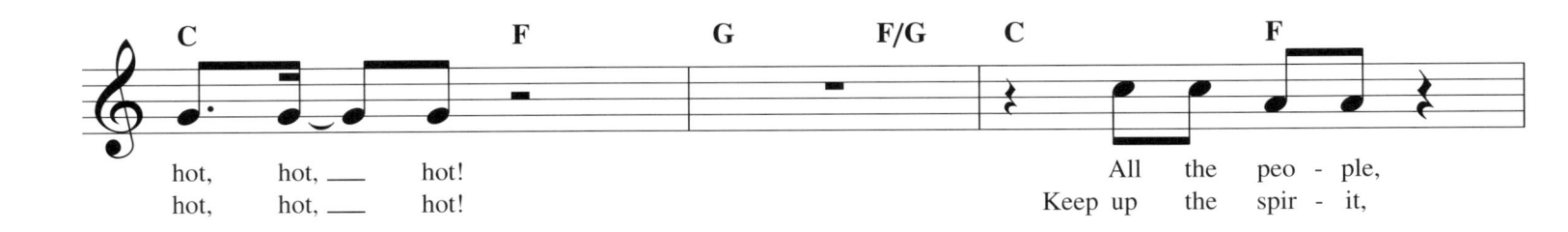

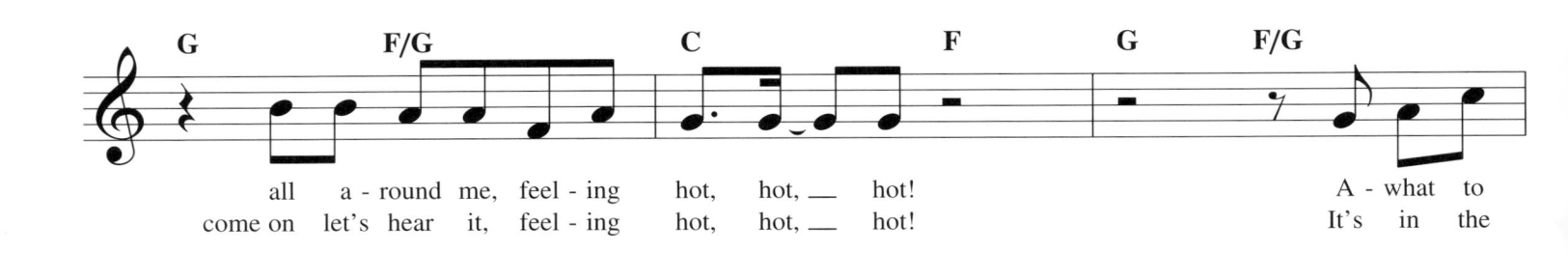

hot, hot, hot! All the peo - ple,
hot, hot, hot! Keep up the spir - it,

all a - round me, feel - ing hot, hot, hot! A - what to
come on let's hear it, feel - ing hot, hot, hot! It's in the

do on a night like this? Is it sweet? I can't re -
air, cel - e - bra - tion time. Is it sweet? Cap - ti - vate your

sist! We need a par - ty sound, a
mind. We need this par - ty sound, this

fun - da - men - tal charm.
fun - da - men - tal charm. So we can rhum - bum - bum - bum.

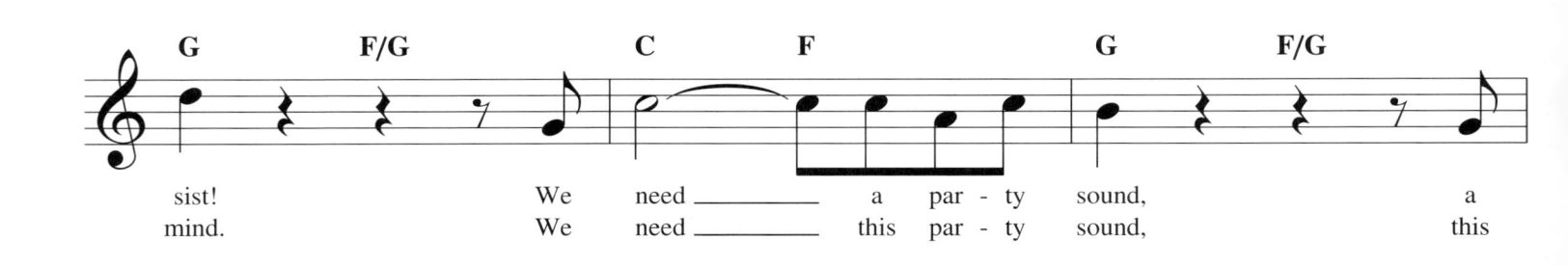

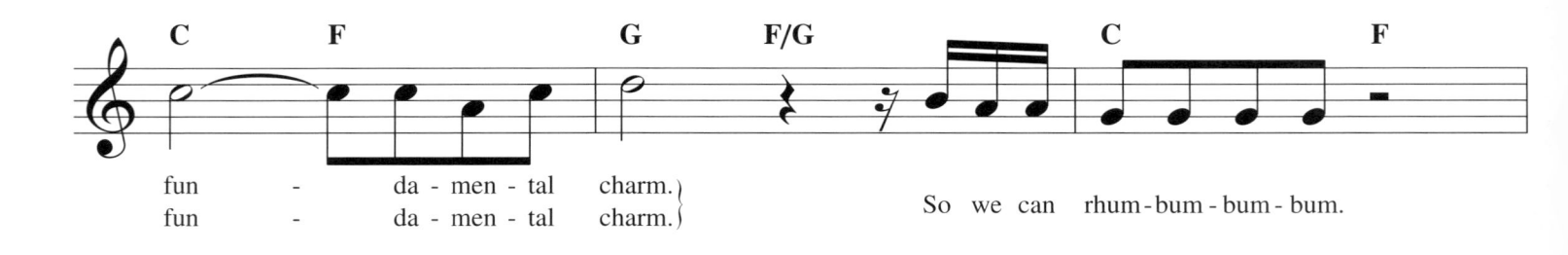

G F/G C F G F/G
Yeah, rhum - bum - bum - bum. Feel - ing
C F G F/G C F
hot, hot, hot! Feel - ing hot, hot, hot!
1 G F/G 2 G F/G C F
Feel - ing hot, hot, hot!
G F/G C F G F/G
Feel - ing hot, hot, hot! (Instrumental)
C F G N.C.
O - lé, o - lé, o -
1–3 4 C F G F/G
lé, o - lé. O - lé, o - lé. (Instrumental) Feel-ing
C F G F/G C
hot, hot, hot! (Instrumental)

HOW WILL I KNOW

Copyright © 1985 IRVING MUSIC, INC., WB MUSIC CORP. and GRATITUDE SKY MUSIC

Words and Music by GEORGE MERRILL, SHANNON RUBICAM and NARADA MICHAEL WALDEN

Moderate Rock

There's a boy I know; he's the one I
dream of.
Looks in - to my eyes;
get e - nough. When I wake from dream -
near me now. Said there's no mis - tak -

takes me to the clouds a - bove. Oh, I lose
in'; tell me, is it real - ly love?
in'; what I feel is real - ly love.

How will I know? (Girl, trust your feel -

- ings.) How will I know? How will I know?

(Love can be de - ceiv - in'.) How will I know?

How will I know if he real - ly loves me? I say a prayer with

G C/G G C/G C Em F G Am
ev - 'ry heart - beat. I fall in love when - ev - er we meet.
C Em F G C/G G C/G C Em F G
I'm ask - in' you, 'cause you know a - bout these things. How will I know if he's
Am C Em F G C/G G C/G C
think - in' of me? I try to phone, but I'm too shy. (Can't speak.)
Em F G Am C Em F
Fall - ing in love is so bit - ter - sweet. This love is strong. Why do
1
D.S.
(take 3rd ending)
2
To next strain
G C/G G C G C/G G C/E F/G
I feel weak? Oh, wake I feel weak? If he loves
3, 4
G C/G G C/G C C/G C/E F/G
I feel weak? me; if he loves
C/G F/G C Dm
me not. If he loves If he loves
D.S.S
(take 3rd ending)
C/D C/E F C/F G
me; if he loves me not. Oh.

HURTS SO GOOD

© 1982 EMI FULL KEEL MUSIC

Words and Music by JOHN MELLENCAMP
and GEORGE GREEN

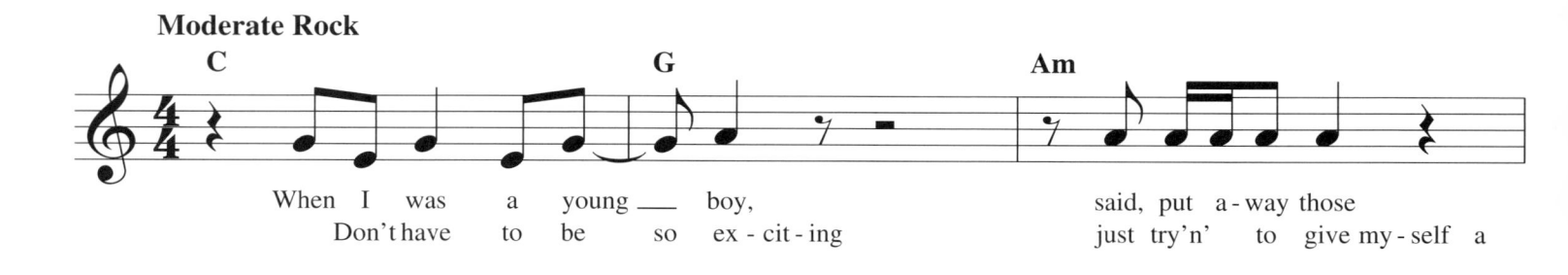

Moderate Rock

When I was a young boy, said, put away those
Don't have to be so exciting just tryn' to give myself a

young boy ways. Now that I'm gettin' older, so much older,
little bit of fun, yeah. You always look so inviting.

I love all those young boy days. With a girl like you,
You ain't as green as you are young. Hey, baby, it's

you.
with a girl like you,
Come on, girl, now, it's you.

Lord knows, there are things we can do, baby, just me and you.
Sink your teeth right through my bones, baby. Let's see what we can do.

Come on and make it }
Come on and make it } hurt so good.

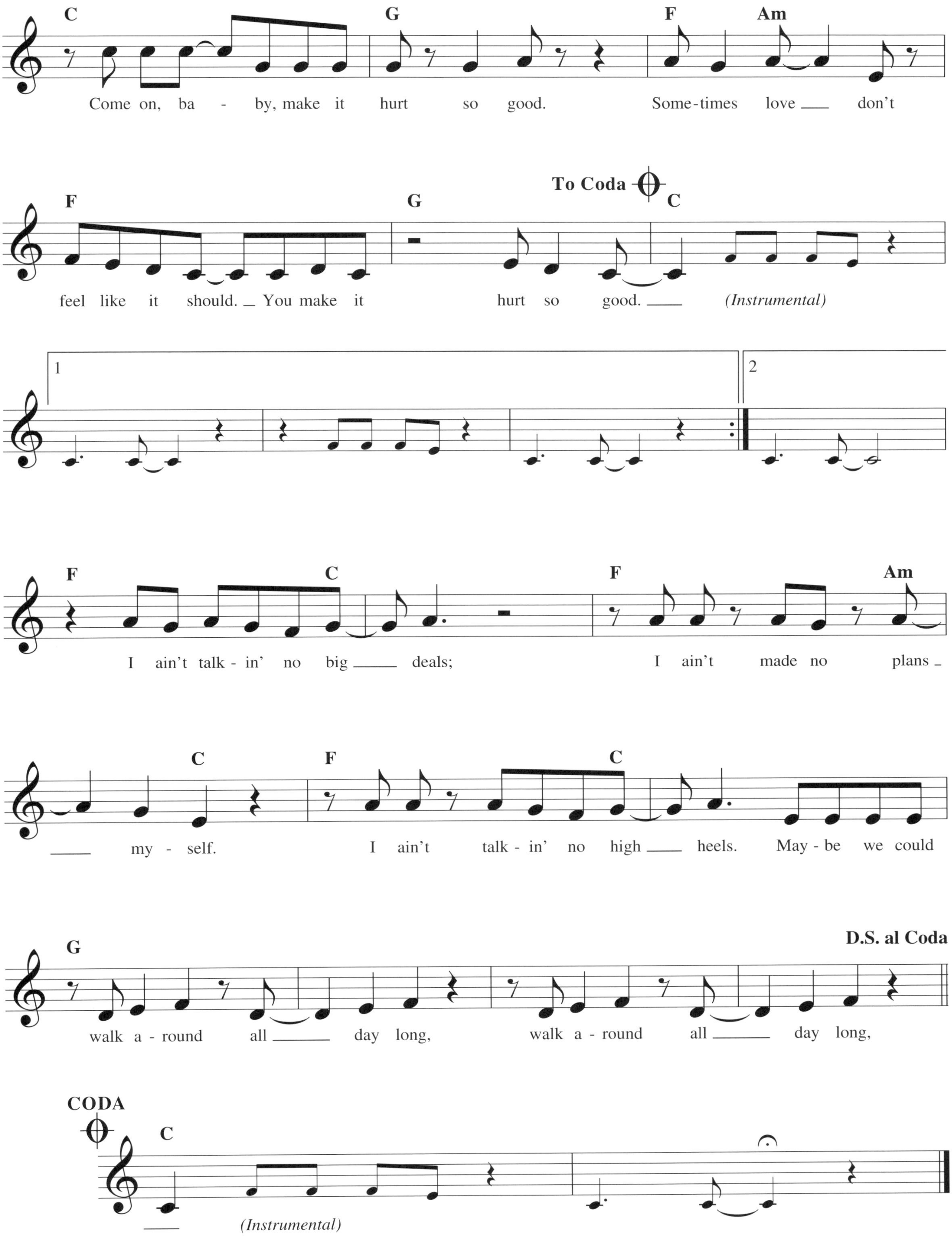
C G F Am
Come on, ba - by, make it hurt so good. Some-times love don't
F G To Coda C
feel like it should. You make it hurt so good. (Instrumental)
1 2
F C F Am
I ain't talk - in' no big deals; I ain't made no plans
C F C
my - self. I ain't talk - in' no high heels. May - be we could
G D.S. al Coda
walk a - round all day long, walk a - round all day long,
CODA
C
(Instrumental)

I JUST CALLED TO SAY I LOVE YOU

Words and Music by
STEVIE WONDER

Dm G C
to say I love you.
Dm G
I just called to say how much I care.
Am Dm
I just called to say
G Am
I love you. And I mean
Dm G7
it from the bot - tom of my
C
heart. No sum - mer's
D.S. al Coda
(Take repeats)
CODA
I just called
Dm G C
to say I love you.

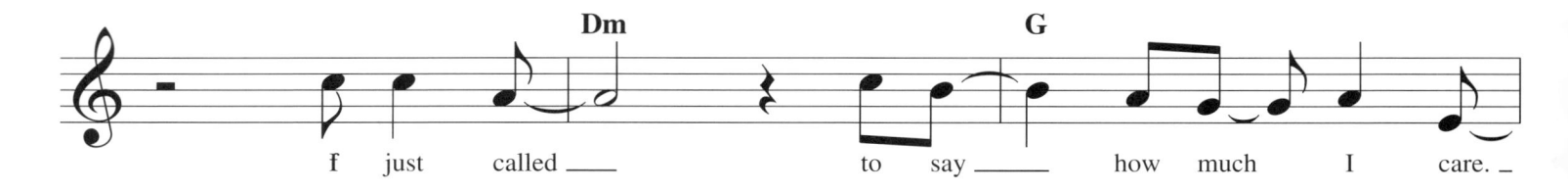

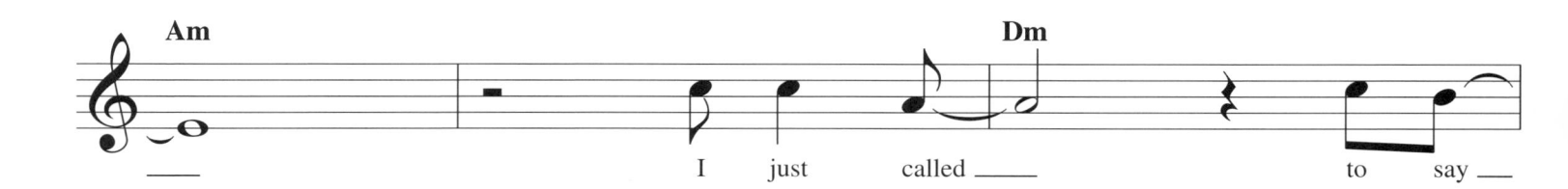

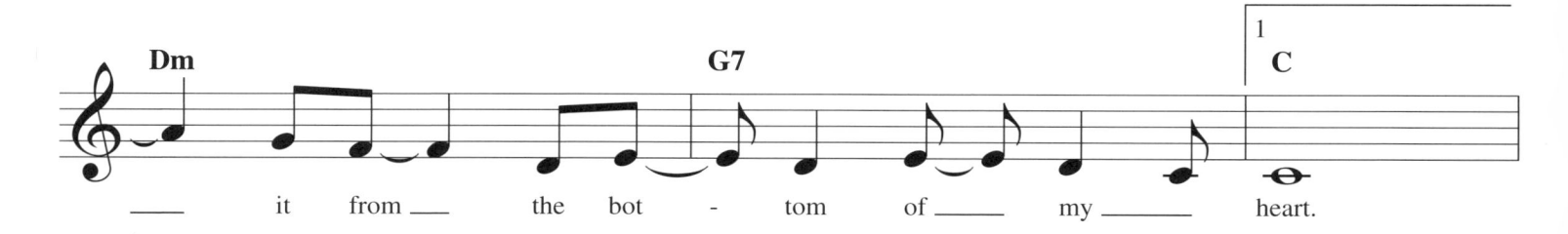

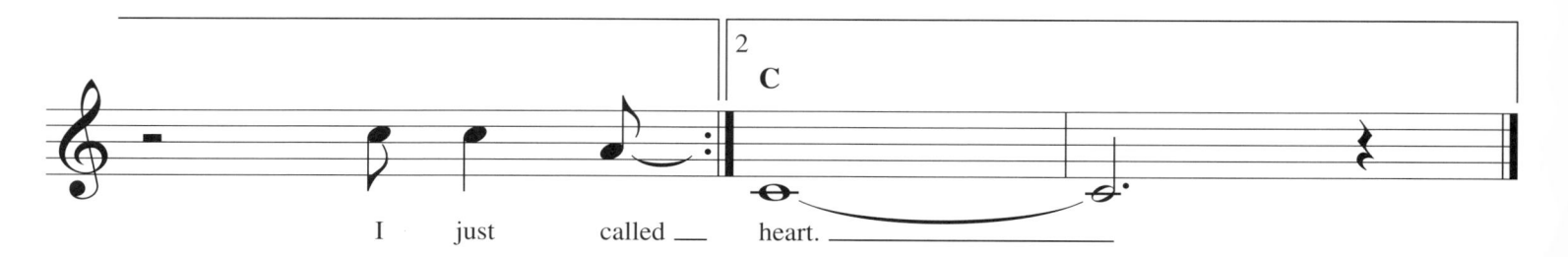

Additional Lyrics

3. No summer's high; no warm July;
   No harvest moon to light one tender August night.
   No autumn breeze; no falling leaves,
   Not even time for birds to fly to southern skies.

4. No Libra sun; no Halloween;
   No giving thanks to all the Christmas joy you bring.
   But what it is, though old so new
   To fill your heart like no three words could ever do.
   Chorus

I Love Rock 'N Roll

Words and Music by ALAN MERRILL
and JAKE HOOKER

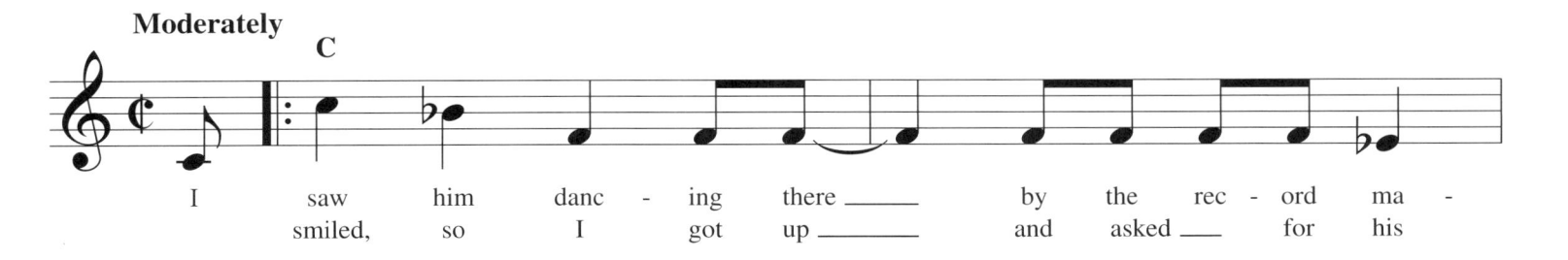

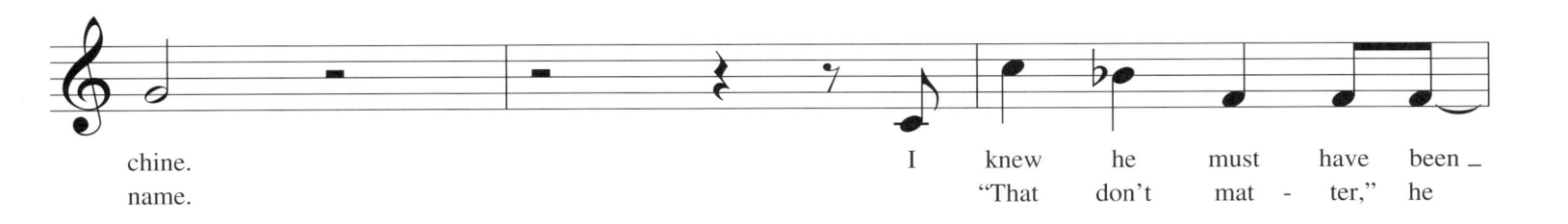

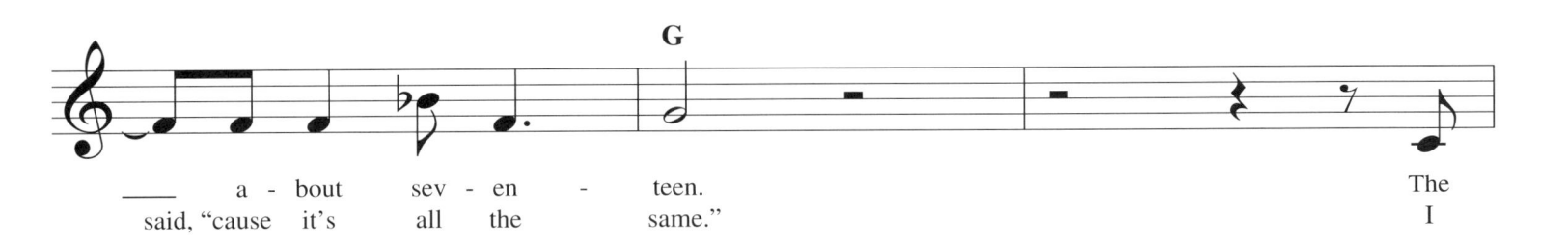

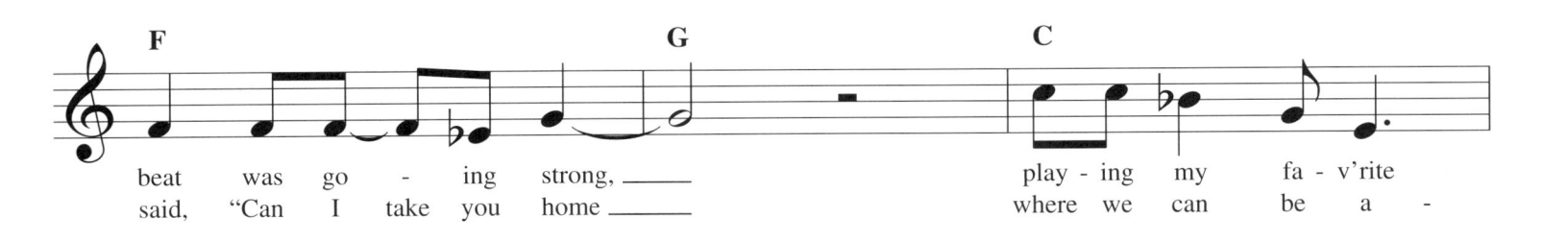

Copyright © 1975, 1982 Rak Publishing Ltd. for the World
Copyright Renewed 2003
All Rights for the U.S.A. and Canada Controlled by Finchley Music Corp.
Administered by Music & Media International, Inc.

Moderately

I saw him danc - ing there ____ by the rec - ord ma -
smiled, so I got up ____ and asked ____ for his

chine. I knew he must have been ____
name. "That don't mat - ter," he

____ a - bout sev - en - teen. The
said, "cause it's all the same." I

beat was go - ing strong, ____ play - ing my fa - v'rite
said, "Can I take you home ____ where we can be a -

song, ____ and I could tell it would - n't be long ____
lone?" And next, we were mov - ing

104

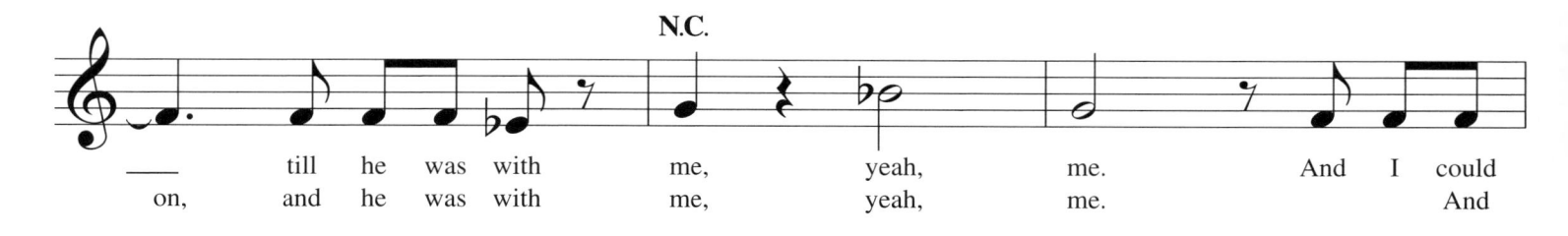

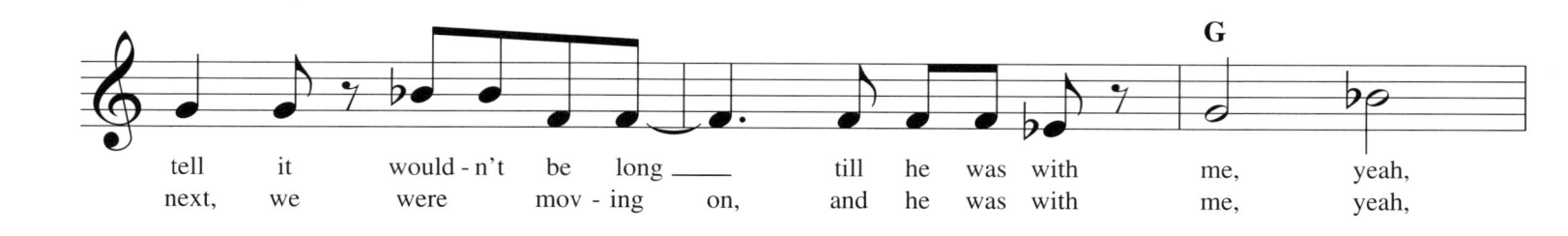

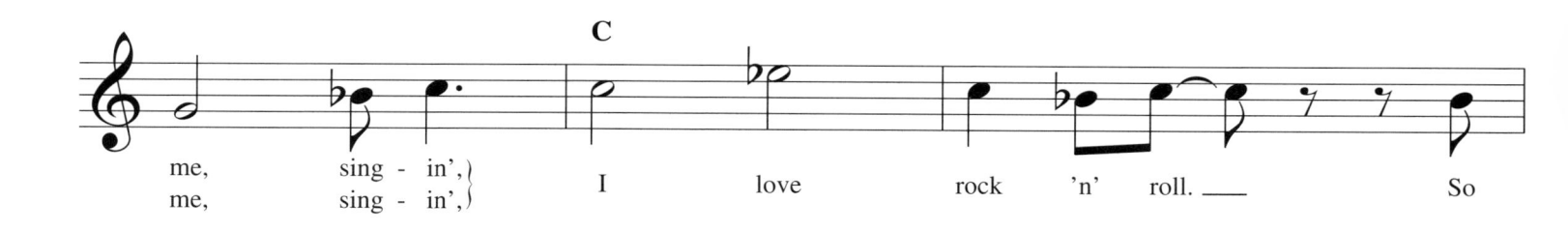

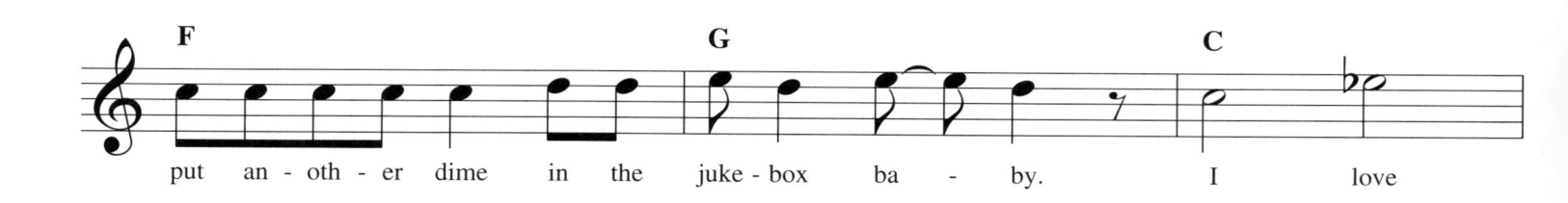

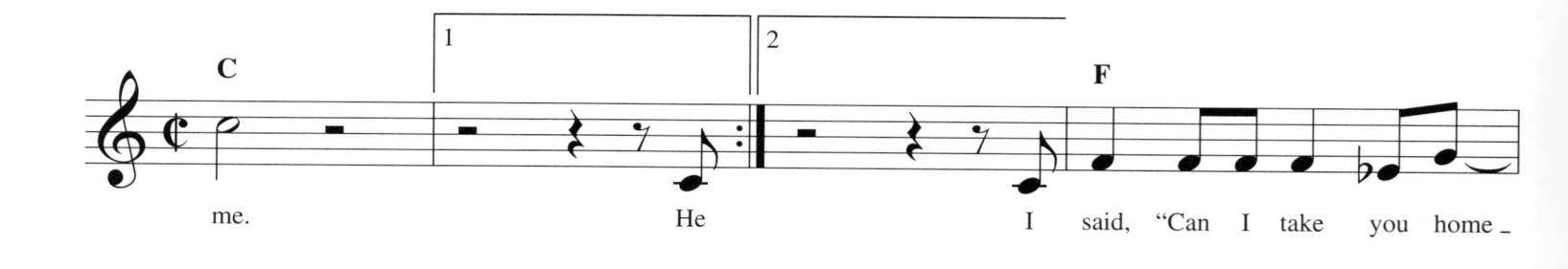

_____ where we can be alone?"

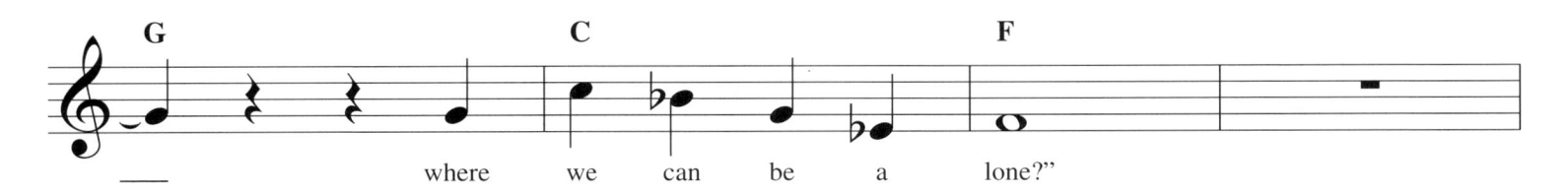

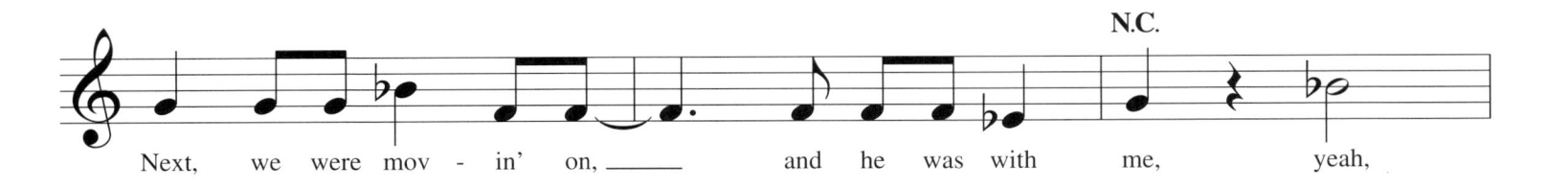

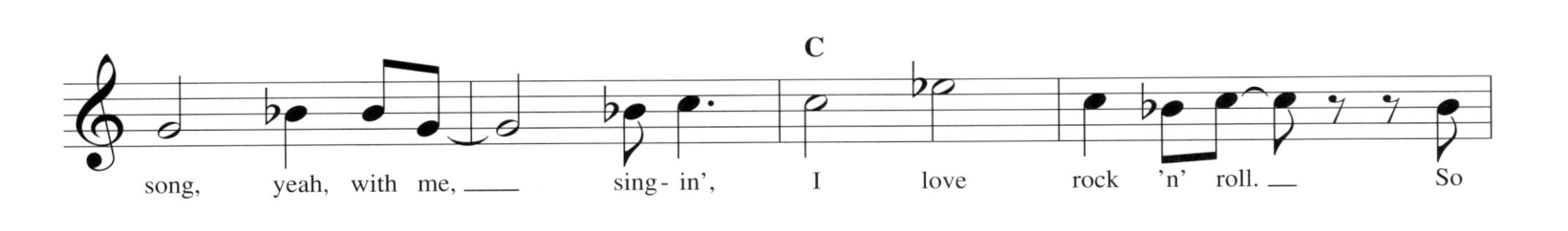

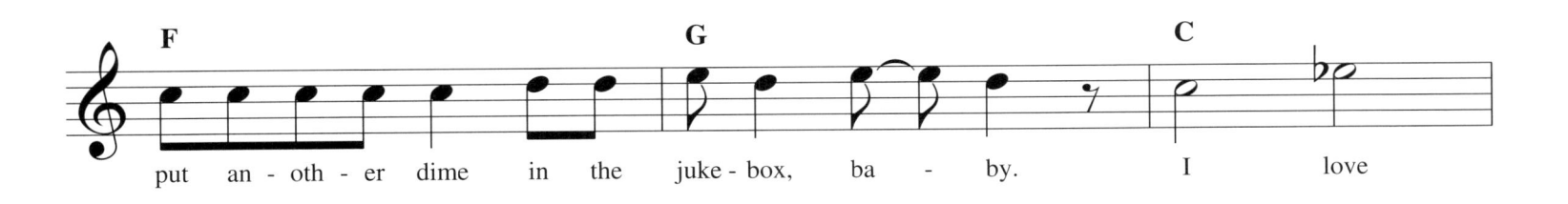

Next, we were movin' on, _____ and he was with me, yeah, me. And we'll be movin' on _____ and singin' that same old song, yeah, with me, _____ singin', I love rock 'n' roll. _____ So put another dime in the jukebox, baby. I love rock 'n' roll. _____ So come and take your time and dance with me.

I'LL BE THERE FOR YOU

Words and Music by JON BON JOVI
and RICHIE SAMBORA

Copyright © 1988 UNIVERSAL - POLYGRAM INTERNATIONAL PUBLISHING, INC.,
BON JOVI PUBLISHING and AGGRESSIVE MUSIC
All Rights for BON JOVI PUBLISHING Controlled and Administered by
UNIVERSAL - POLYGRAM INTERNATIONAL PUBLISHING, INC.
All Rights for AGGRESSIVE MUSIC Administered by
SONY/ATV MUSIC PUBLISHING LLC, 8 Music Square West, Nashville, TN 37203

Slowly

I guess this time you're real-ly leav-ing. I heard your suit-case say good-bye. Well, as my bro-ken heart lies bleed-ing, you say true love, it's su-i-cide. You say you've cried a thou-sand riv-ers, but now you're swim-ming for the shore. You left me drown-ing in my tears, and you won't save me an-y more. I'm pray-ing to God you'll give me one more chance, girl.

I'll be there for you. These five words I swear to you. When you breathe, I want to be the air for you. I'll be there for you. I'd live and I'd die for you.

Am		F	

I'd steal the sun from the sky for you. Words can't say what love can do.

To Coda ⊕ C
| G | | C | |

I'll be there for you.

	Dm	F

I know you know we had some good times; now they have their own hid-ing

C			Dm

place. Well, I can prom-ise you to-mor-row,

F	G	

but I can't buy back yes-ter-day. Yeah, ba-by, you know my hands are

F	G	

dirt-y, but I want-ed to be your val-en-

C G/B Am	F

tine. I'll be the wa-ter when you get thirst-y, ba-by.

D.S. al Coda **CODA** ⊕
G			C

When you get drunk, I'll be the wine. Oh! you.

IF YOU LOVE SOMEBODY SET THEM FREE

© 1985 G.M. SUMNER
Administered by EMI MUSIC PUBLISHING LIMITED

Music and Lyrics by
STING

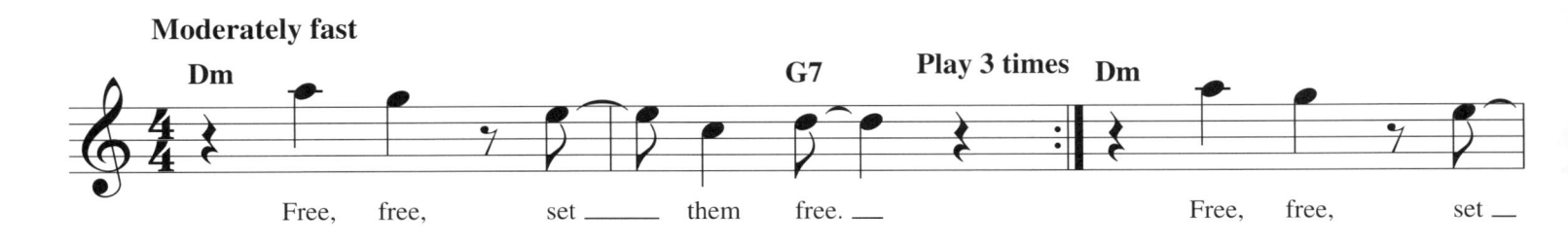

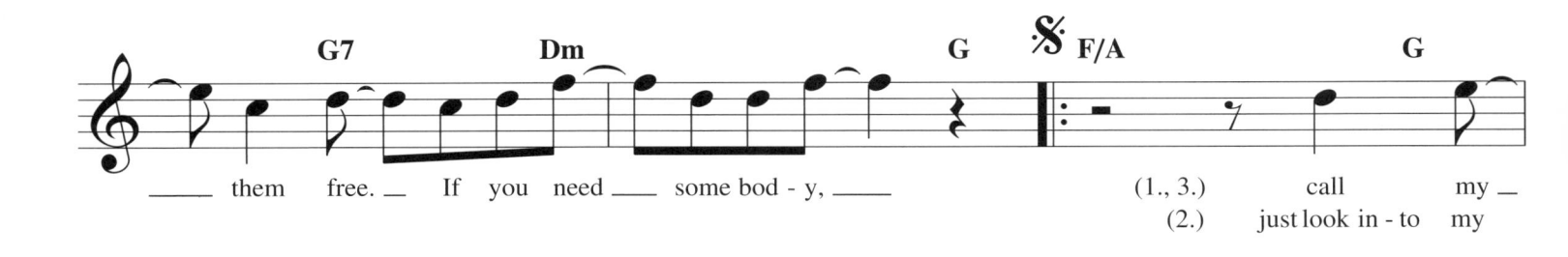

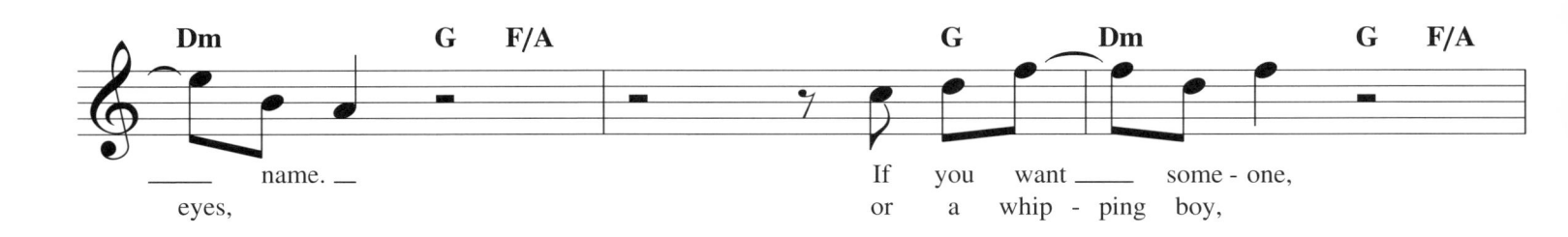

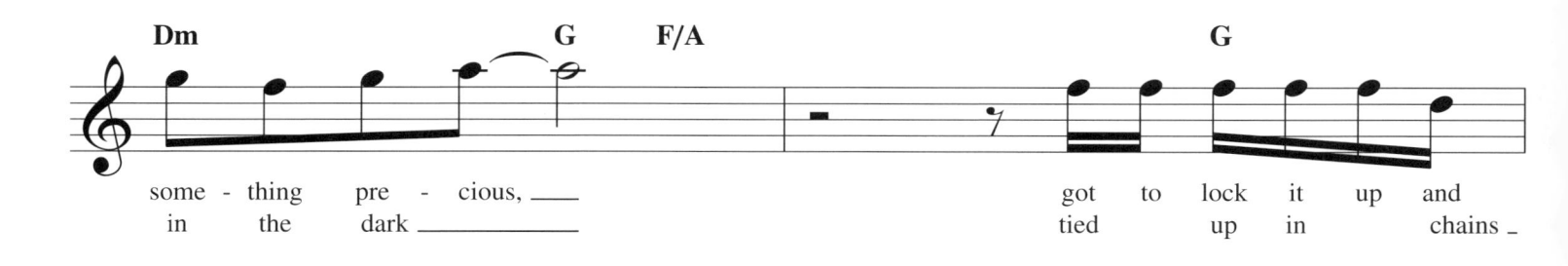

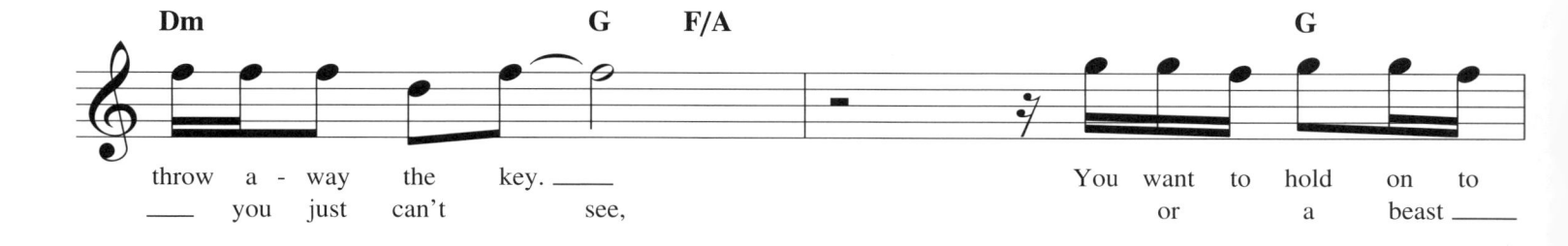

Moderately fast

Dm — G7 — Play 3 times — Dm
Free, free, set them free. Free, free, set

G7 — Dm — G — F/A — G
them free. If you need somebody, (1., 3.) call my
(2.) just look in-to my

Dm — G F/A — G Dm — G F/A
name.
eyes, If you want some-one,
or a whip-ping boy,

G Dm — G F/A — G
you can do the same. If you want to keep
some-one to des-pise, or a pris-'ner

Dm — G F/A — G
some-thing pre-cious, got to lock it up and
in the dark tied up in chains

Dm — G F/A — G
throw a-way the key. You want to hold on to
you just can't see, or a beast

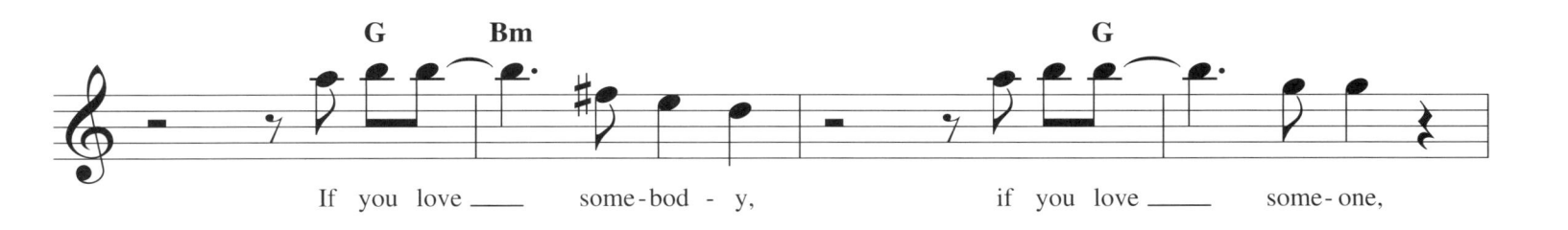

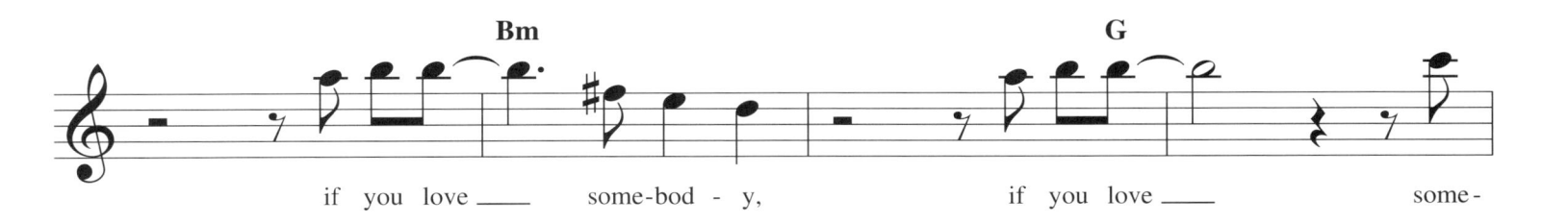

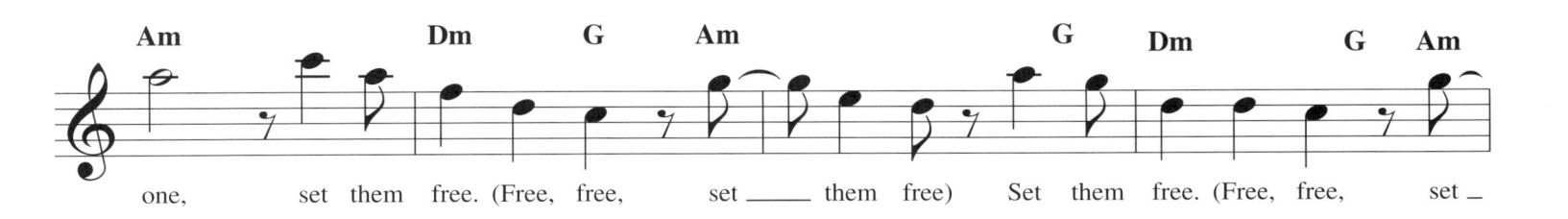

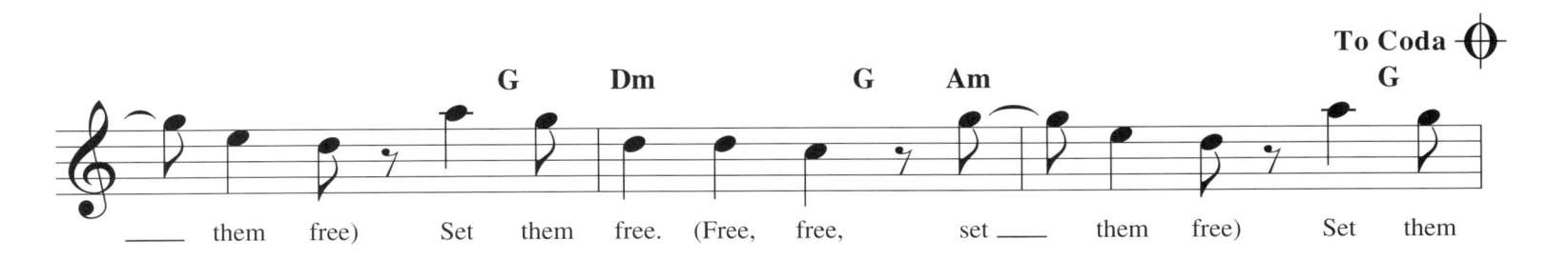

your pos-ses-sion; ___ don't e-ven think a-bout me.
___ in a gild-ed cage; that's all some peo-ple ev-er want to be.

If you love ___ some-bod-y, if you love ___ some-one,

if you love ___ some-bod-y, if you love ___ some-

one, set them free. (Free, free, set ___ them free) Set them free. (Free, free, set

___ them free) Set them free. (Free, free, set ___ them free) Set them

free. (Free, free, set ___ them free) If it's a mir-ror you want,

Sheet Music Transcription

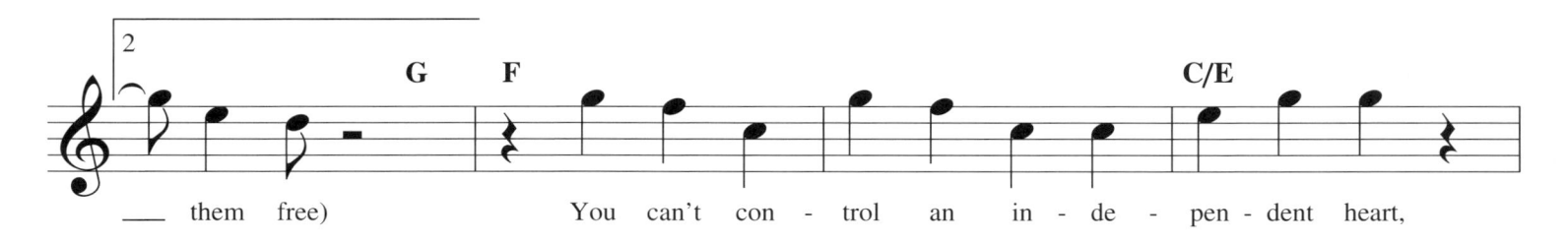

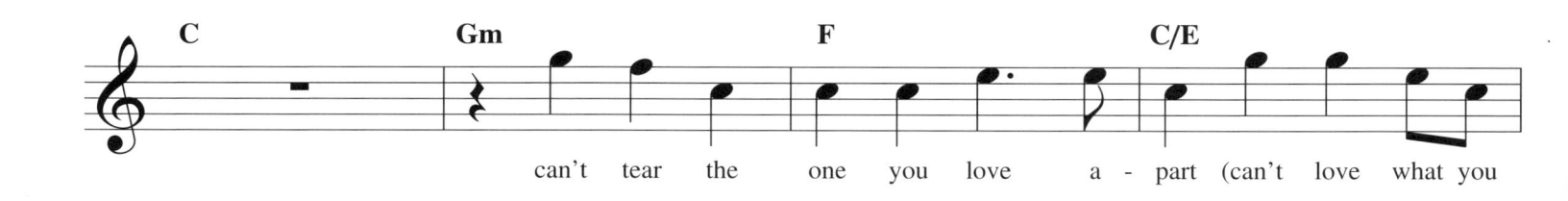

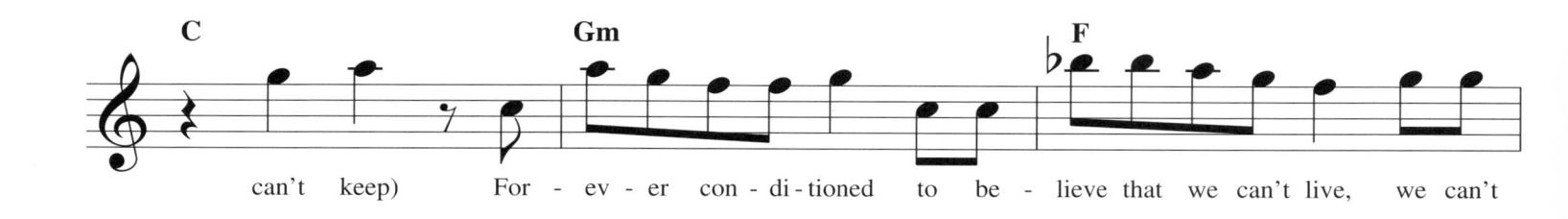

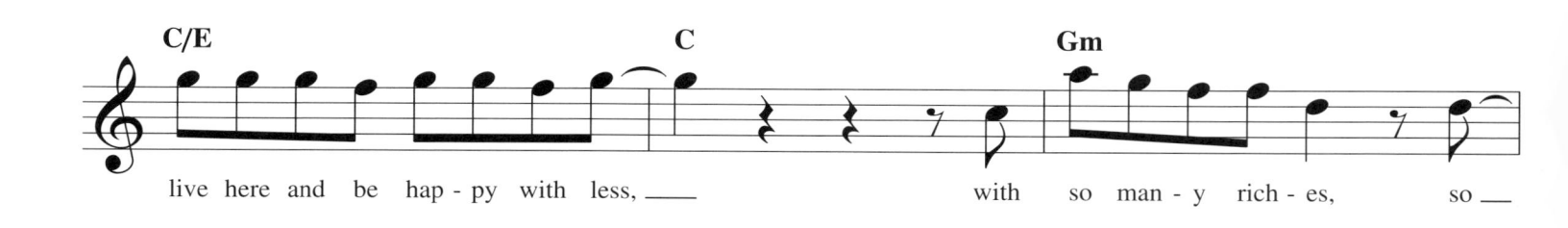

(... them free) You can't control an independent heart, **[G F C/E]**

can't tear the one you love apart *(can't love what you* **[C Gm F C/E]**

can't keep)* For-ev-er con-di-tioned to be-lieve that we can't live, we can't **[C Gm F]**

live here and be hap-py with less, ___ with so man-y rich-es, so ___ **[C/E C Gm]**

___ man-y souls, with ev-'ry-thing we see that we want to pos-sess. If you **[F C/E C]**

need some-bod-y, ___ **[Dm G]** — **D.S. al Coda**

CODA free. (Free, free, set ___ them free) Set them **[Dm G Am G]** — **Repeat and Fade**

IN A BIG COUNTRY

Steady Rock beat

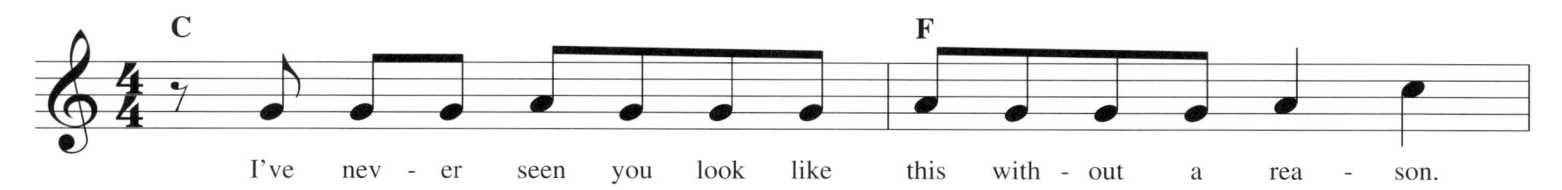

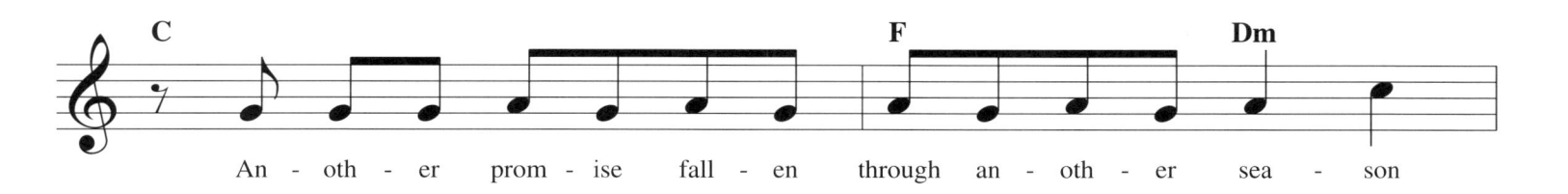

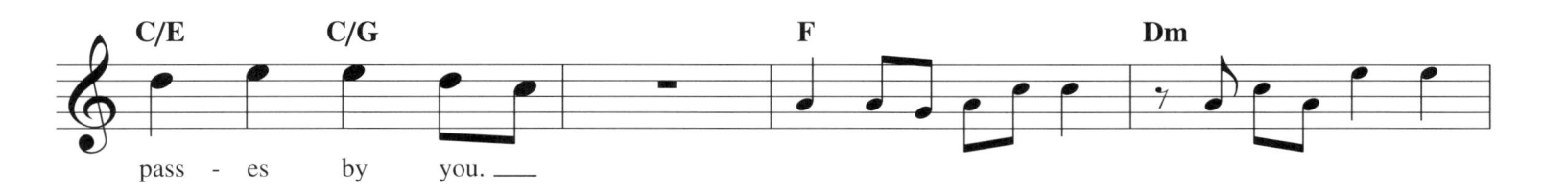

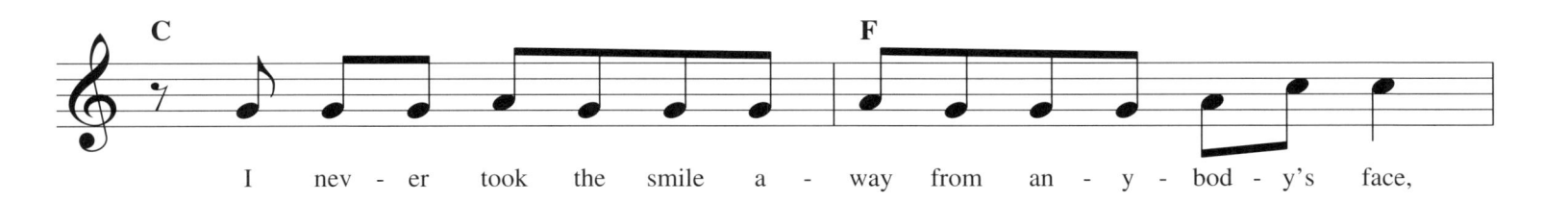

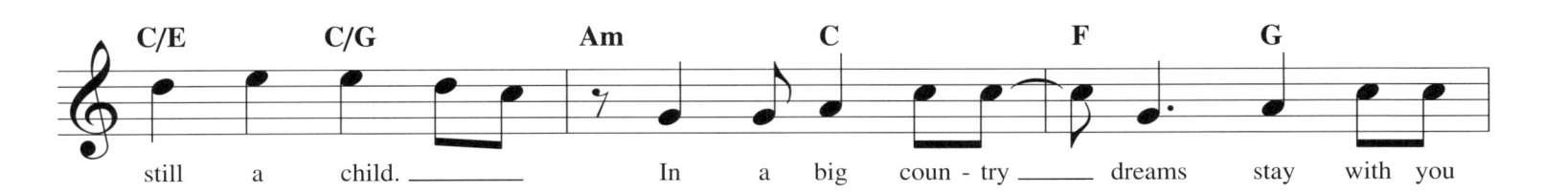

© 1983 EMI 10 MUSIC LTD.
All Rights for the U.S.A. and Canada Controlled and Administered by
EMI VIRGIN MUSIC, INC. and EMI VIRGIN SONGS, INC.

Words ans Music by STUART ADAMSON,
MARK BRZEZICKI, TONY BUTLER and BRUCE WATSON

I've never seen you look like this without a reason.

Another promise fallen through another season

passes by you. I never took the smile away from anybody's face,

and that's a des-p'rate way to look for someone who is

still a child. In a big country dreams stay with you

112

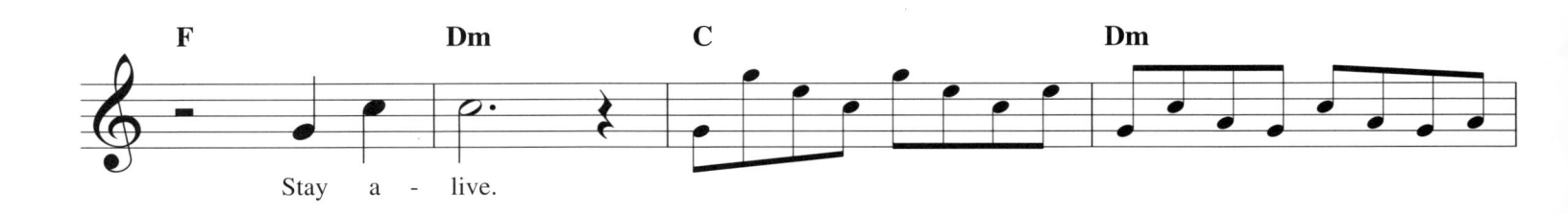

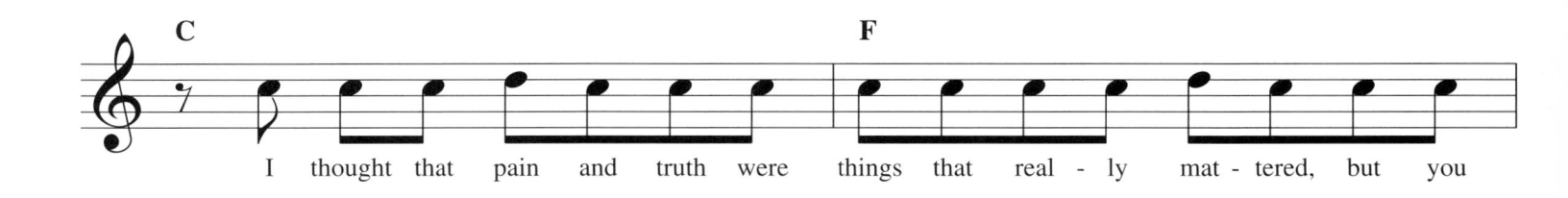

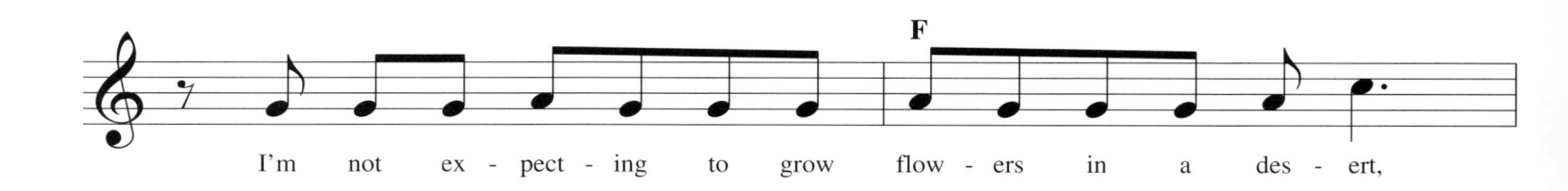

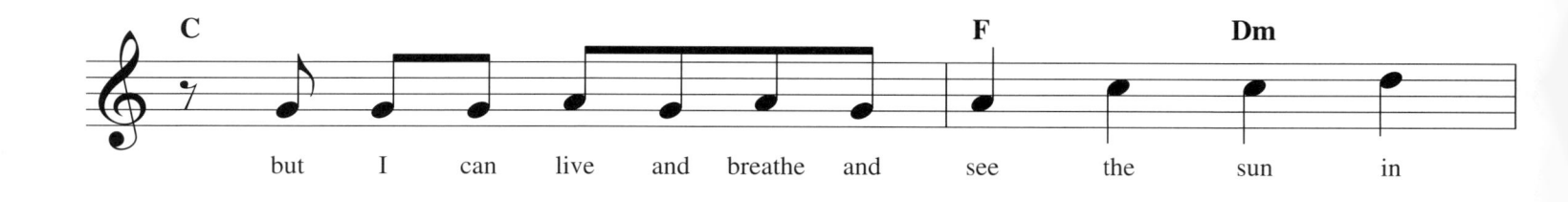

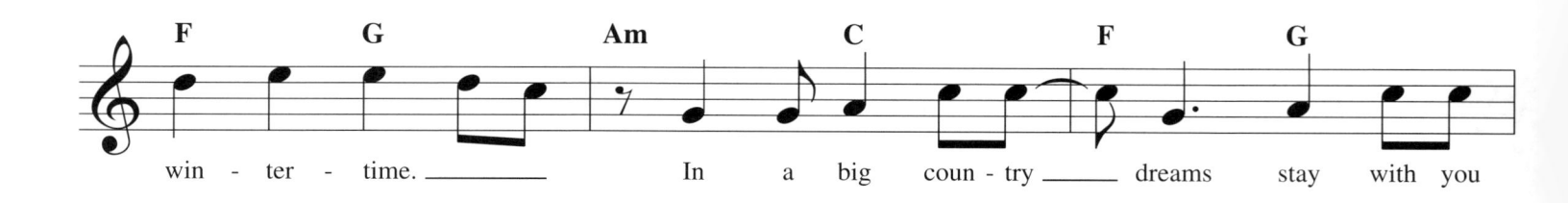

like a lover's voice ___ fires the mountainside.

Stay a-live.

I thought that pain and truth were things that really mattered, but you

can't stay here with ev-'ry single hope you had shattered. ___

I'm not expecting to grow flowers in a desert,

but I can live and breathe and see the sun in

wintertime. ___ In a big country ___ dreams stay with you

like a lov-er's voice ____ fires the moun-tain - side.

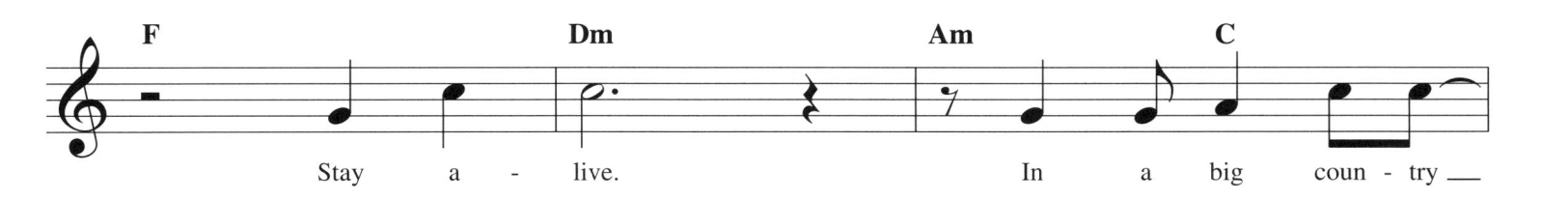

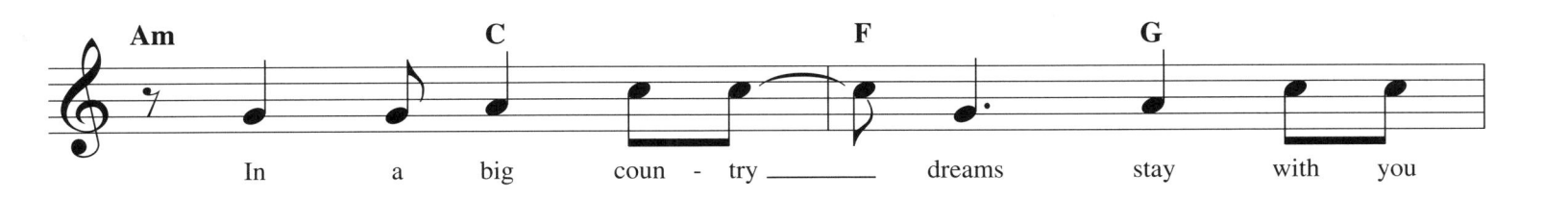

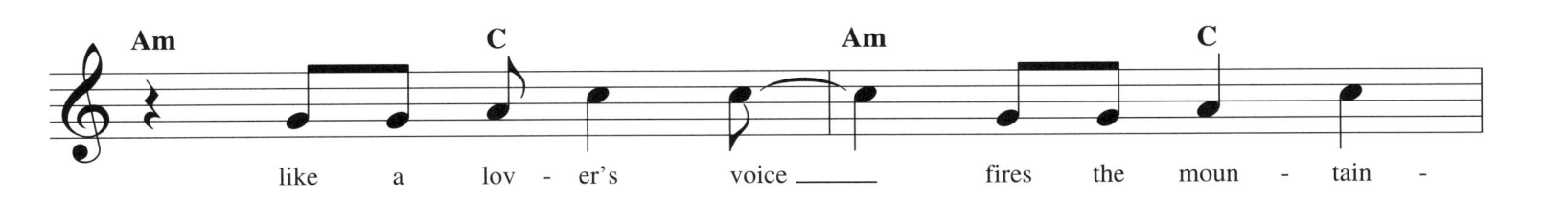

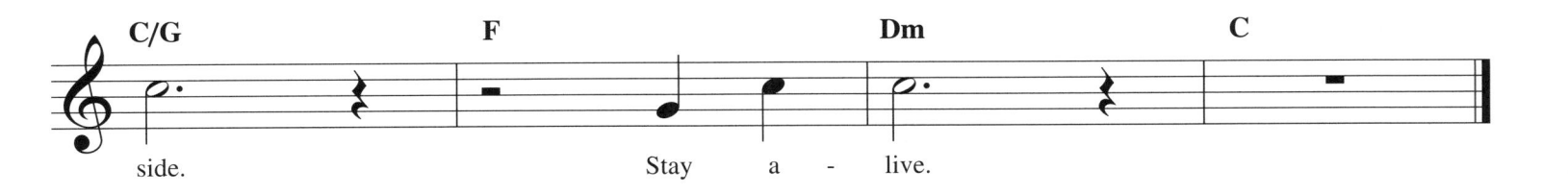

Stay a - live. In a big coun-try ____

____ dreams stay with you like a lov-er's voice ____ fires the moun-tain -

side. Stay a - live.

In a big coun-try ____ dreams stay with you

like a lov-er's voice ____ fires the moun-tain -

side. Stay a - live.

JACK AND DIANE

Words and Music by
JOHN MELLENCAMP

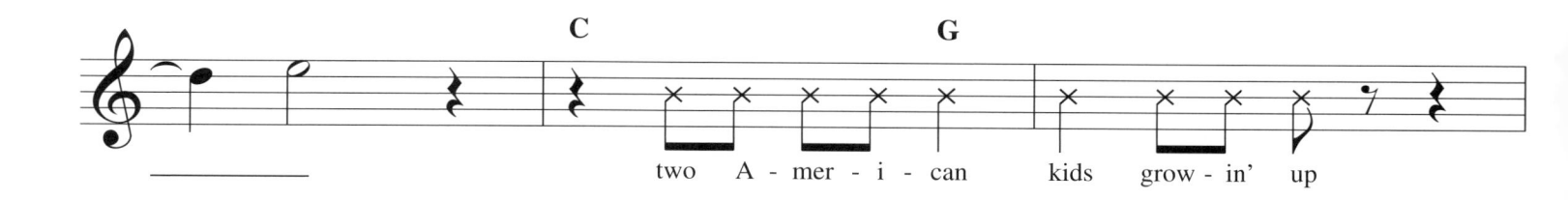

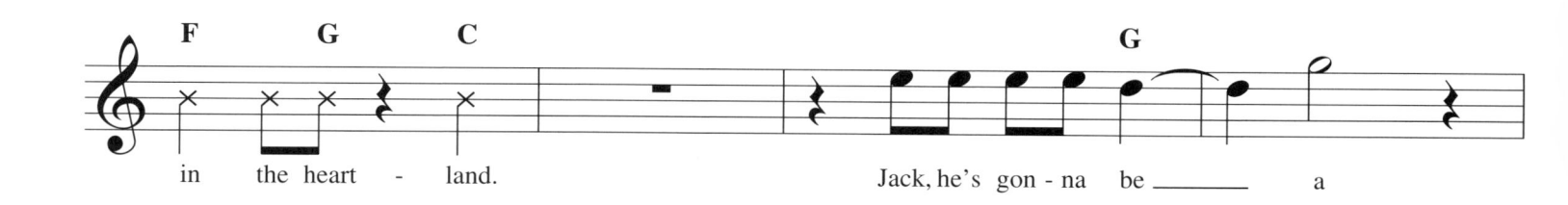

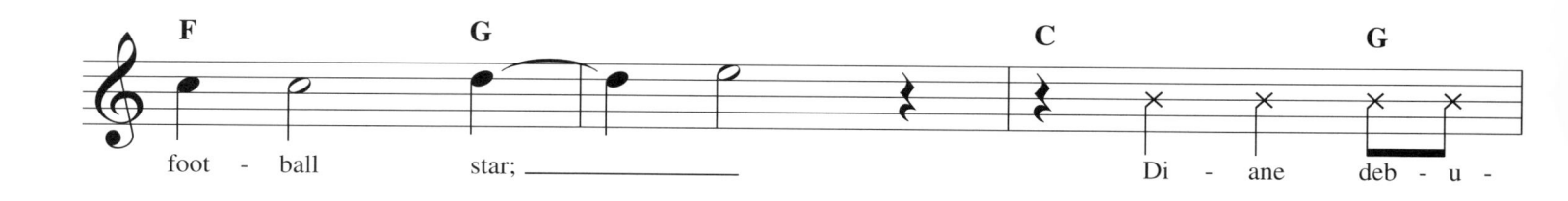

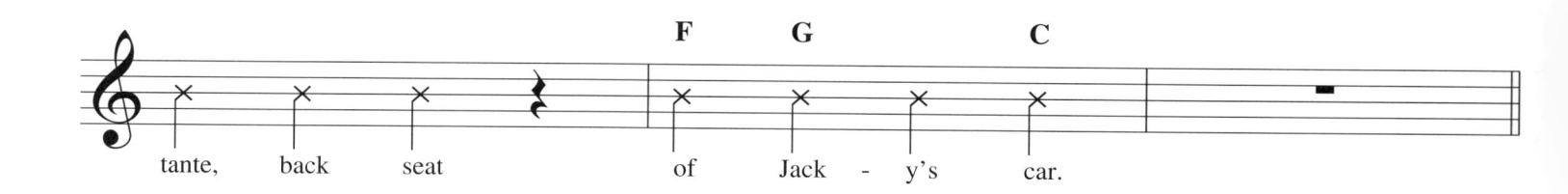

A lit-tle dit-ty a-bout Jack and Di-ane, ___ two A-mer-i-can kids grow-in' up in the heart-land. Jack, he's gon-na be ___ a foot-ball star; ___ Di-ane deb-u-tante, back seat of Jack-y's car.

Suck-in' on a chil-i dog out-side the Tast-ee Freez. ___
Jack, he sits back, col-lects his thoughts for a ___ mo-

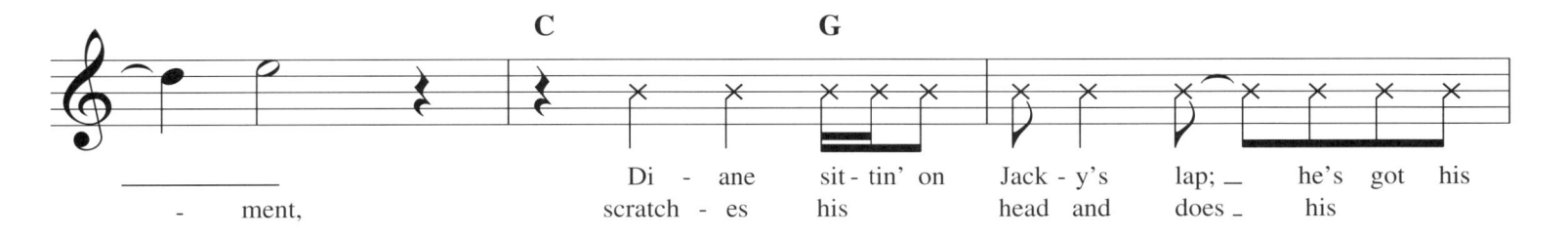

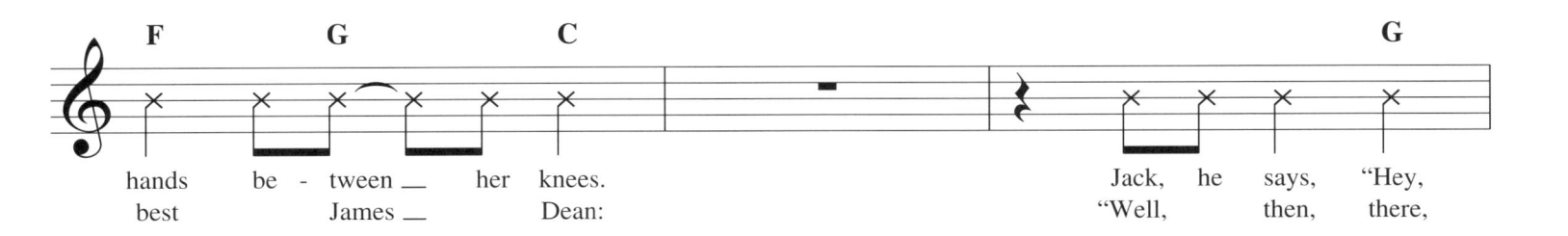

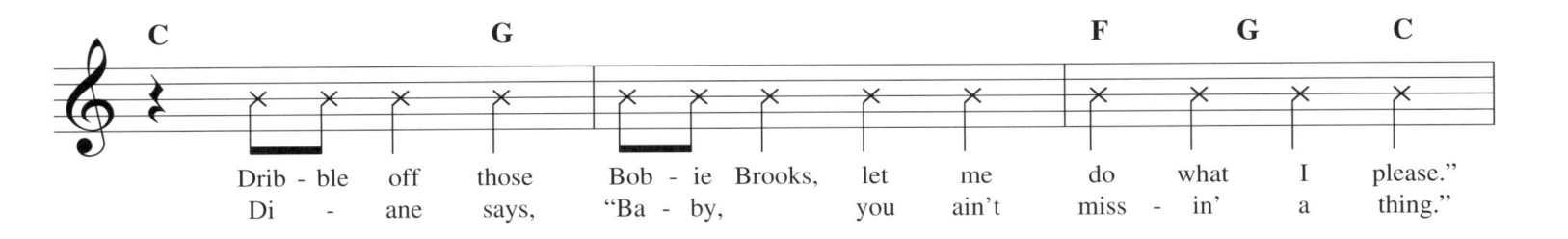

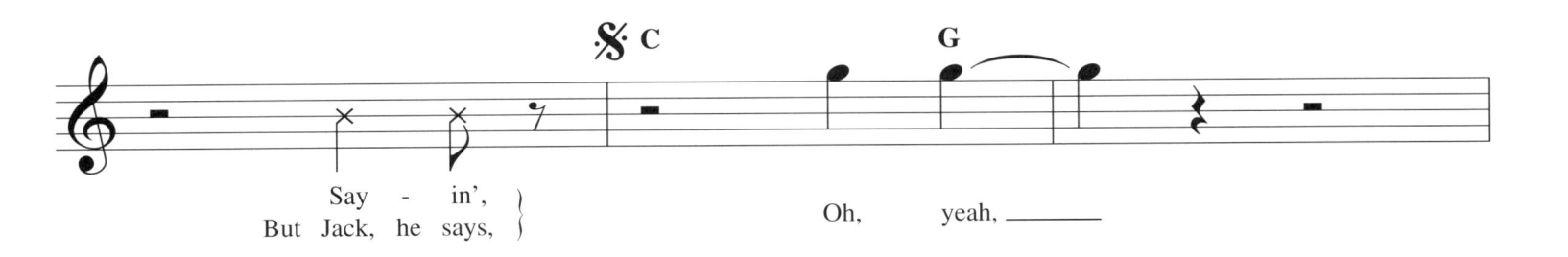

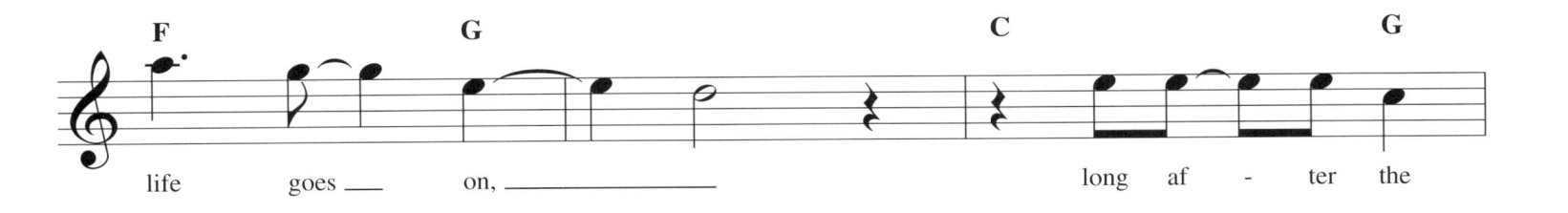

-ment,
Di - ane sit-tin' on Jack - y's lap; he's got his
scratch - es his head and does his

hands be - tween her knees. Jack, he says, "Hey,
best James Dean: "Well, then, there,

Di - ane, let's run off be - hind a shad - y tree.
Di - ane, we got - ta run off to the cit - y."

Drib - ble off those Bob - ie Brooks, let me do what I please."
Di - ane says, "Ba - by, you ain't miss - in' a thing."

Say - in',
But Jack, he says, } Oh, yeah,

life goes on, long af - ter the

F G
thrill of liv - ing is gone. Say - in',
C G F G
oh yeah, life goes on,
To Coda
C G F G C
long af - ter the thrill of liv - ing is gone.
1
Now, walk on.
2
N.C. C/G F/A
Oh, let it rock,
N.C. F/A G/B N.C.
let it roll.
C/G F/A B♭/D F/C
Let the Bi - ble belt come and save my soul.

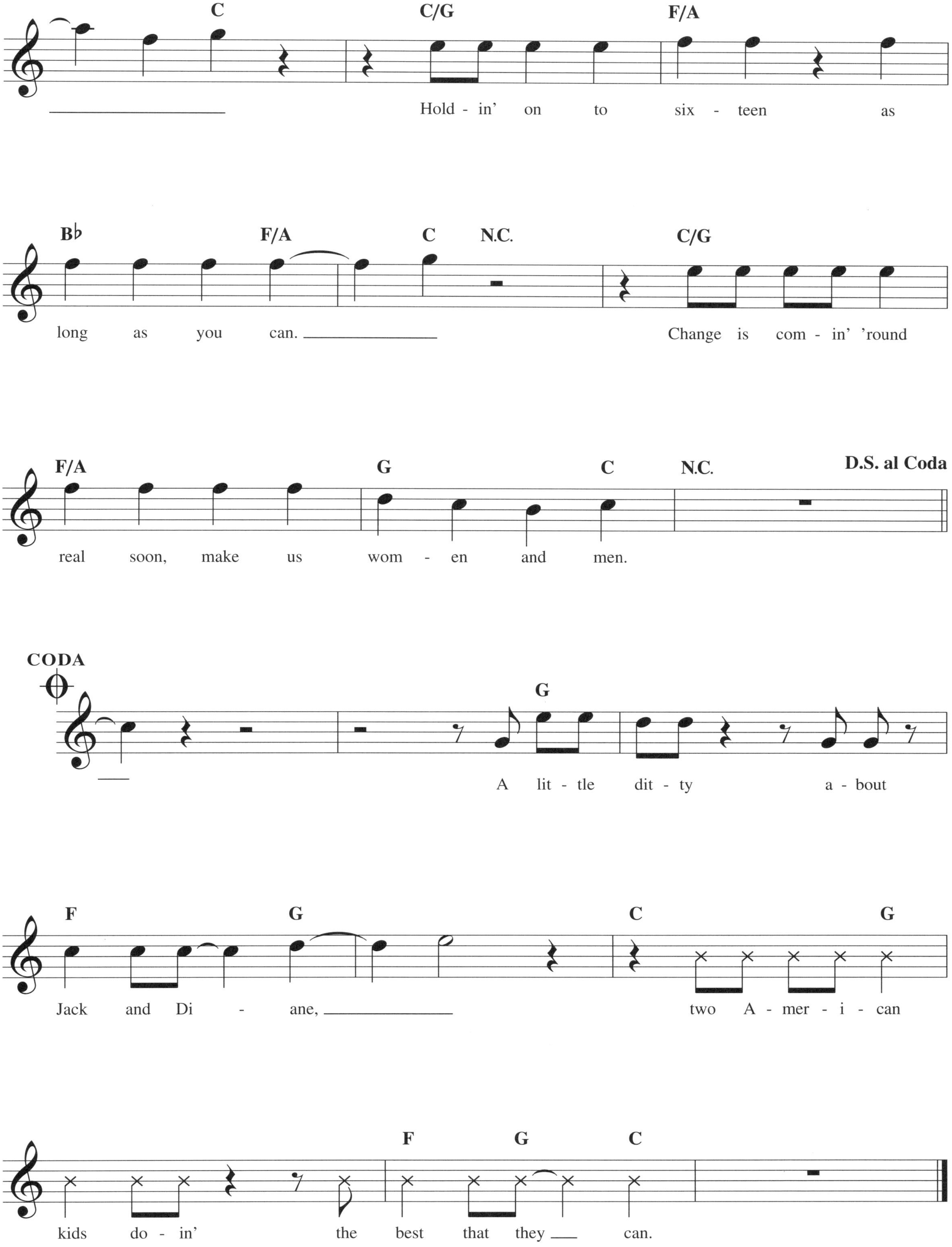
C C/G F/A
Hold - in' on to six - teen as
B♭ F/A C N.C. C/G
long as you can.
Change is com - in' 'round
F/A G C N.C.
D.S. al Coda
real soon, make us wom - en and men.
CODA
G
A lit - tle dit - ty a - bout
F G C G
Jack and Di - ane,
two A - mer - i - can
F G C
kids do - in' the best that they can.

JESSIE'S GIRL

Words and Music by
RICK SPRINGFIELD

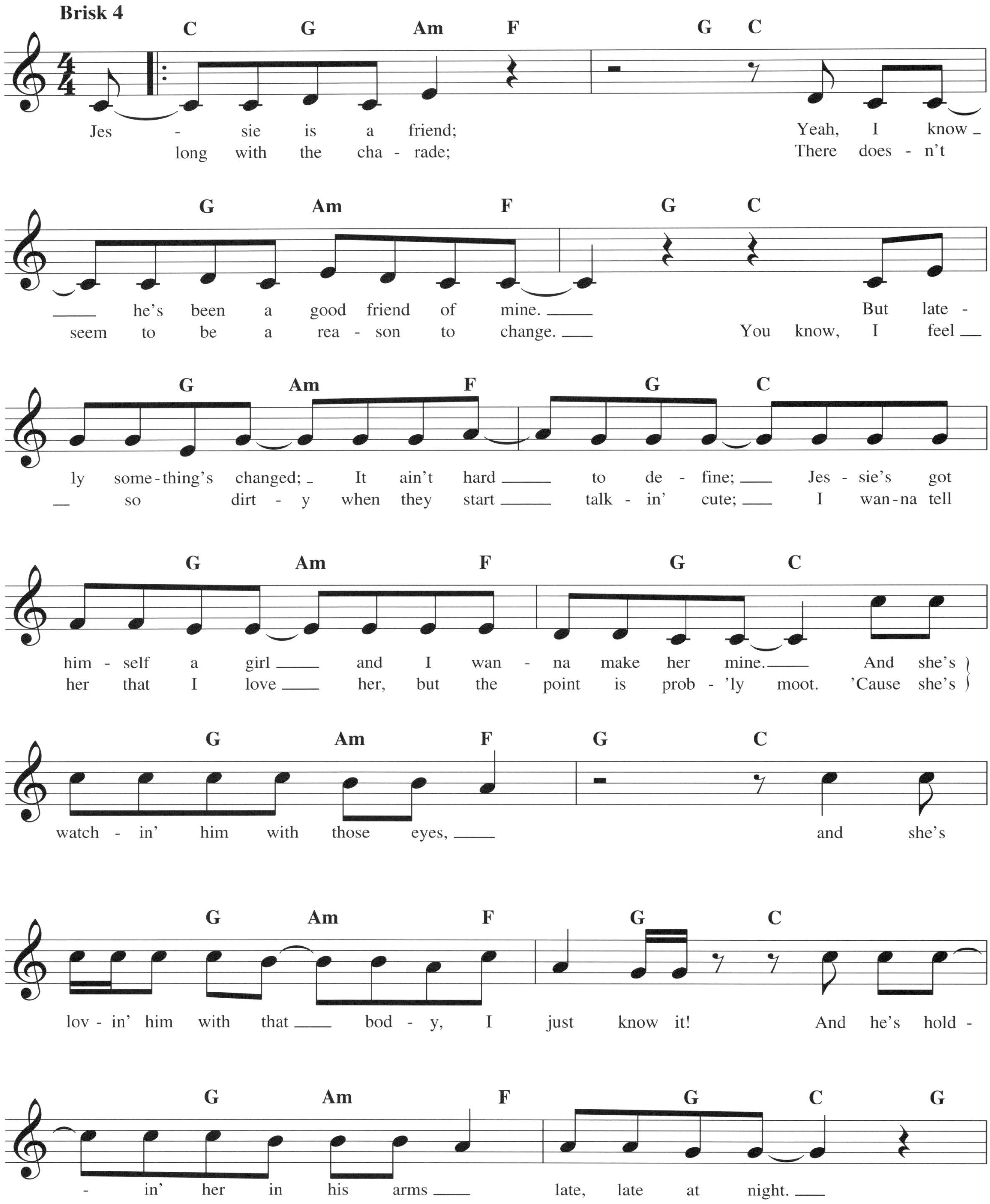

C
You know I wish that I had Jes - sie's Girl,
Am C Am
I wish that I had Jes - sie's Girl,
F G C Am
1
G N.C.
When can I find a wom - an like that? I'll play a -
2
Am G C Am
wom - an like that? Like Jes - sie's Girl, I wish that I had
C Am F G C Am
Jes - sie's Girl, When can I find a
F G C F G C Am G
wom - an... When can I find a wom - an like that?
F C/F G/F F C/F G/F
F C/F G/F
And I'm look - in' in the mir - ror all the time

F C/F G/F F C/F G/F
won-d'rin what she don't see in me. I've been fun - ny I've been cool
with the lines, F C/F G
ain't that the way love's sup - posed
to be? G C G
You know I wish that I had
C Am
Jes - sie's Girl, I wish that I had
C Am C
Jes - sie's Girl, I want Jes - sie's Girl,
Am 1 F G C Am G
When can I find a wom - an like that? Like
2 N.C. Slower C

JUMP

Words and Music by DAVID LEE ROTH,
EDWARD VAN HALEN, ALEX VAN HALEN
and MICHAEL ANTHONY

C/F G
Am
Ah, can't you see me stand - ing here? I got my
F C/E
back a - gainst the rec - ord ma - chine.
Dm F C/E
I ain't the worst that you've seen.
Dm F C/E G
Ah, can't you see what I mean?
To Coda
G/C C F/C G/C
Ah, might as well jump. Might as well
C F/C C/F G G/C C
jump. Go a - head and jump.

123

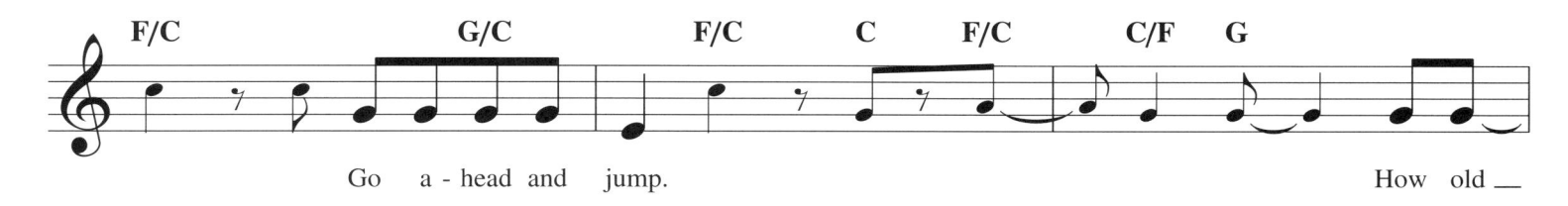

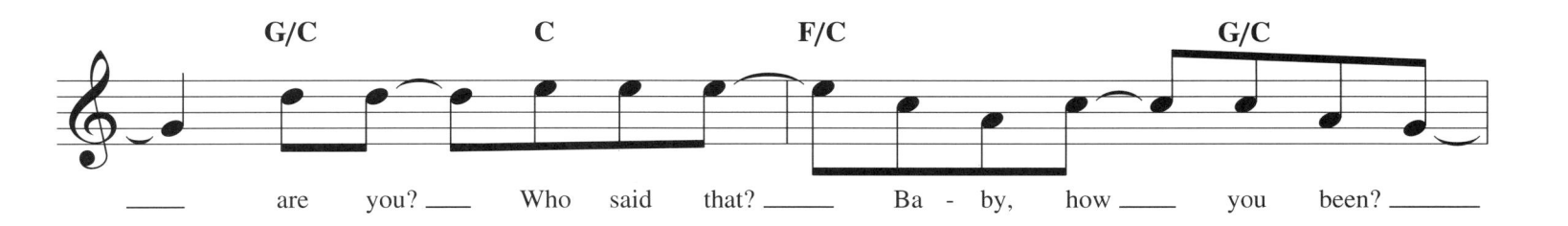

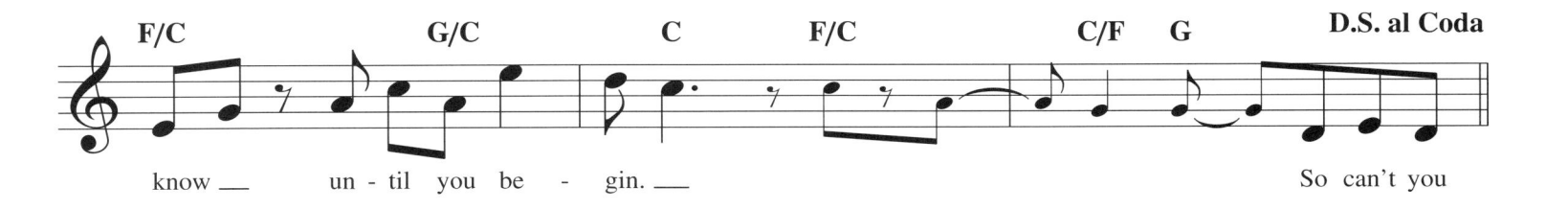

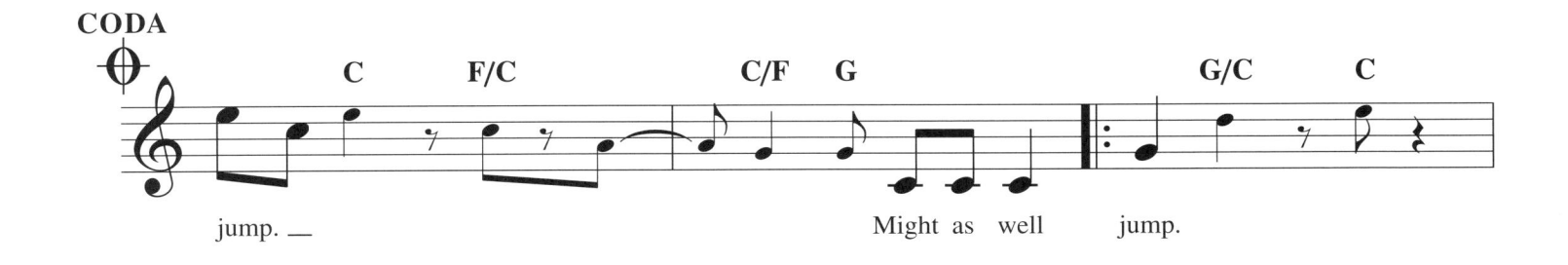

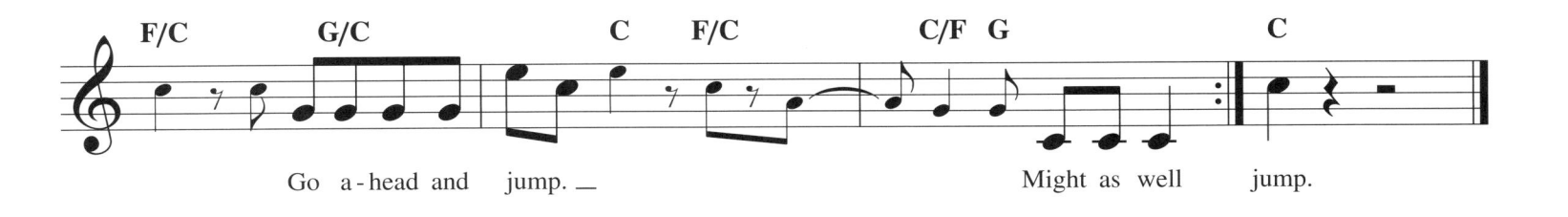

Go a-head and jump. How old _____ are you? _____ Who said that? _____ Ba-by, how _____ you been? _____

You say you don't know. _____ You won't know _____ un-til you be-gin. _____ So can't you

D.S. al Coda

CODA

jump. _____ Might as well jump.

Go a-head and jump. _____ Might as well jump.

JUST CAN'T GET ENOUGH

Words and Music by
VINCE CLARK

Moderately fast

C
When I'm with you, ba - by, I go out of my head, and I
We walk to - geth - er, we're walk - ing down the street, and I
And when it rains, you're shin - ing down for me, and I

F
just can't get e - nough, and I just can't get e - nough.
just can't get e - nough, and I just can't get e - nough.
just can't get e - nough, and I just can't get e - nough.

C
All the things you do to me and ev - 'ry - thing you said, I
Ev - 'ry time I think of you, I know we have to meet, and I
Just like a rain - bow, you know you set me free, and I

F
just can't get e - nough, and I just can't get e - nough.
just can't get e - nough, and I just can't get e - nough.
just can't get e - nough, and I just can't get e - nough.

G   **Am**   **F**
We slip and slide as we fall in love, and I just can't seem to
It's get - ting hot - ter, it's our burn - ing love, and I just can't seem to
You're like an an - gel and you give me your love, and I just can't seem to

get e - nough, ah!
get e - nough, ah! *(Instrumental)*
get e - nough, ah!

Just can't get e - nough,
just can't get e - nough, I
just can't get e - nough, I just can't get e - nough, I
just can't get e - nough. I just can't get e - nough.

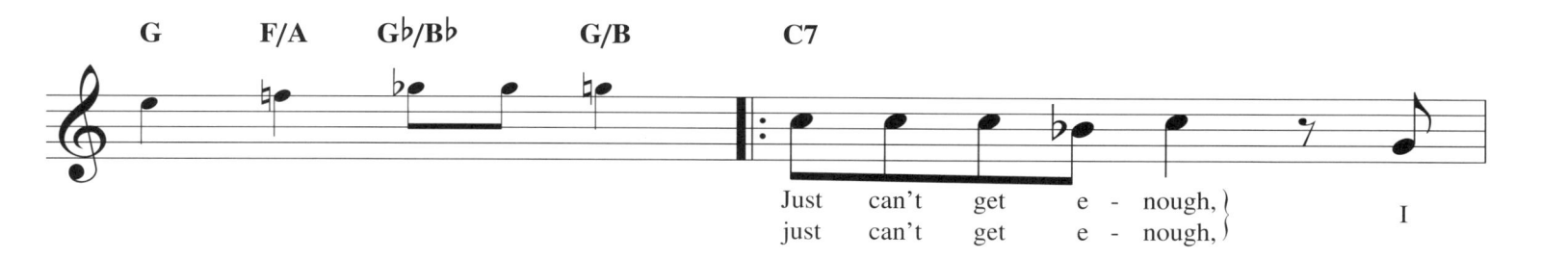

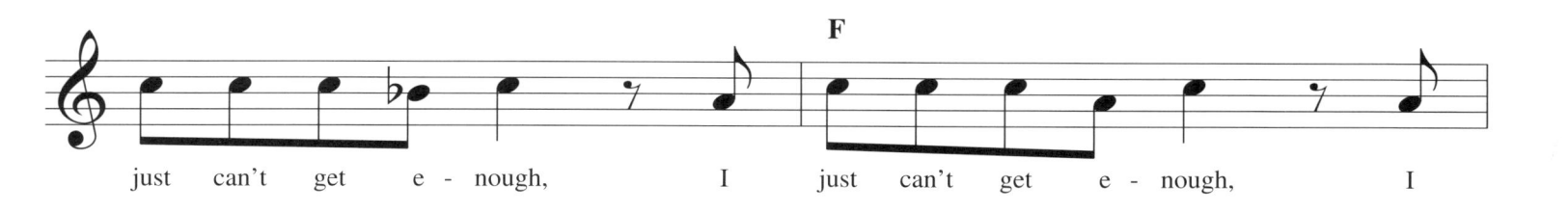

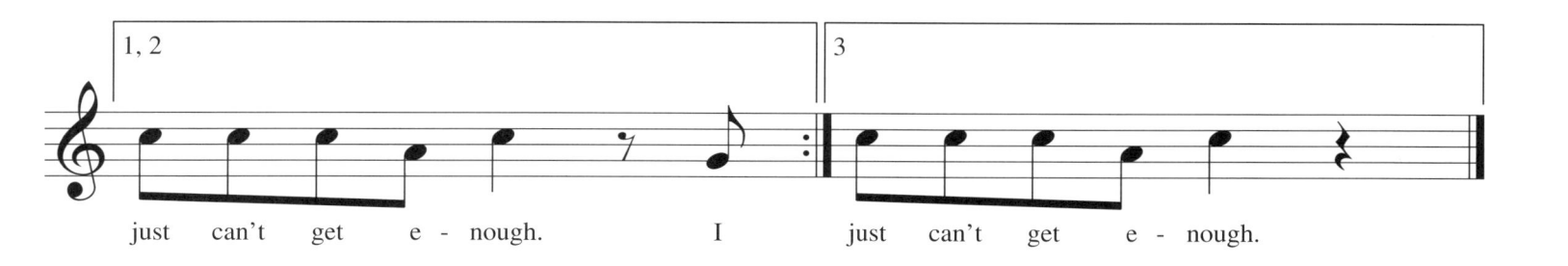

KEEP ON LOVING YOU

Words and Music by
KEVIN CRONIN

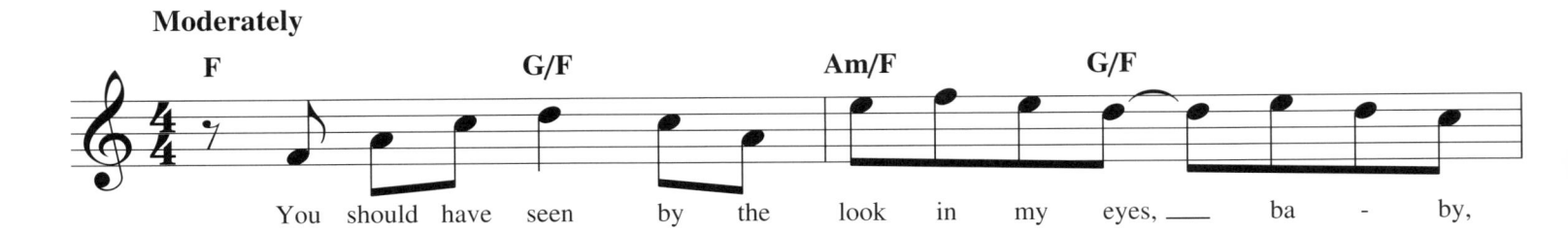

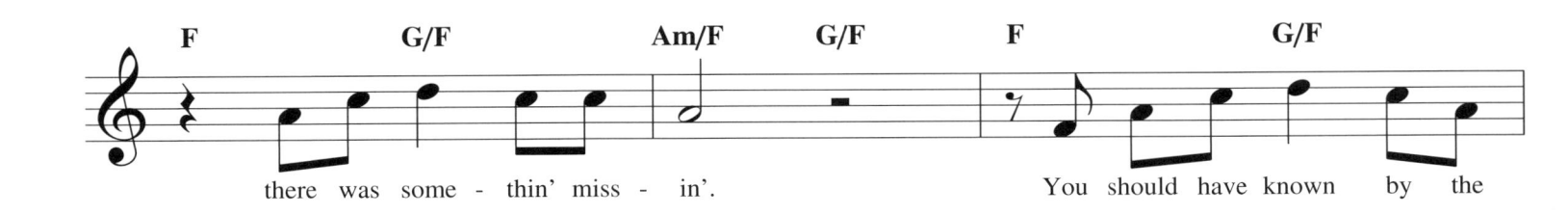

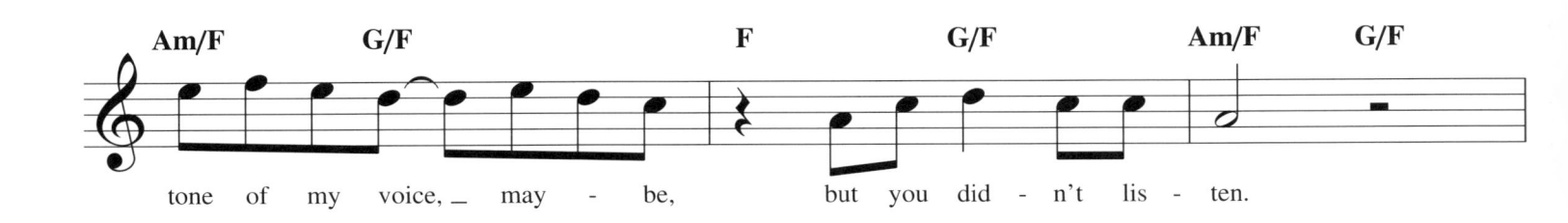

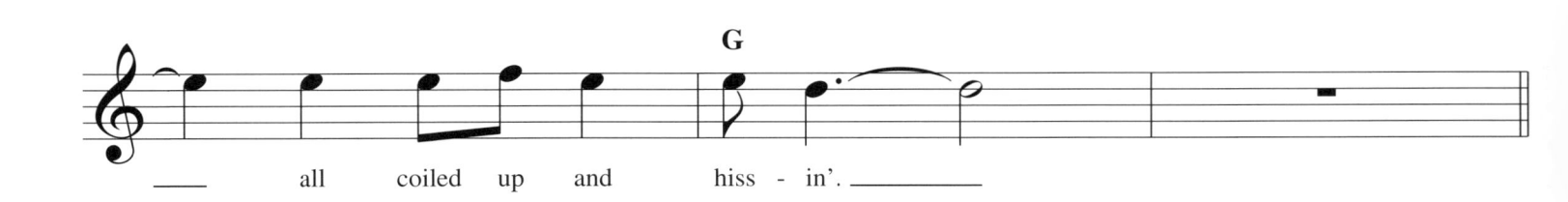

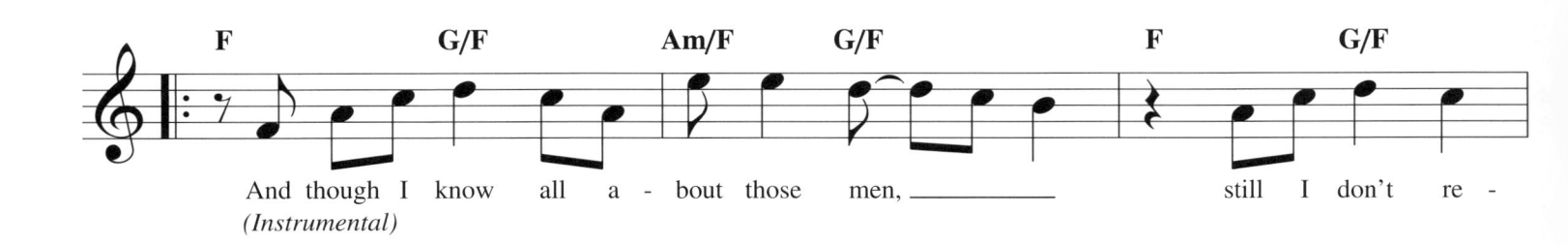

Moderately

You should have seen by the look in my eyes, ba - by, there was some - thin' miss - in'. You should have known by the tone of my voice, may - be, but you did - n't lis - ten.

You played dead, but you nev - er bled. In - stead you laid still in the grass all coiled up and hiss - in'.

And though I know all a - bout those men, still I don't re -
(Instrumental)

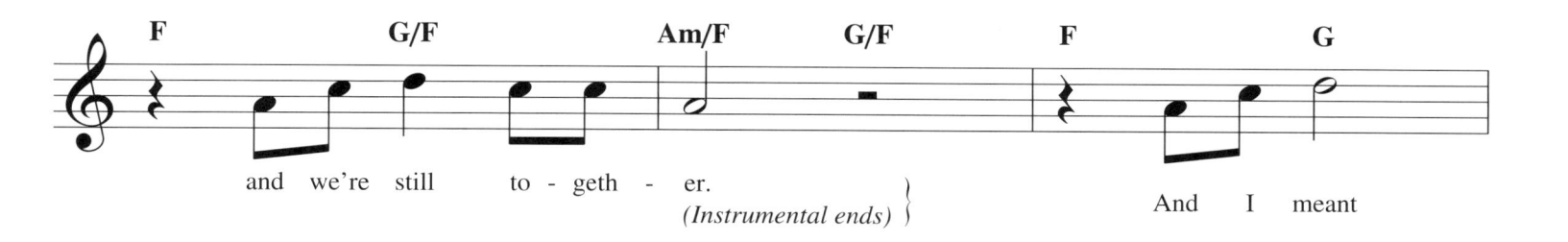

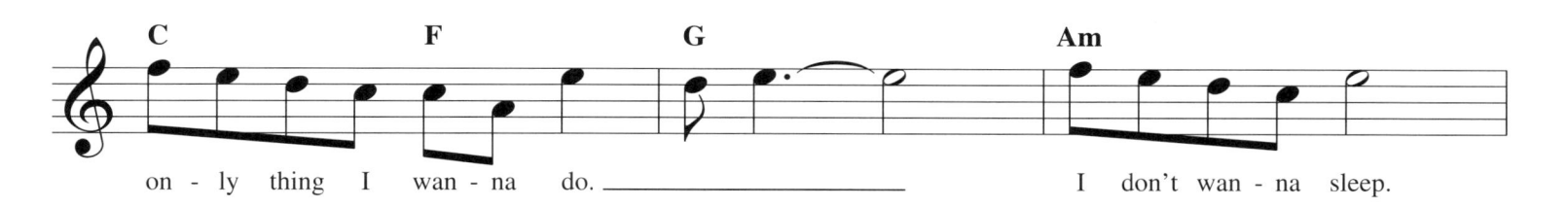

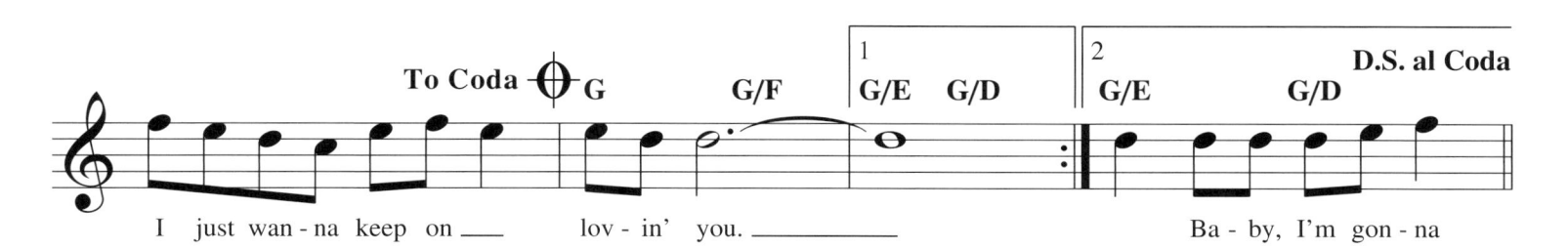

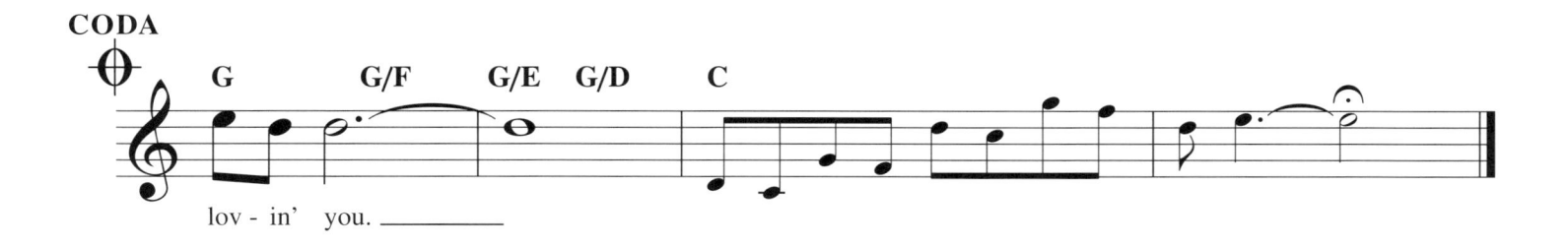

mem - ber. 'Cause it was us, ba - by, way be - fore them, _____ and we're still to - geth - er. *(Instrumental ends)* And I meant ev - 'ry word I said. When I said that I love __ you, I meant __ that I'll love __ you for - ev - er. _____ And I'm gon - na keep on __ lov - in' you, 'cause it's the on - ly thing I wan - na do. _____ I don't wan - na sleep. I just wan - na keep on __ lov - in' you. _____ Ba - by, I'm gon - na lov - in' you. _____

LADY IN RED

Words and Music by
CHRIS DeBURGH

Copyright © 1986 RONDOR MUSIC (LONDON) LTD.
All Rights in the USA and Canada Administered by ALMO MUSIC CORP.

Moderately slow

I've nev-er seen you look-ing so love-ly as you did to-night;
nev-er seen you look-ing so gor-geous as you did to-night;

I've nev-er seen you shine so bright. Mm mm mm. You were a-
I've nev-er seen you shine so bright.

maz-ing. I've nev-er seen so man-y men ask you if you want-ed to dance.
I've nev-er seen so man-y want to be there by your side,

They're look-ing for a lit-tle ro-mance, giv-en half a
and when you turn to me and smiled, it took my breath a-

chance. I have nev-er seen that dress you're wear-ing, or the
way. I have nev-er had such a feel-ing, such a

high-lights in your hair that catch your eyes. I have been blind.
feel-ing of com-plete and ut-ter love. As I do to-night.

The la-dy in red is danc-ing with

Am G/B Am Dm
me, cheek to cheek. There's no - bod - y here;
G C
it's just you and me. It's where I wan - na be.
C7 F E7/G♯ E7
But I hard - ly know this beau - ty by my
Am Am/G D7/F♯ Dm
side. I'll nev - er for - get
1
G C C/E F G C C/E
the way you look to - night.
F G
I've
2
G Am Am/G
the way you look to - night.
D7/F♯ Dm G C C/E
I nev - er will for - get the way you look to - night.
F G C C/E F G C
Play 3 times
The la - dy in red. My la - dy in red.

LONGER

© 1979 EMI APRIL MUSIC INC. and HICKORY GROVE MUSIC
All Rights Controlled and Administered by EMI APRIL MUSIC INC.

Words and Music by
DAN FOGELBERG

Moderate Ballad

Long-er than there've been fish-es in the o-cean, high-er than an-y
Strong-er than an-y moun-tain ca-the-dral, tru-er than, an-y
Through the years as the fi-re starts to mel-low, burn-ing lines in the

bird ev-er flew. Long-er than there've been
tree ev-er grew. Deep-er than an-y
book of our lives. Though the bind-ing cracks and the pag-

stars up in the heav-ens, I've been in love with you.
for-est pri-me-val, I am in love with you.
-es start to yel-low, I'll be in love with you.

I'll bring fi-re in the win-ters; you'll send

show-ers in the springs. We'll fly

D.C. al Coda

through the falls and sum-mers with love on our wings.

CODA

I'll be in love with you. *(Instrumental)*

Long - er than there've been fish - es in the o - cean, high - er than an - y bird ev - er flew. Long - er than there've been stars up in the heav - ens, I've been in love with you, I am in love with you.

Love Shack

© 1989 MAN WOMAN TOGETHER NOW!, INC. and EMI BLACKWOOD MUSIC INC.
All Rights for MAN WOMAN TOGETHER NOW!, INC.
Controlled and Administered by EMI APRIL MUSIC INC.

Words and Music by CATHERINE E. PIERSON,
FREDERICK W. SCHNEIDER, KEITH J. STRICKLAND
and CYNTHIA L. WILSON

Rock

If you see a fad-ed sign at the side of the road that says "Fif-teen miles to the Love Shack." Love Shack yeah, yeah. I'm head-ed down the At-lan-ta High-way. Head-ed for the love get-a-way. Head-ed for the love get-a-way. I got me a car it's as big as a whale and we're head-in' on down to the Love Shack. I got me a Chrys-ler, it seats a-bout twen-ty. So hur-ry up and bring your

Gm C7 E♭ F7
juke - box mon - ey. The Love Shack is a lit - tle old place where we can get
A♭ C7 Gm
to - geth - er. Love Shack, ba - by
C7 Gm C7 Gm
Love Shack, ba - by. Love Shack, ba - by, Love Shack.
C7 Gm C7 Gm
Love Shack, ba - by, Love Shack, Love Shack, ba - by, Love Shack.
C7 Gm C7 Gm
Love Shack, ba - by, Love Shack. Bang, bang, on the door, ba - by.
C7 1 Gm 2 C7 N.C.
Bang, bang, on the door. Your what? Tin roof
C7 Gm C7 Gm
rust - ed. Love Shack, ba - by, Love Shack. Love Shack, ba - by, Love
1 2 C7
Shack. Shack.

134

LOVERGIRL

© 1984 EMI APRIL MUSIC INC. and MIDNIGHT MAGNET MUSIC PUBLISHING
All Rights Controlled and Administered by EMI APRIL MUSIC INC.

Words and Music by
TEENA MARIE

Moderate Dance groove

Cof - fee, tea or me, ba - by, tou - ché o - lé.
Hook, line and sink - er, ba - by, that's how you caught me.

My op - 'ning line might be a bit pas - se, yes.
My sec - ond verse might be a bit old hat. But,

But, don't think that I don't know what I'm feel - in' for ya',
don't think that I don't know what it's do - in' to me,

'cause I got a vibe from you the first time that I saw you, saw you.
'cause I got a vibe on you the first time you saw through me, through me.

I need your love and I won't bring no pain.

A lit - tle bird - ie told me that you feel the same.

I'm for the real and for you I'm true blue.

Dm/A
G/A
G
Let's make a deal, sug - ar, all I want to do is
F
G
Am
be your one and on - ly lov - er. I just want to
F
G
Am
F
G
be your lov - er - girl.
Am
F
G
Am
I just want to rock your world.
F
G
F
G
To Coda
Oh, yeah, hey, hey, hey.
F
G
D.S. al Coda
(Instrumental)
CODA
N.C.
Ba - by, let me groove you.
Let me prove it to you.
Am
G
Let me groove in - to your love.
Ba - by, let me rock your world.

N.C.
1
Am
I just want to be your lov - er - girl.
2
rock your world.
Am
Cof - fee, tea or me, ba - by, tou - ché o - lé. My o - pen - ing line might be
a bit pas - se, but, don't think that I don't know what I'm feel - ing for you 'cause
N.C.
I got a vibe the first time that I saw you, oh, oh.
G Am N.C.
When the push comes to shove and you need a lit - tle love, let me
up, don't be shy for my love will make you high.
Am
put some rock in - to your world.
Call me
I just want to be...

MATERIAL GIRL

© 1984 CANDY CASTLE MUSIC
All Rights Controlled and Administered by EMI BLACKWOOD MUSIC INC.

Words and Music by PETER BROWN
and ROBERT RANS

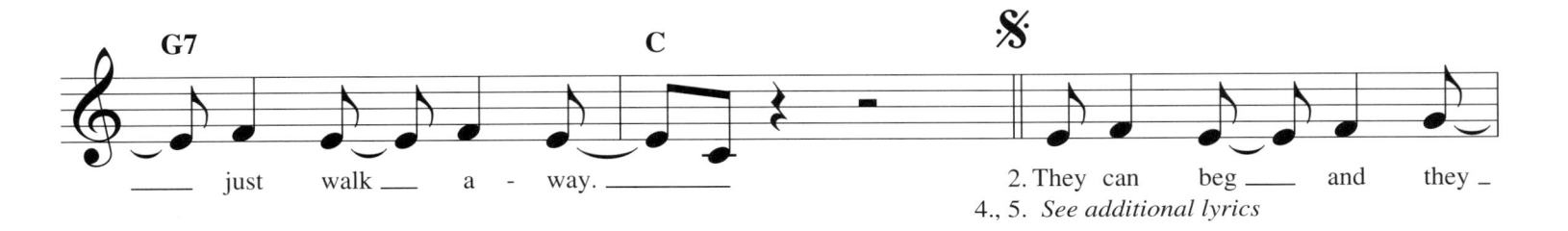

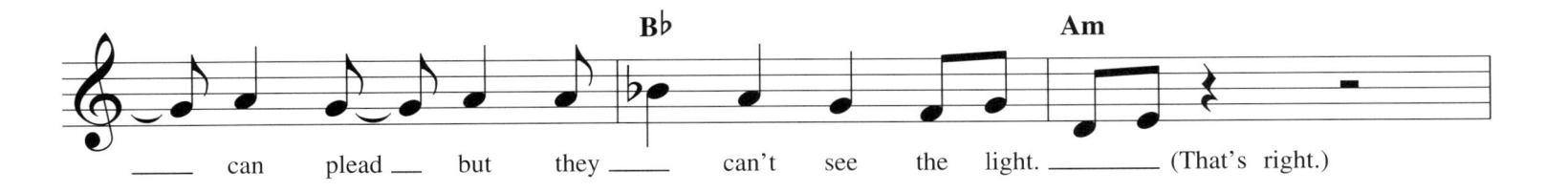

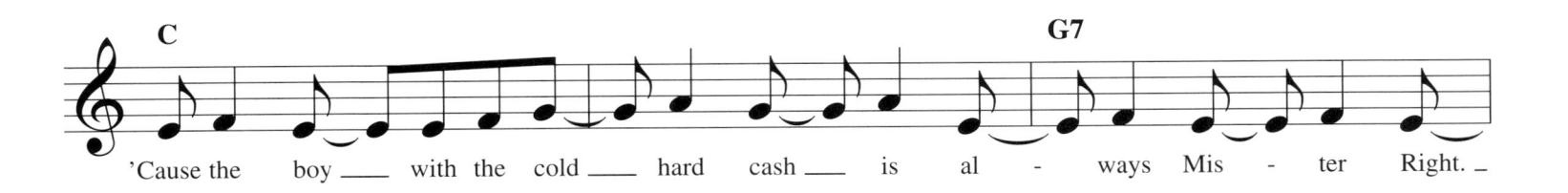

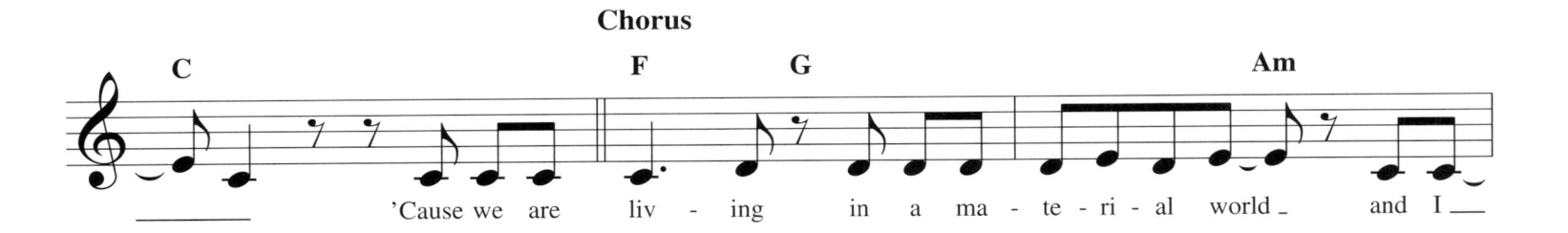

Moderately

1. Some boys kiss me, some boys hug me. I think they're O. K.
3. *See additional lyrics*

If they don't give me prop - er cred - it I

just walk a - way. 2. They can beg and they
4., 5. *See additional lyrics*

can plead but they can't see the light. (That's right.)

'Cause the boy with the cold hard cash is al - ways Mis - ter Right.

Chorus

'Cause we are liv - ing in a ma - te - ri - al world and I

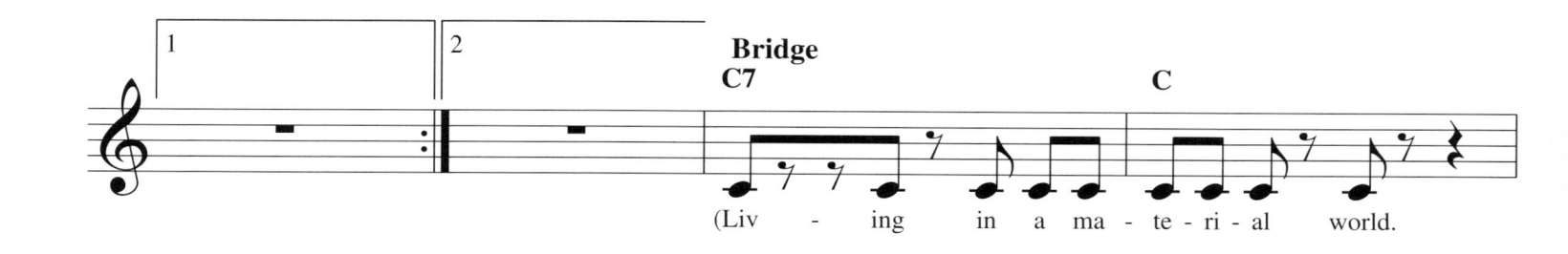

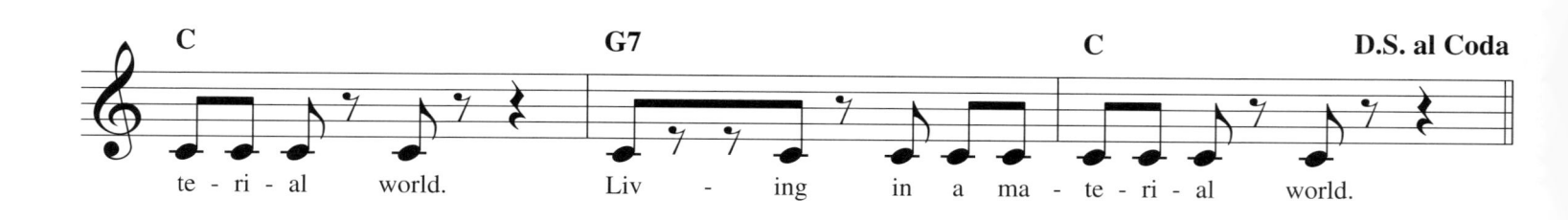

    am a ma-te-ri-al girl. You know that we are living in a ma-terial world and I am a ma-te-ri-al girl.

Bridge

(Living in a material world.

Living in a material world. Living in a material world. Living in a material world.

CODA

Living in a material world and I am a ma-te-ri-al girl.

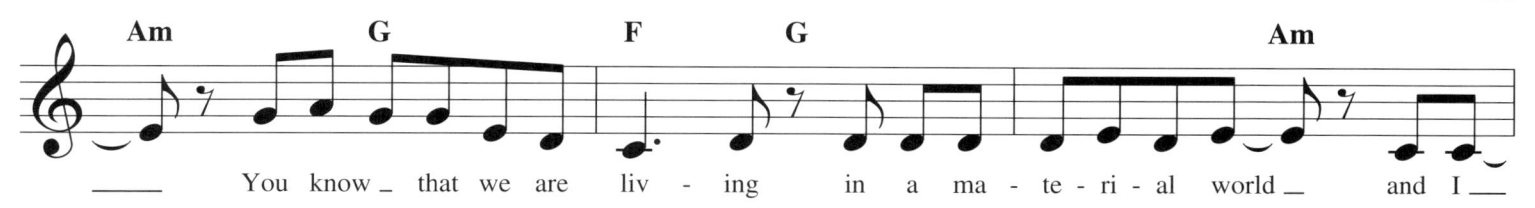

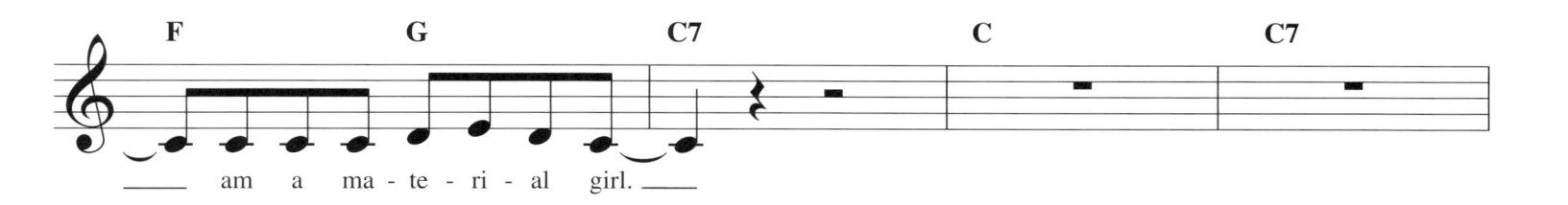

Additional Lyrics

3. Some boys romance, some boys slow dance.
   That's all right with me.
   If they can't raise my int'rest
   Then I have to let them be.

4. Some boys try and some boys lie
   But I don't let them play.
   Only boys who save their pennies
   Make my rainy day.
   Chorus

5. Boys may come and boys may go and
   That's all right, you see.
   Experience has made me rich
   And now they're after me,
   'Cause ev'rybody's living...
   Chorus

MANEATER

Words by SARA ALLEN, DARYL HALL and JOHNA OATES
Music by DARYL HALL and JOHN OATES

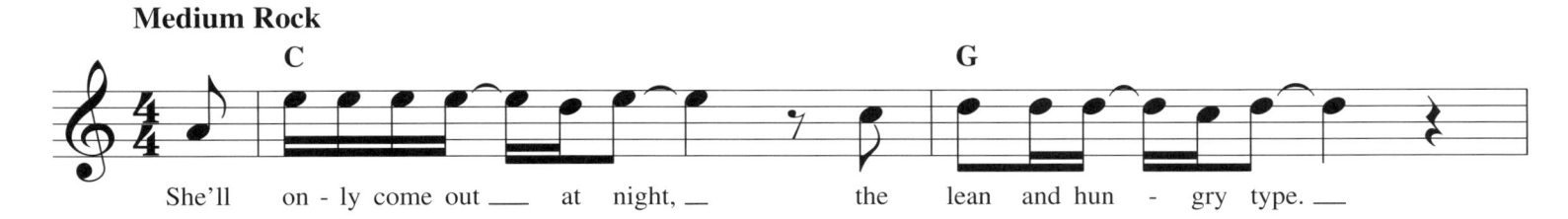

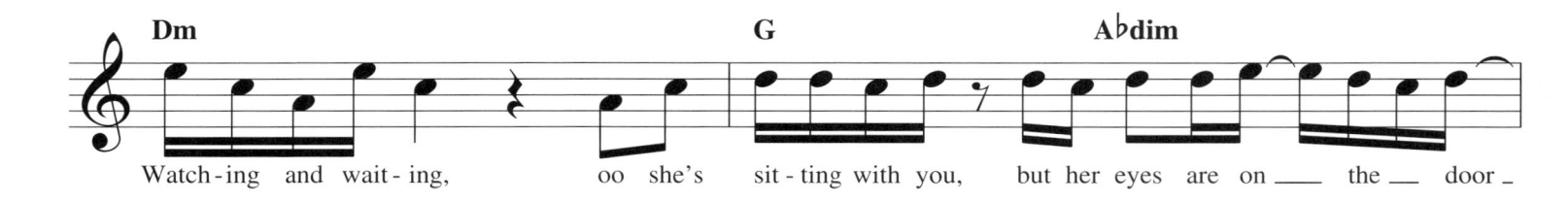

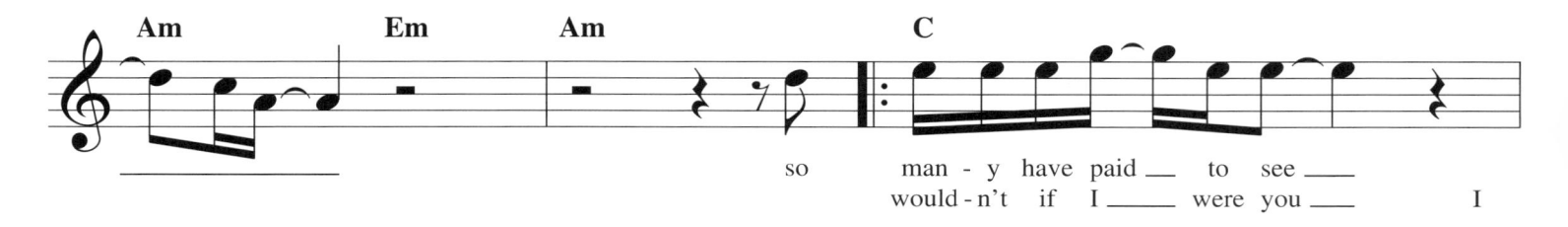

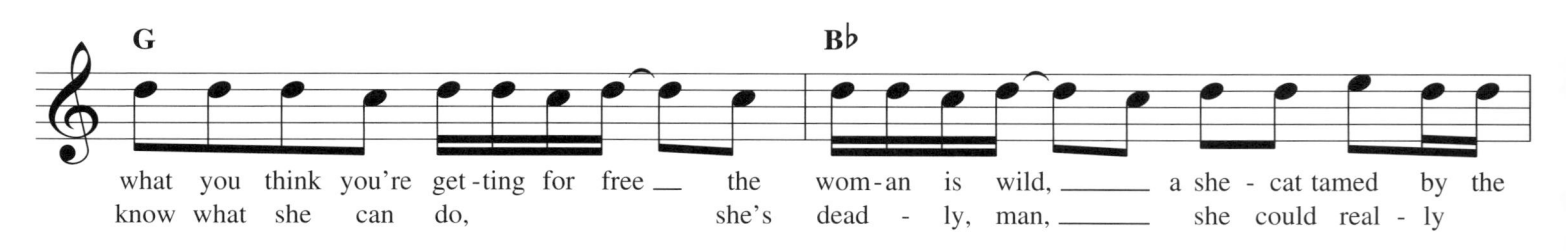

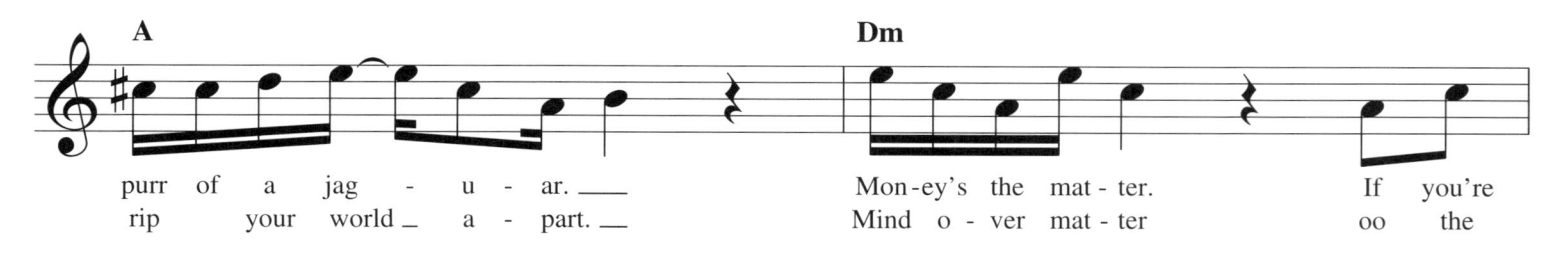

Copyright © 1982 by Unichappell Music Inc., Hot Cha Music Co. and Geomantic Music
All Rights for Hot Cha Music Co. Administered by Unichappell Music Inc.
All Rights for Geomantic Music Controlled and Administered by Irving Music, Inc.

Medium Rock

[C] She'll only come out at night, [G] the lean and hungry type.

[Bb] Nothing is new, I've seen her here [G] before.

[Dm] Watching and waiting, [G] oo she's sitting with you, [Abdim] but her eyes are on the door

[Am] [Em] [Am] [C] so many have paid to see
wouldn't if I were you I

[G] what you think you're getting for free, [Bb] the woman is wild, a she-cat tamed by the
know what she can do, she's deadly, man, she could really

[A] purr of a jaguar. [Dm] Money's the matter. If you're
rip your world apart. Mind over matter oo the

[G] in it for love, you ain't gonna get [Abdim] too far. [Am] [A]
beauty is there. But a beast is in the heart.

Am
G
Oh, here she comes, watch out boy, she'll chew you up.
F
E
Am
Oh, here she comes. She's a Man - eat - er. Oh, here she comes,
G
Dm
watch out boy. She'll chew you up. Oh, here she comes, she a
F
G
Am
3
1
2
Man - eat - er
I
Am
G
Oh, here she comes, watch out boy, she'll chew you up.
F
E
Oh, here she comes, she's a Man - eat - er.
Am
G
Oh, here she comes, watch - out boy, she'll chew you up.
Dm
F
G
Repeat and Fade
Oh, here she comes, she's a Man - eat - er.

MICKEY

Words and Music by MICHAEL CHAPMAN
and NICKY CHINN

Copyright © 1981, 1982 by Universal Music - MGB Songs

Moderately

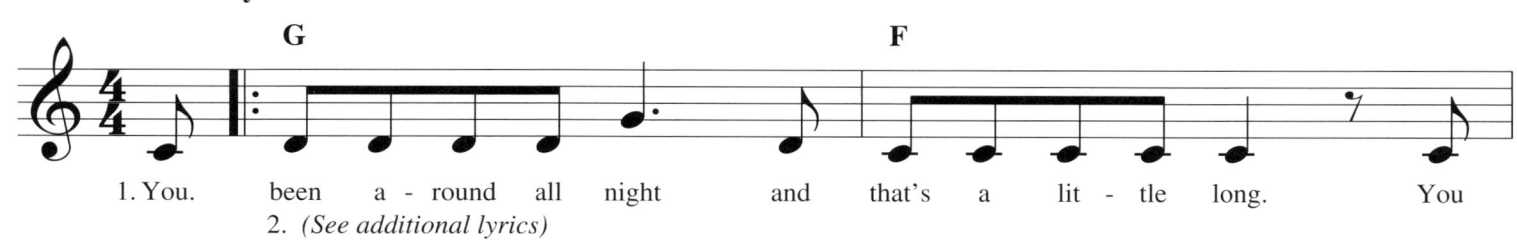

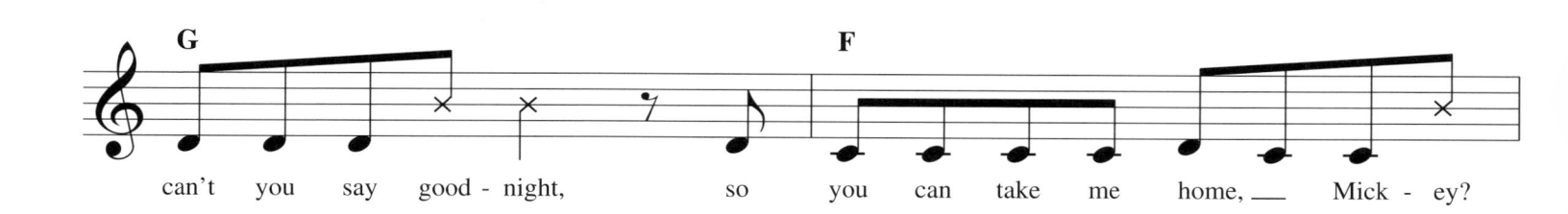

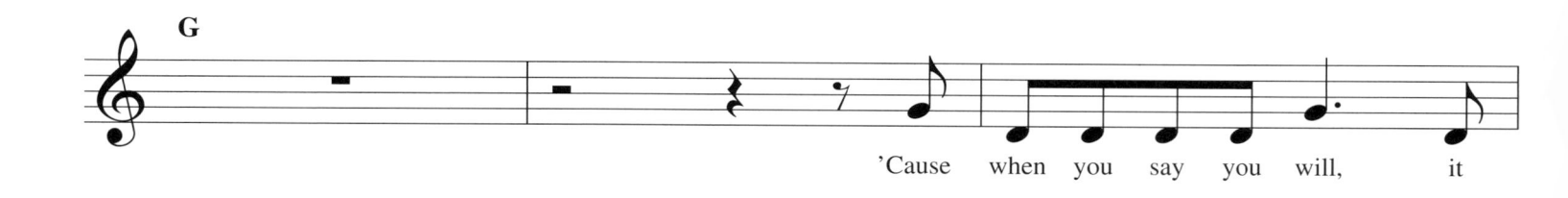

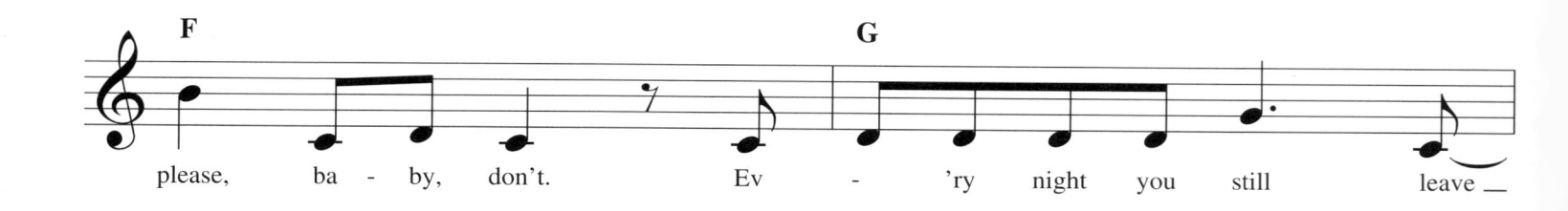

1. You been around all night and that's a little long. You
2. *(See additional lyrics)*

think you got the right, but I think you got it wrong. But

can't you say good-night, so you can take me home, Mick-ey?

'Cause when you say you will, it

al-ways means you won't. You're giv-in' me the chills. Ba-by,

please, ba-by, don't. Ev-'ry night you still leave

___ me all a-lone, ___ Mick-ey.

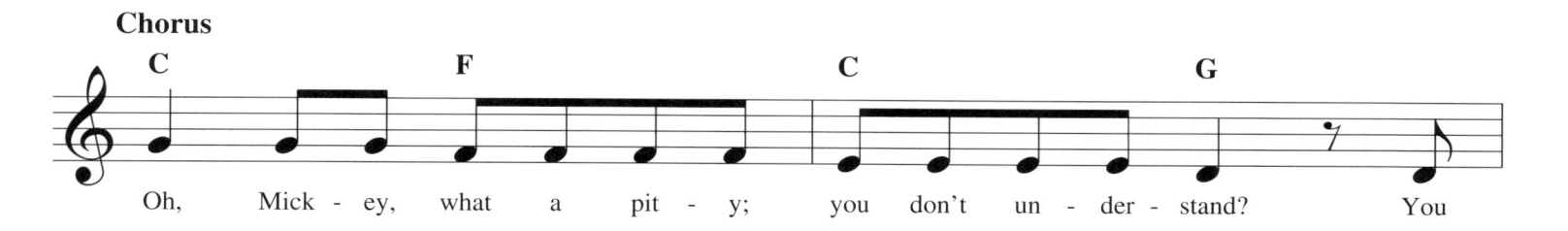

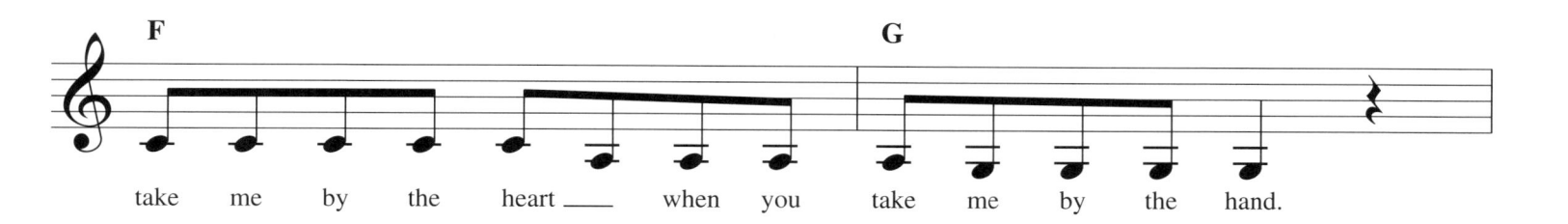

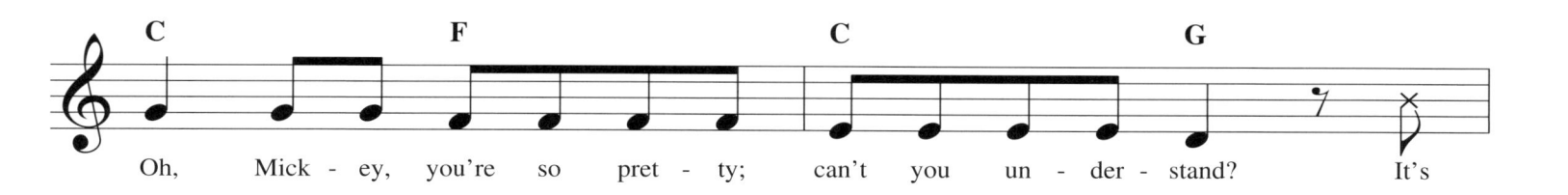

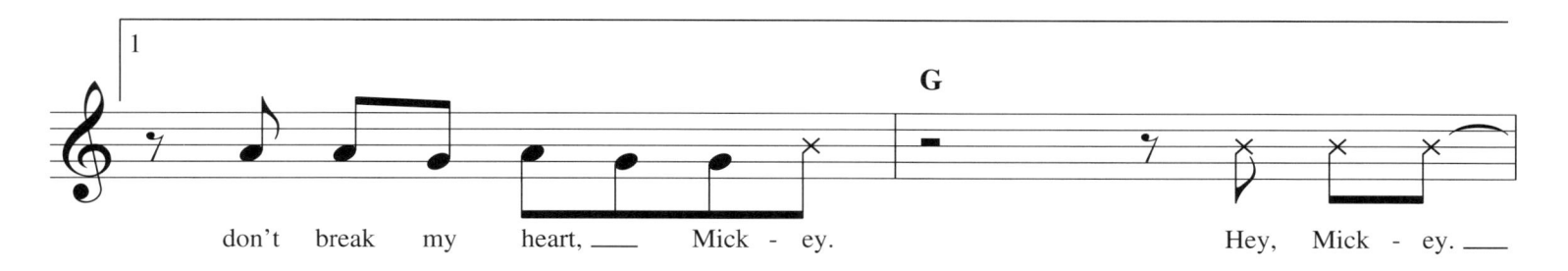

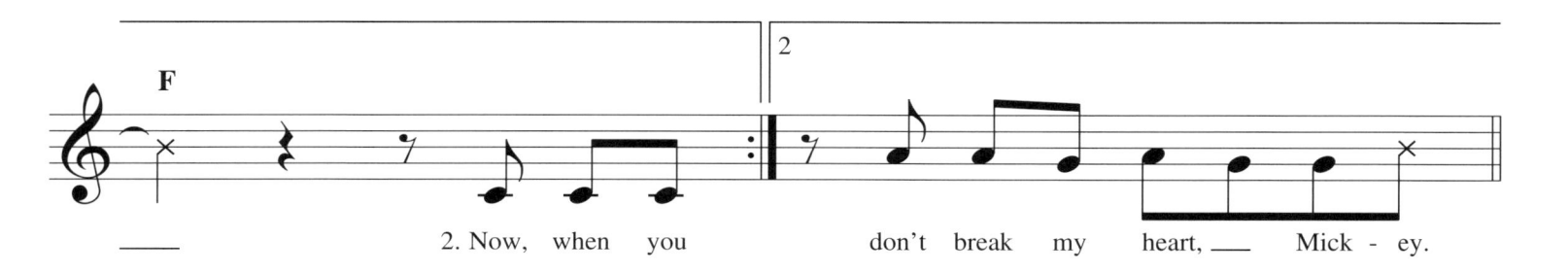

Chorus

Oh, Mick-ey, what a pit-y; you don't un-der-stand? You take me by the heart ___ when you take me by the hand.

Oh, Mick-ey, you're so pret-ty; can't you un-der-stand? It's guys like you, Mick-ey. ___ Oh, what you do ___ Mick-ey, do ___ Mick-ey,

1. don't break my heart, ___ Mick-ey. Hey, Mick-ey. ___

2. Now, when you don't break my heart, ___ Mick-ey.

Chorus

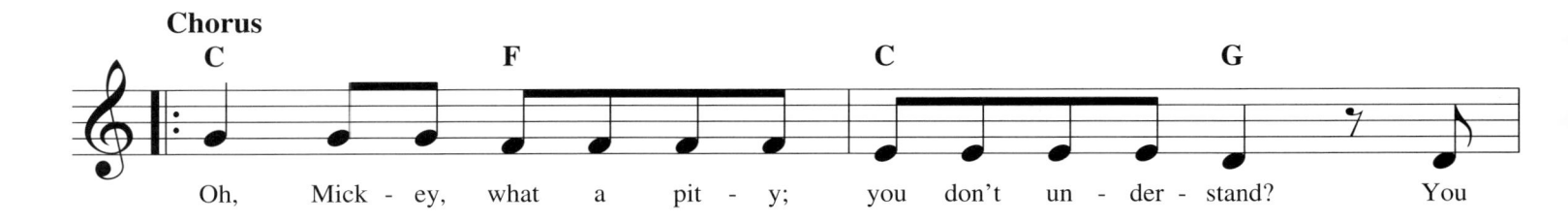

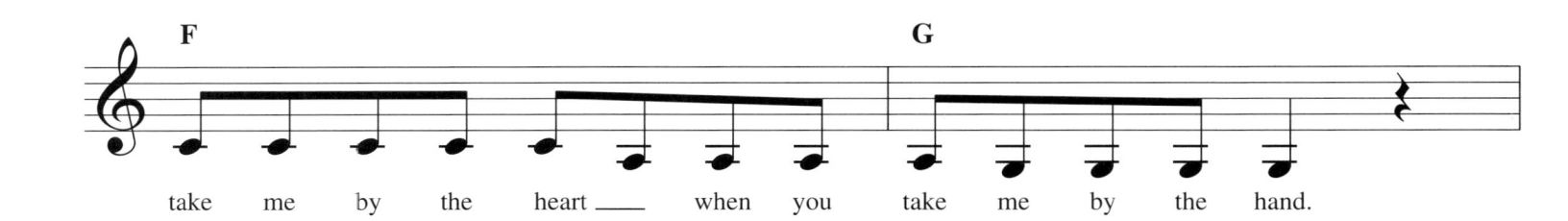

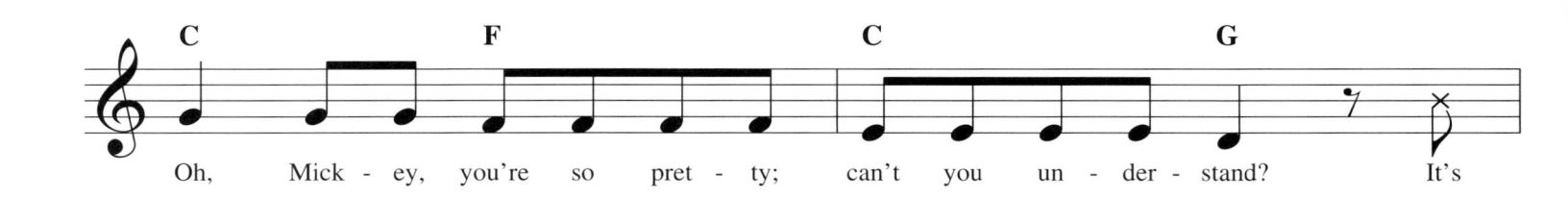

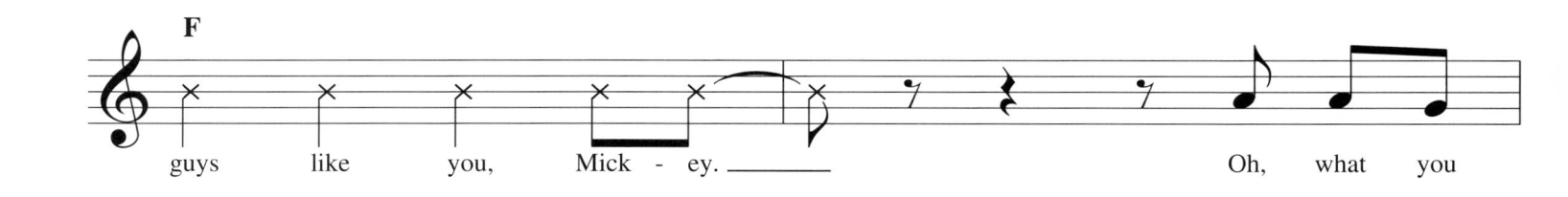

Oh, Mick-ey, what a pit-y; you don't un-der-stand? You take me by the heart when you take me by the hand. Oh, Mick-ey, you're so pret-ty; can't you un-der-stand? It's guys like you, Mick-ey. Oh, what you do Mick-ey, do Mick-ey, don't break my heart, Mick-ey.

Repeat and Fade

Additional Lyrics

2. Now, when you take me by the hand who's ever gonna know?
   Ev'ry time you move I let a little more show.
   There's somethin' you can use so don't say no, Mickey.
   So come on and give it to me any way you can.
   Any way you want to do it, I'll take it like a man.
   Please, baby, please, don't leave me in this jam, Mickey.
   Chorus

MISSING YOU

Words and Music by JOHN WAITE
CHARLES SANFORD and MARK LEONARD

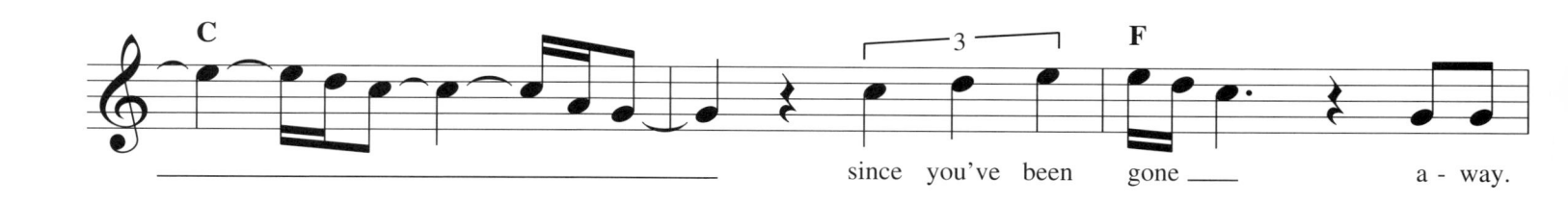

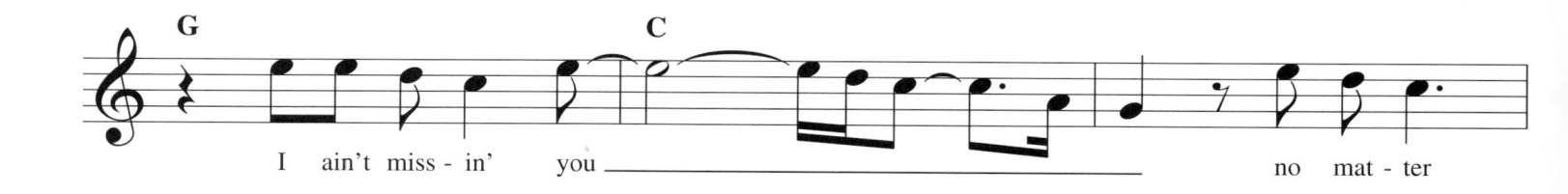

down this long distance line to-night. I ain't miss-in' you since you've been gone a-way. I ain't miss-in' you no mat-ter a-what I might say. There's a mes-sage in the wire and I'm send-in' you this sig-nal to-night. You don't know how des-p'rate I've be-come, and it looks like I'm los-in' this fight. In your world I have no mean-ing. I try so hard to un-der-stand. And it's my say. There's a

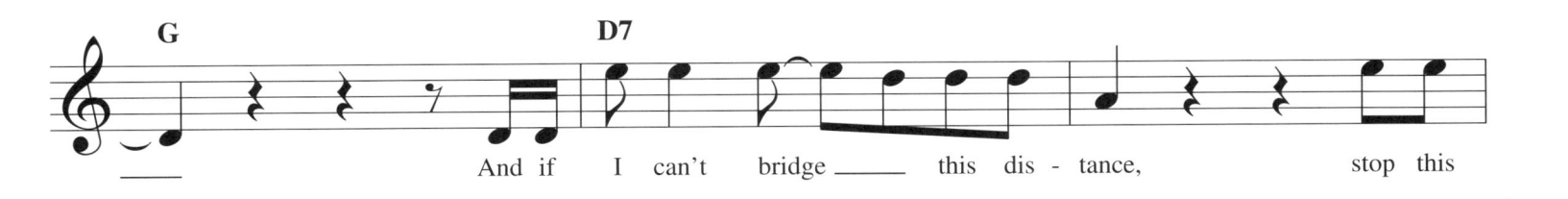

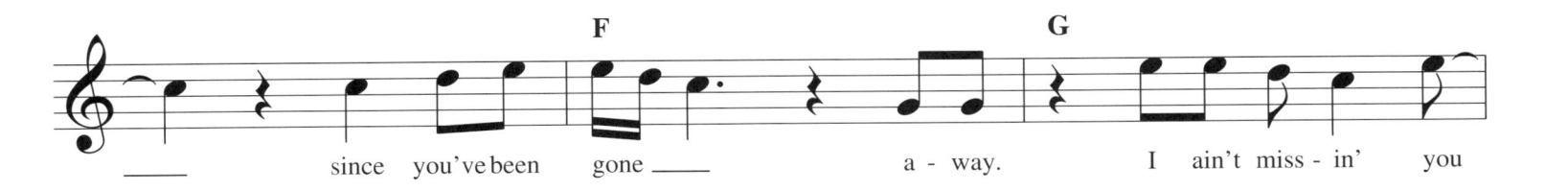

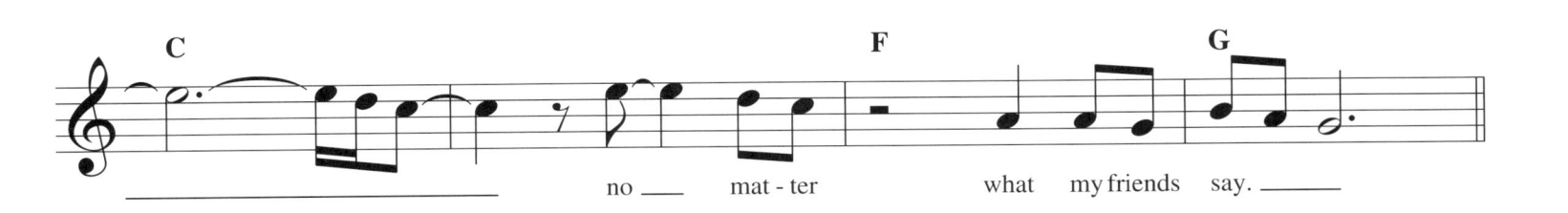

mes-sage that I'm send-in' out like a tel-a-graph to your soul.

And if I can't bridge this dis-tance, stop this

heart-break o-ver-load, I ain't miss-in' you

since you've been gone a-way. I ain't miss-in' you

no mat-ter what my friends say.

Repeat and Fade

I ain't miss-in' you.

NINE TO FIVE
from NINE TO FIVE

Copyright © 1980 Velvet Apple Music and Warner-Tamerlane Publishing Corp.

Words and Music by
DOLLY PARTON

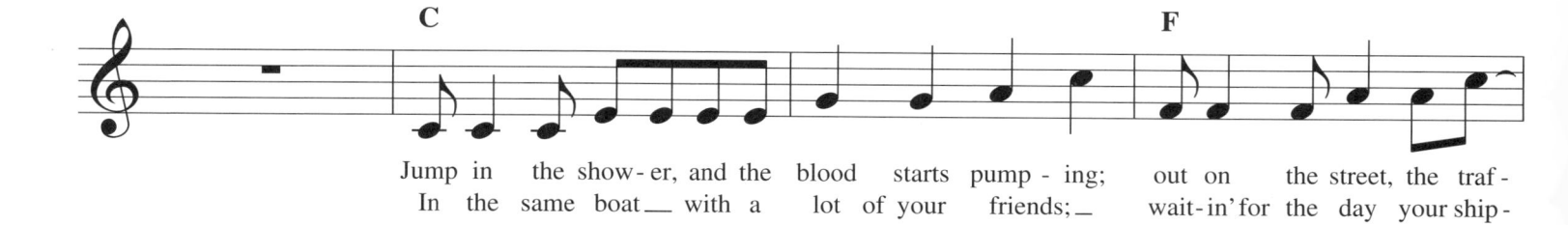

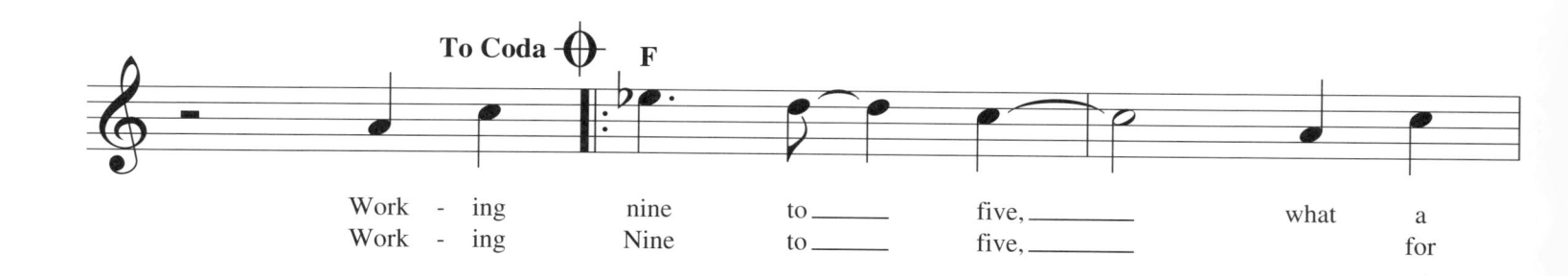

Lively

Tum - ble out of bed and stum - ble to the kitch - en; pour my - self a cup
let__ you__ dream just to watch__ them__ shat - ter; you're just a step on the

__ of am - bi - tion, and yawn, and stretch, and try to come__ to life.__
boss__ man's lad - der, but you've got dreams he'll nev - er take__ a - way.__

Jump in the show - er, and the blood starts pump - ing; out on the street, the traf -
In the same boat__ with a lot of your friends;__ wait - in' for the day your ship -

- fic starts jump - ing, with folks__ like me on the job from nine to five.
- 'll come in,__ and the tide's gon - na turn and it's all gon - na roll your way.

To Coda

Work - ing nine to__ five,__ what a
Work - ing Nine to__ five,__ for

way to make__ a liv - ing; bare - ly get - ting by,__ it's all
ser - vice and__ de - vo - tion; you would think__ that I would de -

taking and no giving. They just use your
serve a fair promotion; want to move a-
mind, and they never give you credit; it's enough to drive
head, but the boss won't seem to let me. I swear sometimes,

1. you crazy, if you let it.
2. that man is out to get

me. *(Instrumental)* They

CODA

nine to five, what a way to make a liv-
Nine to five, they've got you where they want

-ing; barely getting by, it's all taking and no
you; there's a better life, and you dream about it,

giving. They just use your mind, and they never give you
don't you? It's a rich man's game, no matter what they

Repeat and Fade

credit; it's enough to drive you crazy, if you let it.
call it; and you spend your life putting money in his pocket.

OH SHERRIE

Words and Music by STEVE PERRY, RANDY GOODRUM,
BILL CUOMO and CRAIG KRAMPF

Copyright © 1984 Street Talk Tunes (ASCAP), California Phase (ASCAP),
Random Notes (ASCAP), Pants Down Music (BMI) and Phosphene Music (BMI)
All Rights for California Phase Controlled and Administered in the U.S.,
 Canada and Mexico by Universal Music Corp.
All Rights for Random Notes Controlled and Administered in the
 United States and Canada by Universal Music Corp.
All Rights for Pants Down Music Controlled and Administered by Bug Music

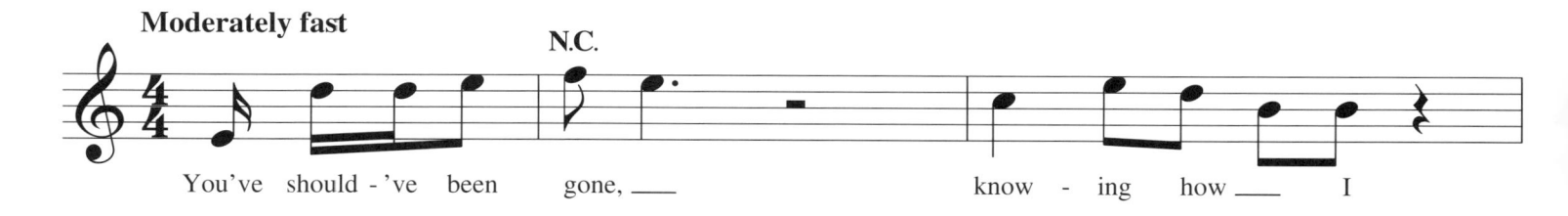

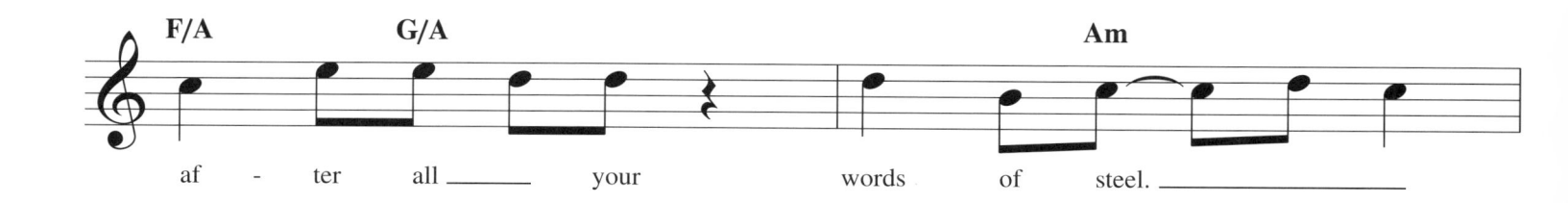

Moderately fast

You've should-'ve been gone, knowing how I made you feel. And I should-'ve been gone after all your words of steel.

Oh, I must-'ve been a dream-er

And I must-'ve been some-one else.

And we should-'ve been o-ver.

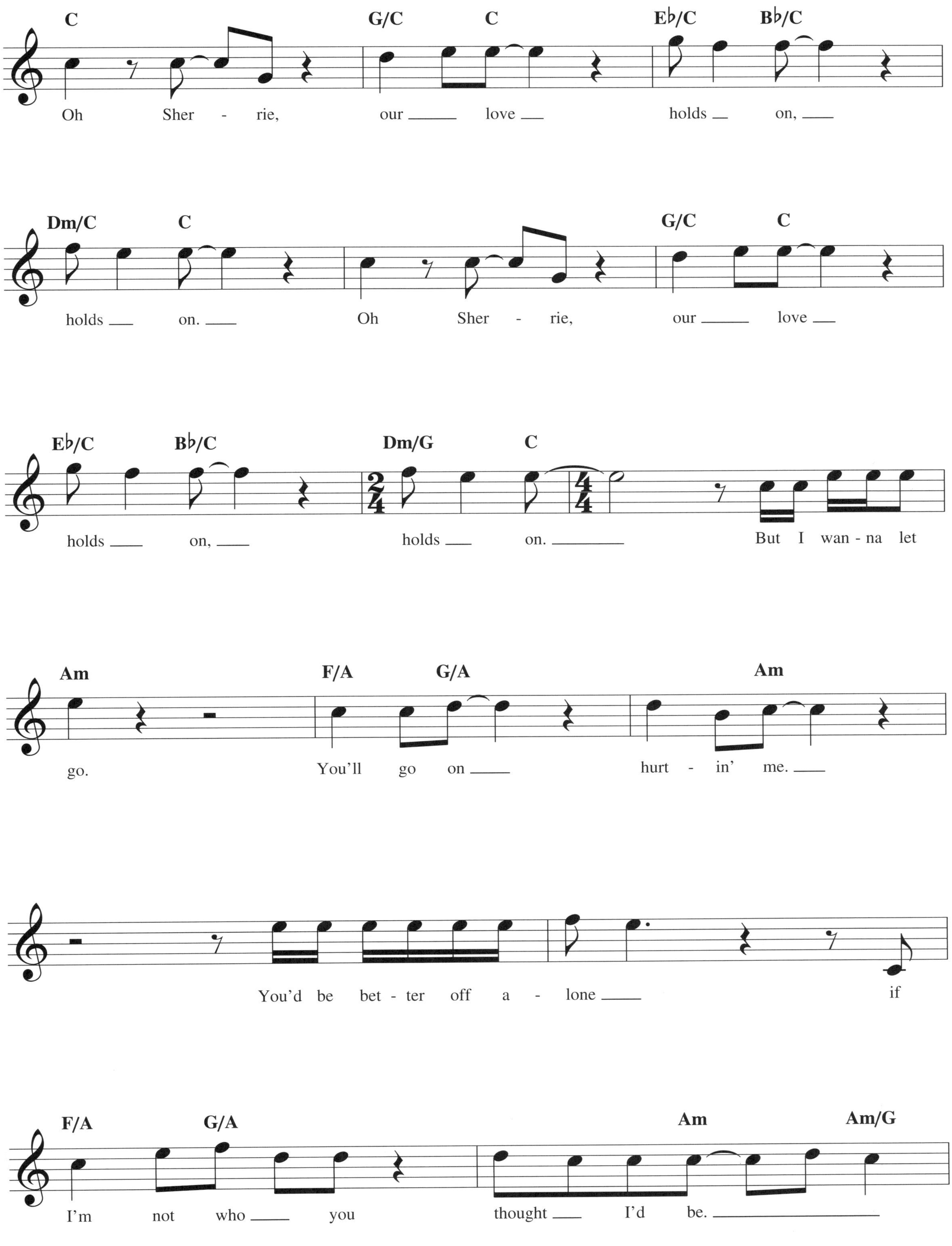
C G/C C Eb/C Bb/C
Oh Sher - rie, our love holds on,
Dm/C C G/C C
holds on. Oh Sher - rie, our love
Eb/C Bb/C Dm/G C
holds on, holds on. But I wan - na let
Am F/A G/A Am
go. You'll go on hurt - in' me.
You'd be bet - ter off a - lone if
F/A G/A Am Am/G
I'm not who you thought I'd be.

F
C/G
G
But you know that there's a fe - ver,
F
C/G
G
oh, that you'll nev - er find no - where else.
F
C/G
Can't you feel it burn - ing on and on?
C
G/C
C
Eb/C
Bb/C
Oh, Sher - rie, our love holds on,
Dm/C
C
G/C
C
holds on. Oh Sher - rie, our love
Eb/C
Bb/C
Dm/C
C
holds on, holds on.

ONCE IN A LIFETIME

Copyright © 1980 by EG Music Ltd., WB Music Corp. and Index Music, Inc.
All Rights for EG Music Ltd. in the United States and Canada
Administered by Universal Music - MGB Songs
All Rights for Index Music, Inc. Administered by WB Music Corp.

Words and Music by BRIAN ENO,
DAVID BYRNE, CHRISTOPHER FRANTZ,
JERRY HARRISON and TINA WEYMOUTH

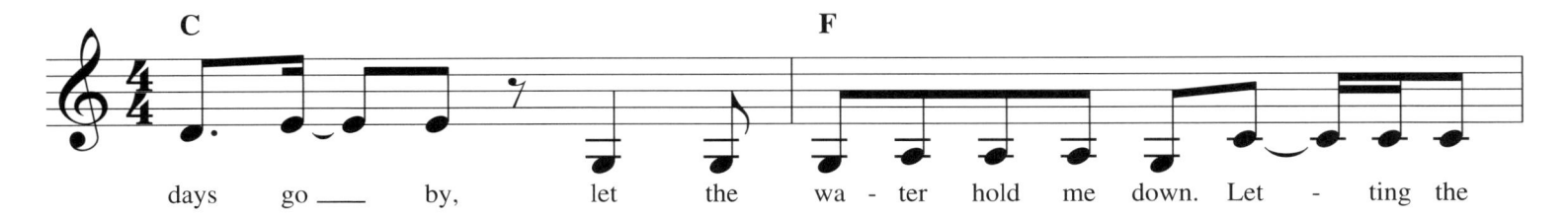

Moderately bright

And you may find yourself living in a shotgun shack. And you may find yourself in another part of the world. And you may find yourself behind the wheel of a large automobile. And you may find yourself in a beautiful house, with a beautiful wife. And you may ask yourself, "Well, how did I get here?" Letting the days go by, let the water hold me down. Letting the

[C] days go by, water flowing underground. [F] Into the
[C] blue again, after the money's gone. [F] Once in a
[C] lifetime, water flowing underground. [F] And you may
[G7] ask yourself, "How do I work this?" And you may
ask yourself, "Where is that large automobile?" And you may
tell yourself, "This is not my beautiful house." And you may
tell yourself, "This is not my beautiful wife." Letting the

days go __ by, let the wa-ter hold me down. Let-ting the

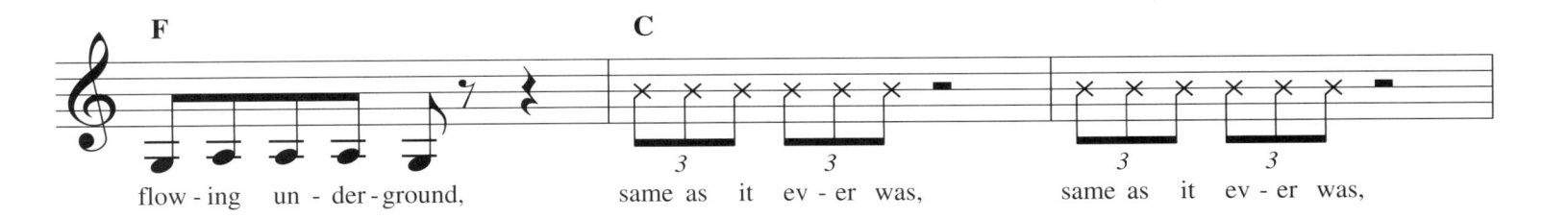

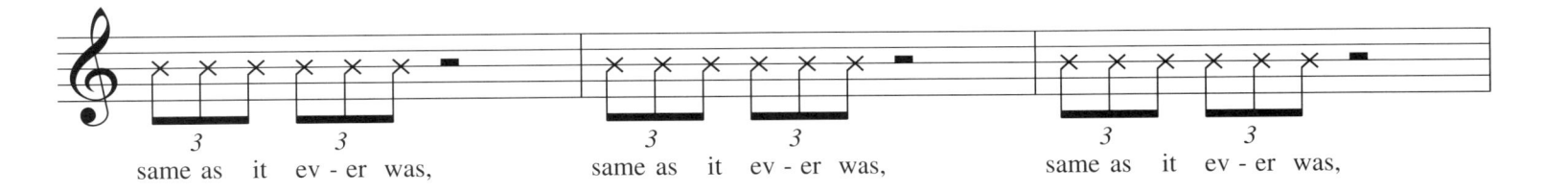

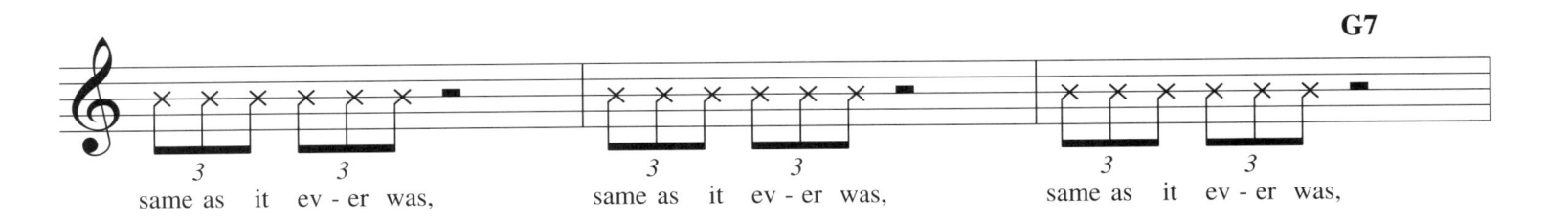

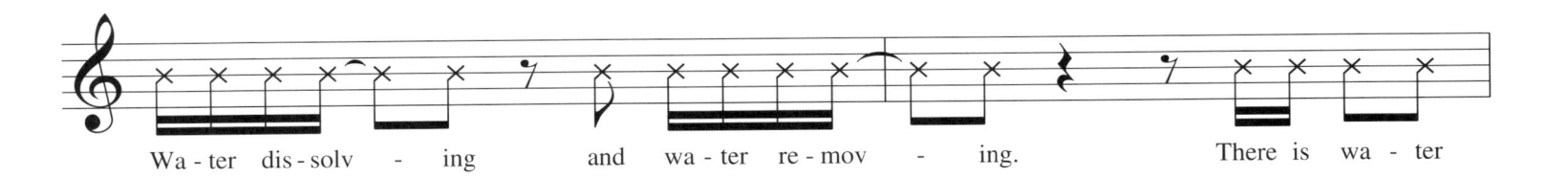

days go __ by, wa-ter flow-ing un-der-ground. In - to the

blue a-gain, af-ter the mon-ey's gone. Once __ in a life-time, __ wa-ter

flow-ing un-der-ground, same as it ev-er was, same as it ev-er was,

same as it ev-er was, same as it ev-er was, same as it ev-er was,

same as it ev-er was, same as it ev-er was, same as it ev-er was,

Wa-ter dis-solv-ing and wa-ter re-mov-ing. There is wa-ter

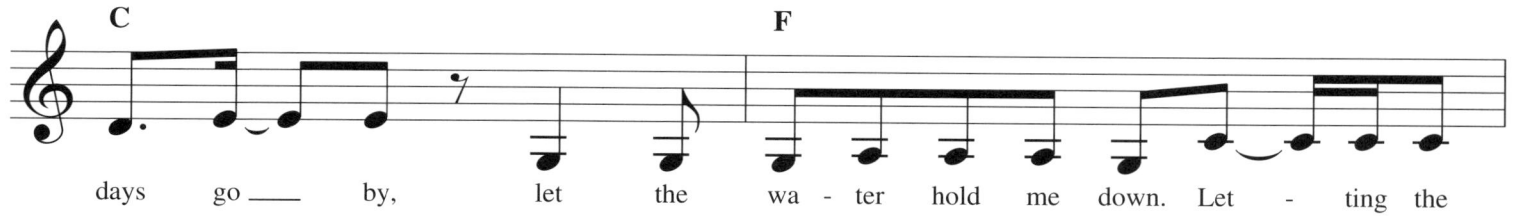

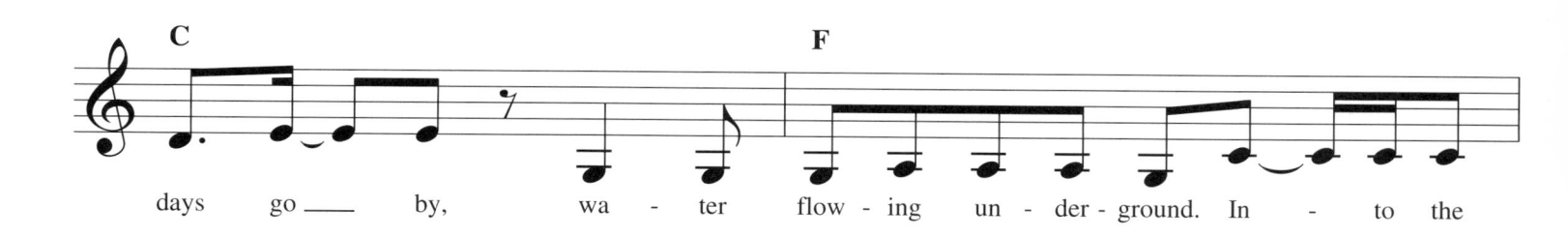

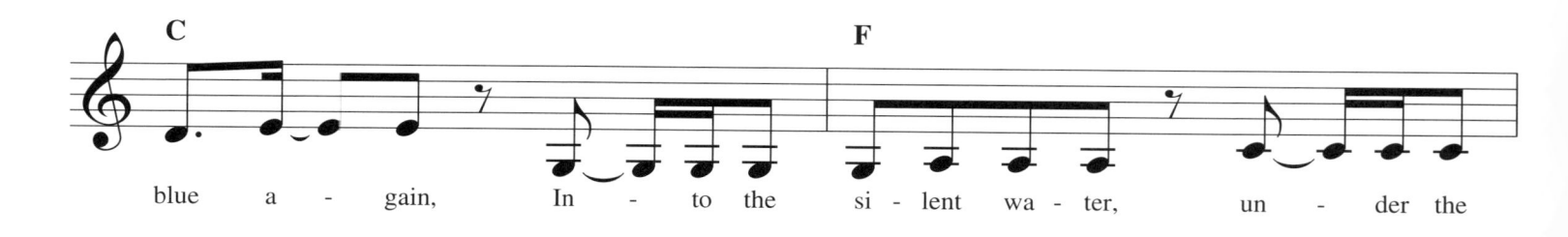

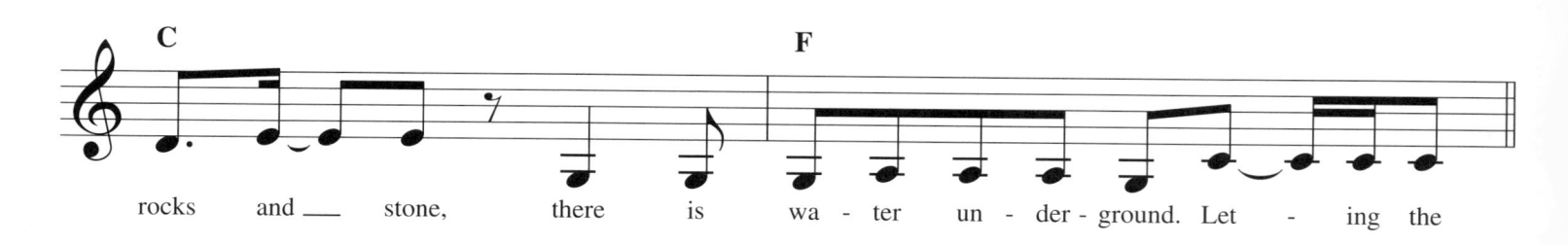

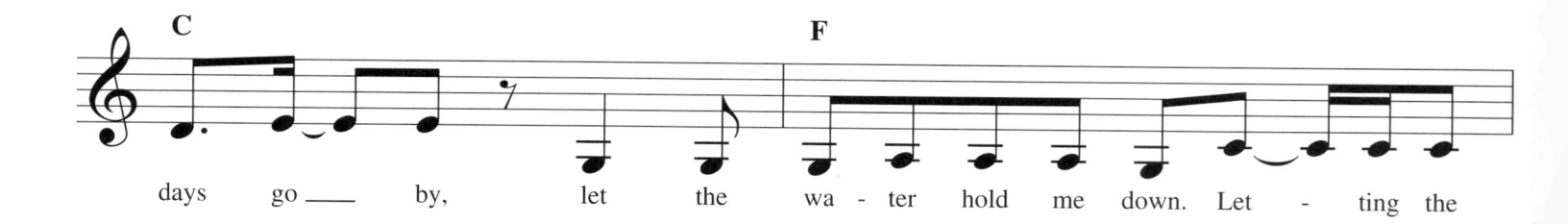

at the bot-tom of the o-cean. Un-der the wa-ter, car-ry the wa-ter. Let - ting the days go ___ by, let the wa-ter hold me down. Let - ting the days go ___ by, wa-ter flow-ing un-der-ground. In - to the blue a-gain, In - to the si-lent wa-ter, un-der the rocks and ___ stone, there is wa-ter un-der-ground. Let - ing the days go ___ by, let the wa-ter hold me down. Let - ting the

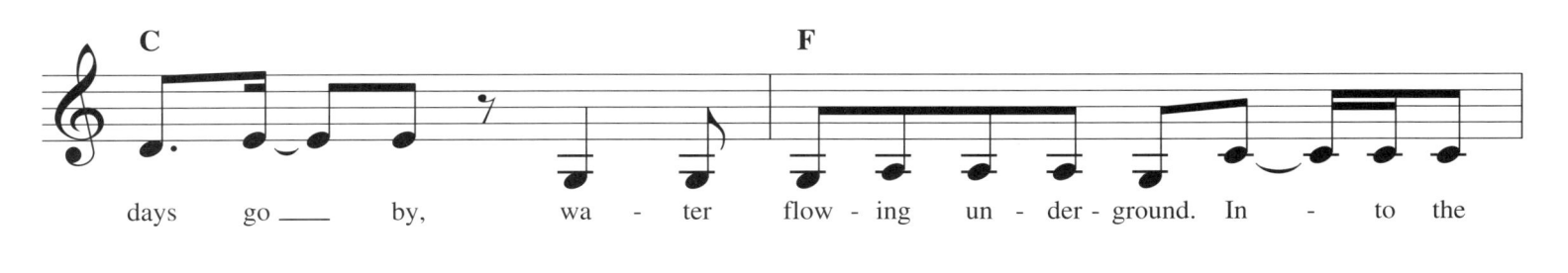

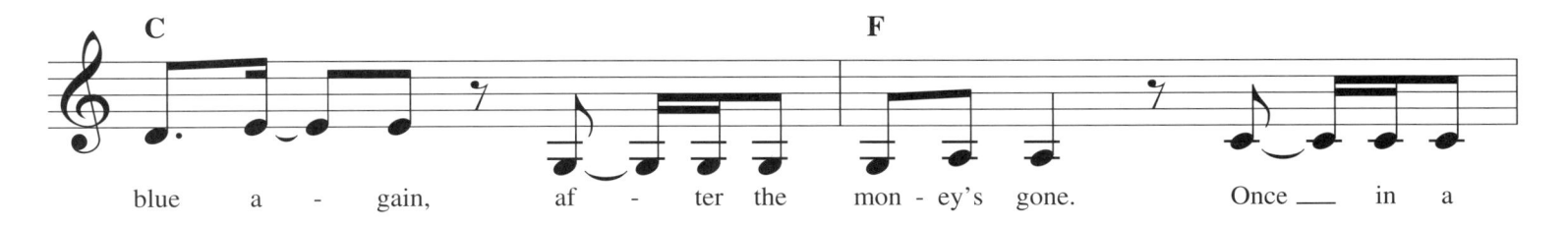

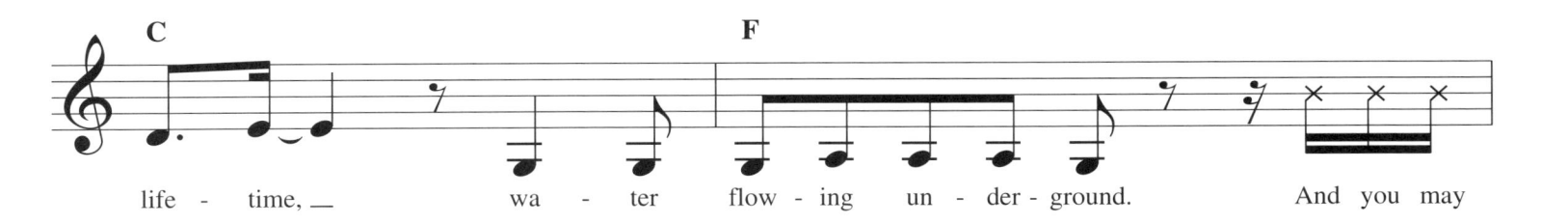

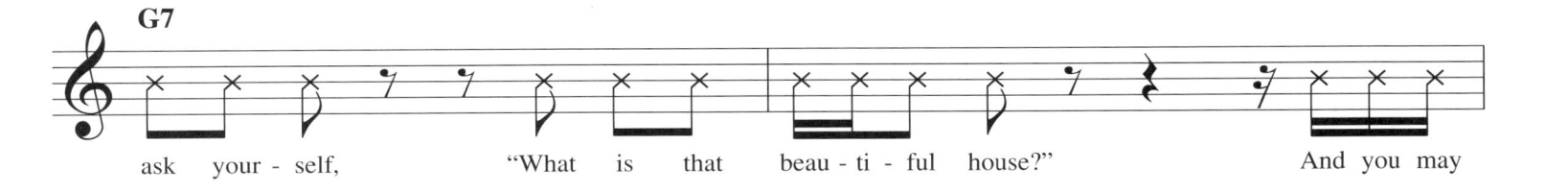

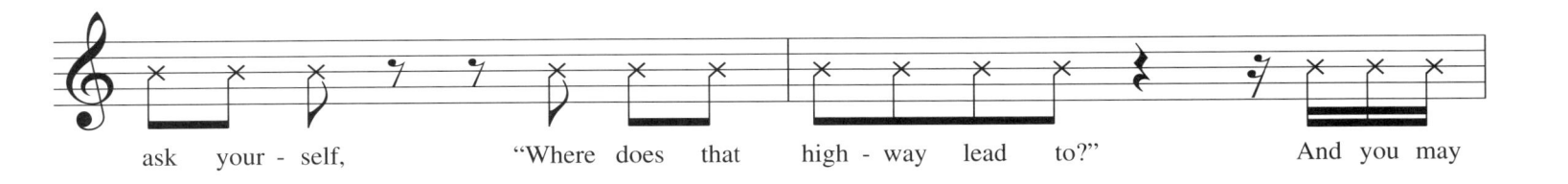

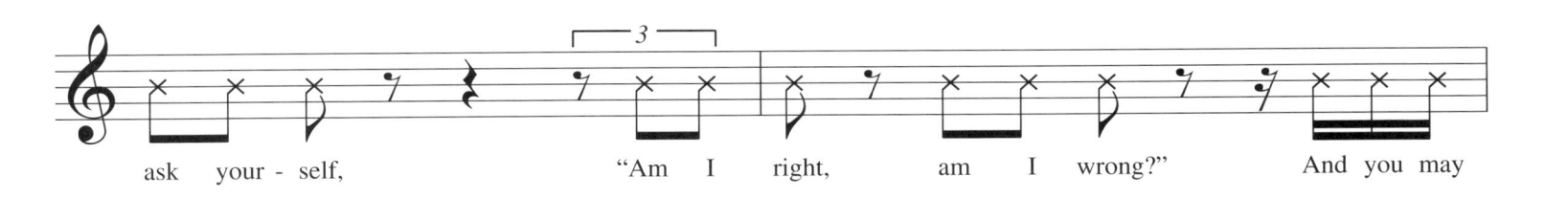

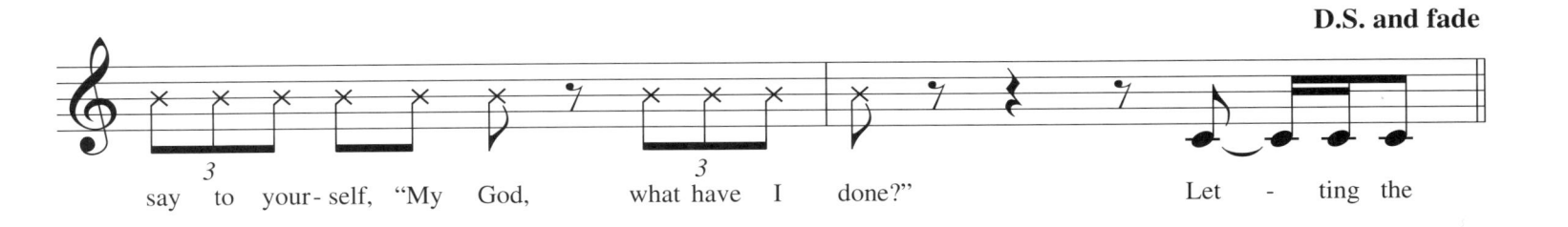

C		F	
days go — by, water flowing un-der-ground. In - to the

C		F	
blue a-gain, af - ter the mon-ey's gone. Once — in a

C		F	
life - time, — water flow-ing un-der-ground. And you may

G7

ask your-self, "What is that beau-ti-ful house?" And you may

ask your-self, "Where does that high-way lead to?" And you may

ask your-self, "Am I right, am I wrong?" And you may

D.S. and fade

say to your-self, "My God, what have I done?" Let - ting the

ON MY OWN

Words and Music by CAROLE BAYER SAGER and BURT BACHARACH

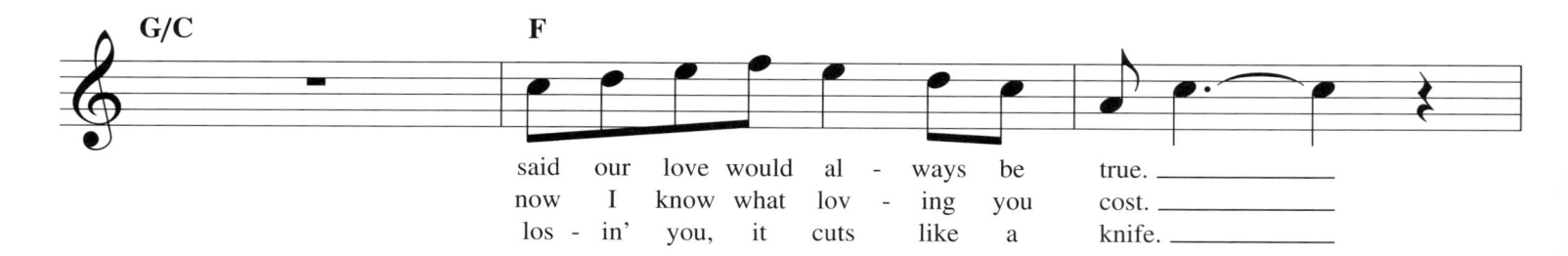

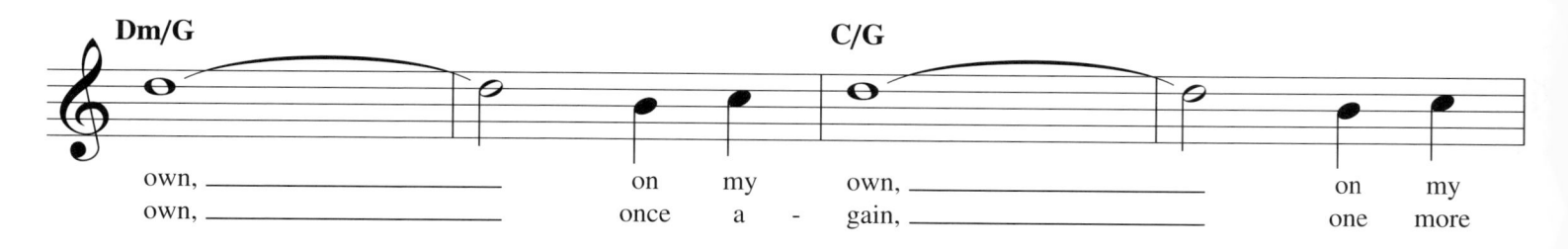

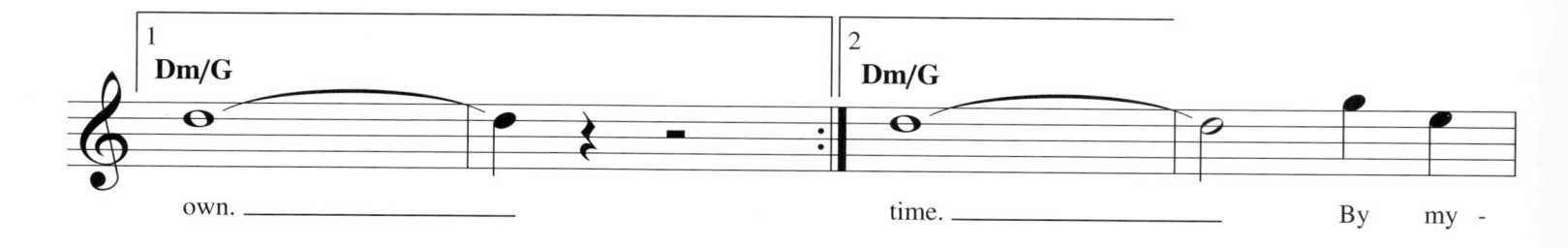

Copyright © 1985 CAROLE BAYER SAGER MUSIC and NEW HIDDEN VALLEY MUSIC
All Rights for CAROLE BAYER SAGER MUSIC Controlled and Administered by SONGS OF UNIVERSAL, INC.

Moderately slow

So man-y times, said it was for-ev-er; said our love would al-ways be true. Some-thing in my heart al-ways knew I'd be ly-ing here be-side you. On my own, on my own, on my own

So man-y prom-is-es nev-er should be spo-ken; now I know what lov-ing you cost. Now we're up to talk-in' di-vorce and we were-n't e-ven mar-ried. On my own, once a-gain, one more

So man-y times, I know I could have told you; los-in' you, it cuts like a knife. You walked out and there went my life; I don't want to live with-out you. On my

own. time. By my-

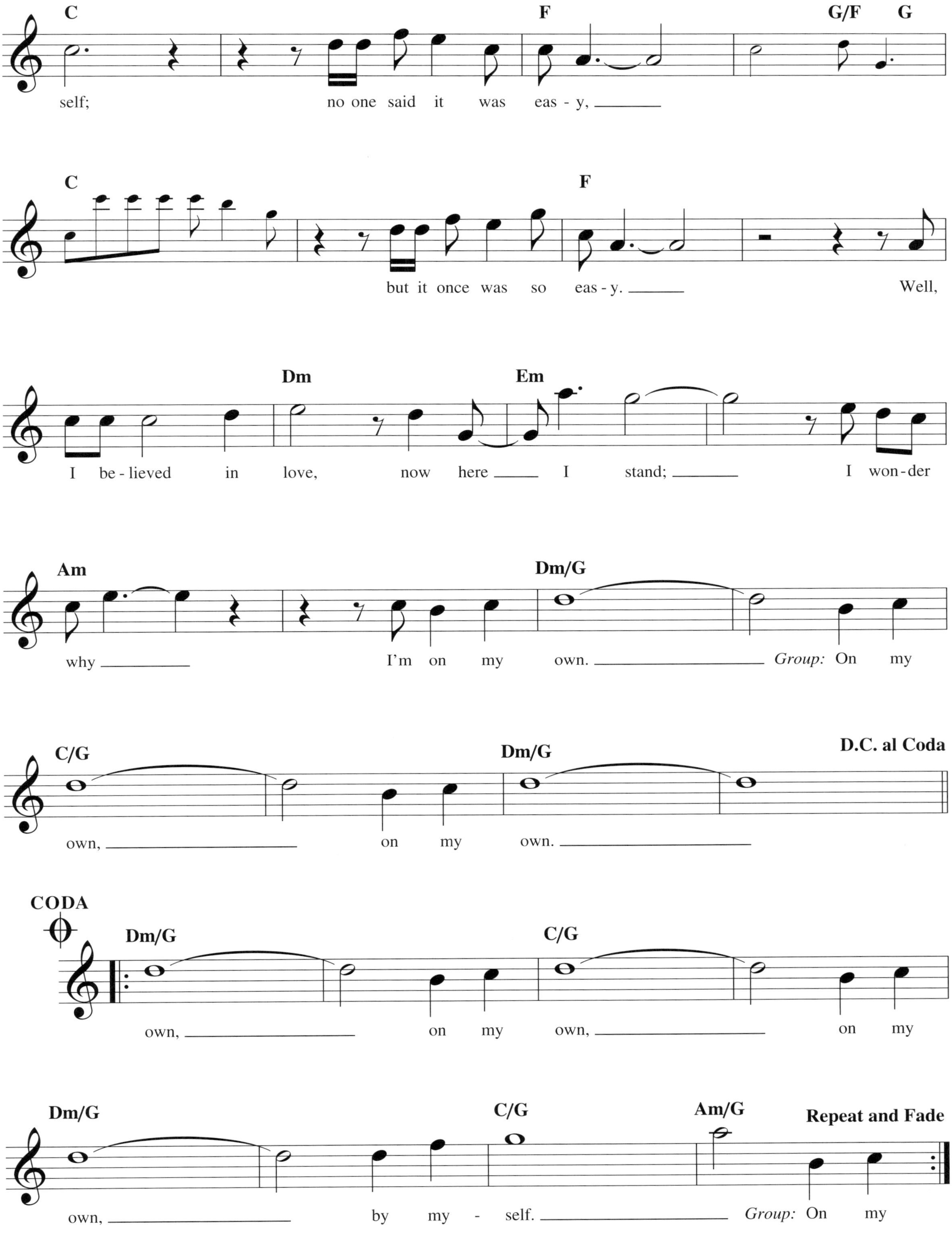
C
F
G/F
G
self; no one said it was eas - y,
C
F
but it once was so eas - y. Well,
Dm
Em
I be - lieved in love, now here I stand; I won - der
Am
Dm/G
why I'm on my own. Group: On my
C/G
Dm/G
D.C. al Coda
own, on my own.
CODA
Dm/G
C/G
own, on my own, on my
Dm/G
C/G
Am/G
Repeat and Fade
own, by my - self. Group: On my

ONE THING LEADS TO ANOTHER

© 1983 EMI MUSIC PUBLISHING LTD.
All Rights for the U.S. and Canada Controlled and
Administered by COLGEMS-EMI MUSIC INC.

Words and Music by CY CURNIN, JAMIE WEST-ORAM,
ADAM WOODS, RUPERT GREENALL and ALFRED AGIUS

Moderately fast

The de-cep - tion with tact; just
- sion that you sell
- sy to be - lieve

what are you try - ing to say? You got a black face which
pass - es in and out like a scent. But the long face
some-bod-y's been ly - ing to me. But when the wrong word goes in the

ir - ri - tates. Com - mu - ni - cate; pull out your par - ty
that you see comes from liv - ing close to your fears.
right ear I know you've been ly - in' to me.

piece. You see di - men - sions in
If this is up, then I'm up, but you're
It's get - ting rough off the cuff. I've got to

two. State your case in black or white,
run - ning out of sight. You've seen your name on the
say e - nough's e - nough. Big - ger, the hard - er he

but when one lit - tle cross leads to
walls. And when one lit - tle bump leads to
falls. But when the wrong an - ti - dote is like a

shots, grit your teeth, you run for cov - er, so dis -
shock, miss a beat, you run for cov - er and there's
bulge on the throat, you run for cov - er in the

creet.
heat. } Why don't they do what they say; say what you mean?
heat.

One thing leads to an - oth - er. You told me some - thing

wrong; I know I lis - ten too long, but then one thing leads to an - oth -

1 - er. The im - pres - - er, yeah, yeah, yeah. *(Instrumental)*
2

One thing one thing leads to an -

D.S. al Coda **CODA**

oth - er. Then it's eas - - er, yeah, yeah.

Repeat and Fade

One thing, one thing leads to an - oth - er.

OWNER OF A LONELY HEART

Words and Music by TREVOR HORN, JON ANDERSON,
TREVOR RABIN and CHRIS SQUIRE

Copyright © 1983 by Carlin Music Corp., Unforgettable Songs and Affirmative Music
All Rights for Carlin Music Corp. in the U.S. and Canada Administered by Carbert Music Inc.
All Rights for Affirmative Music Administered by Warner-Tamerlane Publishing Corp.

Moderately bright

Move your-self. You al-ways live your life
Say you don't want to change it.
nev-er think-ing of the fu-ture. Prove your-self.
You've been hurt so be-fore. Watch it now,
You are the move you make. Take your chan-ces, win or los-er.
the ea-gle in the sky, how he danc-in' one and on - ly.
See your-self. You are the steps you take. You and you, and that's the on-
You lose your-self. No, not for pit-y's sake. There's no real rea-son to be
- ly way. Shake, shake your-self. You're ev-'ry move you make.
lone - ly. Be your-self. Give your free will a chance.
So the sto - ry goes. Own-er of a lone-ly heart.
You've got to want to suc-ceed.
Own-er of a lone-ly heart. (Much bet-ter than a)

owner of a broken heart. Owner of a lonely heart. Owner of a lonely heart. Owner of a lonely heart. After my own indecision, they confused me so. My love said never question your will at all. In the end you've got to go. Look before you leap and don't you hesitate at all. No, no. Owner of a lonely heart. Owner of a lonely heart. (Much better than a)

Am Bm C D G
Own - er of a bro - ken heart.
1
Am Bm C D G
Own - er of a lone - ly heart.
2
Am Bm C D A Am
Own - er of a lone - ly heart.
G/A A Am G/A A Am
Own - er of a lone - ly heart.
G/A A Am G/A
Soon er or lat - er each con - clu - sion will de - cide the lone - ly heart.
A Am G/A A Am/G
It will ex - cite it, will de - light it, will give a bet - ter start.
F Eb/F
Don't de - ceive your free will at all.
Don't de - ceive your free will at all.
F Eb/F F Eb/F
Don't de - ceive your free will at all.
F Eb/F
Just re - ceive it. Just re - ceive it.
Repeat and Fade

D G D G
Come on... Take a bot - tle, shake it up.
Give a lit-tle more.
C F C F G
Break the bub - ble; break it up.
C F G
Pour some sug - ar on me, ooh, in the name of love.
C F G
Pour some sug - ar on me. C' - mon, fire me up.
C F G
Pour your sug - ar on me. I can't get e - nough.
A N.C.
I'm hot, stick - y sweet
1
from my head to my feet, yeah.
2
from my head to my feet, yeah. (You got the peach - es, I got the cream.)

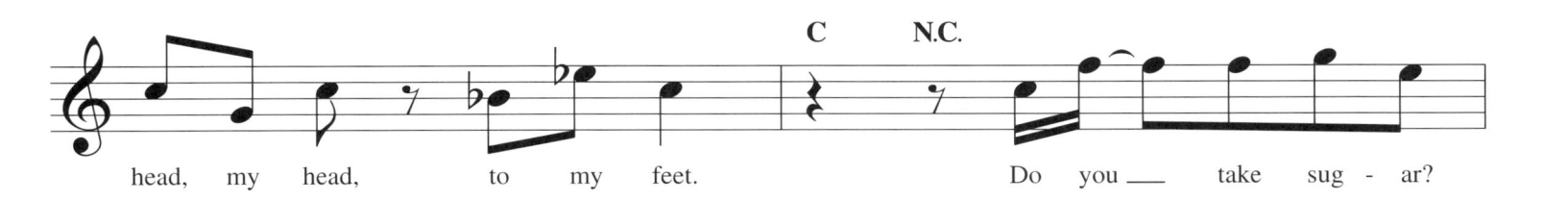

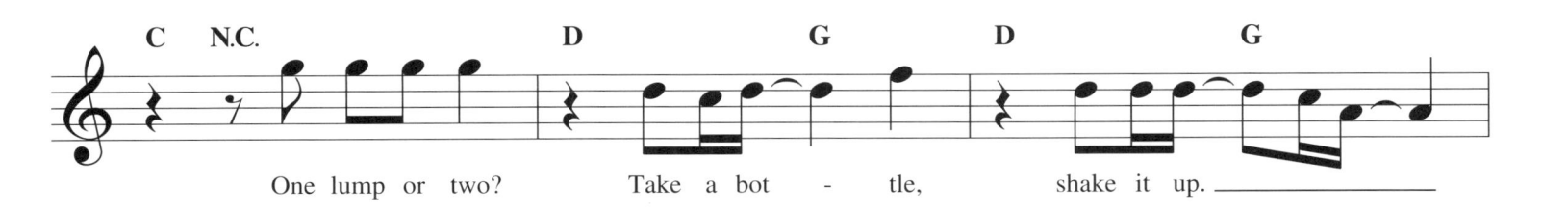

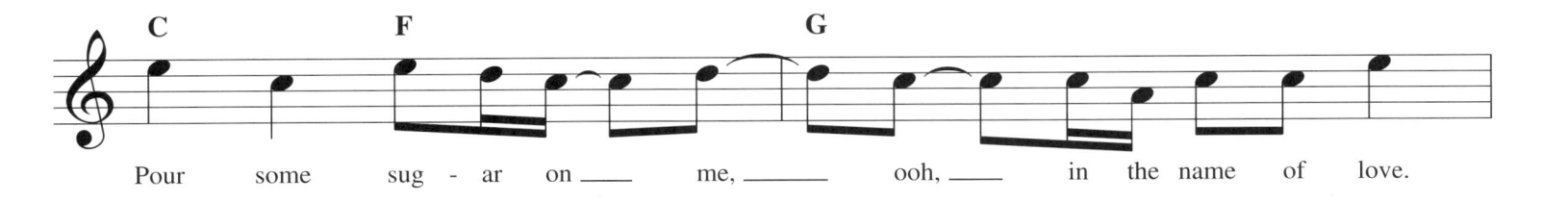

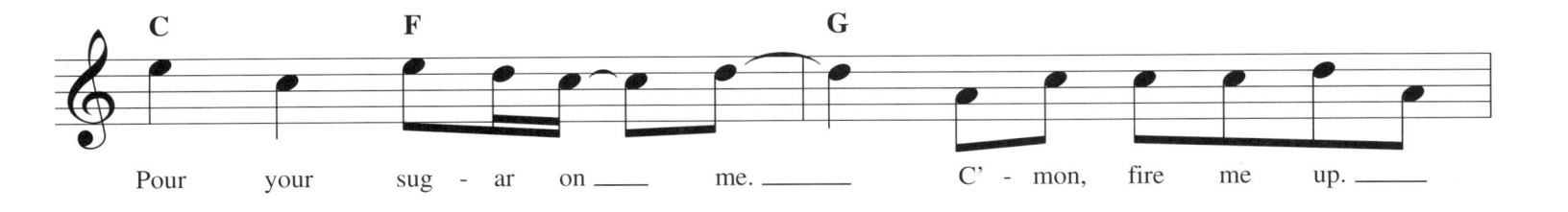

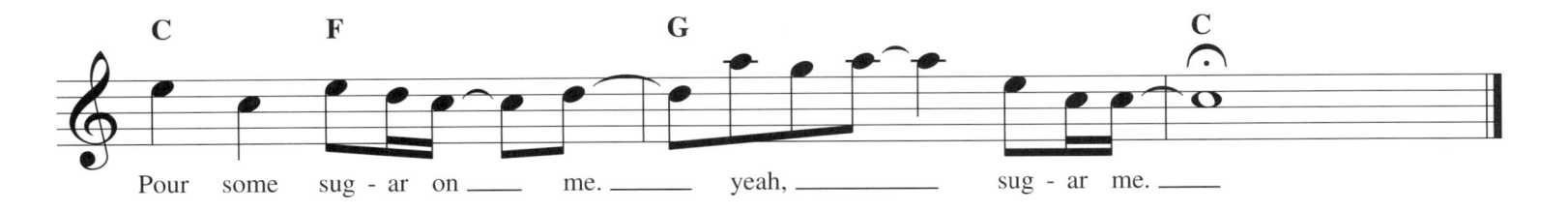

Sweet to taste; __ (sac-cha-rine.) __ 'Cause I'm hot, so hot, stick-y sweet, _ from my head, my head, to my feet.

Do you __ take sug-ar? One lump or two? Take a bot-tle, shake it up. __

Break the bub - ble; __ break it up. __

Pour some sug-ar on __ me, __ ooh, __ in the name of love.

Pour your sug-ar on __ me. __ C'-mon, fire me up. __

Pour some sug-ar on __ me. __ yeah, __ sug-ar me. __

PHYSICAL

Words and Music by STEPHEN A. KIPNER
and TERRY SHADDICK

© 1981 EMI APRIL MUSIC INC., STEPHEN A. KIPNER MUSIC
and TERRY SHADDICK MUSIC
All Rights for STEPHEN A. KIPNER MUSIC Controlled and Administered
by EMI APRIL MUSIC INC.

Moderately

I'm say-in' all the things that I know you'll like, mak-
I've been pa-tient, I've been good, try'n

-in' good con-ver-sa-tion. I got-ta han-dle
to keep my hands on the ta-ble. It's get-tin hard, this

you just right;   you know what I mean.   I
hold-in' back;   you know what I mean.   I'm

took you to an in-ti-mate res-tau-rant,   then
sure you'll un-der-stand my point of view,   we

to a sug-ges-tive mov-ie,
know each oth-er men-tal-ly,

there's noth-ing left to talk a-bout 'less it's
you've got-ta know that you're bring-in' out the

hor-i-zon-tal-ly.
an-i-mal in me.   Let's get phys-i-cal, phys-i-cal,

I wan - na get phys - i - cal, let's get in - to phys - i - cal.
Am
Let me hear your bod - y talk, your bod - y talk,
let me hear your bod - y talk.
1., 3. Let's get
2. Let's get
F
phys - i - cal, phys - i - cal, I wan - na gat phys - i - cal, let's
an - i - mal, an - i - mal, I wan - na get an - i - mal, let's
get in - to phys - i - cal.
get in - to an - i - mal.
Am
Let me hear your bod - y talk,
To Coda
your bod - y talk, let me hear your bod - y talk.
1
2
D.S. al Coda
Oh, let's get
CODA

PRIVATE EYES

Copyright © 1981 GNARLY DUDE MUSIC, GEOMANTIC MUSIC,
ALMO MUSIC CORP., UNICHAPPELL MUSIC INC. and HOT-CHA MUSIC CO.
All Rights for GNARLY DUDE MUSIC and GEOMANTIC MUSIC Administered by IRVING MUSIC, INC.
All Rights for HOT-CHA MUSIC CO. Administered by UNICHAPPELL MUSIC INC.

Words and Music by JANNA ALLEN,
SARA ALLEN, WARREN PASH
and DARYL HALL

Steady

I see you, you see me; watch you
You play with love. You can

blow-ing the lines when you're mak-ing a scene. Oh girl,
twist it a-round, ba-by, that ain't e-nough. 'Cause girls,

you've got to know, what my head o-ver-looks, the
I'm gon-na know if you're let-ting me in or

sens-es will show to my heart, when it's watch-ing for lies.
let-ting me go. Don't lie when you're hurt-ing in-side. } 'Cause

you can't es-cape my pri-vate eyes. They're watch-ing you.

They see your ev'-ry move. Pri-vate eyes,

they're watch-ing you. Pri-vate eyes, they're

A♭
watch-ing you, watch-ing you, watch-ing you, watch-ing you,
1
Am
You play with words.
2
Am
(Instrumental)
Dm G
Dm
Don't know why you try to put up a front for me.
I'm a spy, but on your side, you see.
Gm
Slip on in-to an-y dis-guise;
I'll still know you.
E7
Look in-to my pri-vate eyes.
Am Em Am
They're watch-ing you.
They see your
C Dm F
ev-'ry move.
Oh, babe, pri-vate eyes,
Am Em Am
they're watch-ing you.
Repeat and Fade
Dm
Pri-vate eyes,
G E7 Am
they're watch-ing you. Pri-vate eyes.

REBEL YELL

Copyright © 1983 Chrysalis Music, Boneidol Music and WB Music Corp.
All Rights for Boneidol Music Administered by Chrysalis Music

Words and Music by BILLY IDOL
and STEVE STEVENS

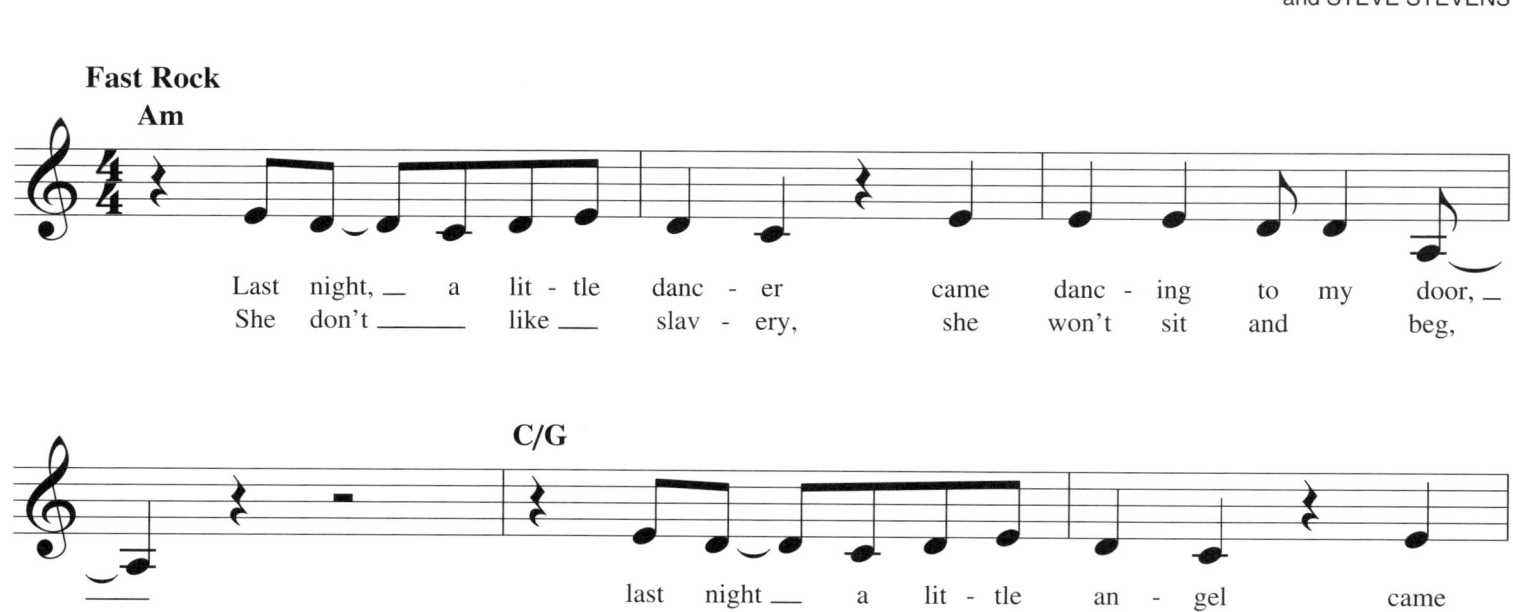

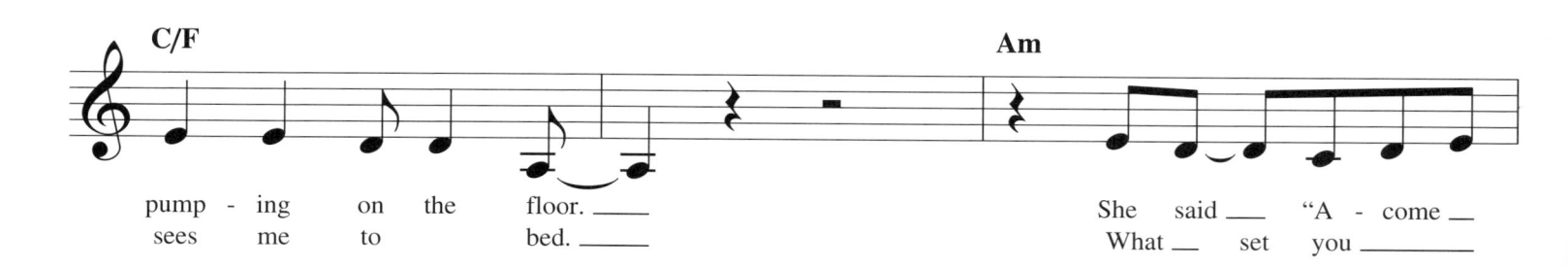

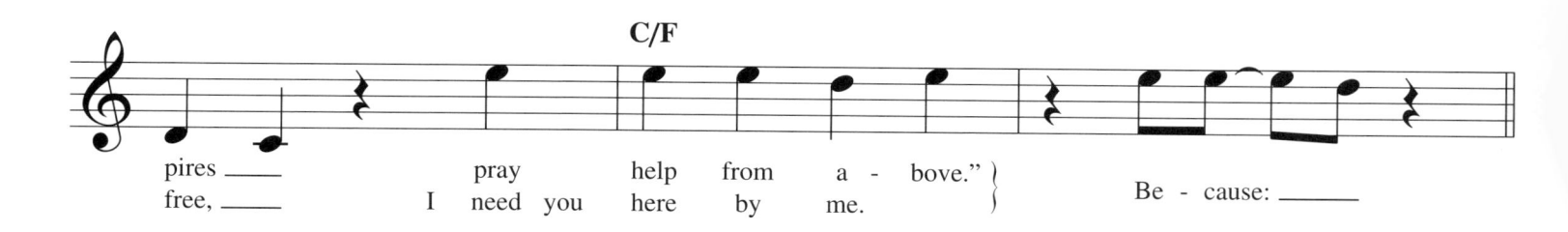

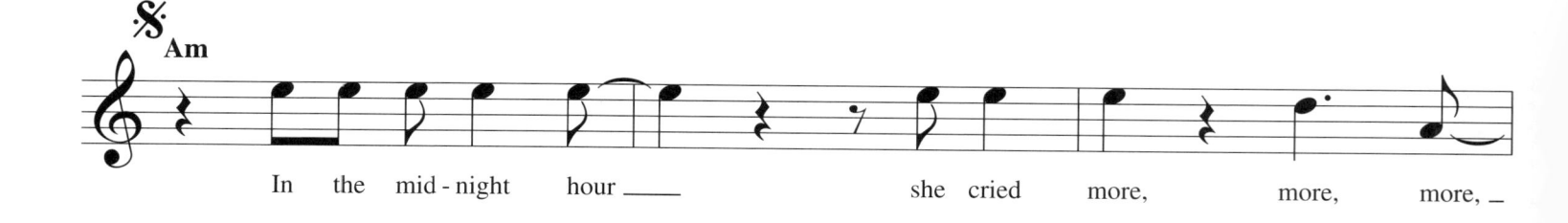

Fast Rock

Am

Last night, a lit-tle danc-er came danc-ing to my door,
She don't like slav-ery, she won't sit and beg,

C/G

last night a lit-tle an-gel came
but when I'm tired and lone-ly she

C/F   Am

pump-ing on the floor.   She said "A-come
sees me to bed.   What set you

                                                C/G

ba-by, got a li-cense for love,   and if it ex-
free and brought you to me babe?   What set you

                        C/F

pires   pray help from a-bove." }
free,   I need you here by me.   }   Be-cause:

𝄋 Am

In the mid-night hour she cried more, more, more,

C/G
with a re - bel yell
she cried
F
more, more, more.
Am
In the mid - night hour,
babe, more, more, more,
C/G
with a re - bel yell,
F
To Coda
more, more, more,
1
more, more, more.
2
Em
Am/D
A - he lives in a - his own hea - ven,

| F | Em | Am/D |

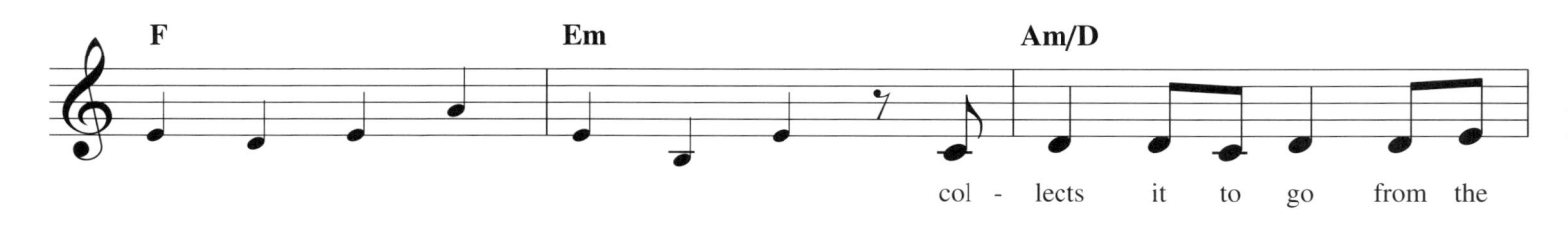

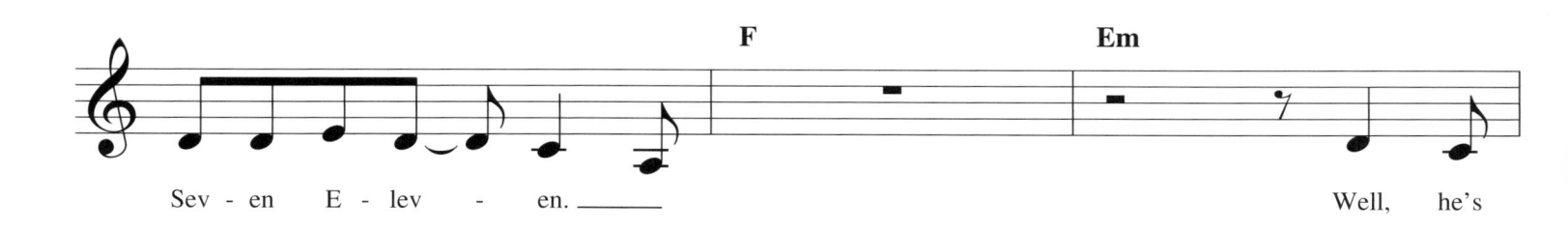

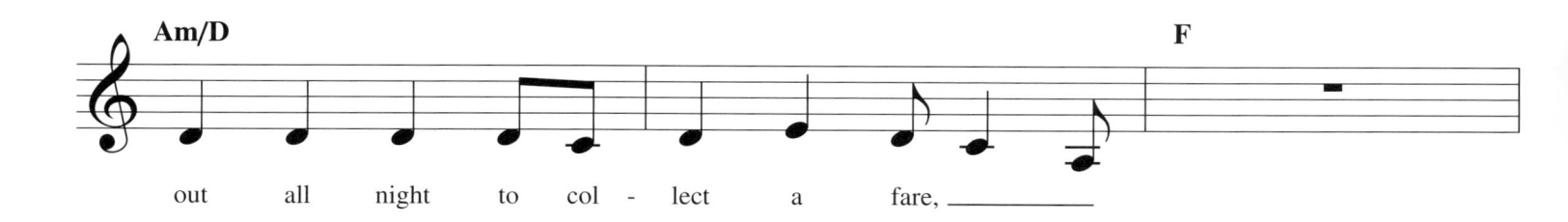

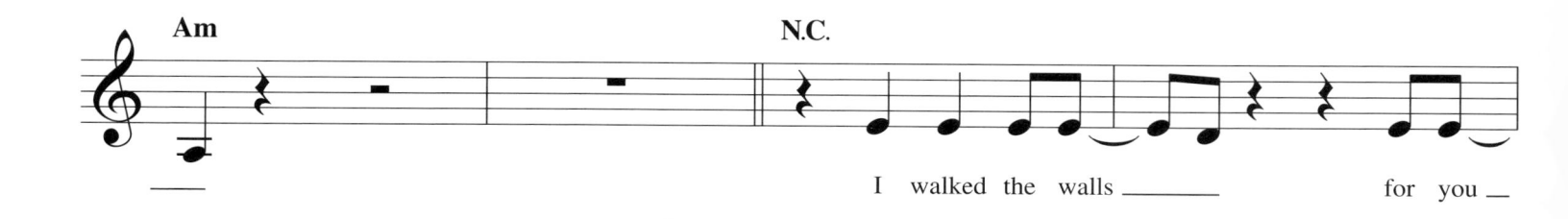

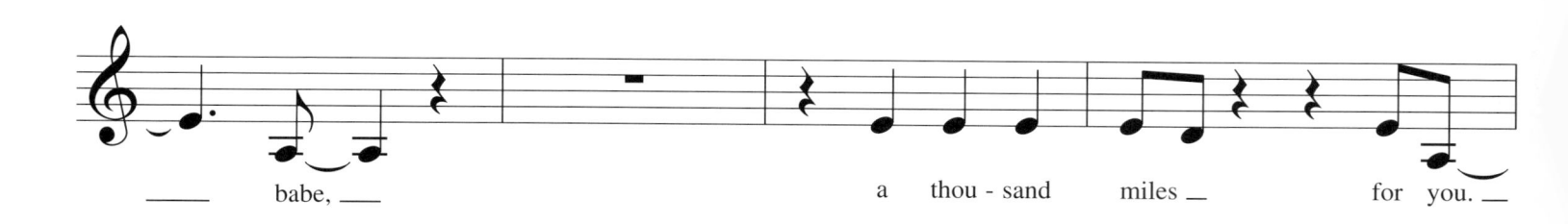

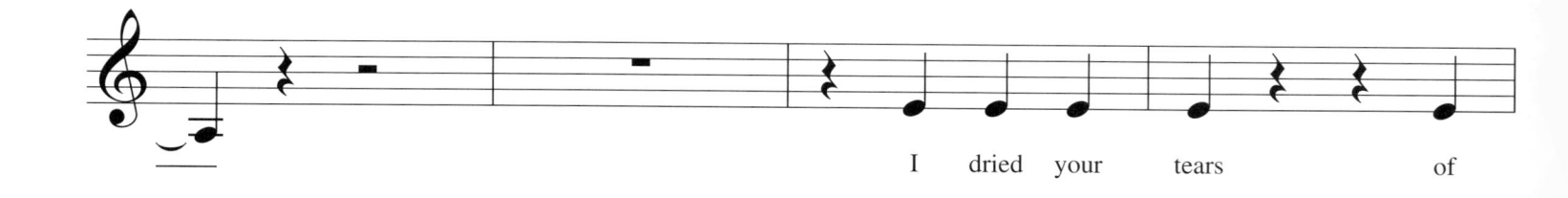

col - lects it to go from the

| | F | Em |

Sev - en E - lev - en. ____ Well, he's

| Am/D | | F |

out all night to col - lect a fare, ____

| Em | Am/D | C G |

just so long, just so long it don't mess up his hair. ____

| Am | N.C. | |

____ I walked the walls ____ for you ____

____ babe, ____ a thou - sand miles ____ for you. ____

I dried your tears of

pain, a mil-lion times for you.

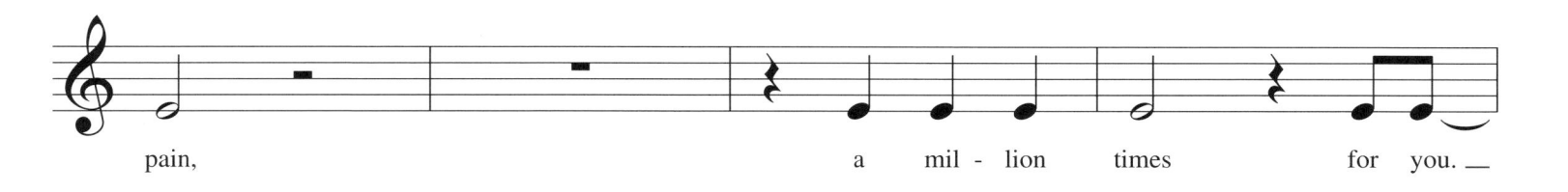

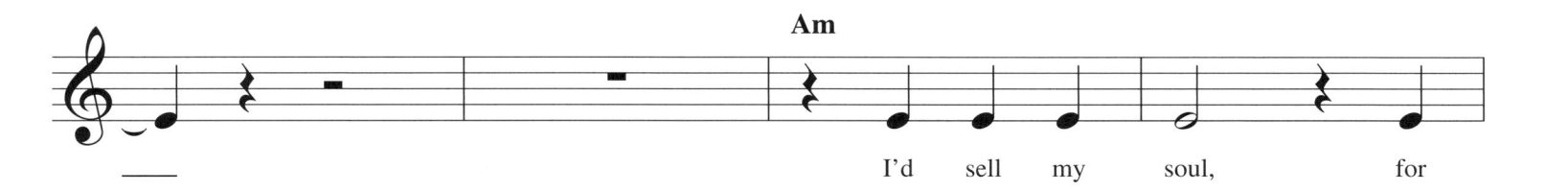

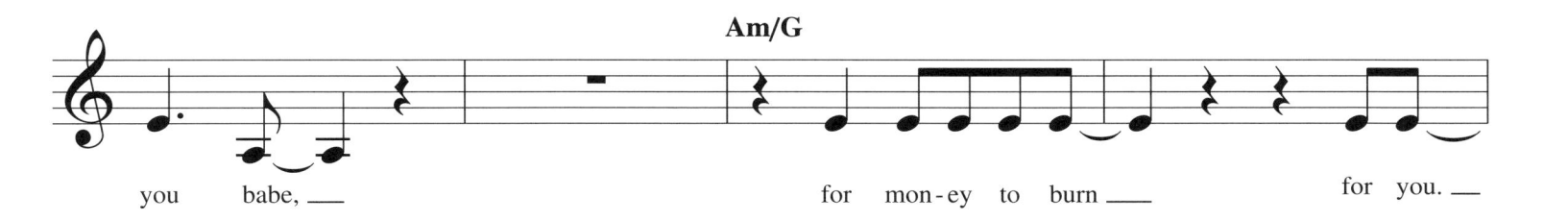

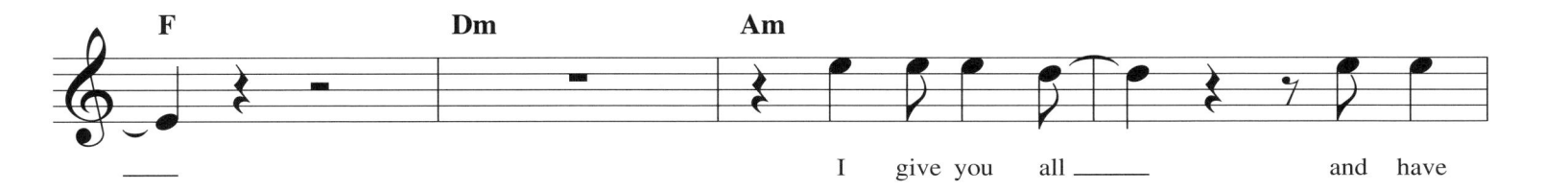

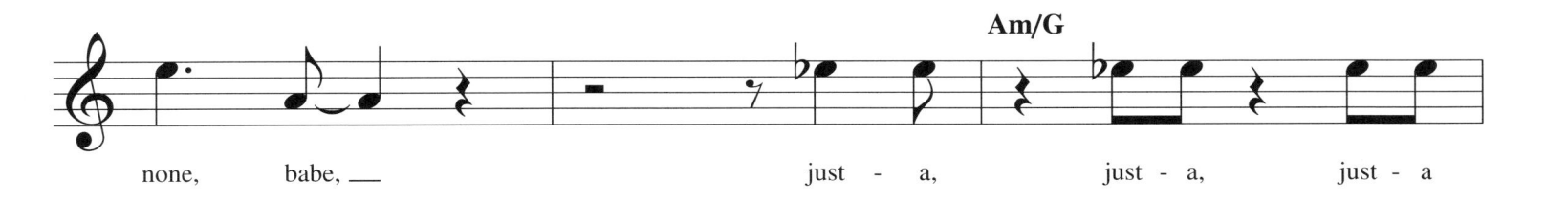

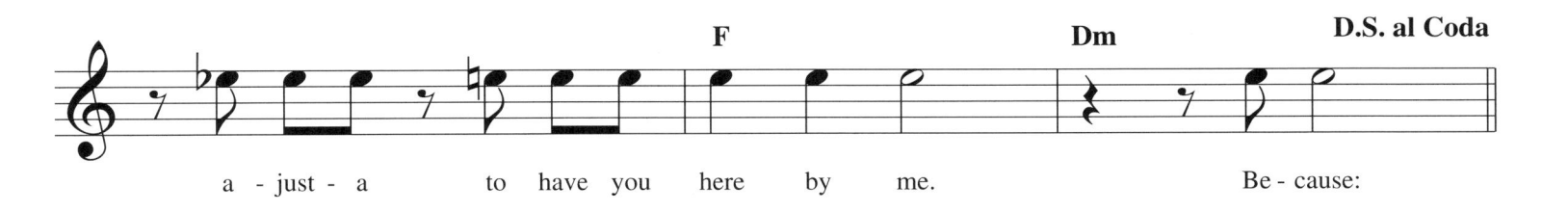

Am
I'd sell my soul, for

Am/G
you babe, for mon-ey to burn for you.

F **Dm** **Am**
I give you all and have

Am/G
none, babe, just-a, just-a, just-a

F **Dm** **D.S. al Coda**
a-just-a to have you here by me. Be-cause:

CODA
Dm **Am**
more, more, more.

RED, RED WINE

© 1966 (Renewed), 1978 TALLYRAND MUSIC, INC.

Words and Music by
NEIL DIAMOND

Slow Country beat

Red, red wine, go to my head. Make me for-
wine, it's up to you. All I can

get that I still need her so. Red, red
do, I've done. But mem-'ries won't

go. No, mem-'ries won't go. I'd have

thought that with time, thoughts of her would leave my head. I was

wrong, and I find just one thing makes me for-get. Red, red

wine, stay close to me.

Don't let me be a-lone. It's tear-ing a-part

my blue, blue heart.

Rock the Casbah

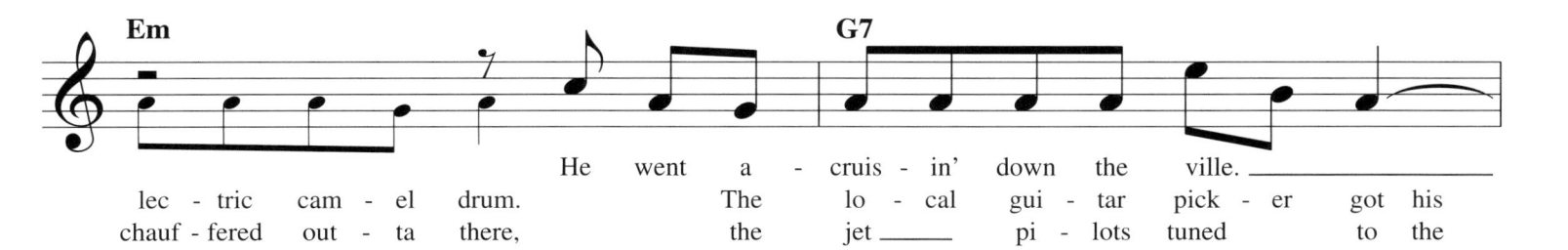

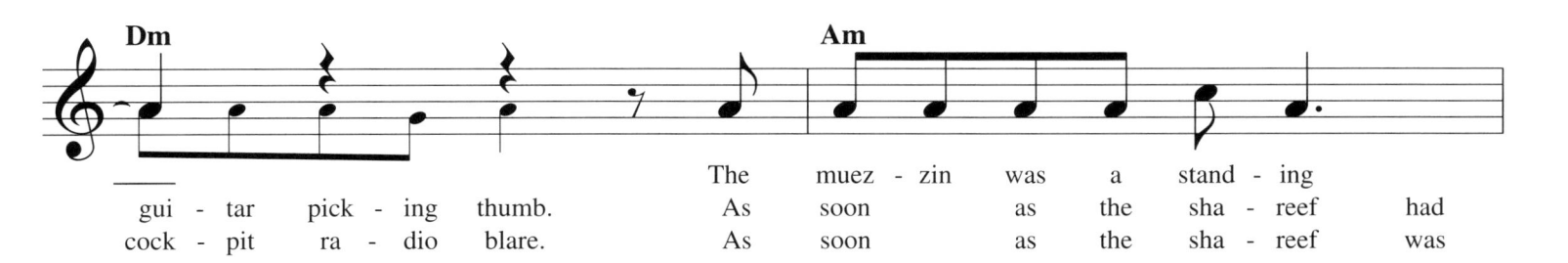

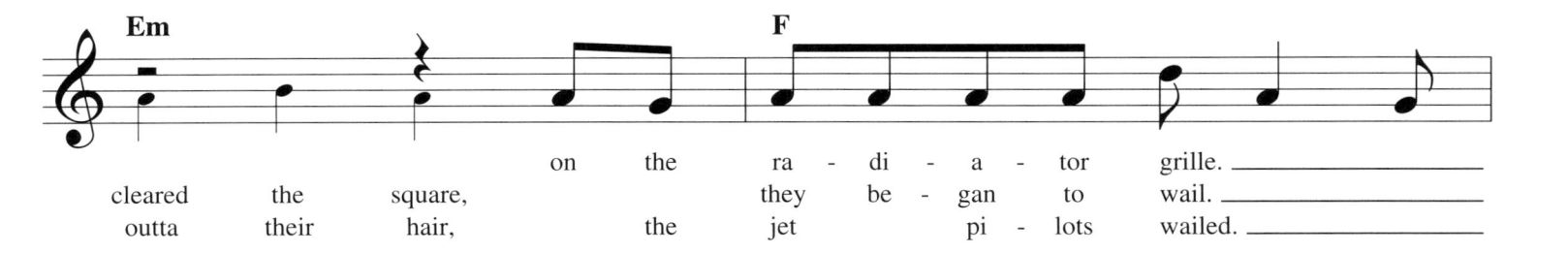

Words and Music by JOE STRUMMER, MICK JONES and TOPPER HEADON

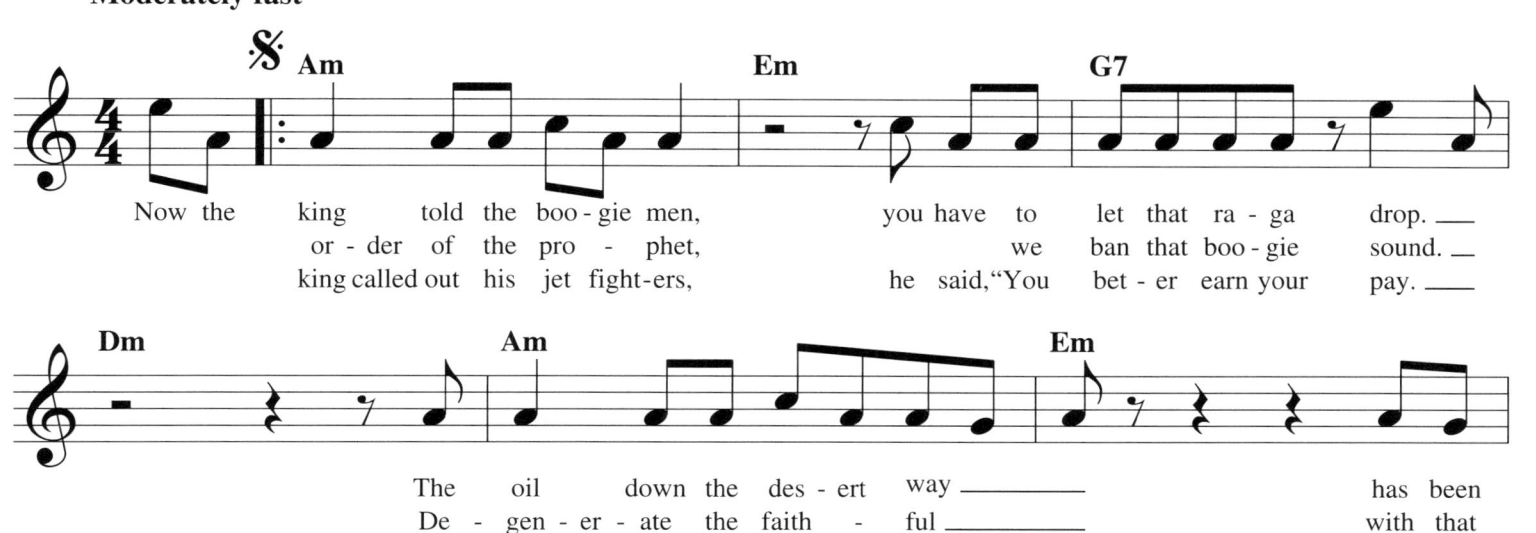

Copyright © 1982 NINEDEN LTD.
All Rights in the U.S. and Canada Controlled and Administered by
UNIVERSAL - POLYGRAM INTERNATIONAL PUBLISHING, INC.

Moderately fast

[Am] Now the king told the boo-gie men, [Em] you have to [G7] let that ra-ga drop.
[Am] or-der of the pro-phet, [Em] we [G7] ban that boo-gie sound.
[Am] king called out his jet fight-ers, [Em] he said,"You [G7] bet-ter earn your pay.

[Dm] The oil down the des-ert [Am] way has been [Em] shak-in' to the top.
[Dm] De-gen-er-ate the faith-[Am]ful with that [Em] cra-zy Cas-bah sound.
[Dm] Drop your bombs be-tween the min-a-[Am]rets down the [Em] Cas-bah way.

[G7] The sheik, he drove his [Dm] Ca-dil-lac. [Am] He went a-cruis-in' down the ville.
[G7] But the Bed-ou-in, they brought out the e-[Dm]lec-tric cam-el drum. [Am] The lo-cal gui-tar pick-er got his
[G7] As soon as the sha-reef was [Dm] chauf-fered out-ta there, [Am] the jet pi-lots tuned to the

[Em] [G7]

[Dm] The muez-zin was a stand-ing [Am] on the ra-di-a-tor grille.
[Dm] gui-tar pick-ing thumb. As soon as the sha-reef had [Am] they be-gan to wail.
[Dm] cock-pit ra-dio blare. As soon as the sha-reef was [Am]

[Em] cleared the square, [F]
outta their hair, the jet pi-lots wailed.

Dm
G7
Sha - reef don't like it.
Em F
Em Am
Dm
Rock - in' the Cas - bah. Rock the Cas - bah. Sha - reef don't like it.
G7
Em F
To Coda
1
Em Am
Rock - in' the Cas - bah. Rock the Cas - bah. By
2
Em Am
Rock the Cas - bah. Now, o - ver at the tem - ple, oh, they
real - ly pack 'em in. The in crowd say it's cool
to dig this chant - ing thing. But as the

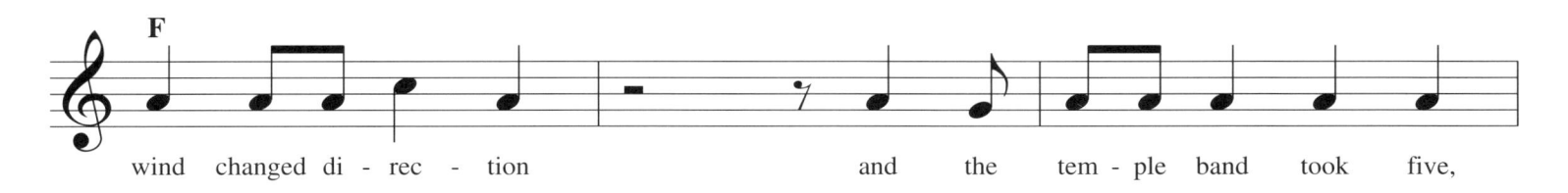

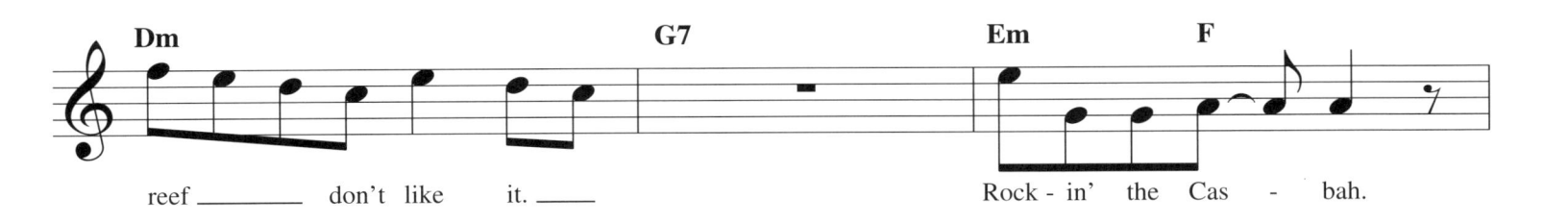

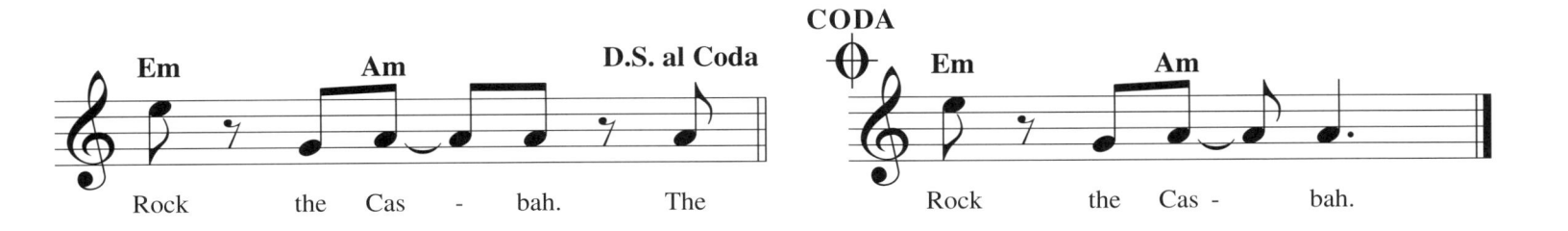

wind changed di-rec-tion and the tem-ple band took five, the crowd caught a wiff of that cra-zy Cas-bah jive. Sha-reef don't like it. Rock-in' the Cas-bah. Rock the Cas-bah. Sha-reef don't like it. Rock-in' the Cas-bah. Rock the Cas-bah. The

D.S. al Coda

CODA

Rock the Cas-bah.

SAILING

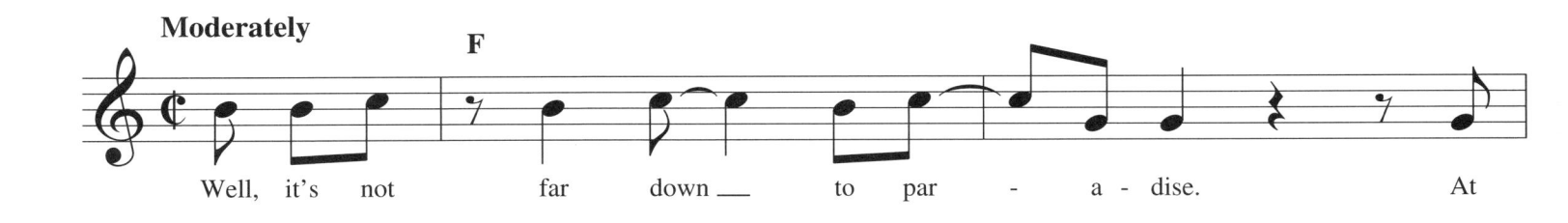

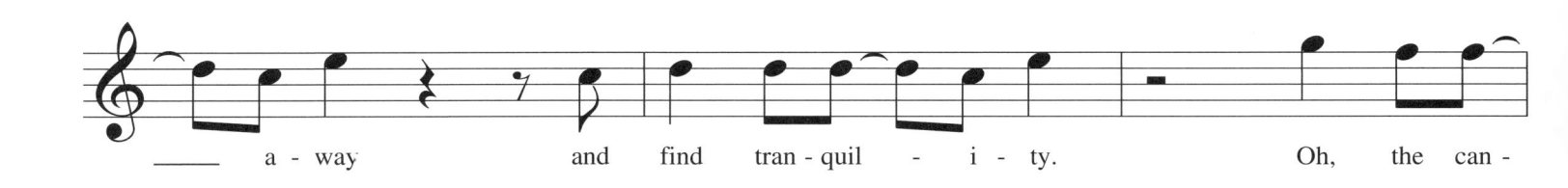

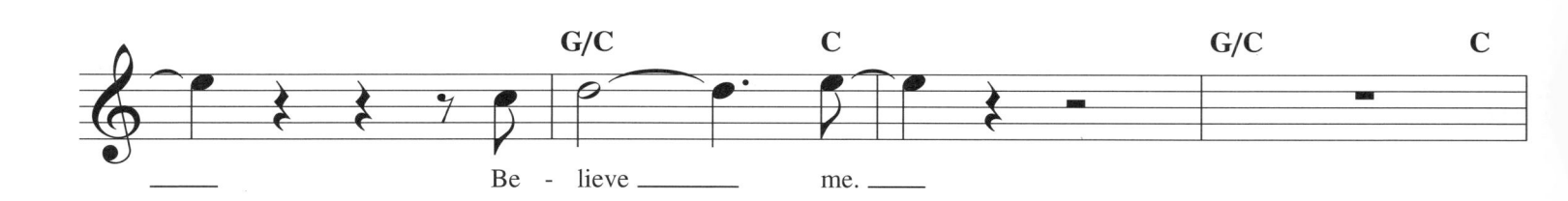

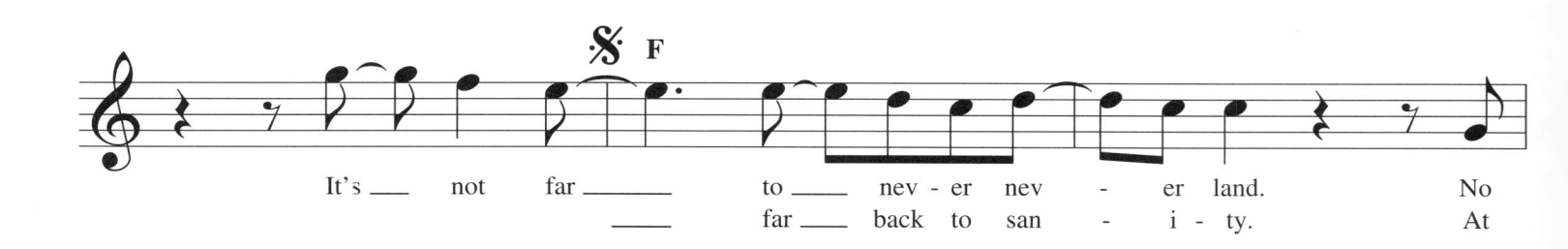

Words and Music by
CHRISTOPHER CROSS

Copyright © 1979 by Universal Music - MGB Songs

Moderately

Well, it's not far down to par - a - dise. At least it's not for me. And if the wind is right, you can sail a - way and find tran - quil - i - ty. Oh, the can - vas can do mir - a - cles. Just you wait and see. Be - lieve me.

It's not far to nev - er nev - er land. No
far back to san - i - ty. At

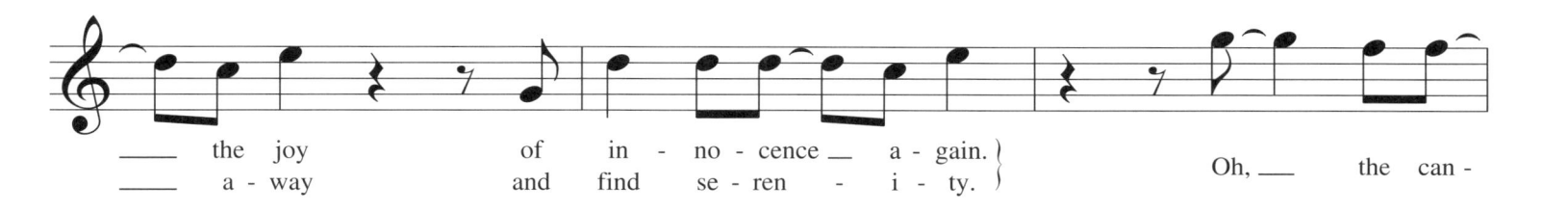

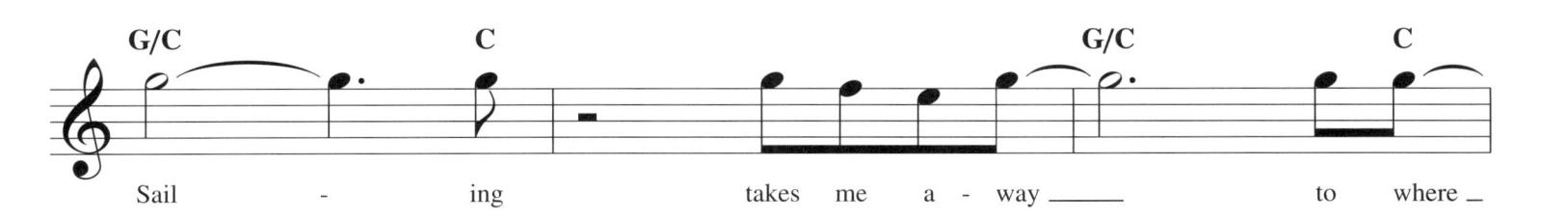

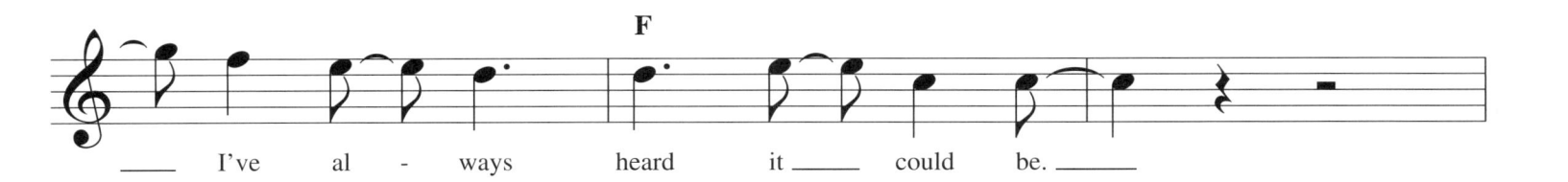

reason to pretend. And if the wind is right, you can find
least it's not for me. And if the wind is right, you can sail

the joy of innocence again.
away and find serenity.
Oh, the can-

vas can do miracles. Just you wait and see.

Believe me.

Sailing takes me away to where

I've always heard it could be.

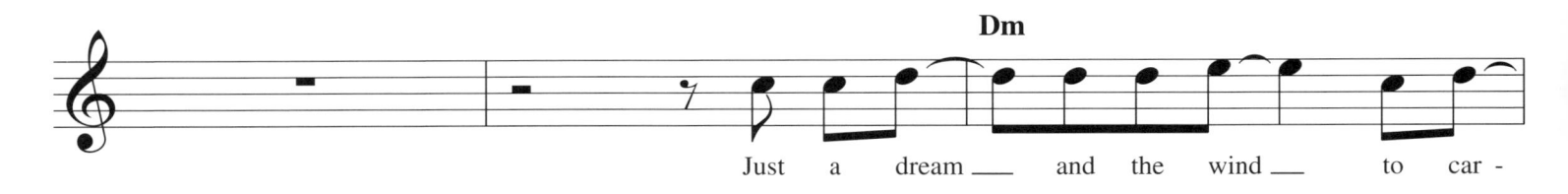

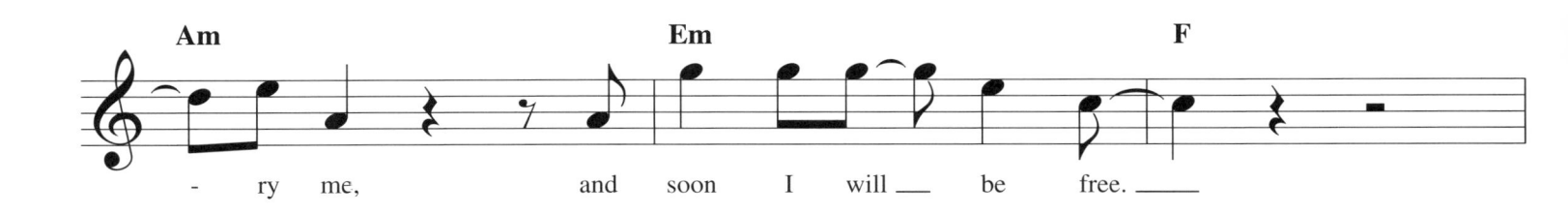

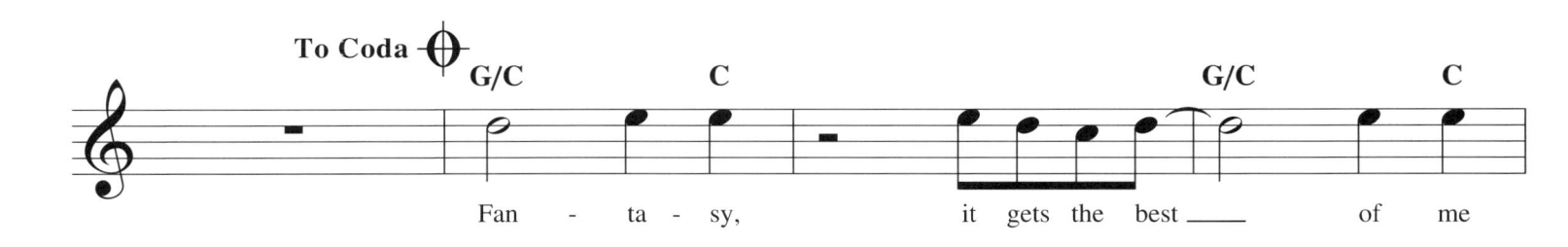

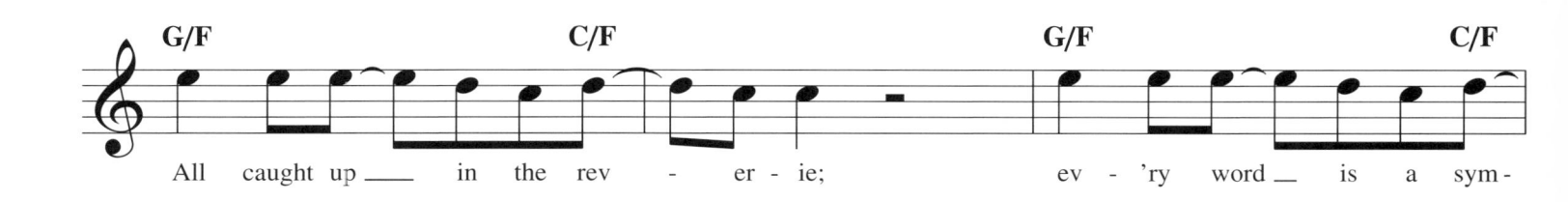

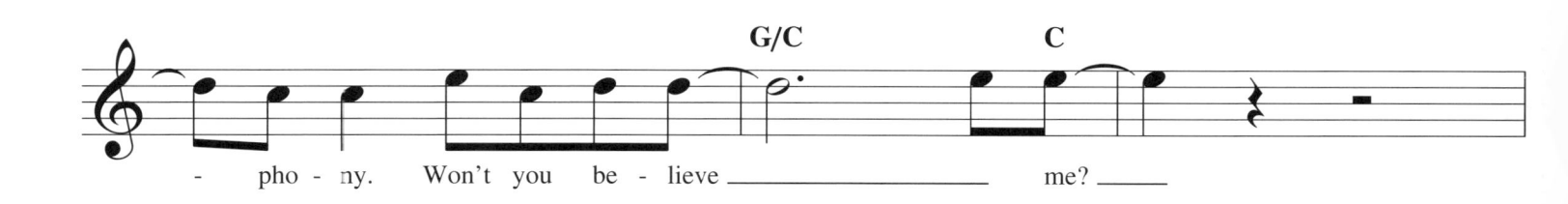

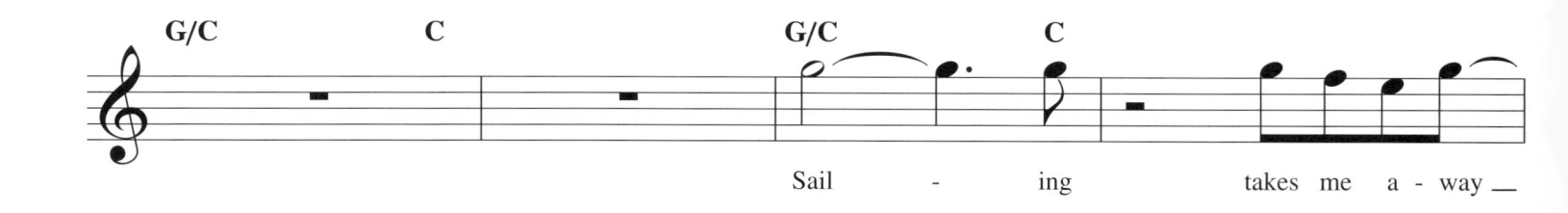

Just a dream and the wind to car-ry me, and soon I will be free.

Fan-ta-sy, it gets the best of me when I'm sail-ing.

All caught up in the rev-er-ie; ev-'ry word is a sym-pho-ny. Won't you be-lieve me?

Sail-ing takes me a-way

| G/C | C | F |

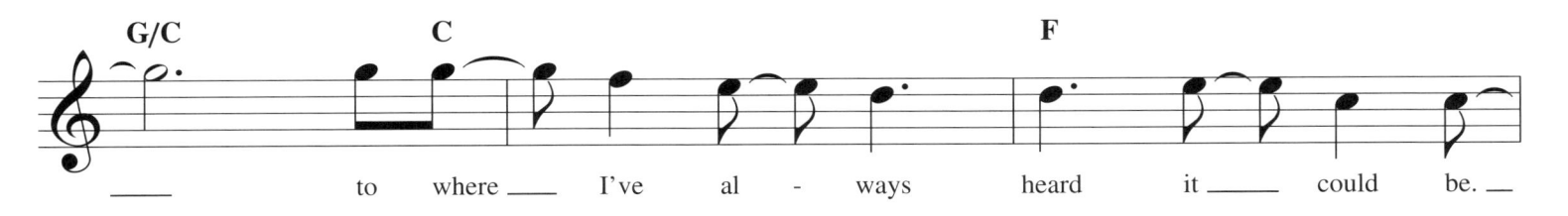

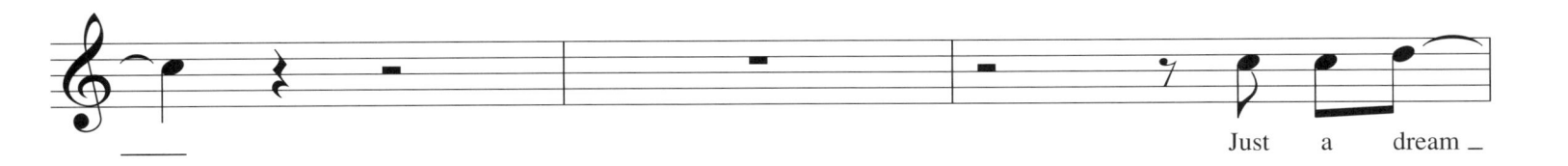

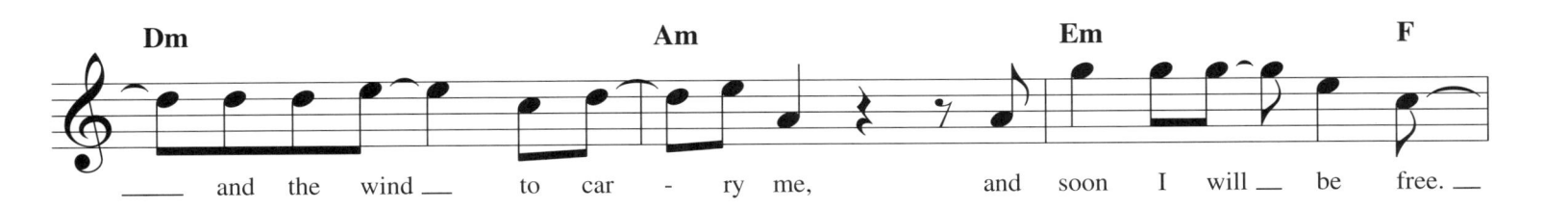

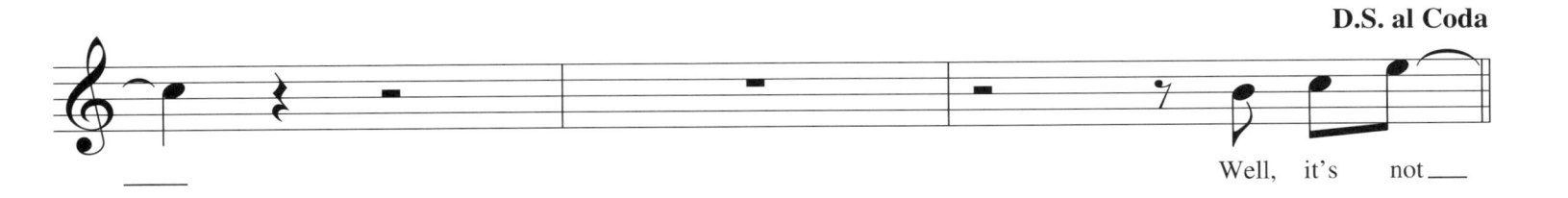

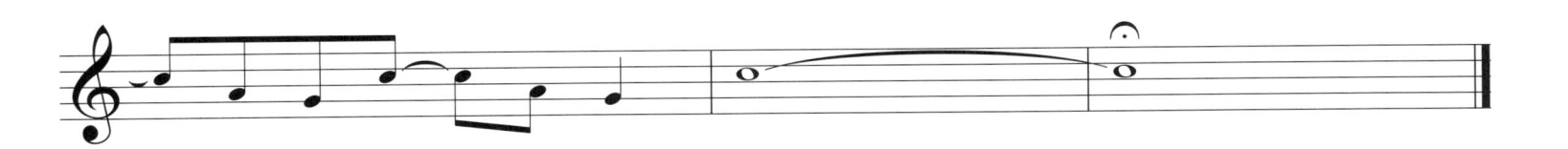

___ to where ___ I've al - ways heard it ___ could be. ___

Just a dream ___

| Dm | Am | Em | F |

___ and the wind ___ to car - ry me, and soon I will __ be free. ___

D.S. al Coda

Well, it's not ___

CODA

F

(Instrumental)

SISTER CHRISTIAN

Words and Music by
KELLY KEAGY

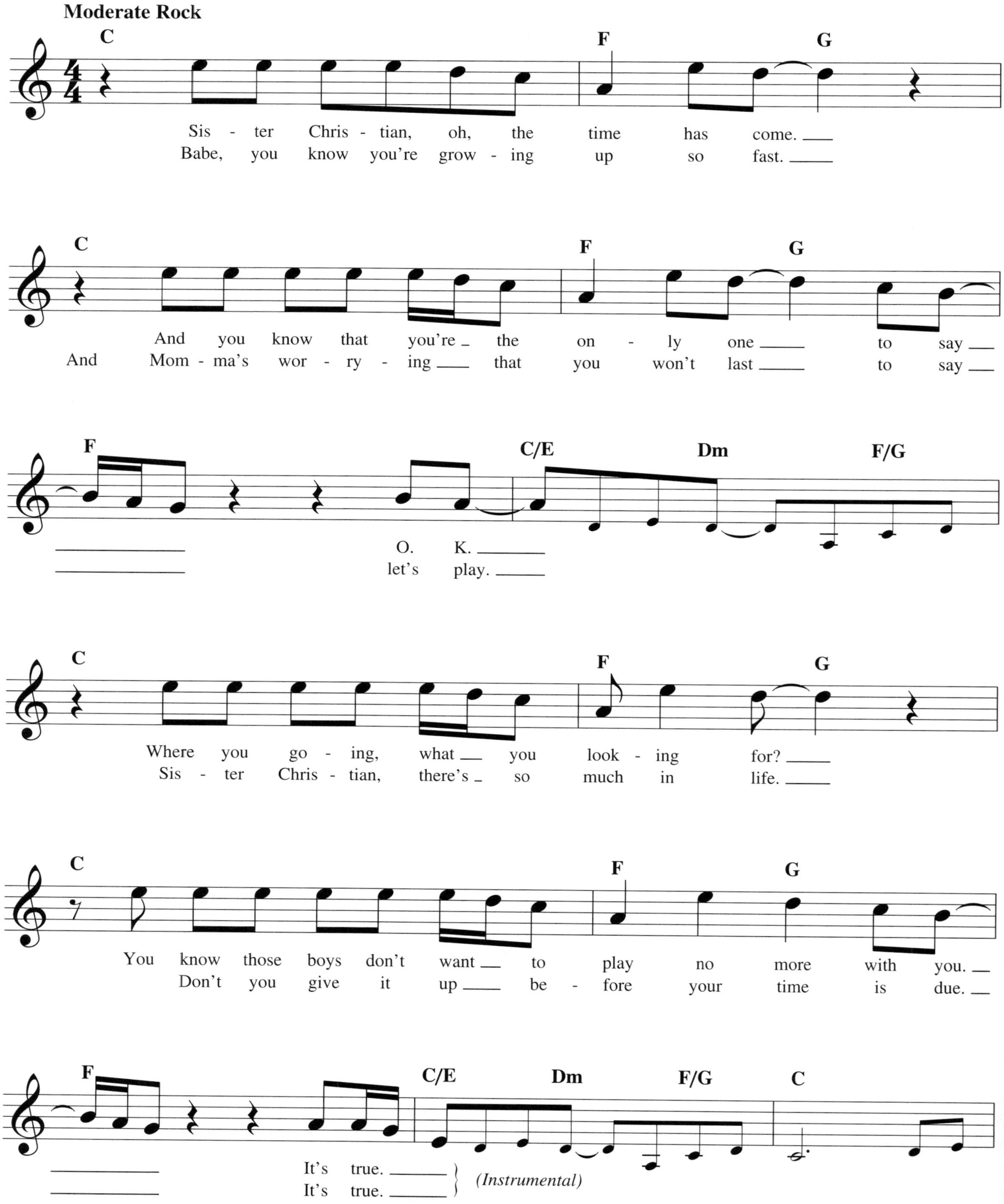

You're mo-tor-ing. What's your price for flight? In find-ing Mis-ter Right, you'll be all right to-night. Sis-ter Chris-tian, oh, the time has come. And you know that you're the on-ly one to say O. K. But you're mo-tor-ing. You're mo-tor-ing.

SMOOTH OPERATOR

Words and Music by HELEN ADU
and RAY ST. JOHN

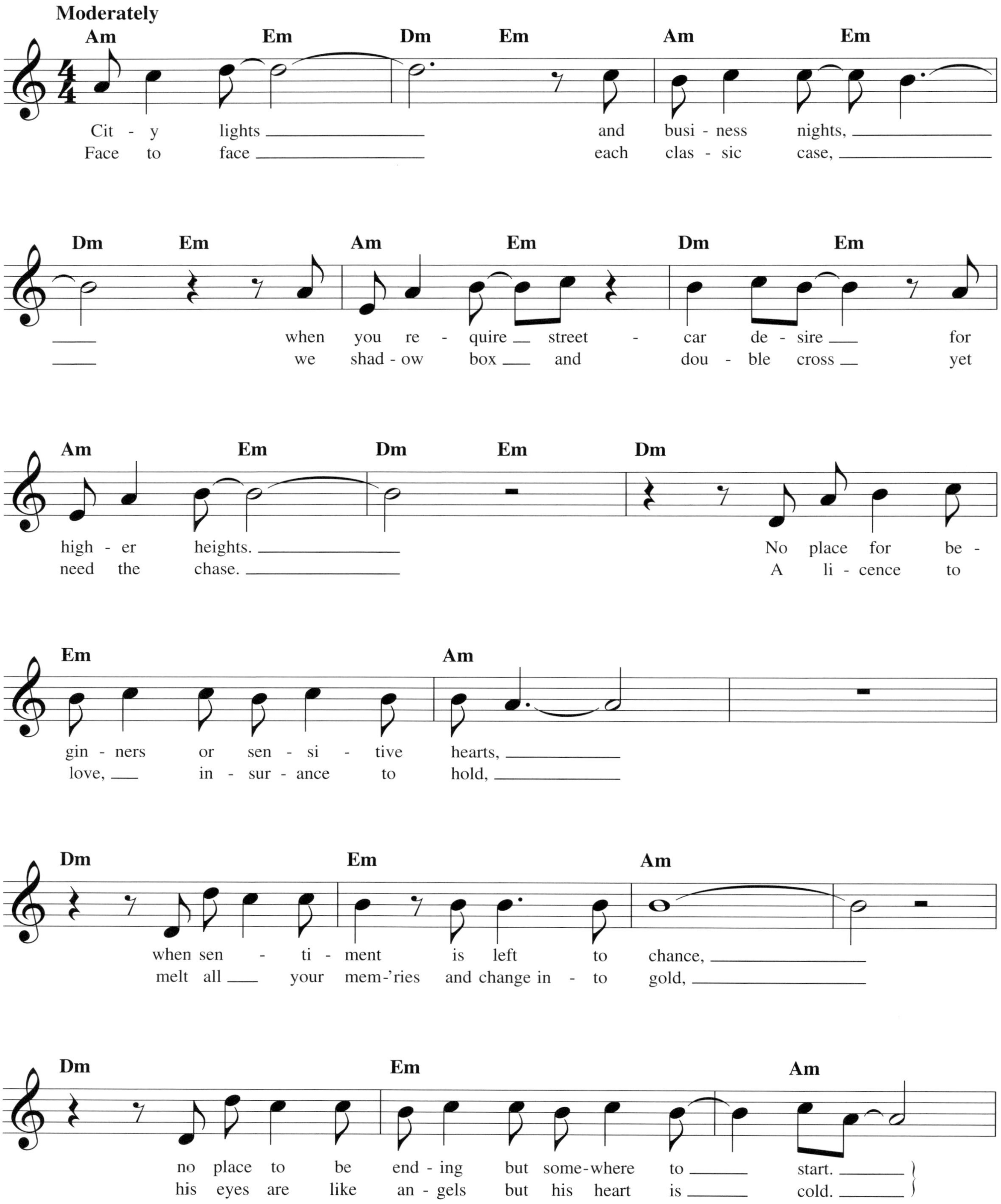

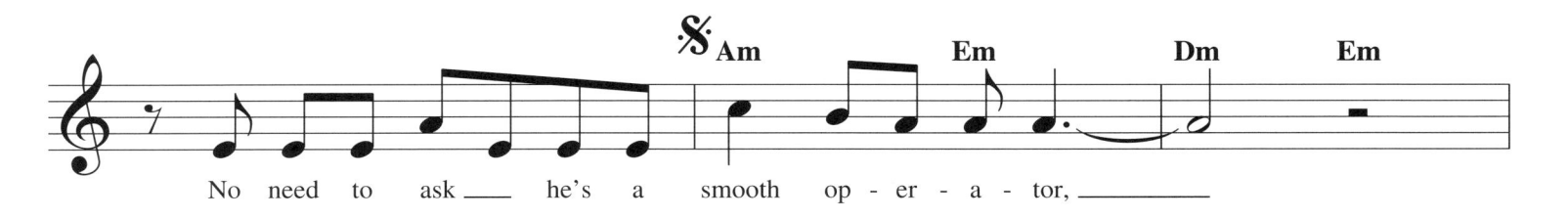

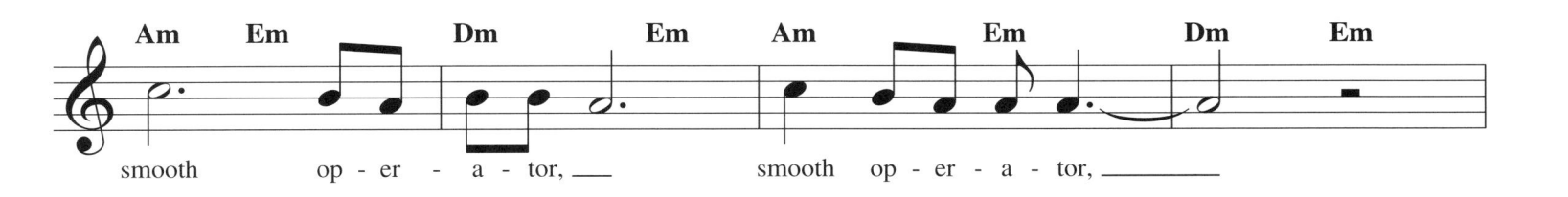

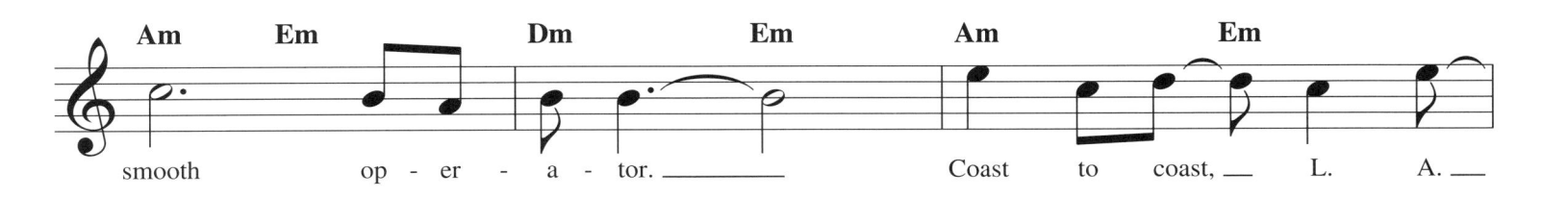

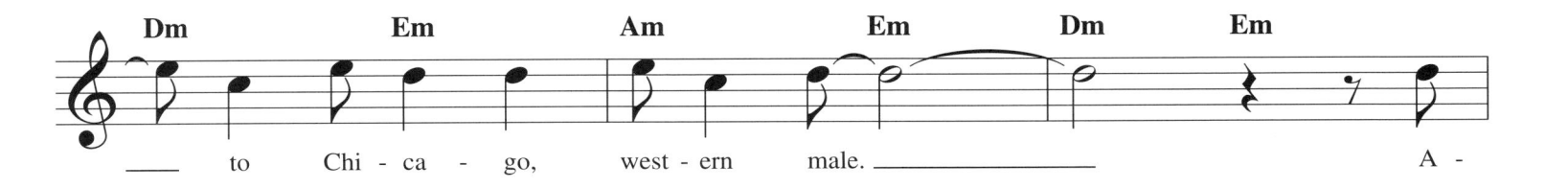

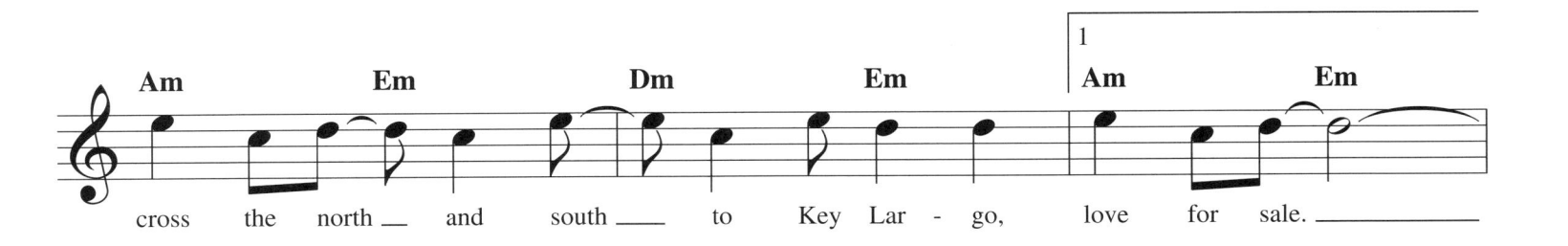

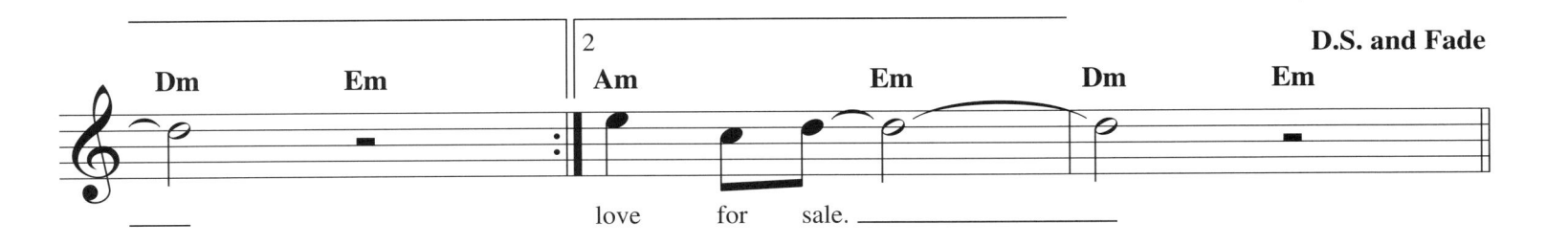

No need to ask — he's a smooth op-er-a-tor, smooth op-er-a-tor, smooth op-er-a-tor, smooth op-er-a-tor. Coast to coast, L.A. to Chi-ca-go, west-ern male. A-cross the north and south to Key Lar-go, love for sale.

D.S. and Fade

love for sale.

SOMEWHERE OUT THERE
from AN AMERICAN TAIL

Music by BARRY MANN and JAMES HORNER
Lyric by CYNTHIA WEIL

Somewhere out there beneath the pale moonlight
someone's thinkin' of me and loving me tonight.
Somewhere out there someone's saying a prayer
that we'll find one another in that big somewhere out there.
And even though I know how very far apart we are,
it helps to think we might be wishin' on the same bright star.
And when the night wind starts to sing that lonesome lullaby,
it helps to think we're sleeping underneath the same big sky.
Somewhere out there if love can see us through,
then we'll be together somewhere out there, out where dreams come true.

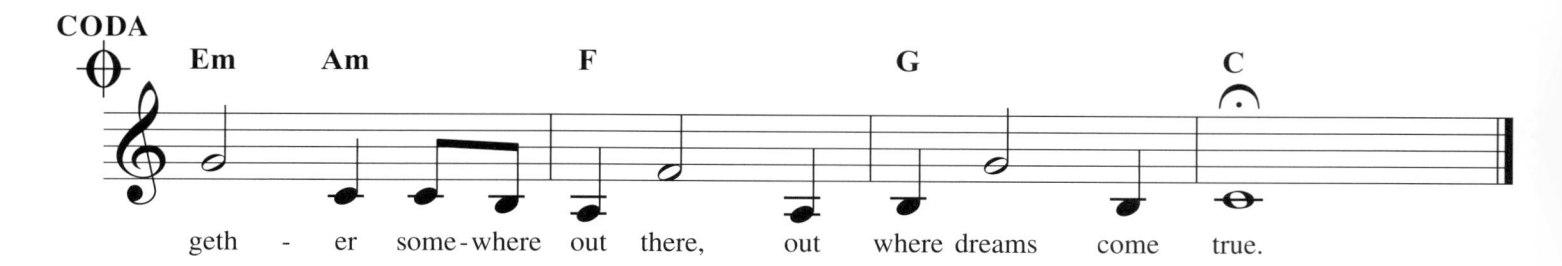

SOUTHERN CROSS

Words and Music by STEPHEN STILLS,
RICHARD CURTIS and MICHAEL CURTIS

B♭ F C
A - va - lon, I tried to call you. But on the mid-night watch I
all her flags are a - fly - ing. She is all that I have
B♭ F Dm C
re - al - ized why twice you ran a - way.
left, and mu - sic is her name.
B♭ F B♭ C
Think a - bout how man - y times I have fall - en.
B♭ F B♭ C
Spi - rits are us - in' me; larg - er voic - es call - in'.
B♭ F B♭ C
What heav - en brought you and me can - not be for - got -
- ten. I have been a - round
F G C F G
the world, look - in' for that wom - an - girl
C F G
who knows love can en - dure.

F C
And you know it will.
When you see
So we cheat -
B♭ F
the South - ern Cross for the first time, you
- ed and we lied and we test - ed. And
C B♭ F
un - der - stand now why you came this way.
we nev - er failed to fail. It was the eas-i-est thing to do.
C B♭
'Cause the truth you might be run - nin' from is
You will sur - vive be - ing
F C
so small. But it's as big as the
best - ed. Some - bod - y fine will
B♭ F Dm C
prom - ise, the prom - ise of a com - in' day.
come a - long, make me for - get a - bout lov - ing you
1 2 B♭
So I'm in the South - ern Cross.
(Instrumental)
F C B♭ F

STAGES

Words and Music by BILLY F GIBBONS,
DUSTY HILL and FRANK LEE BEARD

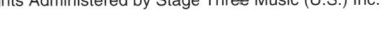

Copyright © 1985 Stage Three Songs
All Rights Administered by Stage Three Music (U.S.) Inc.

Moderate Rock

It's a fine time to fall in love with you.
Then you left me stand-ing all a-lone.
Now you're back and say you're gon-na stay.

I ain't got a sin-gle thing to do.
I could-n't e-ven get you on the phone.
I would-n't have it an-y oth-er way.

Hap-pened be-fore I knew what was go-ing on.
Were you just con-fused and did-n't know
Tell me it's for real and let me know

I fell out and knew that I was gone.
if you should stay or if you had to go?
why does lov-in' have to come and go.

Stag-es keep on chang-ing. Stag-es re-

To Coda

-ar-rang-ing love.

D.S. al Coda

CODA

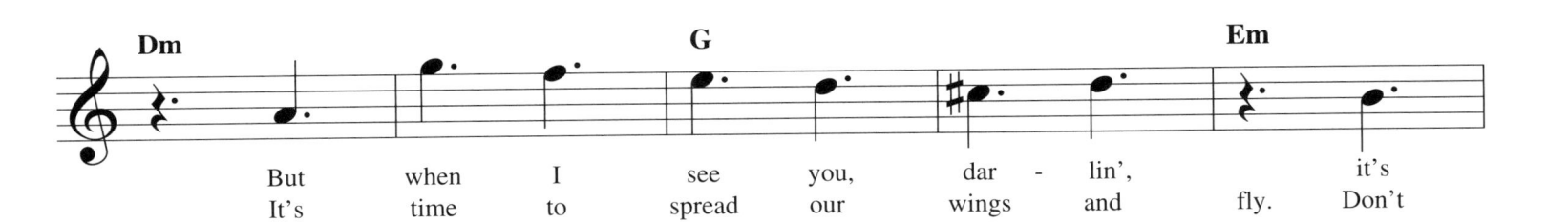

(Just Like) STARTING OVER

© 1980 LENONO.MUSIC
All Rights Controlled and Administered by EMI BLACKWOOD MUSIC INC.

Words and Music by
JOHN LENNON

Freely

Our life together is so precious together. We have grown. We have grown. Although our love is still special, let's take a chance and fly away somewhere alone. It's

Moderately, with a strong beat

been too long since we took the time. No one's to blame. I know time flies so quickly! But when I see you, darlin', it's

day we used to make it, love. Why can't we be makin' love nice and easy? It's time to spread our wings and fly. Don't

like we both are fall-ing in love ___ a-gain. It-'ll
let an-oth-er day go by, ___ my love. It-'ll

be just like start-ing o-ver,
be just like start-ing o-ver,

start-ing o-ver. ___ Ev-'ry
start-ing o-ver. ___

Why don't we take off a-
lone, take a trip some-where far,
far a-way. ___ We'll be to-geth-er all a-
lone ___ a-gain, like we used to ___ in the
ear-ly days. ___ Well, well, dar-lin'. It's

CODA

Our life to- geth-er is so pre-cious to- geth-er. We have grown.

We have grown. Al-though our love is still spe-cial, let's take a chance and fly a-way some-where.

Repeat and Fade

(Instrumental)

STRAIGHT UP

© 1988 EMI VIRGIN MUSIC, INC. and ELLIOT WOLFF MUSIC
All Rights Controlled and Administered by EMI VIRGIN MUSIC, INC.

Words and Music by
ELLIOT WOLFF

Moderate R & B Shuffle

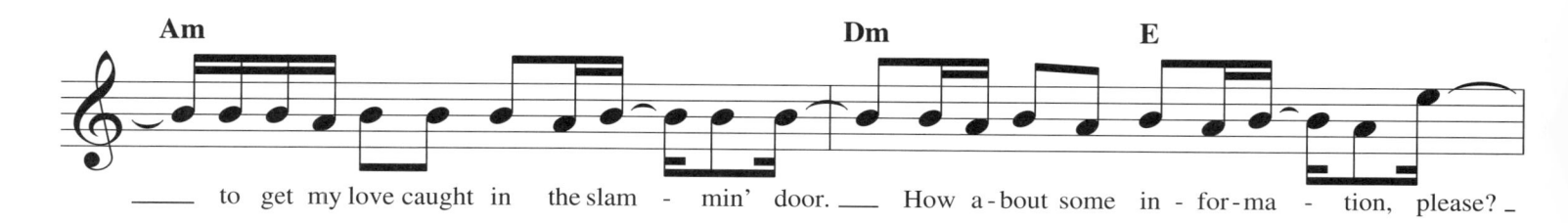

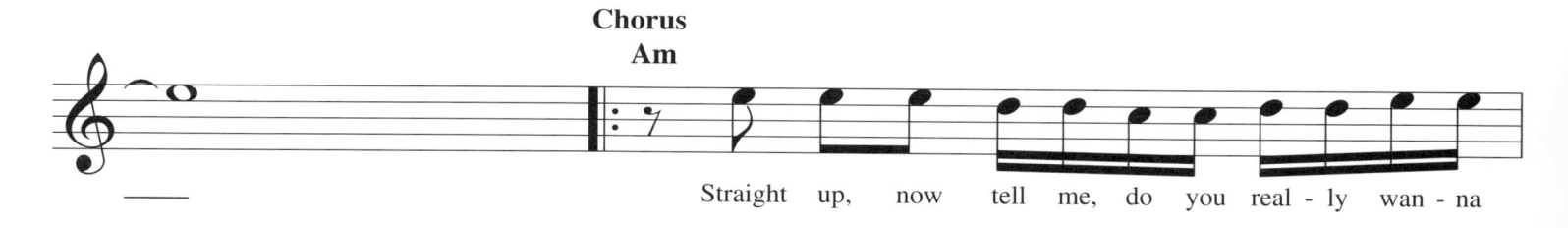

1. Lost in a dream; I don't know which way to go. A-let me say if you are all that you seem, then ba-by, I'm mov-in' way too slow. I've been fooled be-fore; would-n't like to get my love caught in the slam - min' door. How a-bout some in-for-ma-tion, please?

2. (*See additional lyrics*)

Chorus

Straight up, now tell me, do you real-ly wan-na love me for-ev-er, oh, oh, or am I caught in a hit and run? Straight up, now tell me, is it gon-na be you and me to-geth-er, oh, oh,

Additional Lyrics

2. Time's standing still waiting for some small clue.
   I keep getting chills when I think your love is true.
   I've been a fool before;
   Wouldn't like to get my love caught in the slammin' door.
   How about some information, please?
   Chorus

Stray Cat Strut

© 1981 EMI LONGITUDE MUSIC and ROCKIN' BONES MUSIC
All Rights Controlled and Administered by EMI LONGITUDE MUSIC

Words and Music by
BRIAN SETZER

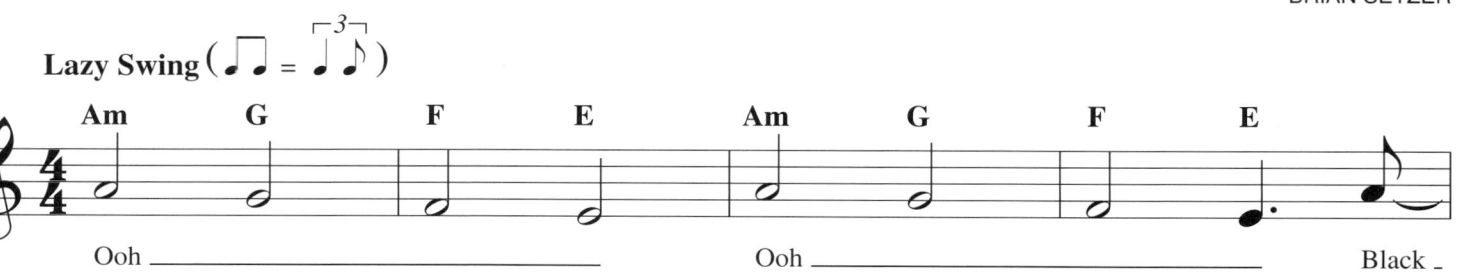

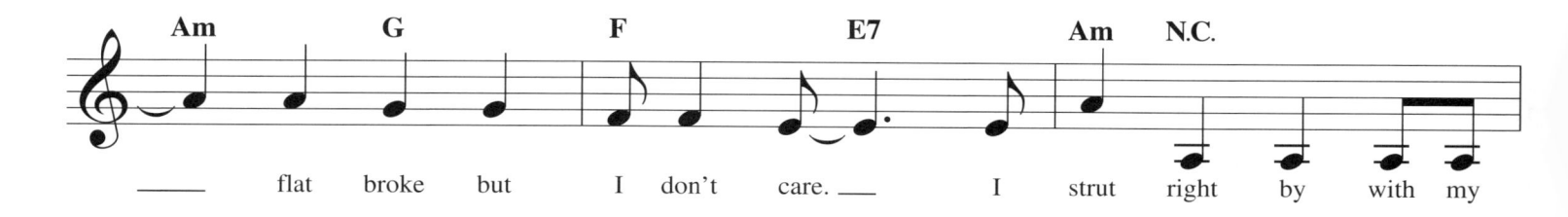

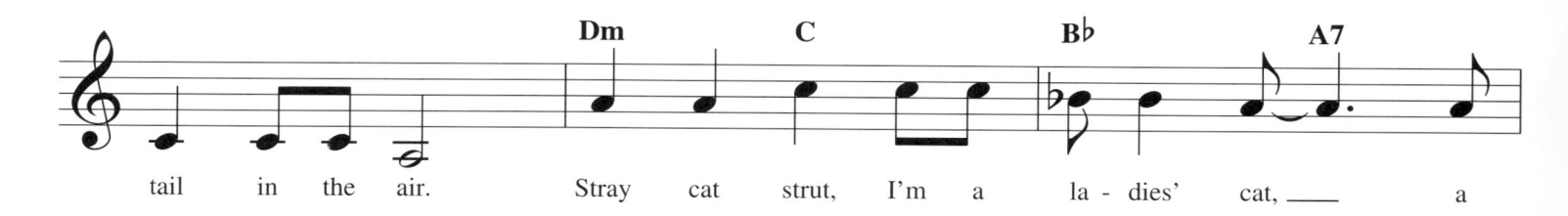

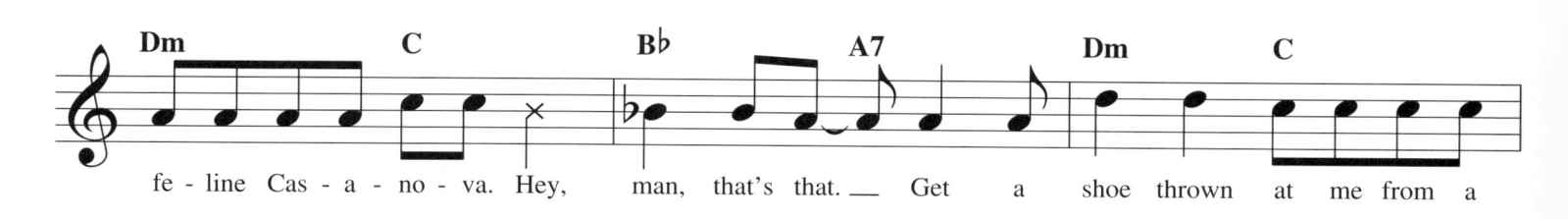

Lazy Swing

Ooh _____ Ooh _____ Black _____ and orange stray cat sit-tin' on a fence. Ain't _____ got e-nough dough to pay the rent. _____ I'm _____ flat broke but I don't care. _____ I strut right by with my tail in the air. Stray cat strut, I'm a la-dies' cat, _____ a fe-line Cas-a-no-va. Hey, man, that's that. _____ Get a shoe thrown at me from a mean old man. _____ Get my din-ner from a gar-bage can. _____

(Instrumental)

I don't bother chasing mice around. I slink down the alley, lookin' for a fight, howlin' to the moonlight on a hot summer night, singin' the blues while the lady cats cry. Wild stray cat, you're a real gone guy. I wish I could be as carefree and wild but I got cat class and I got class style.

(Instrumental)

CODA
(Instrumental)

SWEET DREAMS
(Are Made of This)

Words and Music by DAVID STEWART
and ANNIE LENNOX

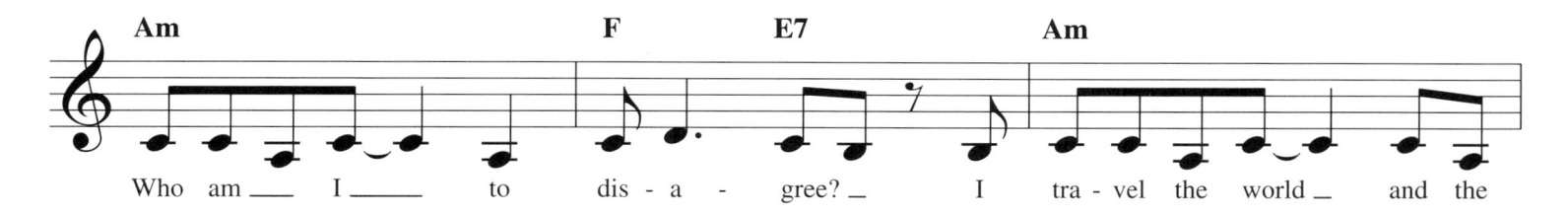

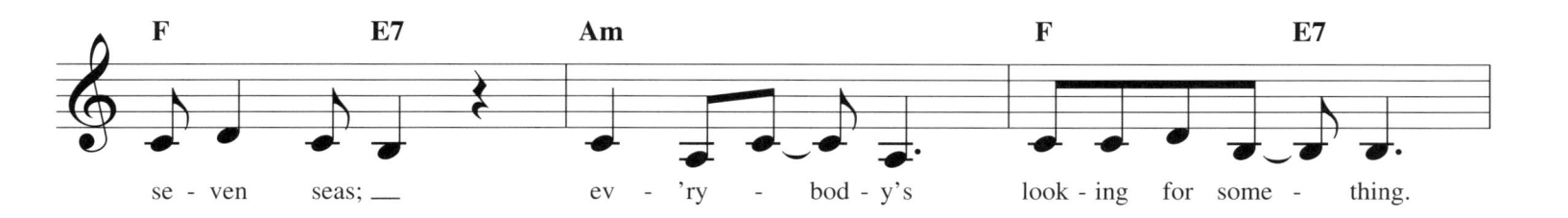

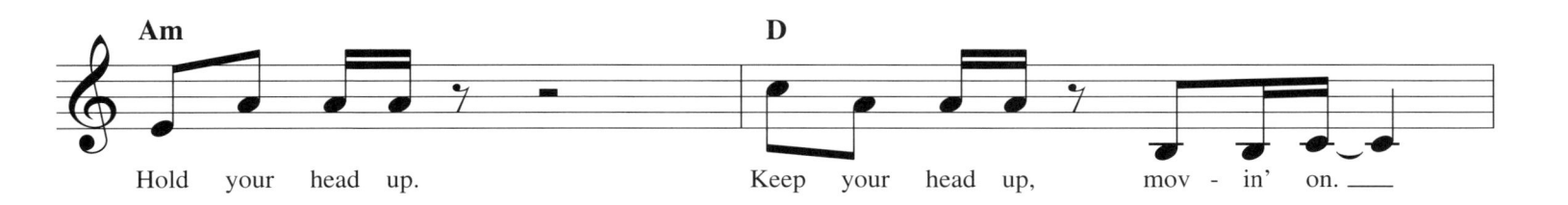

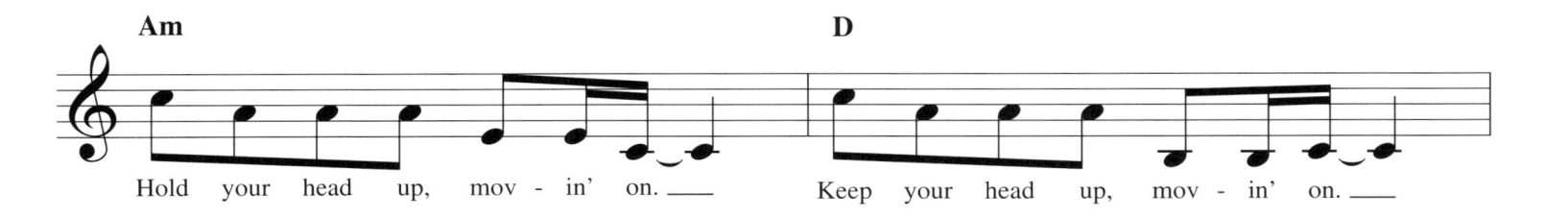

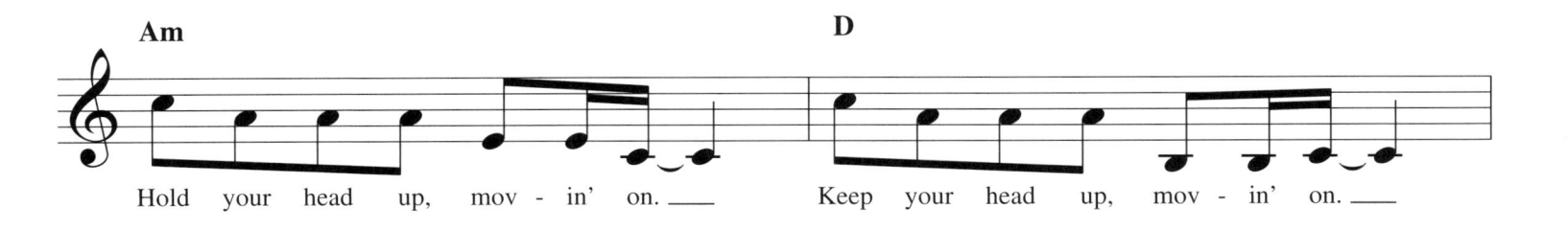

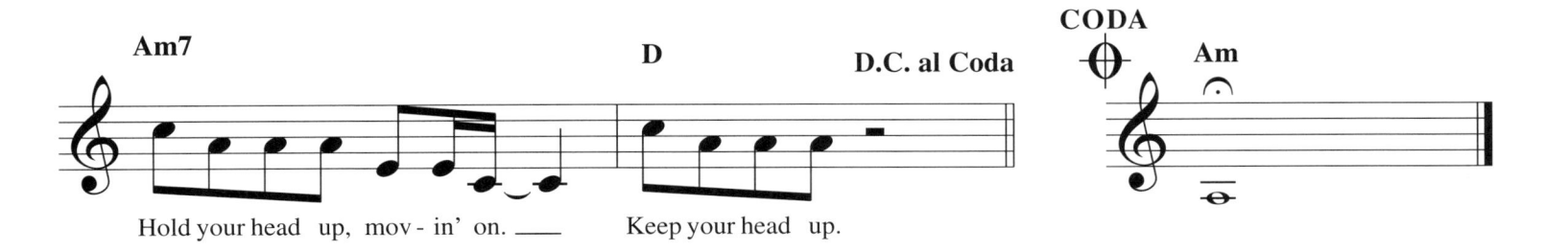

Who am I to disagree? I travel the world and the seven seas; ev'rybody's looking for something.

Hold your head up. Keep your head up, movin' on.

Hold your head up, movin' on. Keep your head up, movin' on.

Hold your head up, movin' on. Keep your head up, movin' on.

Hold your head up, movin' on. Keep your head up.

D.C. al Coda

CODA

TAKE MY BREATH AWAY
(Love Theme)
from the Paramount Picture TOP GUN

Words and Music by GIORGIO MORODER
and TOM WHITLOCK

Moderately slow

1. Watch-ing ev-ery mo-tion in my fool-ish lov-er's game;
2., 3. *(See additional lyrics)*

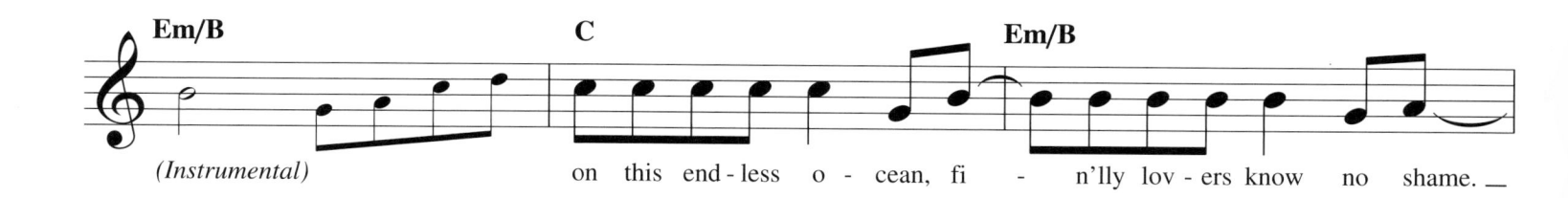

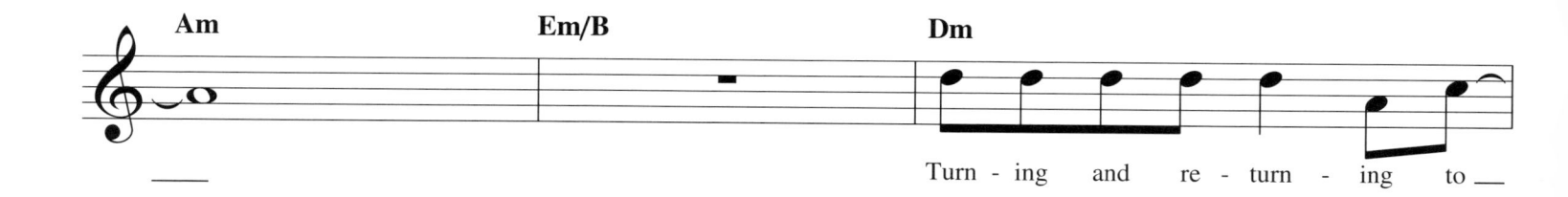

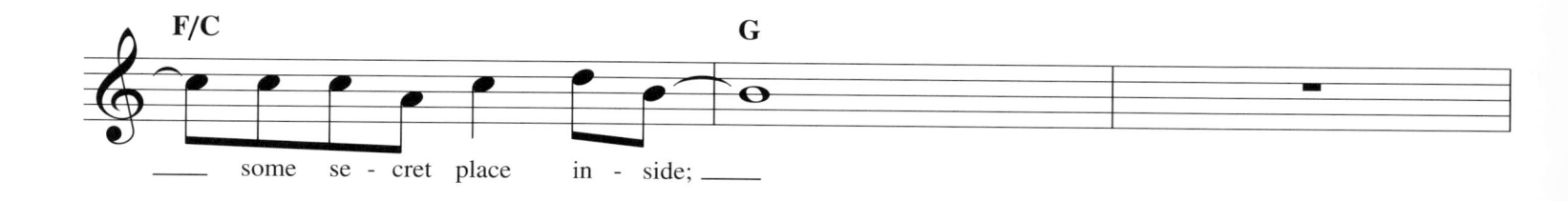

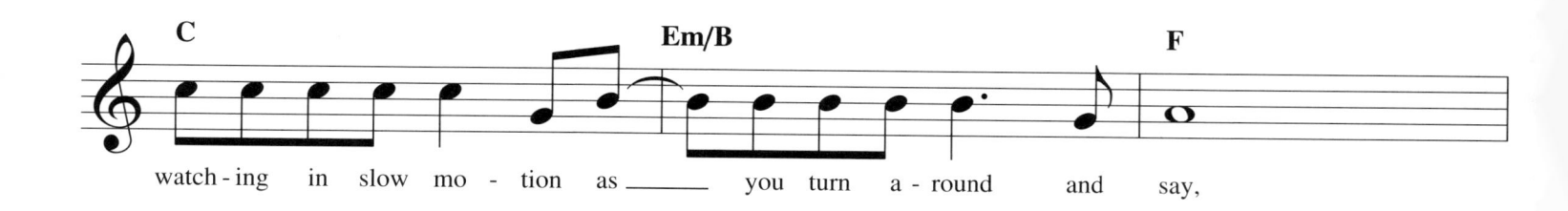

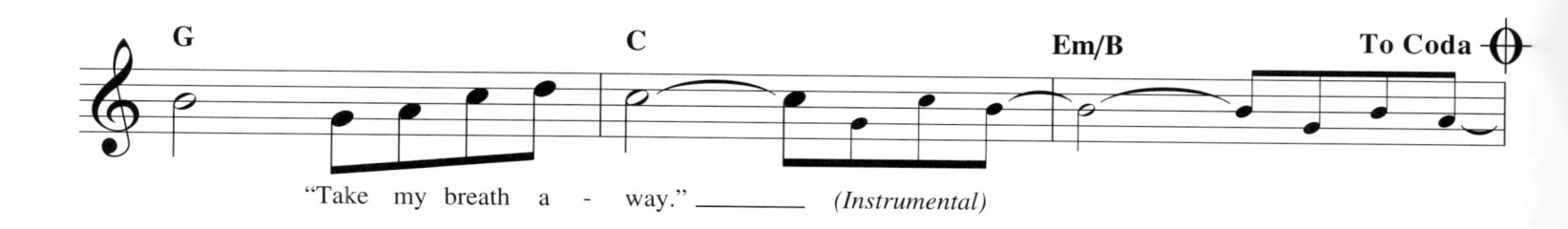

(Instrumental) on this end-less o-cean, fi-n'lly lov-ers know no shame.

Turn-ing and re-turn-ing to some se-cret place in-side;

watch-ing in slow mo-tion as you turn a-round and say, "Take my breath a-way." *(Instrumental)*

To Coda

203

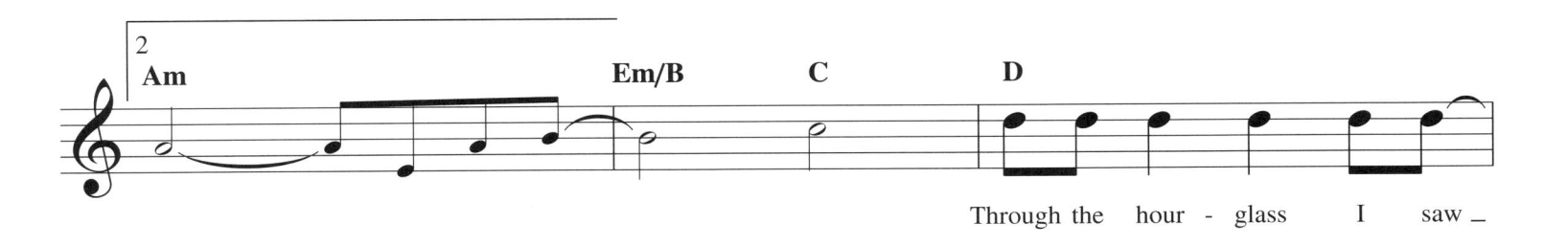

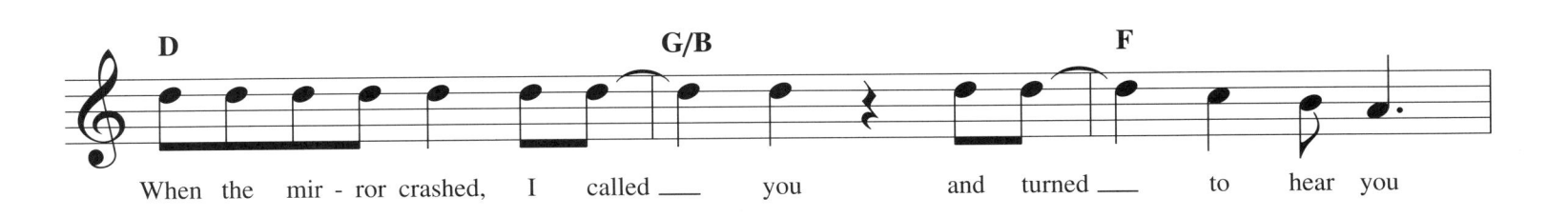

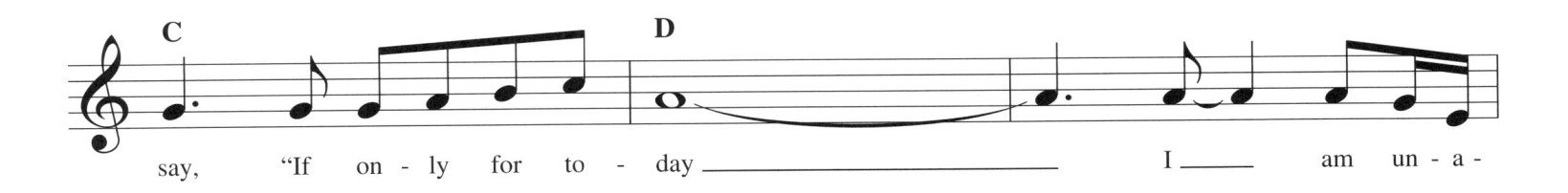

1. F | G | C
"Take my breath a-way." ____ *(Instrumental)*

Em/B | F | G

2. Am | Em/B C | D
Through the hour-glass I saw

G/B | F | C
___ you. In time ___ you slipped a - way. ___

D | G/B | F
When the mir-ror crashed, I called ___ you and turned ___ to hear you

C | D
say, "If on-ly for to-day ___ I ___ am un-a-

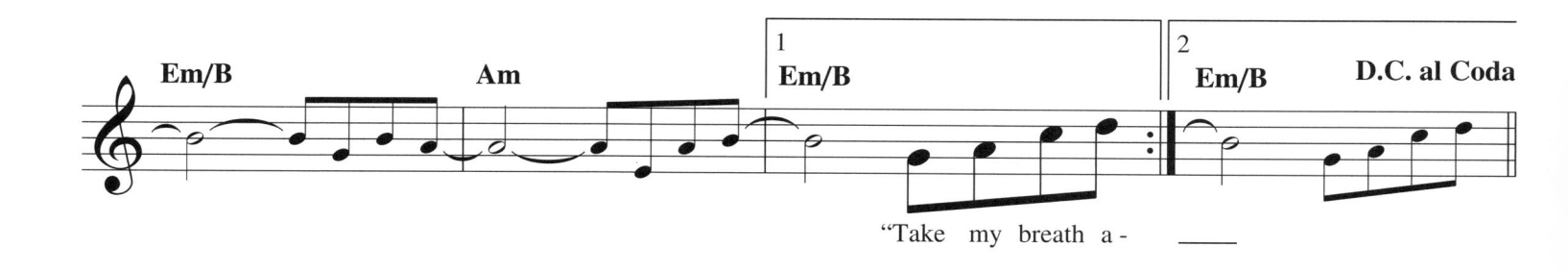

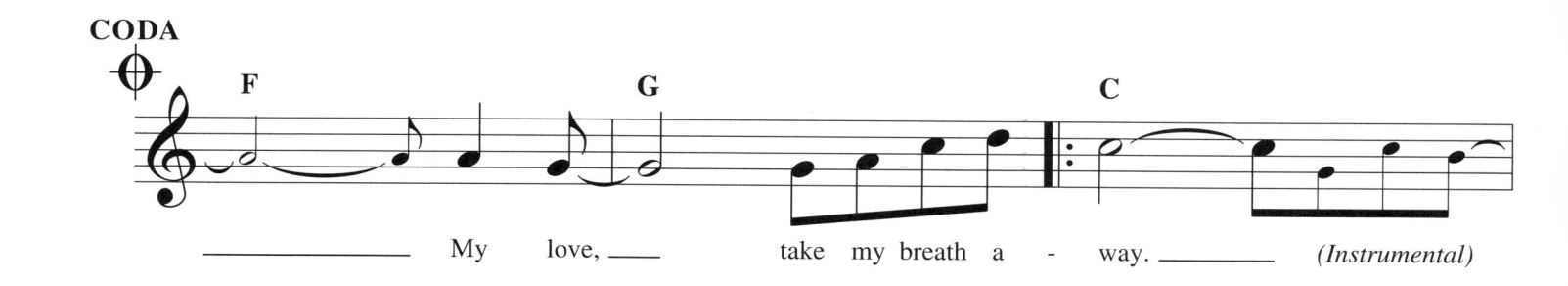

Additional Lyrics

2. Watching, I keep waiting, still anticipating love,
   Never hesitating to become the fated ones.
   Turning and returning to some secret place to hide;
   Watching in slow motion as you turn to me and say,
   "Take my breath away."
   (To Bridge)

3. Watching every motion in this foolish lover's game;
   Haunted by the notion somewhere there's a love in flames.
   Turning and returning to some secret place inside;
   Watching in slow motion as you turn my way and say,
   "Take my breath away."
   (To Coda)

THRILLER

Copyright © 1982 RODSONGS
All Rights Controlled and Administered by ALMO MUSIC CORP.

Words and Music by
ROD TEMPERTON

Moderately bright

D7

It's close to mid - night, and
You hear the door slam and
They're out to get you. There's

Am

some - thin' e - vil's lurk - in' in the dark.
re - al - ize there's no - where left to run.
de - mons clos - in' in on ev - 'ry side.

D7

Un - der the moon - light you
You feel the cold hand, and
They will pos - sess you un -

Am

see a sight that al - most stops your heart. You try to scream,
won - der if you'll ev - er see the sun. You close your eyes,
less you change that num - ber on your dial. Now is the time

D7

but ter - ror takes the sound be - fore you
and hope that this is just i - mag - i -
for you and I to cud - dle close to -

Am

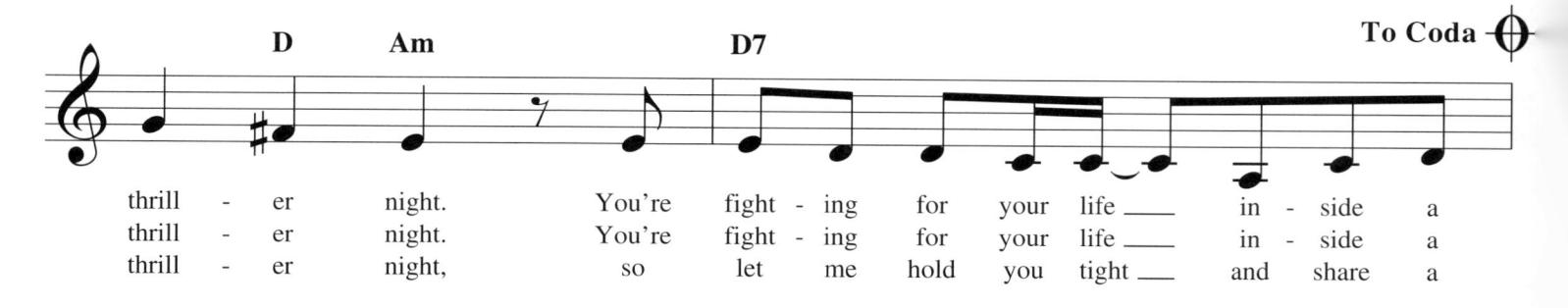

make it. You start to freeze
na - tion. But all the while,
geth - er. All through the night

D7

as hor - ror looks you right be - tween the
you hear the crea - ture creep - in' up be -
I'll save you from the ter - ror on the

Am **F** **Em** **Am** **C**

eyes. You're par - a - lyzed. 'Cause this is thrill - er,
hind. You're out of time. 'Cause this is thrill - er,
screen. I'll make you see that this is thrill - er,

D **Am** **D7**

thrill - er night, and no one's gon - na save you from the
thrill - er night. There ain't no sec - ond chance a - gainst the
thrill - er night, 'cause I could thrill you more than an - y

Dm **Am** **C**

beast a - bout to strike. You know, it's thrill - er,
thing with for - ty eyes. You know, it's thrill - er,
ghost would care to try. Girl, this is thrill - er,

D **Am** **D7** **To Coda**

thrill - er night. You're fight - ing for your life in - side a
thrill - er night. You're fight - ing for your life in - side a
thrill - er night, so let me hold you tight and share a

kill - er, thrill - er to - night.

kill - er, thrill - er to - night.

Night crea - tures call and the dead start to walk in their mas - quer - ade. There's no es - cap - in' the jaws of the a - lien this time.

This is the end of your life.

D.C. al Coda

CODA

kill - er, thrill - er.

TAKE ON ME

Music by PAL WAAKTAAR and MAGNE FURUHOLMNE
Words by PAL WAAKTAAR, MAGNE FURUHOLMNE and MORTON HARKET

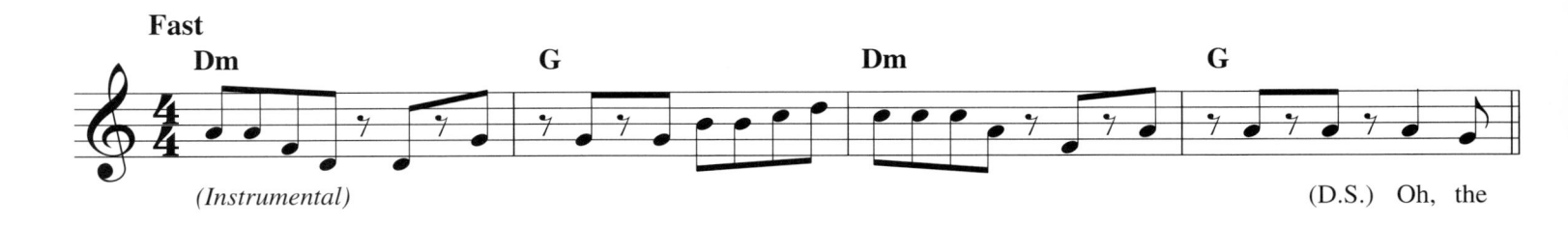

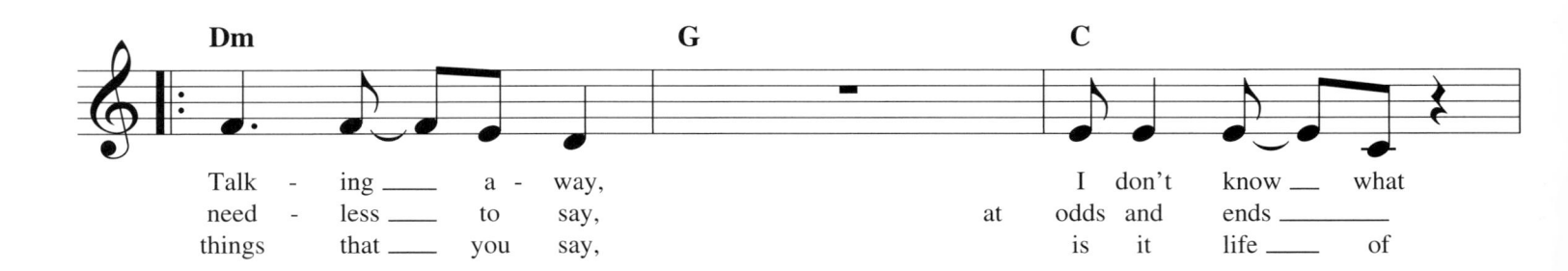

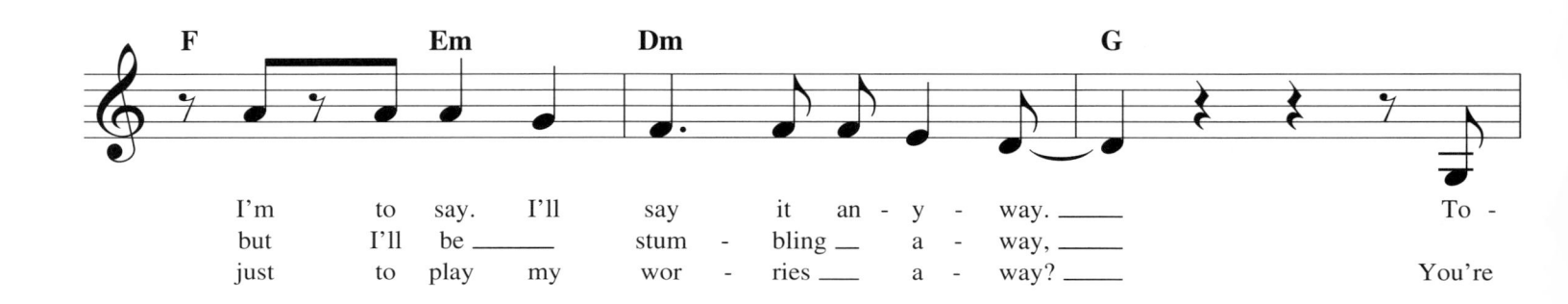

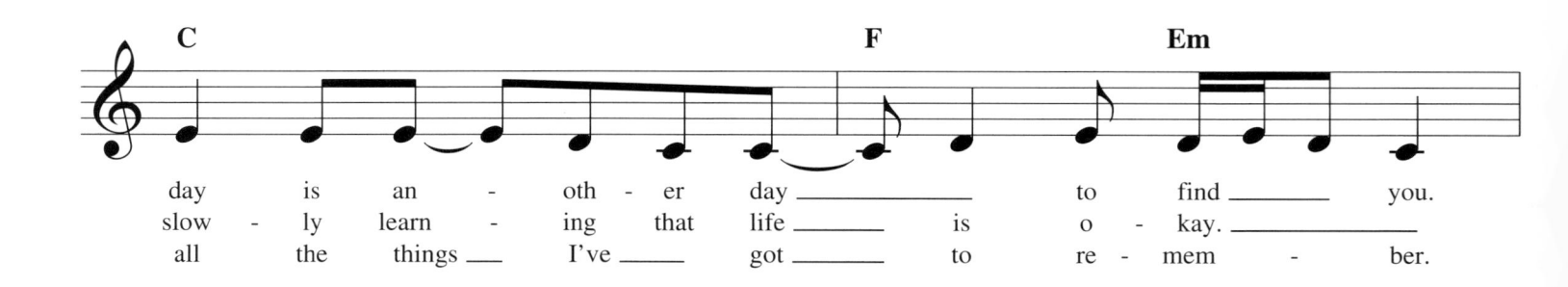

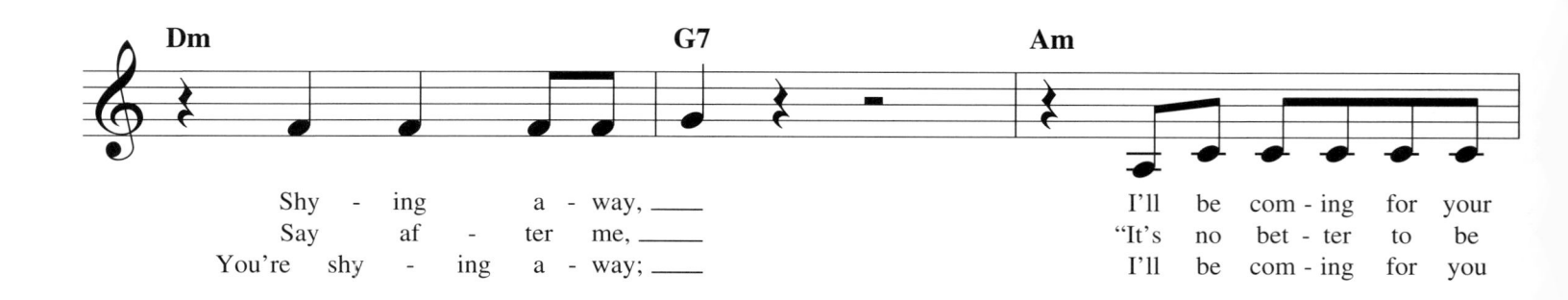

(Instrumental)

(D.S.) Oh, the

Talk - ing a - way, I don't know what
need - less to say, at odds and ends
things that you say, is it life of

I'm to say. I'll say it an - y - way. To-
but I'll be stum - bling a - way, You're
just to play my wor - ries a - way?

day is an - oth - er day to find you.
slow - ly learn - ing that life is o - kay.
all the things I've got to re - mem - ber.

Shy - ing a - way, I'll be com - ing for your
Say af - ter me, "It's no bet - ter to be
You're shy - ing a - way; I'll be com - ing for you

F C Em Am
love o - kay.
safe than sor - ry."
an - y way.
Take on me.
F C Em Am
(Take on me.) Take me on.
To Coda
F C Em Am
(Take on me.) I'll be gone
F G C G F
in a day or two.
1 G
2 G
D.C. al Coda
So,
CODA
F C
in a day.
Em/B Am F C
Take on me.

This Could Be the Night

Words and Music by PAUL DEAN, MIKE RENO,
BILL WRAY and JONATHAN CAIN

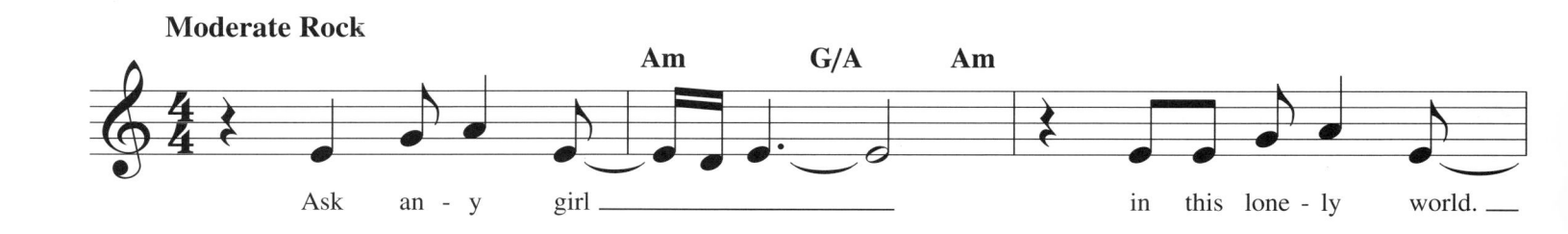

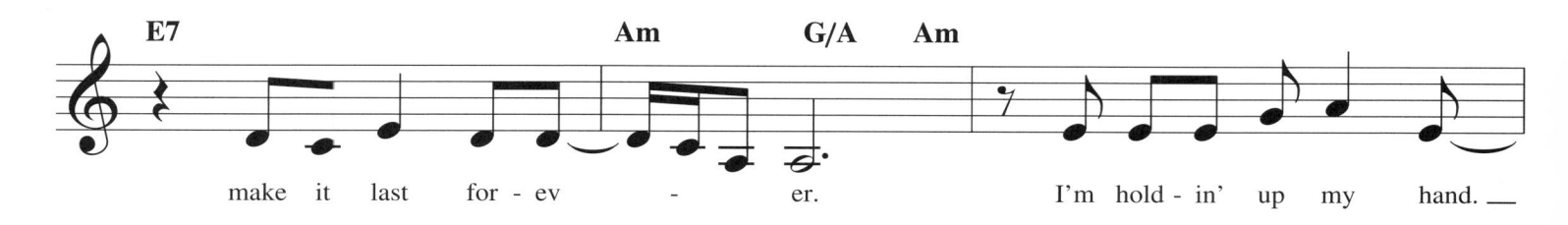

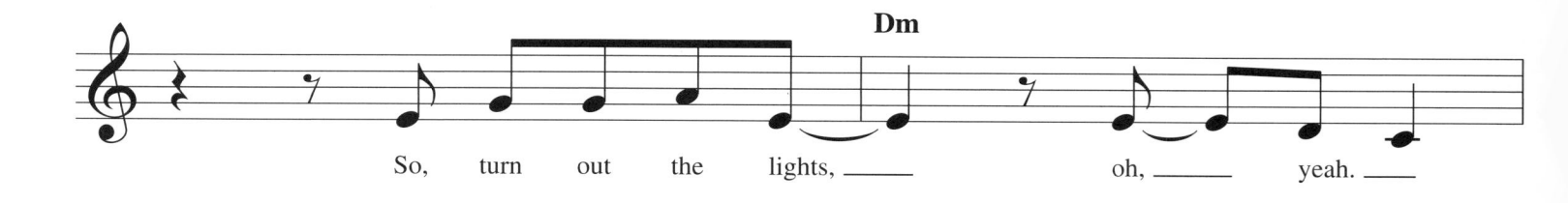

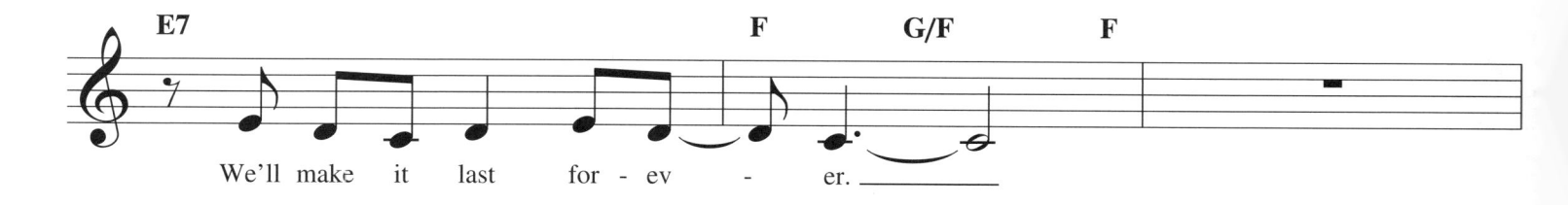

© 1985 EMI BLACKWOOD MUSIC (CANADA) LTD., DEAN OF MUSIC, EMI APRIL MUSIC
(CANADA) LTD., DUKE RENO MUSIC, MEL-DAVIS MUSIC INC. and FRISCO KID MUSIC
All Rights for EMI BLACKWOOD MUSIC (CANADA) LTD. and DEAN OF MUSIC
  Controlled and Administered by EMI BLACKWOOD MUSIC INC.
All Rights for EMI APRIL MUSIC (CANADA) LTD. and DUKE RENO MUSIC
  Controlled and Administered by EMI APRIL MUSIC INC.

Moderate Rock

Ask an-y girl _____ in this lone-ly world. _____

Ask an-y girl, _____ she'll say _____ make it last for-ev-er. I'm hold-in' up my hand. _____

I fi-n'lly un-der-stand. _____

So, turn out the lights, _____ oh, _____ yeah. _____

We'll make it last for-ev- er. _____

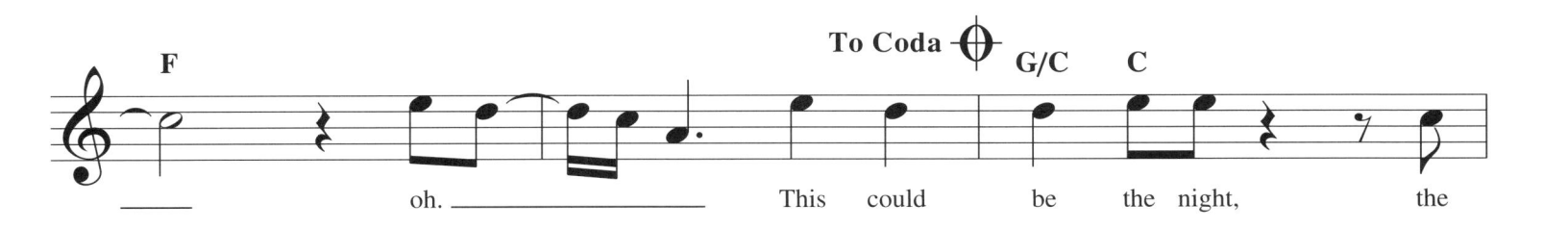

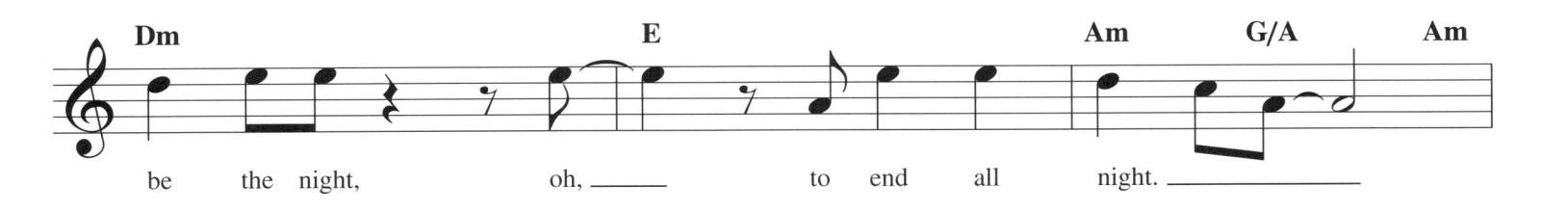

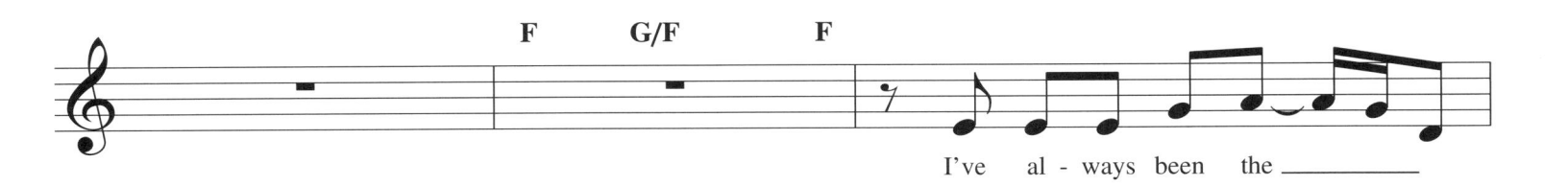

I've been down the street of desire. Sometimes I was so un-in-spired. You found what was locked up inside of me, oh. This could be the night, the night to remember. We'll make it last forever. This could be the night, oh, to end all night. I've always been the one lov - in' on the run.

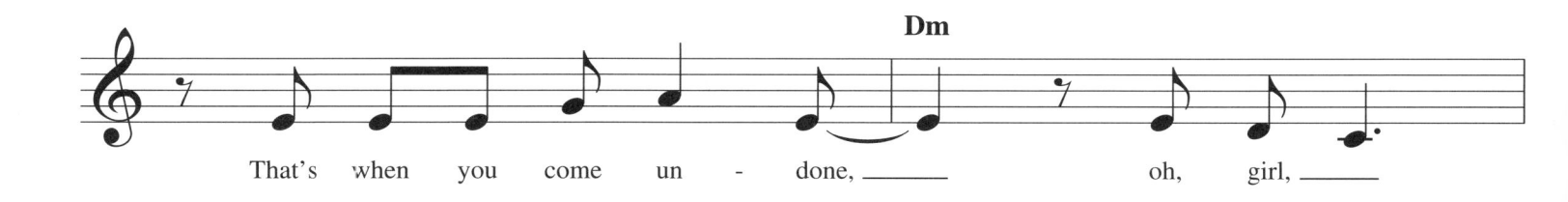

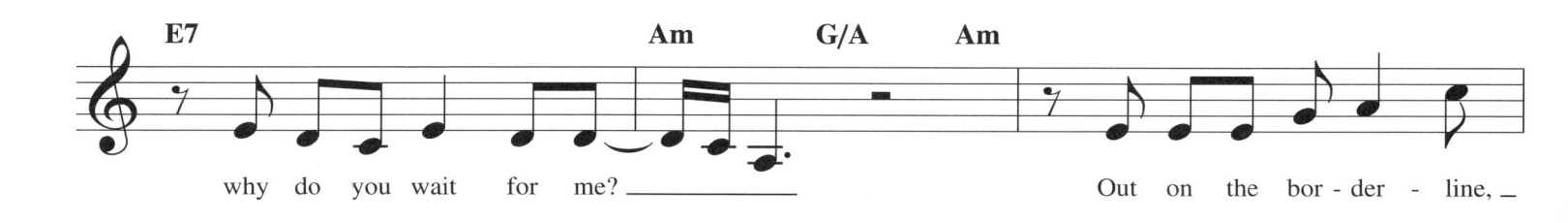

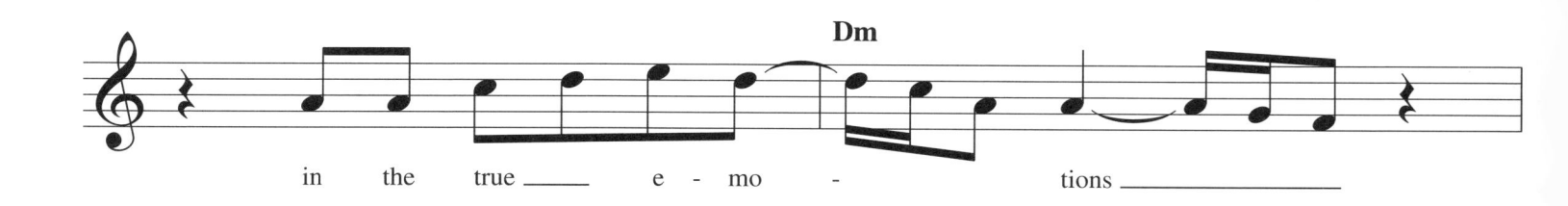

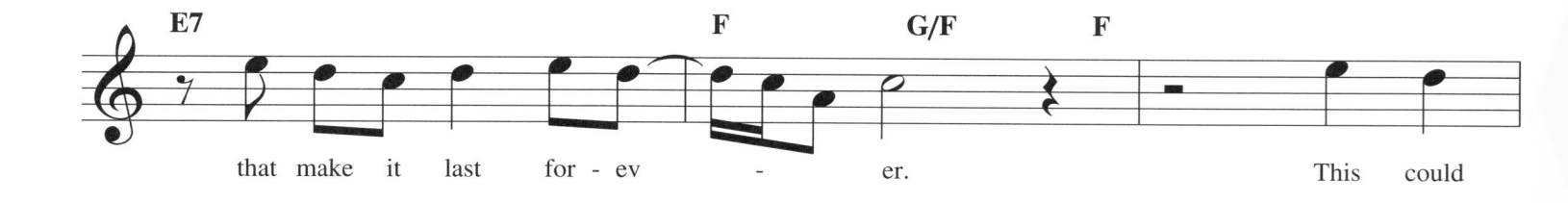

That's when you come un - done, _____ oh, girl, _____

why do you wait for me? _____ Out on the bor - der - line, ___

be - tween the hurt ___ and lies, _____

in the true ___ e - mo - tions _____

that make it last for - ev - er. This could

G/C C
be the night, the night to re - mem - ber.
F Dm
We'll make it last for - ev - er. This could be the night, oh,
E Am D.S. al Coda
to end all night.
CODA
G/C C
be the night, the night to re - mem - ber.
F
We'll make it last for - ev - er. This could
Dm E Am
be the night, oh, to end all night.

TIME AFTER TIME

Words and Music by CYNDI LAUPER and ROB HYMAN

Copyright © 1983 Rellla Music Co., WB Music Corp. and Dub Notes
All Rights for Rella Music Co. Administered by Sony/ATV Music Publishing LLC,
 8 Music Square West, Nashville, TN 37203
All Rights for Dub Notes Administered by WB Music Corp.

Moderately fast Rock

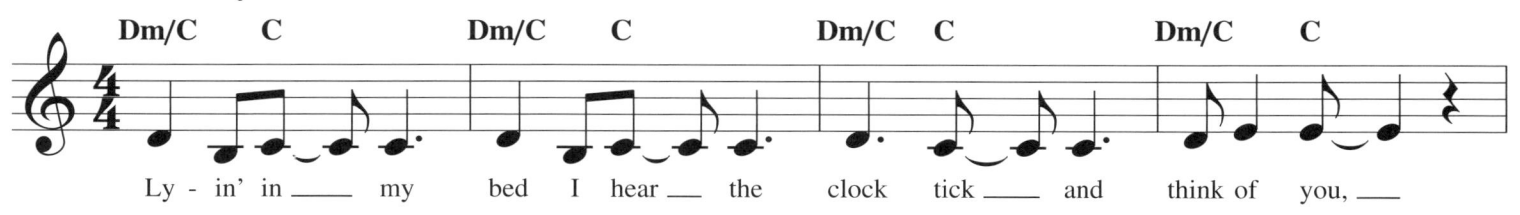

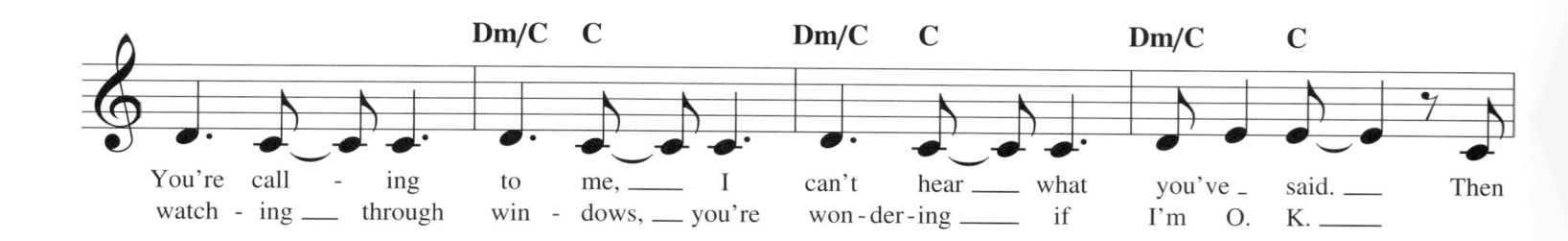

Ly-in' in my bed I hear the clock tick and think of you,

caught up in cir-cles con-fu-sion is noth-ing new.

Flash back warm nights, al-most left be-hind.

Suit-case of mem-o-ries time af-ter.

Some-times you pic-ture me. I'm walk-ing too far a-head.
Af-ter my pic-ture fades and dark-ness has turned to gray,

You're call-ing to me, I can't hear what you've said. Then
watch-ing through win-dows, you're won-der-ing if I'm O. K.

(1.,3.) you say go slow. I fall behind.
Secrets stolen from deep inside.

The second hand unwinds.
The drum beats out of time.
If you're lost, you can look and you will find me, time after time.

If you fall, I will catch you; I'll be waiting, time after time.

If you're lost, you can look and you will find me, time after time.

If you fall, I will catch you; I'll be waiting, time after time.

CODA

Time after time.

(I've Had) THE TIME OF MY LIFE
from DIRTY DANCING

Copyright © 1987 Knockout Music, RU Cyrius Publishing,
Donald Jay Music Ltd. and Sony/ATV Music Publishing LLC
All Rights for Donald Jay Music Ltd. Controlled and Administered by EMI April Music Inc.
All Rights for Sony/ATV Music Publishing LLC Administered by
Sony/ATV Music Publishing LLC, 8 Music Square West, Nashville, TN 37203

Words and Music by FRANKE PREVITE,
JOHN DeNICOLA and DONALD MARKOWITZ

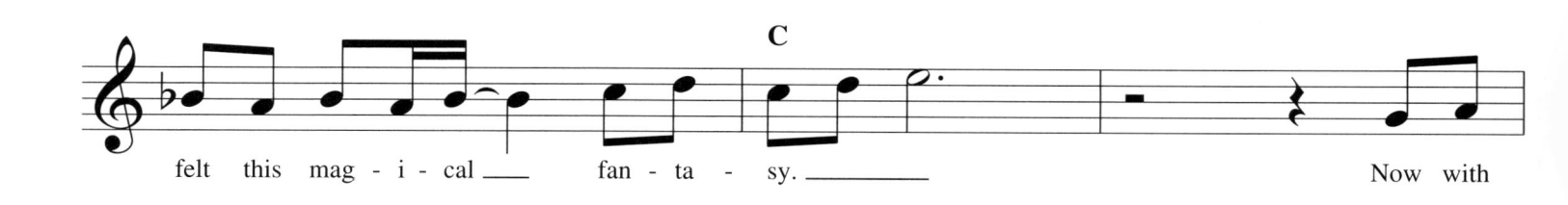

Moderately

1. I've been waiting for so long, now I've fi-n'lly found some-one to stand by me. We saw the writ-ing on the wall as we felt this mag-i-cal fan-ta-sy. Now with

2. (See additional lyrics)

Omit these measures 2nd time

pas-sion in our eyes there's no way we could dis-guise it secret-ly. So we take each oth-er's hand, 'cause we seem to un-der-stand __ the ur-gen-cy. Just __ re-mem-ber:

Bridge
You're the one thing I can't get e-nough of, so I'll tell you some-thing, this could be love. Be-cause I've had the time of my
I've had the time of my

life; _____ no, I nev-er felt __ this way be-fore. Yes, I
life; _____ and I've searched __ through ev-'ry o-pen door till I've

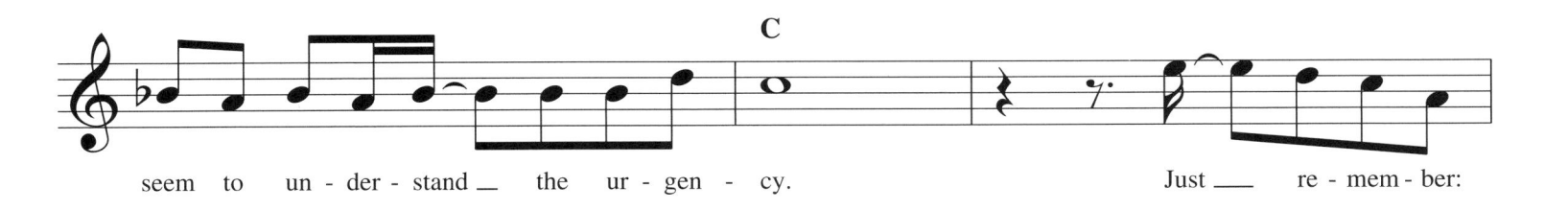

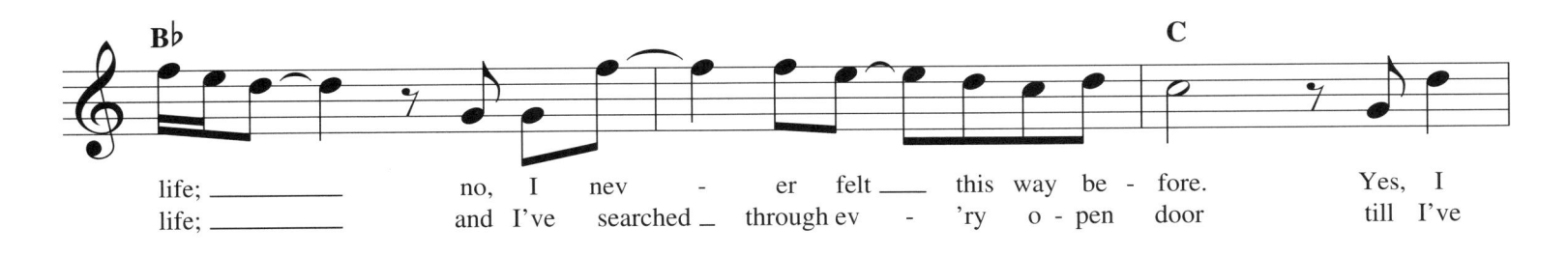

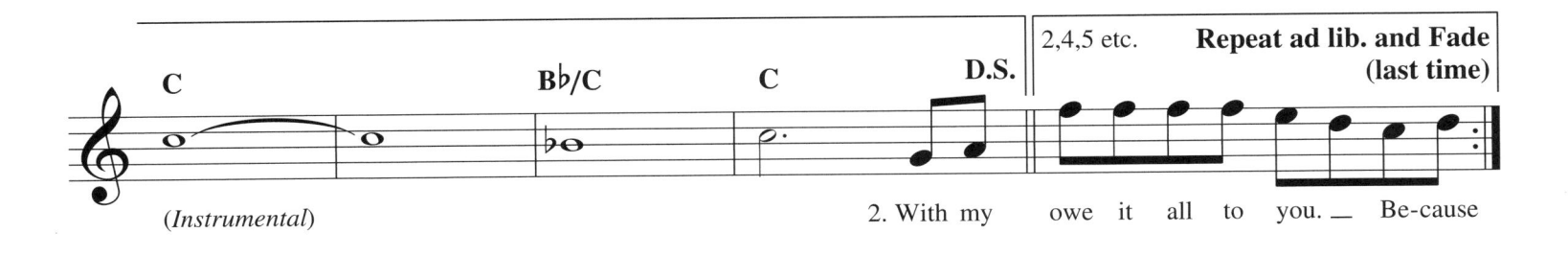

swear it's the truth, _____ and I owe it all to you. __
found the truth, _____

(Instrumental)

2,4,5 etc. Repeat ad lib. and Fade (last time)
2. With my owe it all to you. __ Be-cause

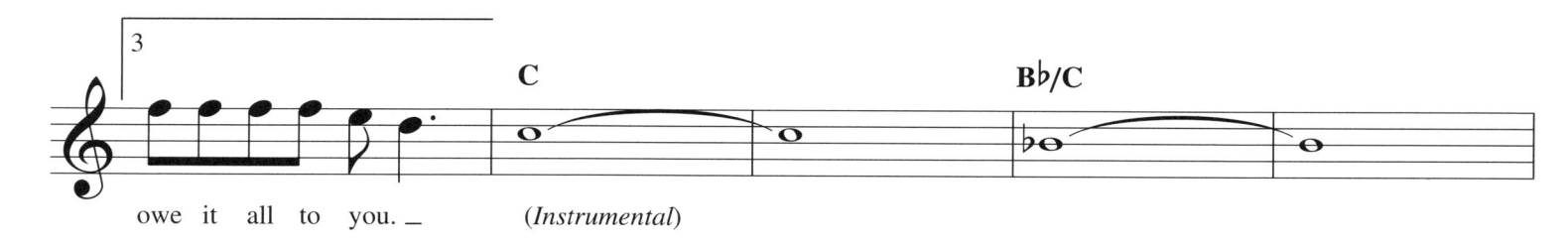

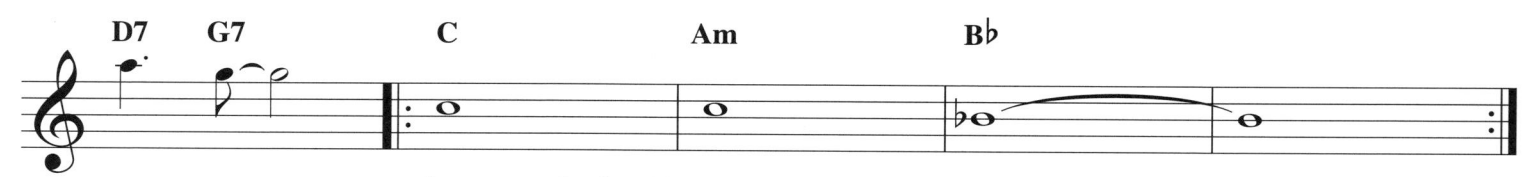

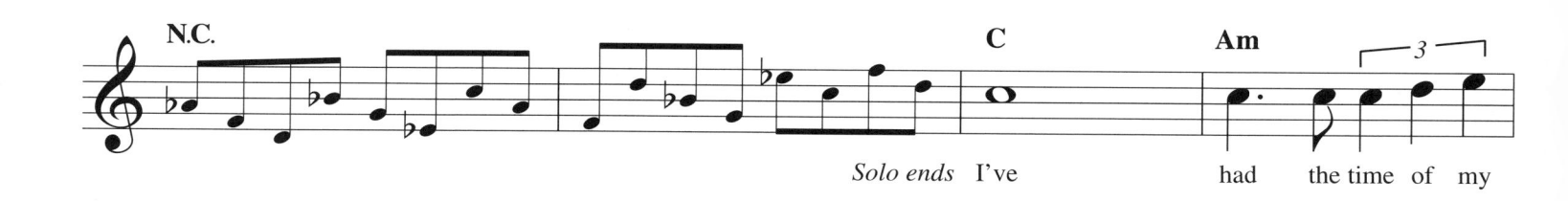

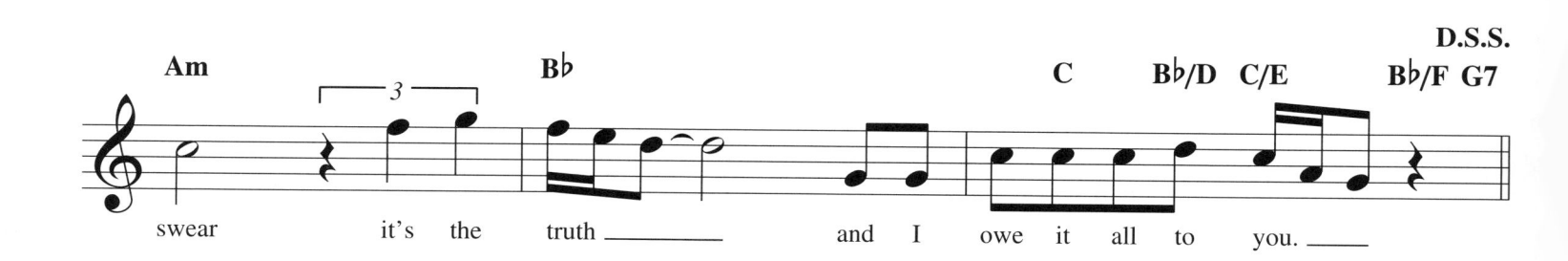

Additional Lyrics

2. With my body and soul
   I want you more and more than you'll ever know.
   So we'll just let it go,
   Don't be afraid to lose control.
   Yes, I know what's on your mind
   When you say "Stay with me tonight."
   Just remember…
   Bridge

TOTAL ECLIPSE OF THE HEART

Copyright © 1982 by Lost Boys Music
All Rights for the United States and Canada
Administered by Edward B. Marks Music Company

Words and Music by
JIM STEINMAN

Rock Ballad

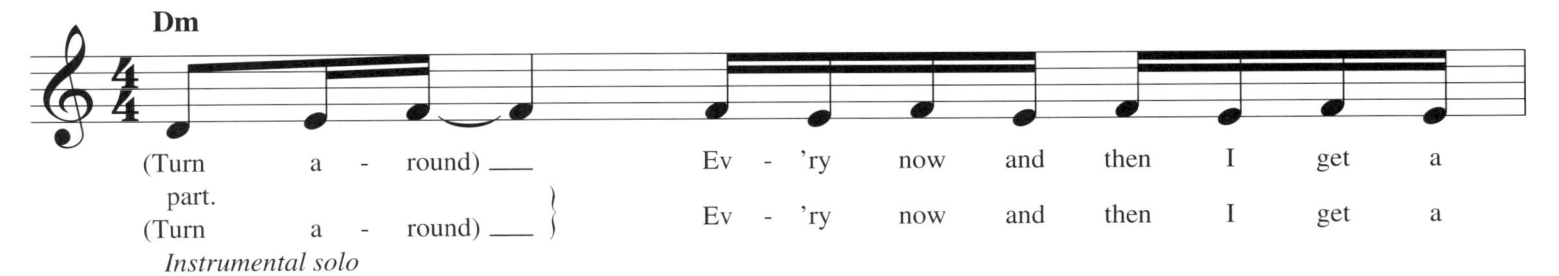

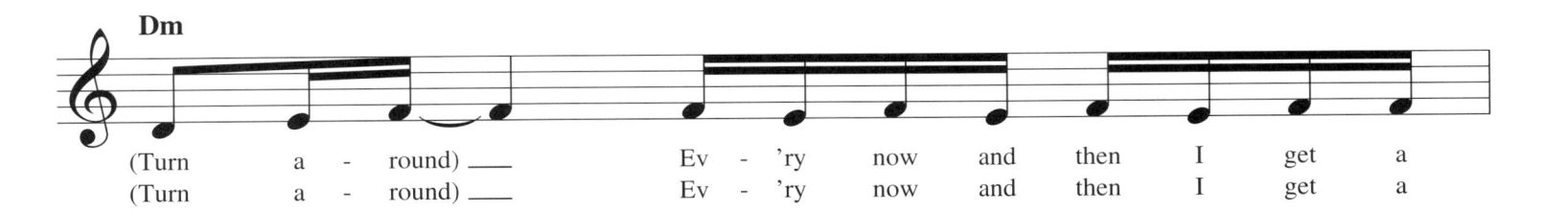

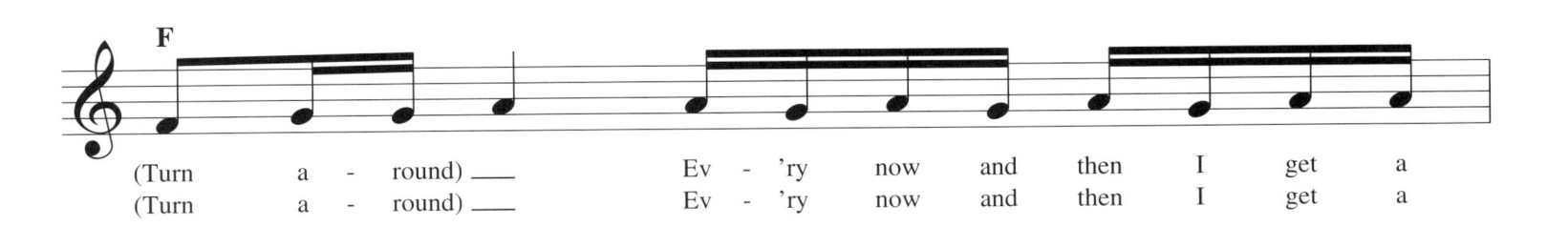

(Turn a - round) ___ Ev - 'ry now and then I get a
part.
(Turn a - round) ___ Ev - 'ry now and then I get a
Instrumental solo

lit - tle bit lone - ly and you're nev - er com - ing 'round. ___
lit - tle bit rest - less and I dream of some - thing wild. ___

(Turn a - round) ___ Ev - 'ry now and then I get a
(Turn a - round) ___ Ev - 'ry now and then I get a

lit - tle bit tired ___ of lis - t'ning to the sound of my tears.
lit - tle bit help - less and I'm ly - ing like a child in your arms.

(Turn a - round) ___ Ev - 'ry now and then I get a
(Turn a - round) ___ Ev - 'ry now and then I get a

lit - tle bit ner - vous that the best of all the years have gone by.
lit - tle bit an - gry and I know I've got to get out and cry.

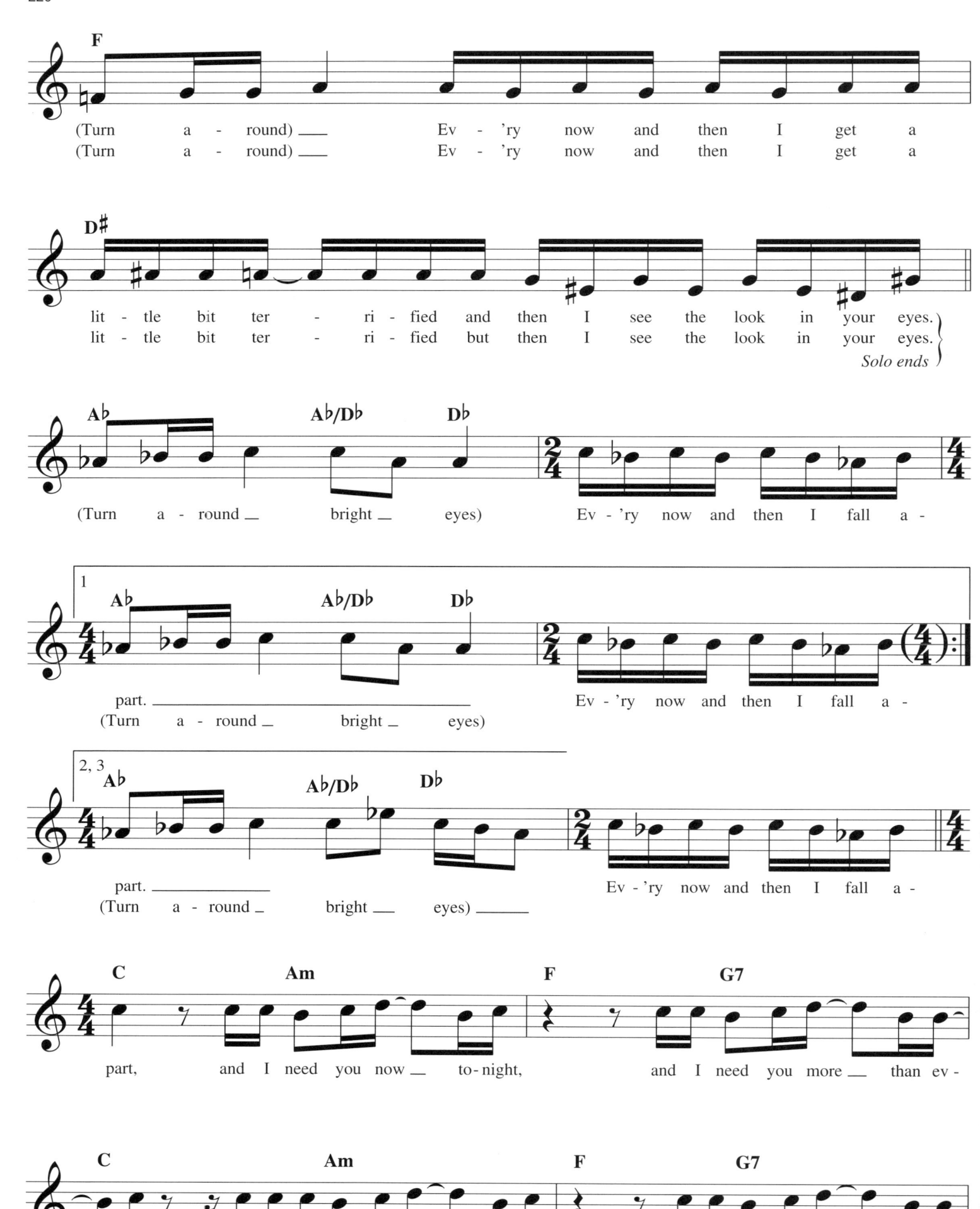

(Turn a-round) ___ Ev-'ry now and then I get a
(Turn a-round) ___ Ev-'ry now and then I get a

lit-tle bit ter-ri-fied and then I see the look in your eyes.
lit-tle bit ter-ri-fied but then I see the look in your eyes.
Solo ends

(Turn a-round bright eyes) Ev-'ry now and then I fall a-

1.
part. _____
(Turn a-round bright eyes) Ev-'ry now and then I fall a-

2, 3.
part. _____
(Turn a-round bright eyes) ___ Ev-'ry now and then I fall a-

part, and I need you now __ to-night, and I need you more __ than ev-

-er. And if you on-ly hold __ me tight, we'll be hold-ing on ____ for-

C				Am			

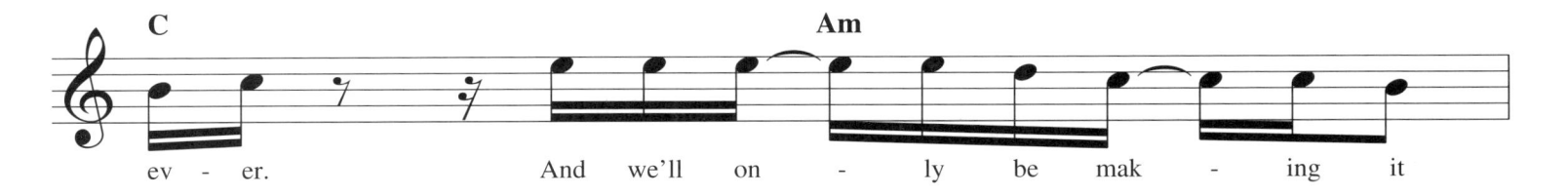

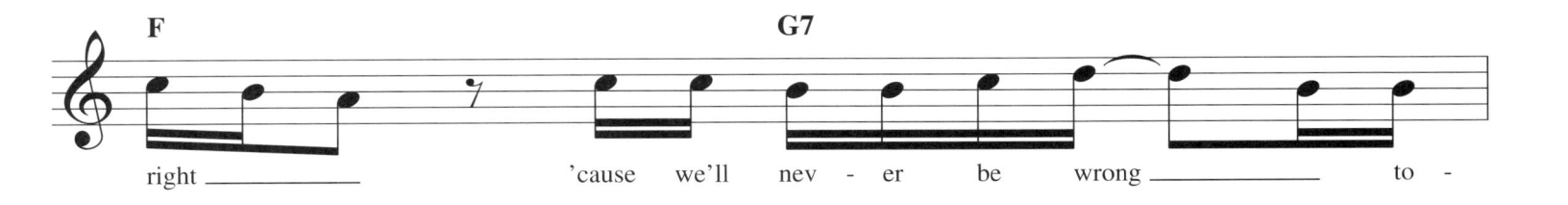

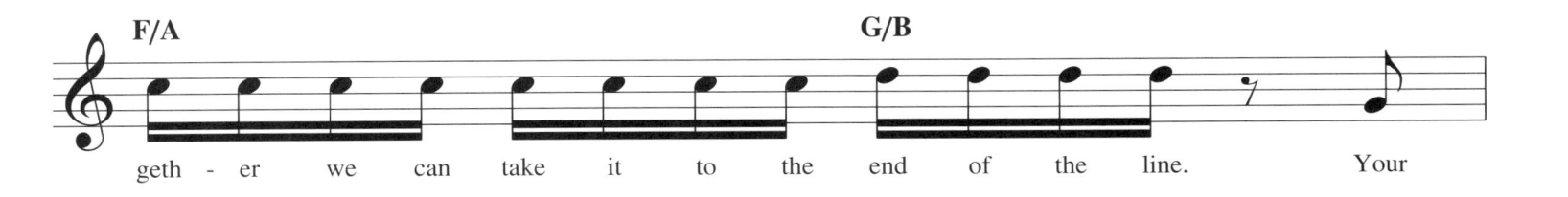

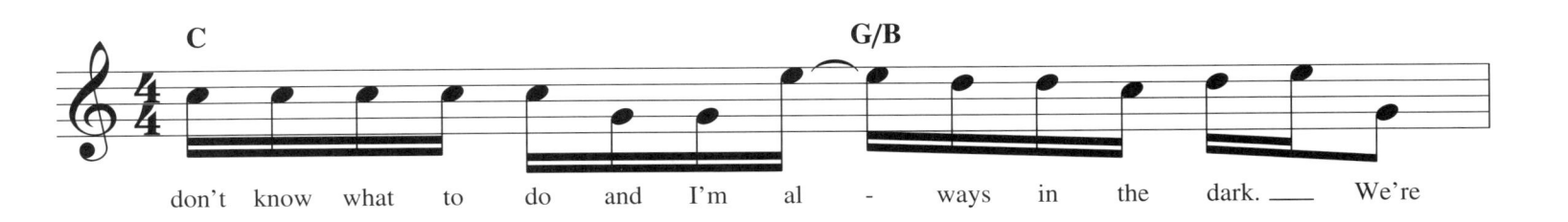

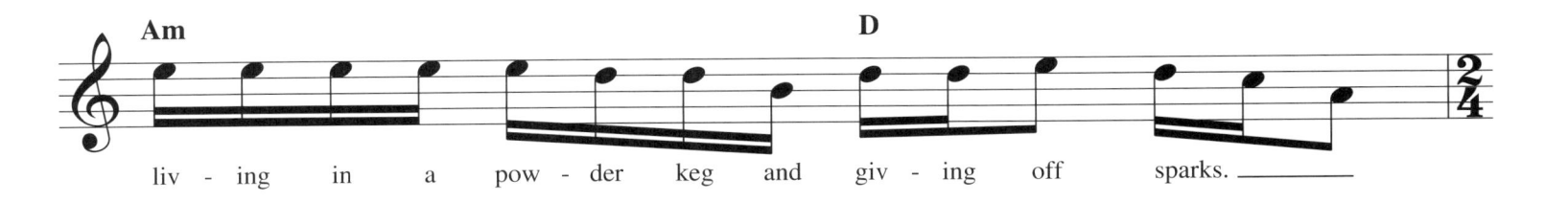

ev - er. And we'll on - ly be mak - ing it

F		G7	

right _____ 'cause we'll nev - er be wrong _____ to -

F/A		G/B	

geth - er we can take it to the end of the line. Your

Am		D	

love is like a shad - ow on me all of the time. _____ I

C		G/B	

don't know what to do and I'm al - ways in the dark. ____ We're

Am		D	

liv - ing in a pow - der keg and giv - ing off sparks. _____

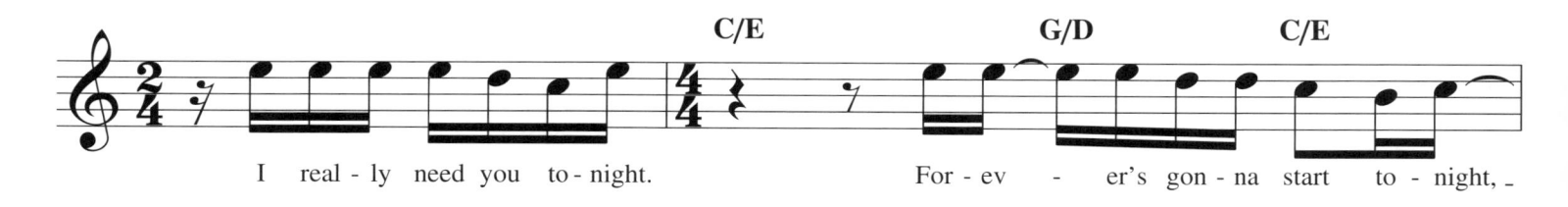

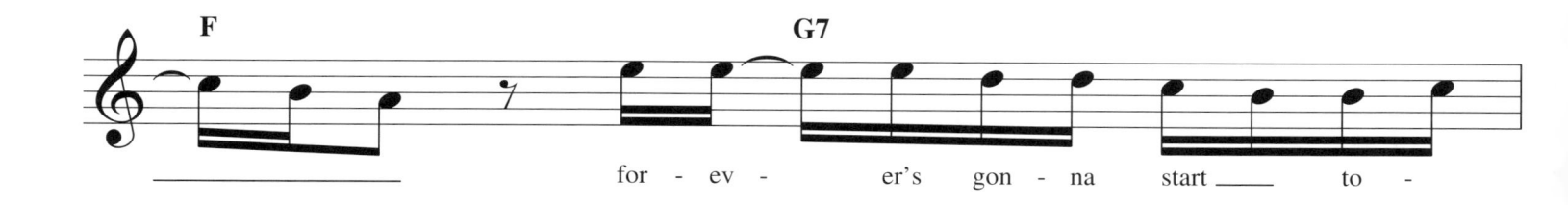

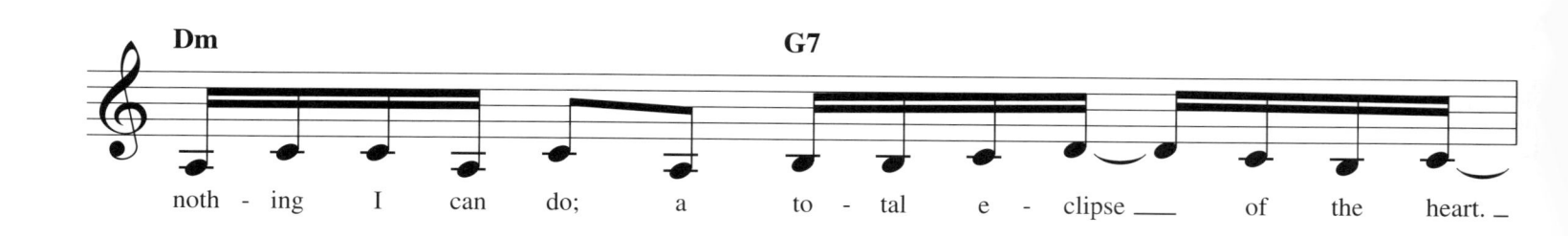

I real-ly need you to-night. For-ev-er's gon-na start to-night, for-ev-er's gon-na start to-night.

Once up-on a time I was fall-ing in love, but now I'm on-ly fall-ing a-part. There's noth-ing I can do; a to-tal e-clipse of the heart.

(Instrumental)

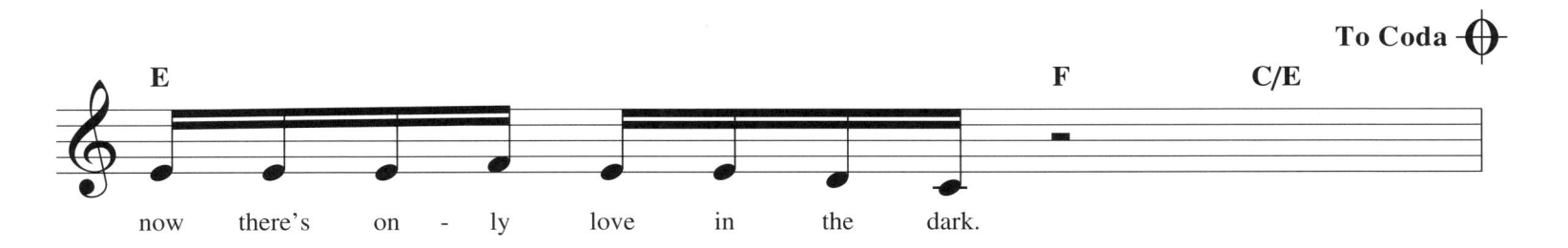

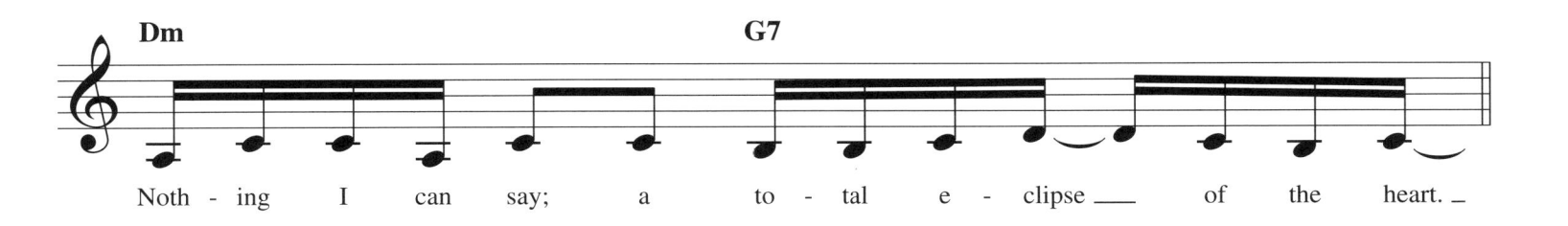

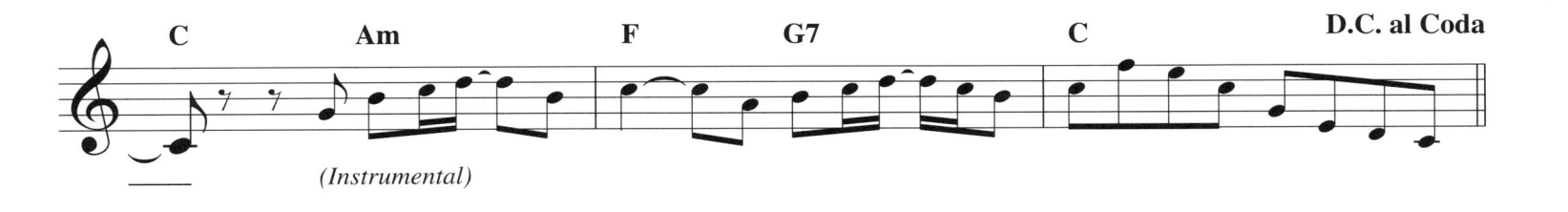

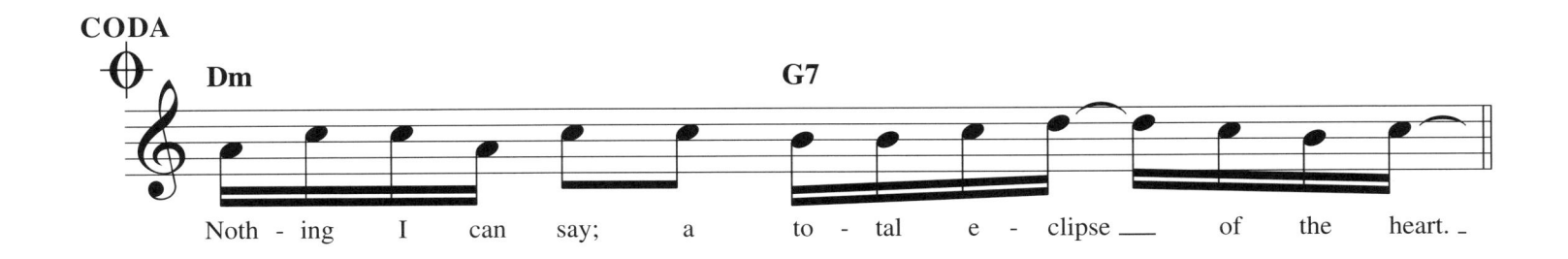

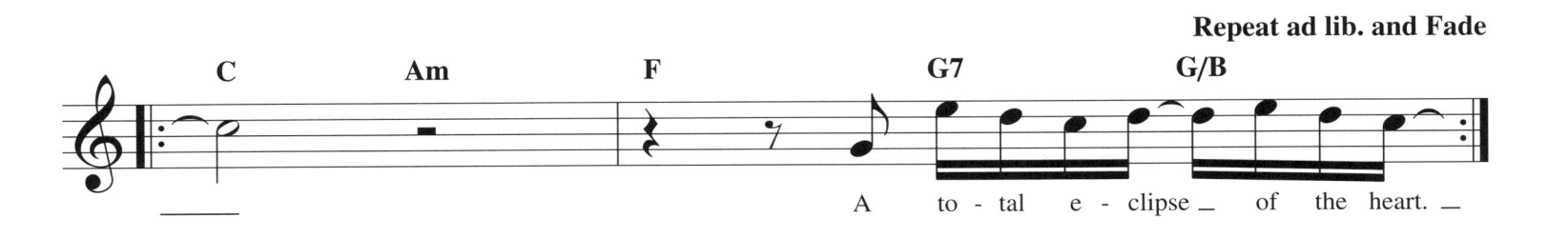

Once upon a time there was light in my life, but now there's only love in the dark. Nothing I can say; a total eclipse of the heart.

(Instrumental)

CODA

Nothing I can say; a total eclipse of the heart.

Repeat ad lib. and Fade

A total eclipse of the heart.

TWO HEARTS

Words and Music by PHIL COLLINS
and LAMONT DOZIER

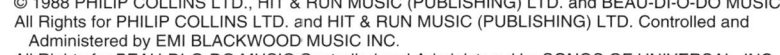

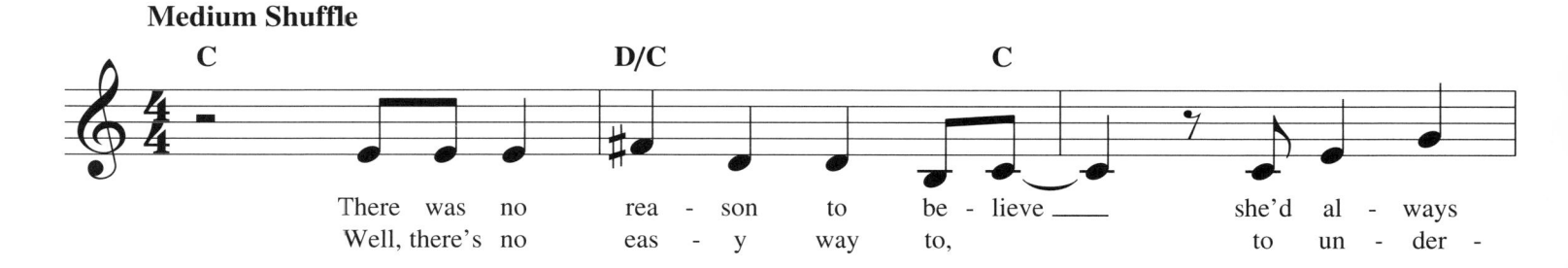

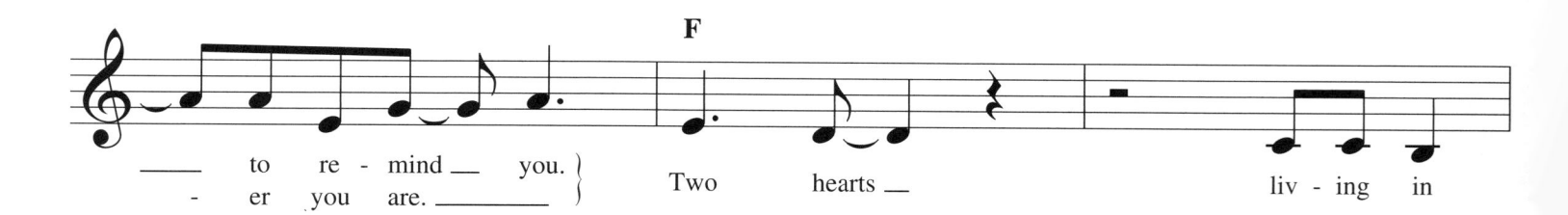

© 1988 PHILIP COLLINS LTD., HIT & RUN MUSIC (PUBLISHING) LTD. and BEAU-DI-O-DO MUSIC
All Rights for PHILIP COLLINS LTD. and HIT & RUN MUSIC (PUBLISHING) LTD. Controlled and
Administered by EMI BLACKWOOD MUSIC INC.
All Rights for BEAU-DI-O-DO MUSIC Controlled and Administered by SONGS OF UNIVERSAL, INC.

Medium Shuffle

There was no rea-son to be-lieve ___ she'd al-ways be there. ___ But if you don't put faith in what you be-lieve in, it's get-ting you no-where. ___ 'Cause it helps, you nev-er give up, ___ don't look down, ___ just look up. ___ 'Cause she's al-ways there be-hind ___ you, ___ just to re-mind ___ you.

Well, there's no eas-y way to, to un-der-stand it. ___ There's so much of my life in her and it's like I planned it. ___ And it teach-es you to nev-er let go, ___ there's so much ___ love you'll nev-er know. ___ She can reach you no mat-ter how far, ___ wher-ev-er you are. ___

Two hearts ___ liv-ing in

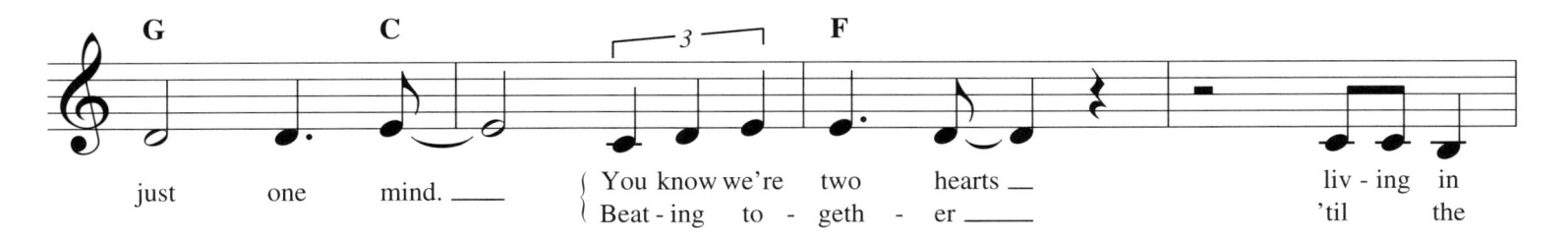

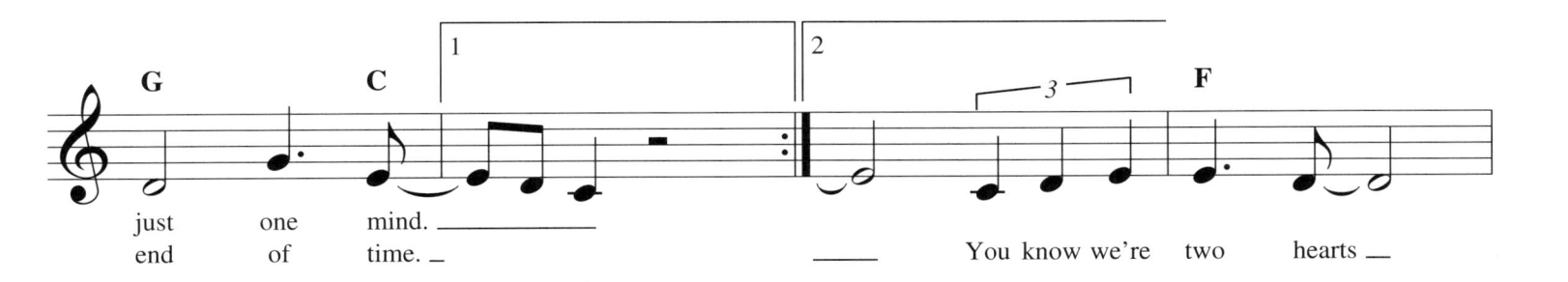

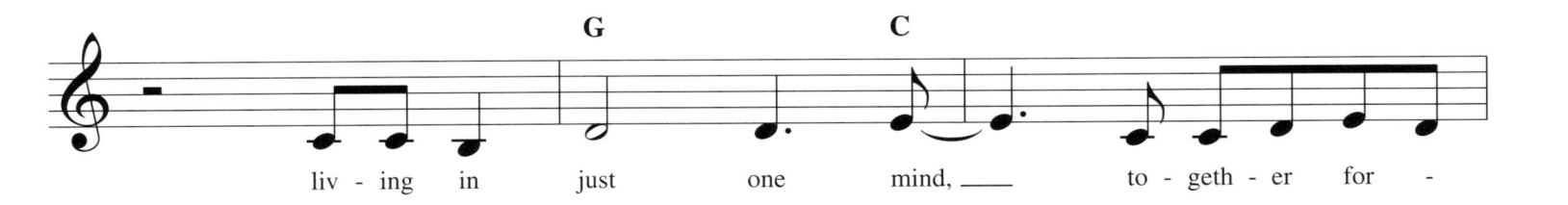

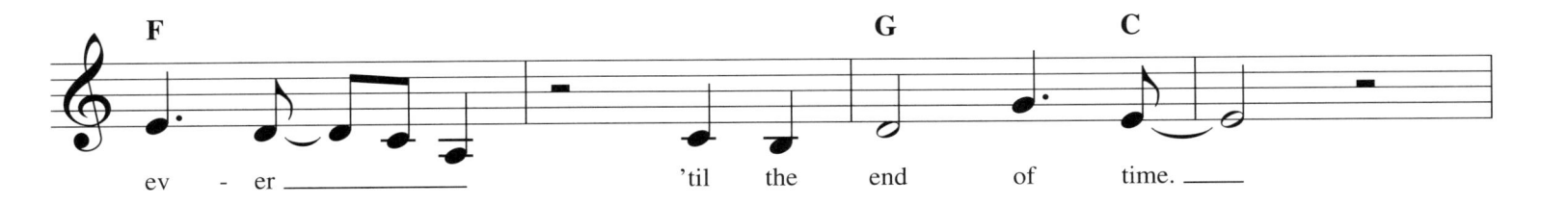

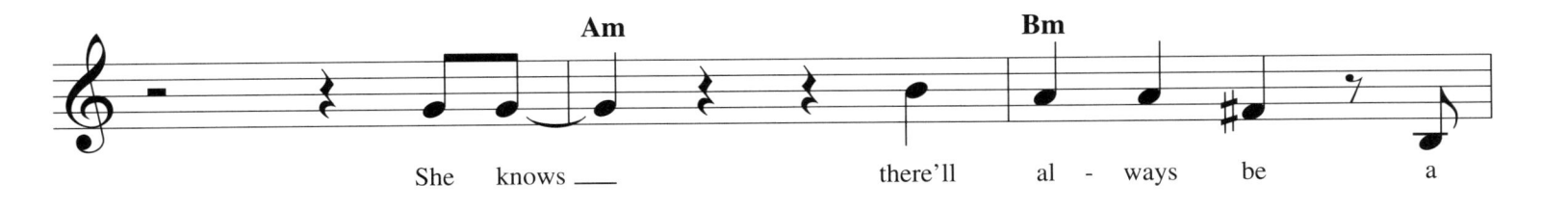

just one mind. You know we're two hearts living in
Beating together 'til the

just one mind.
end of time. You know we're two hearts

living in just one mind, together for-

ever 'til the end of time.

She knows there'll always be a

special place in my heart for her,

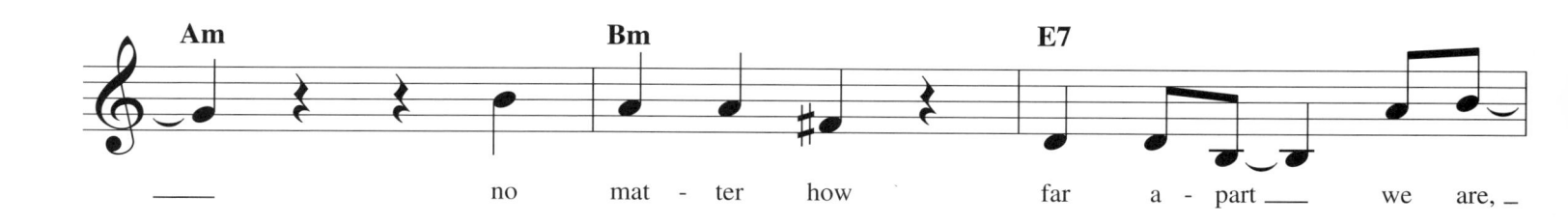

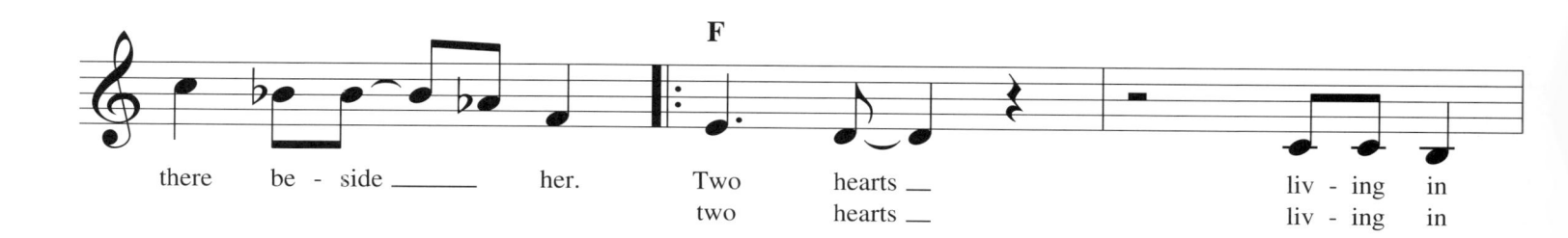

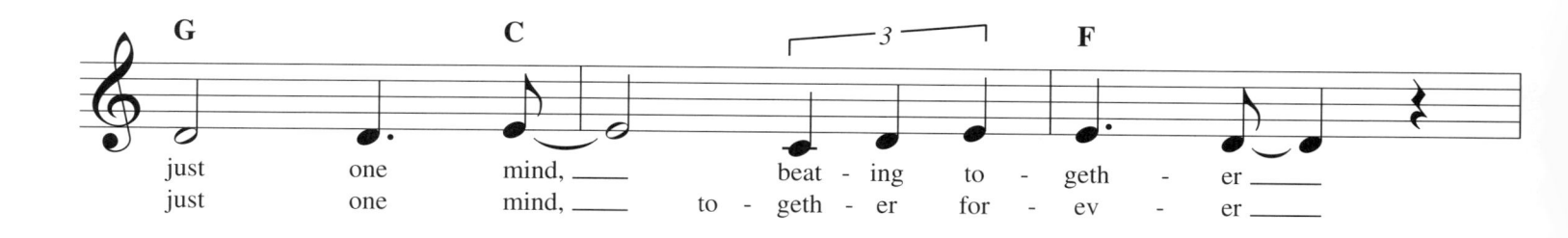

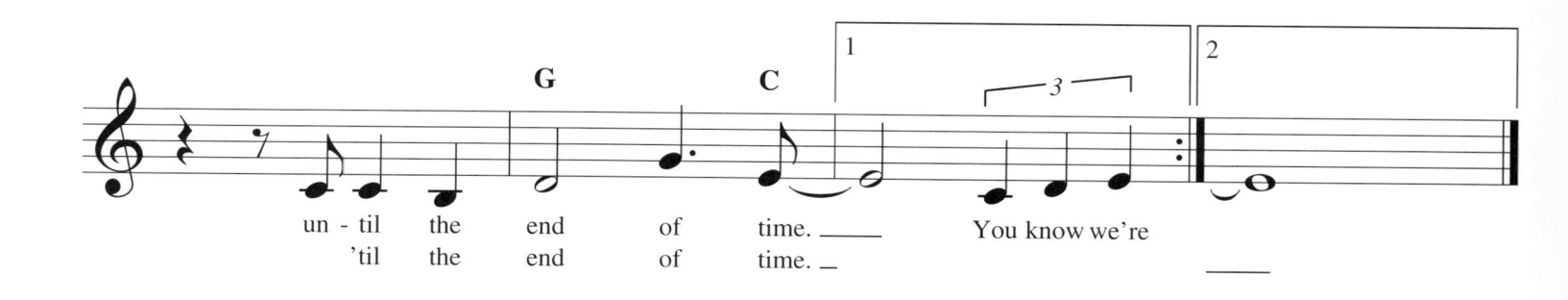

she knows, she knows, she knows. Yeah, she knows no matter how far apart we are, she knows I'm always right there beside her. Two hearts living in just one mind, beating together two hearts living in just one mind, together forever until the end of time. You know we're 'til the end of time.

VIDEO KILLED THE RADIO STAR

Words and Music by BRUCE WOOLLEY,
TREVOR HORN and GEOFF DOWNES

C/E F G
I met your chil - dren. Oh, oh. What did you tell them?
You were the first one. Oh, oh. You were the last one.
C F C
Vid - e - o killed the ra - di - o star. Vid - e - o killed the ra -
F 1 C G/B F/A
- di - o star. Pic - tures came and broke your heart.
G Am 2 C G/B
Oh, uh uh uh oh. In my mind and
F/A C G/B F/A
in my car, we can't re - wind; we've gone too far.
G Am G
Oh, uh uh uh oh. Oh, uh uh uh oh.

Am C F
Vid - e - o killed the ra - di - o star.
C F C G/B
Vid - e - o killed the ra - di - o star. In my mind and
F/A C G/B F/A
in my car, we can't re - wind; we've gone too far.
C G/B F/A C/G G
Pic - tures came and broke your heart. Put the blame on
F C/E F G
V. C. R. You are
C/E F G
1
a ra - di - o star. You
2
C F
Repeat and Fade
Vid - e - o killed the ra - di - o star.

UP WHERE WE BELONG

from the Paramount Picture AN OFFICER AND A GENTLEMAN

Words by WILL JENNINGS
Music by BUFFY SAINTE-MARIE and JACK NITZSCHE

C C/E F Am
Love lift us up where we be - long, far from the
Dm C/E E/G♯ Am Fm C F/C G/C
world we know; up where the clear winds blow.
F/C Fm/C F/G G E♭ B♭/D
clear winds blow. Time goes by,
D♭ A♭/C C♭ G♭/B♭ A♭ E♭m/A♭ D♭
no time to cry, life's you and I, a - live, to - day.
D♭ D♭/F G♭ B♭m
Love lift us up where we be - long where the
E♭m D♭/F C♭ G♭ A♭
ea - gles cry, on a moun - tain high.
D♭ D♭/F G♭ B♭m
Love lift us up where we be - long, far from the
Repeat ad lib. and Fade
E♭m D♭/F F/A B♭m G♭m
world we know; where the clear winds blow.

WALK LIKE AN EGYPTIAN

Words and Music by
LIAM STERNBERG

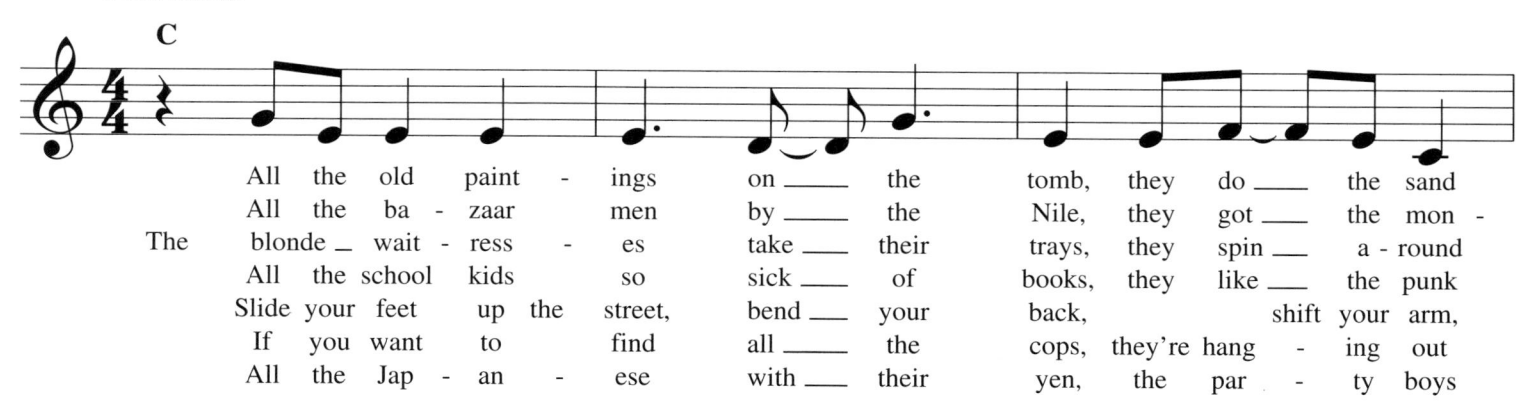

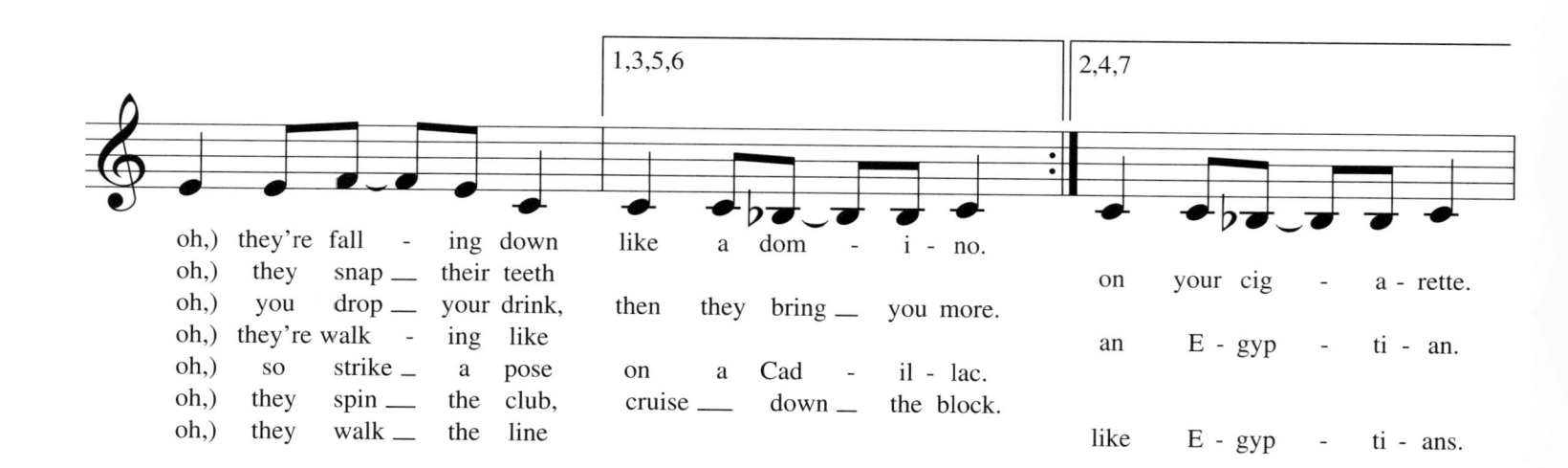

Copyright © 1986 by Peer International Corporation

Fast Rock

C

All the old paint-ings on the tomb, they do the sand
All the ba-zaar men by the Nile, they got the mon-
The blonde wait-ress-es take their trays, they spin a-round
All the school kids so sick of books, they like the punk
Slide your feet up the street, bend your back, shift your arm,
If you want to find all the cops, they're hang-ing out
All the Jap-an-ese with their yen, the par-ty boys

dance, don't you know. If they move too quick, (oh way
ey on a bet. Gold croc-o-diles, (oh way
and they cross the floor. They've got the moves, (oh way
and the met-al bands. When the buzz-er rings (oh way
then you pull it back. Life's hard, you know (oh way
in the do-nut shop. They sing and they dance (oh way
call the "Krem-el-in." And the Chin-ese know, (oh way

1, 3, 5, 6

oh,) they're fall-ing down like a dom-i-no.
oh,) they snap their teeth
oh,) you drop your drink, then they bring you more.
oh,) they're walk-ing like
oh,) so strike a pose on a Cad-il-lac.
oh,) they spin the club, cruise down the block.
oh,) they walk the line

2, 4, 7

on your cig-a-rette.

an E-gyp-ti-an.

like E-gyp-ti-ans.

For-eign types with the hook-ah pipes say,
All the kids in the mar-ket-place say,
All the cops in the do-nut shop say, } "Way oh way oh, way oh way oh,"

Walk like an E-gyp-tian.

(Instrumental)

D.C. al Coda (take 5th ending)

CODA

Walk like an E-gyp - tian.

(Instrumental)

Repeat and Fade

WALKING ON SUNSHINE

© 1985 KYBOSIDE MUSIC LTD. and SCREEN GEMS-EMI MUSIC INC.
All Rights Controlled and Administered by SCREEN GEMS-EMI MUSIC INC.

Words and Music by
KIMBERLEY REW

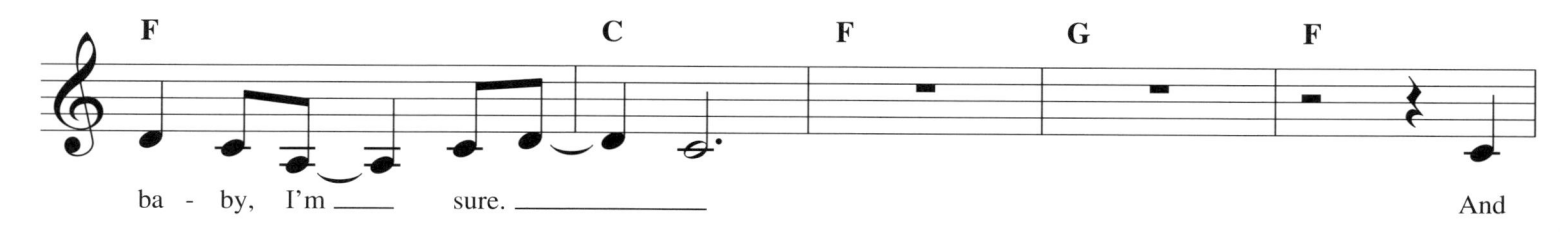

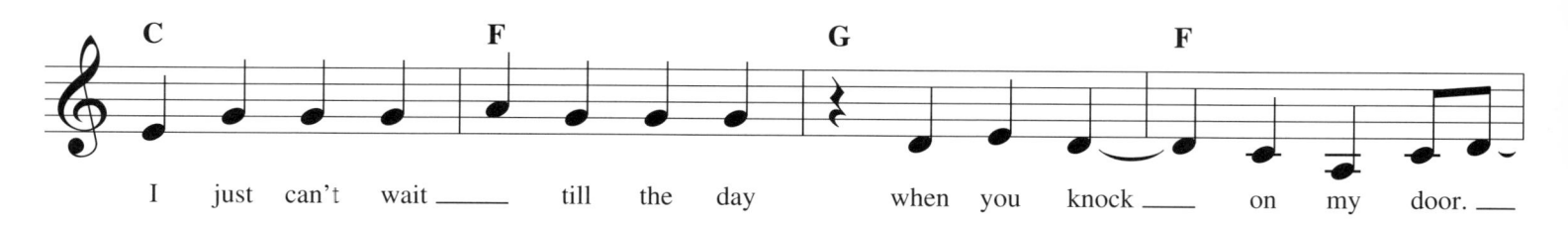

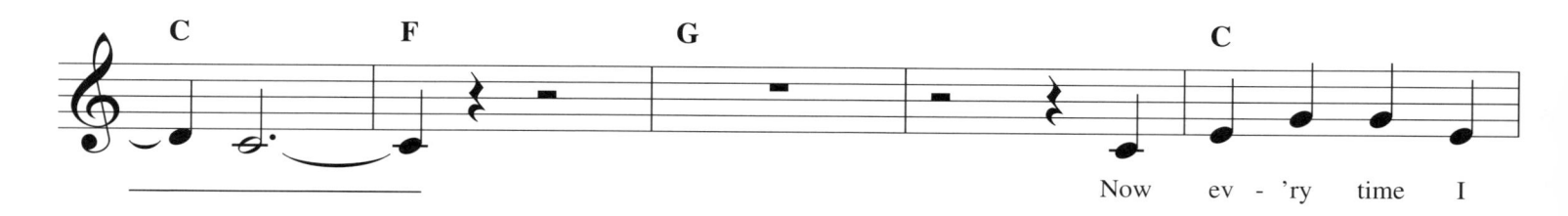

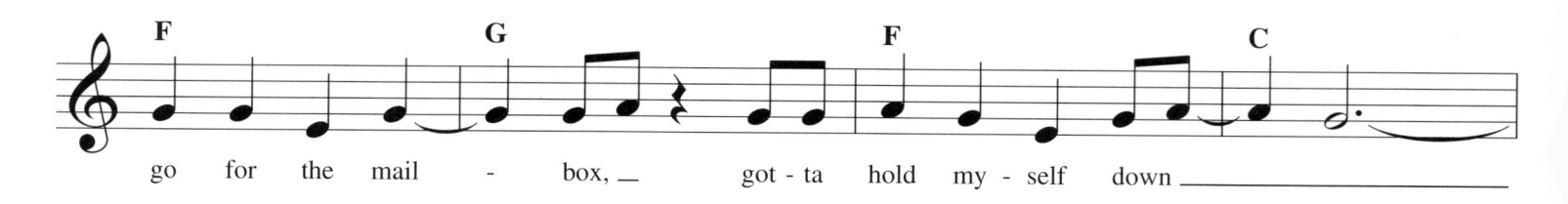

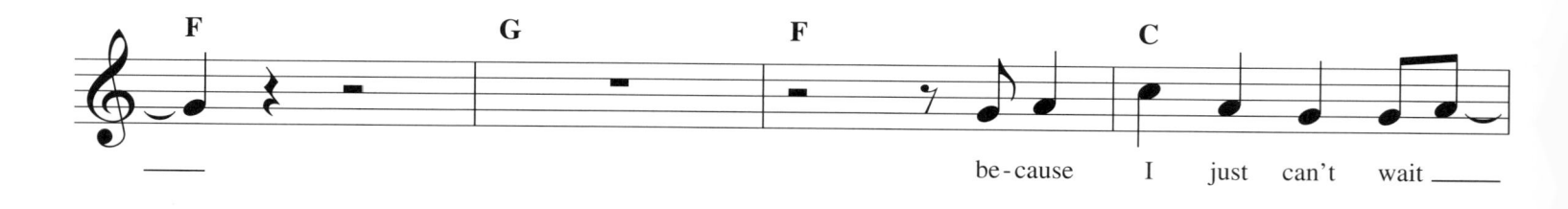

Moderately fast

1. I used to think may - be you loved ___ me, ___ now,
2. *(See additional lyrics)*

ba - by, I'm ___ sure. ___ And

I just can't wait ___ till the day when you knock ___ on my door. ___

Now ev - 'ry time I

go for the mail - box, ___ got - ta hold my - self down ___

be - cause I just can't wait ___

___ till you write ___ me you're com - ing a - round. ___

To Coda 1
F G F
Now I'm walk - ing on sun -
Chorus
G F
- shine. Whoa, I'm walk - ing on sun -
G F
- shine. Whoa, I'm walk - ing on sun -
G F
- shine. Whoa, and don't it feel good?
C F G F
Hey. All right, now. And don't it feel good?
C F G F
D.S. al Coda 1
Hey. Yeah. 2. I
CODA 1
Chorus
G
walk - ing on sun - shine. Whoa,
F G
I'm walk - ing on sun - shine.

F
Whoa, I'm walk - ing on sun -
G F
- shine. Whoa, and don't it feel good?
C F G F
Hey. All right, now. And don't it feel good?
C F G F To Coda 2
Yeah. Oh, yeah.
I'll say it, I'll say it, I'll say it a - gain, now.
And don't it feel good?
C F C F
Walk - ing on sun - shine.
G F C F
Walk - ing on sun - shine.
G F C
Yeah. I feel a - live. I feel the love.

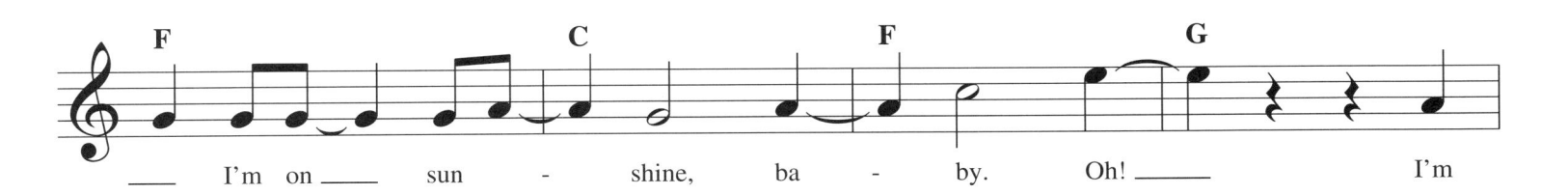

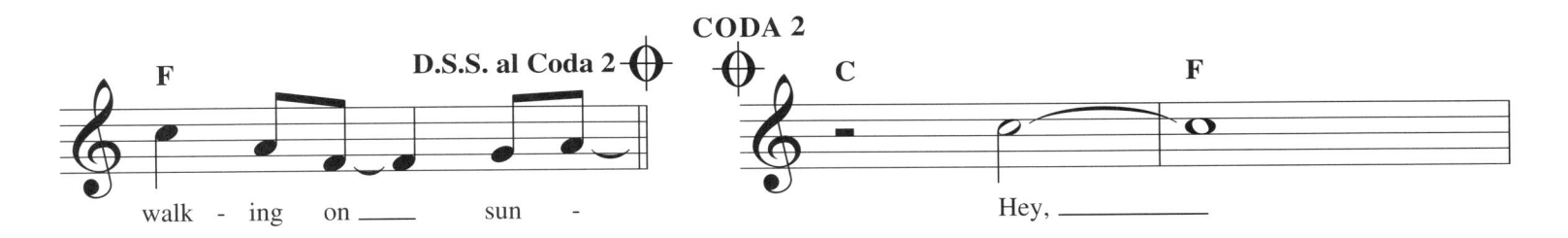

Additional Lyrics

2. I used to think maybe you loved me,
    Now I know that it's true.
    And I don't want to spend my whole life
    Just a waiting for you.
    Now I don't want you back for the weekend,
    Not back for a day. Uh, no, no, no.
    I said, baby, I just want you back
    And I want you to stay. Whoa, yeah, now.
    Chorus

THE WARRIOR

238

Words and Music by NICK GILDER
and HOLLY KNIGHT

Copyright © 1984 Chrysalis Songs and Mike Chapman Publishing Enterprises
All Rights for Mike Chapman Publishing Enterprises
Administered by Music & Media International, Inc.

Moderate Rock

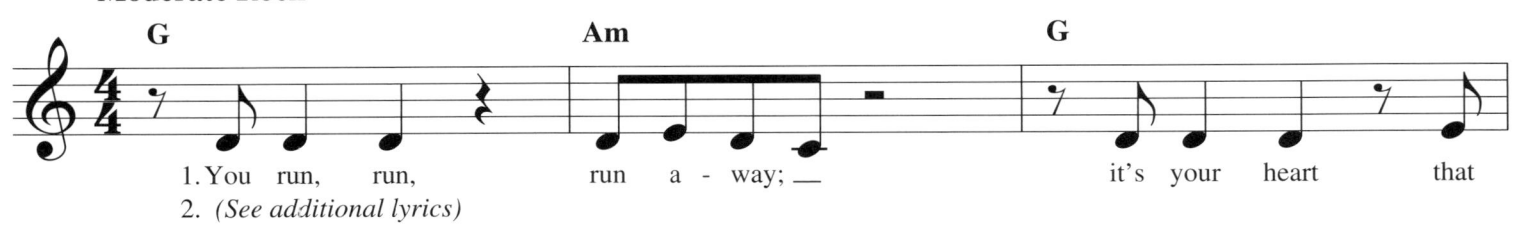

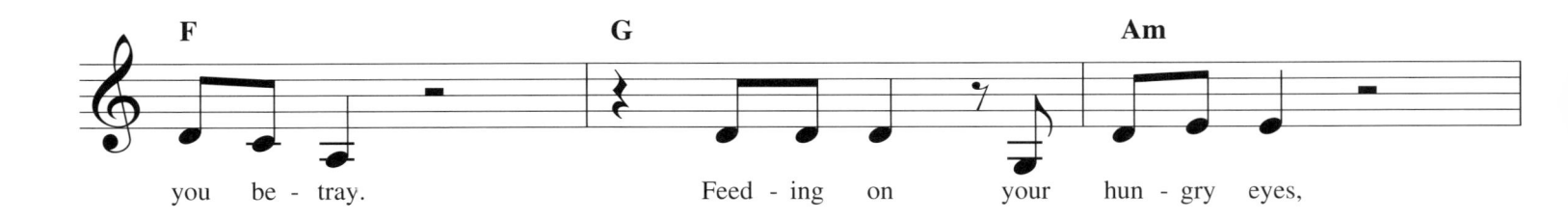

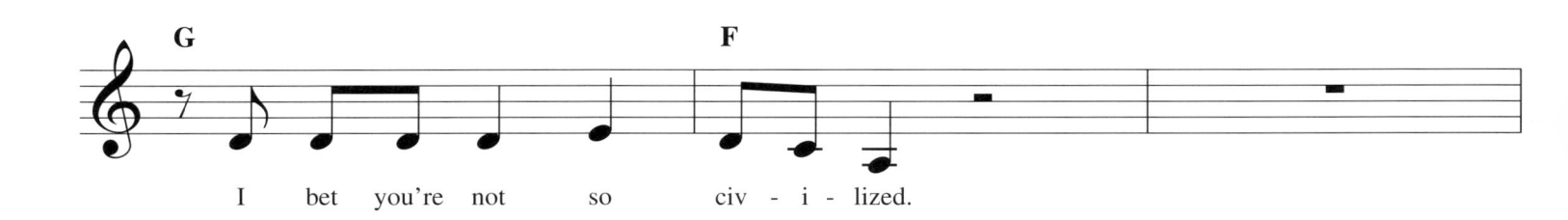

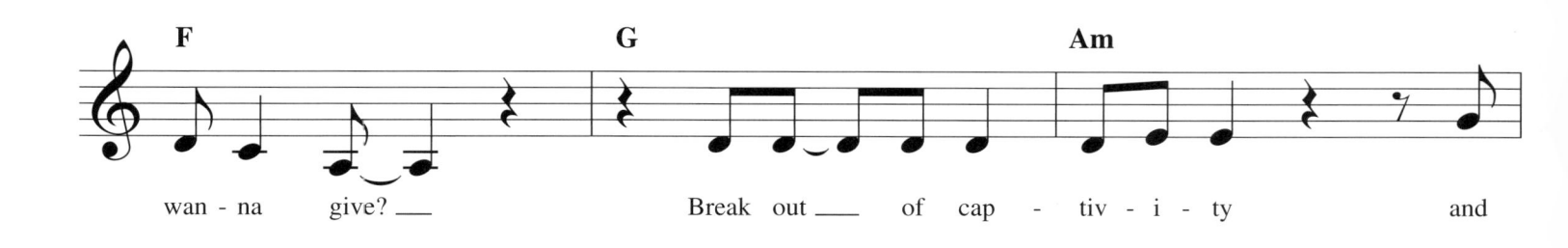

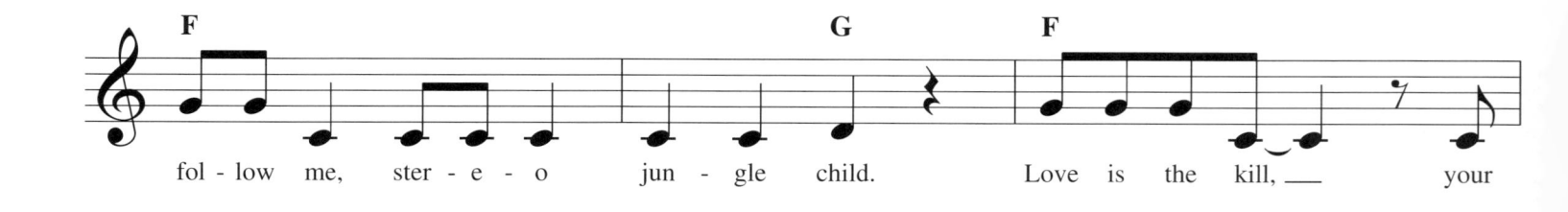

1. You run, run, run a-way; — it's your heart that
2. *(See additional lyrics)*

you be-tray. Feed-ing on your hun-gry eyes,

I bet you're not so civ-i-lized.

Well, is-n't love prim-i-tive, a wild gift that you

wan-na give? — Break out — of cap-tiv-i-ty and

fol-low me, ster-e-o jun-gle child. Love is the kill, — your heart's still wild. Shoot-ing at the walls of heart - ache, bang, bang.

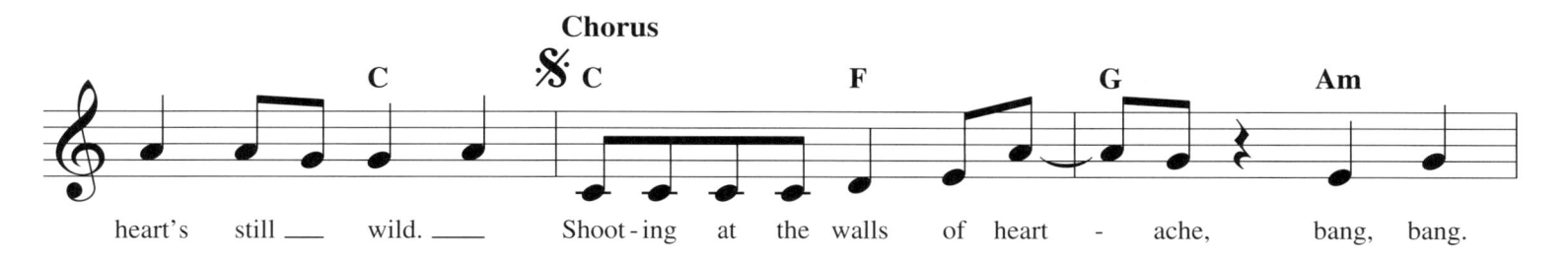

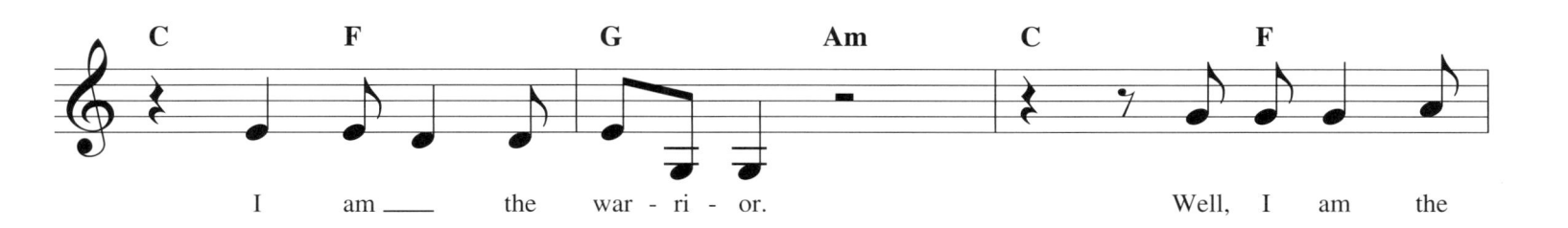

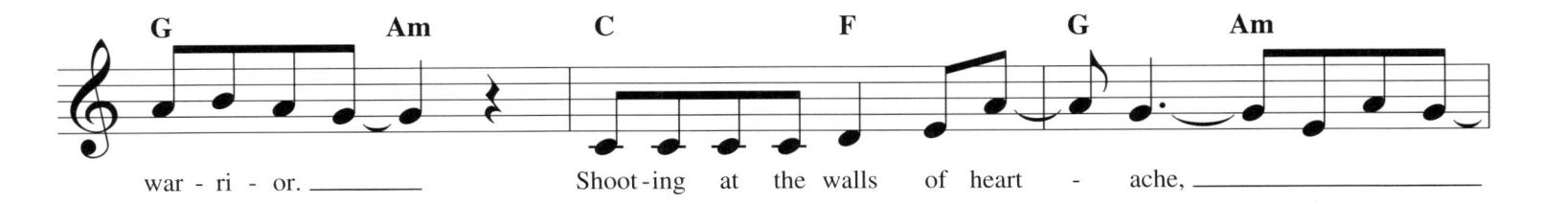

I am the war - ri - or. Well, I am the

war - ri - or, and heart to heart you'll win, if you sur - vive

the war - ri - or, the

1. war - ri - or.
2. war - ri - or. I am the

war - ri - or. Shoot-ing at the walls of heart - ache,

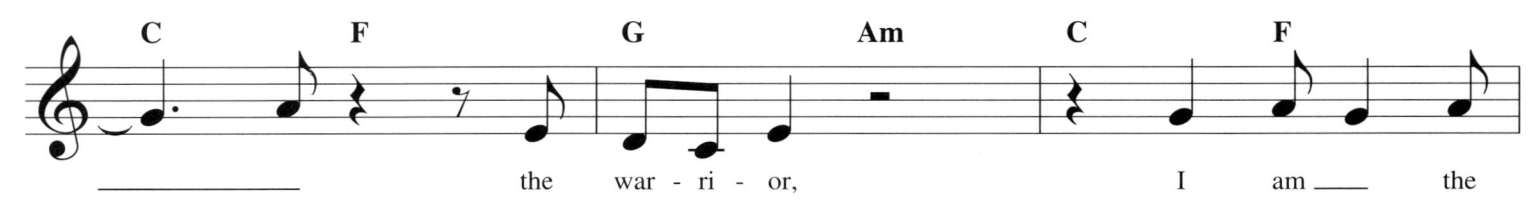

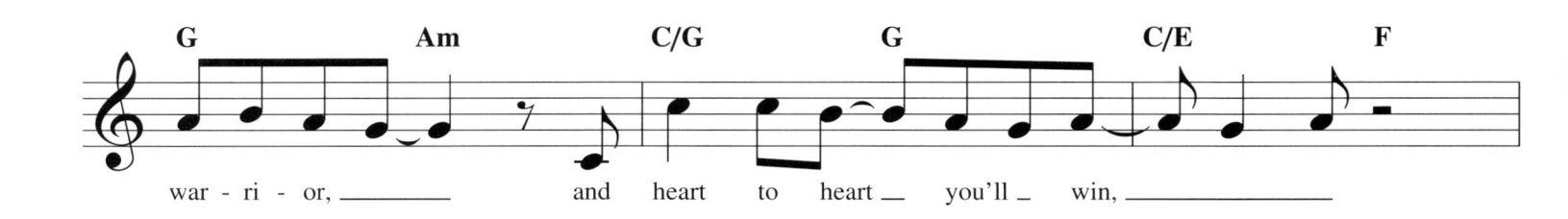

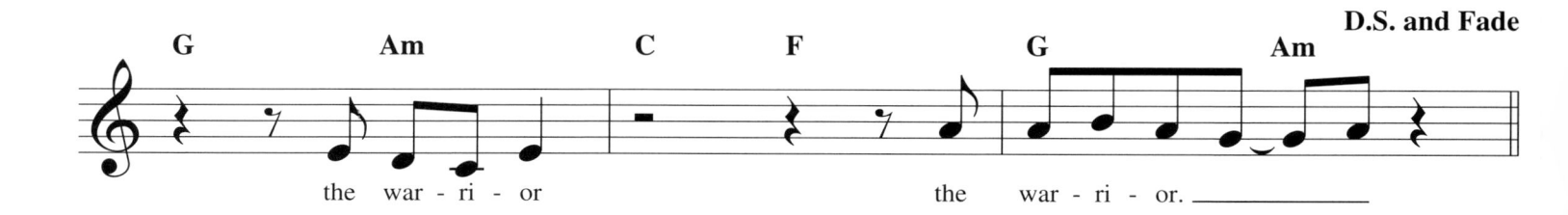

Additional Lyrics

2. You talk, talk, you talk to me,
   Your eyes touch me physically.
   Stay with me, we'll take the night
   As passion takes another bite.
   Who's the hunter, who's the game?
   I feel the beat, call your name.
   I hold you close in victory.
   I don't wanna tame your animal style;
   You won't be caged in the call of the wild.
   Chorus

WE ARE THE WORLD

Words and Music by LIONEL RICHIE
and MICHAEL JACKSON

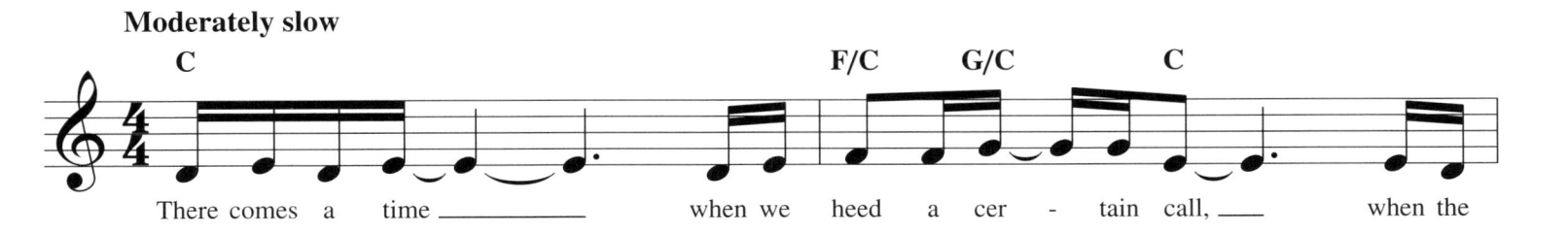

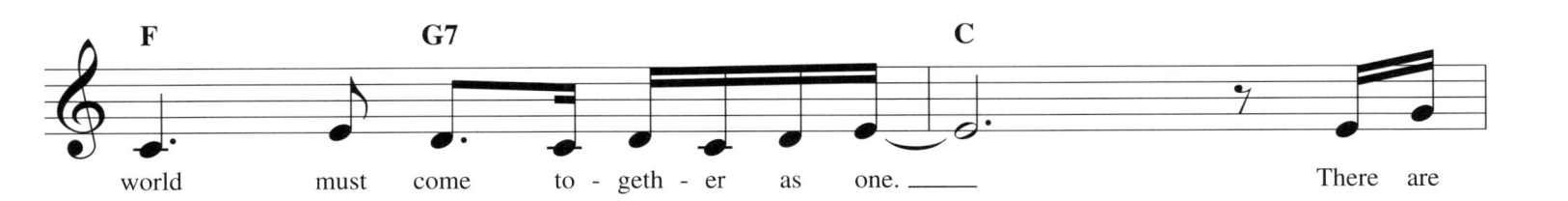

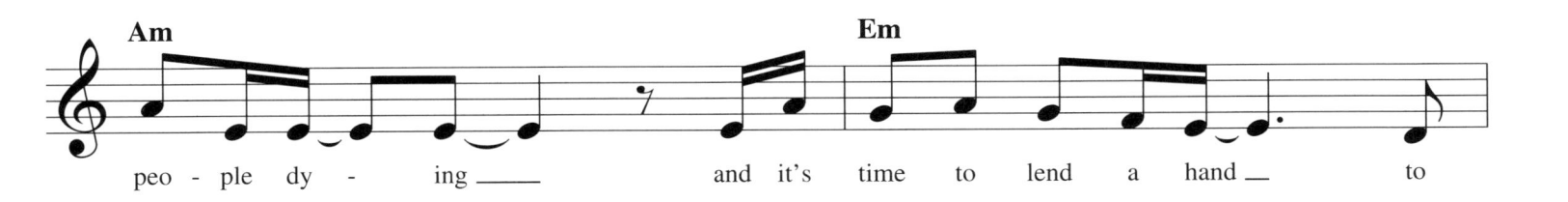

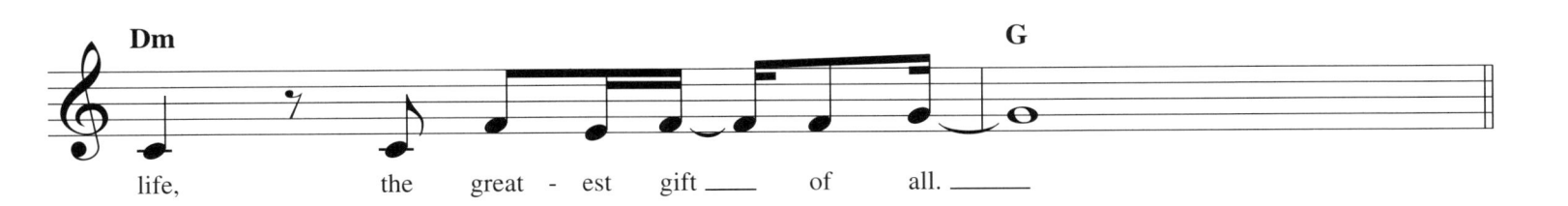

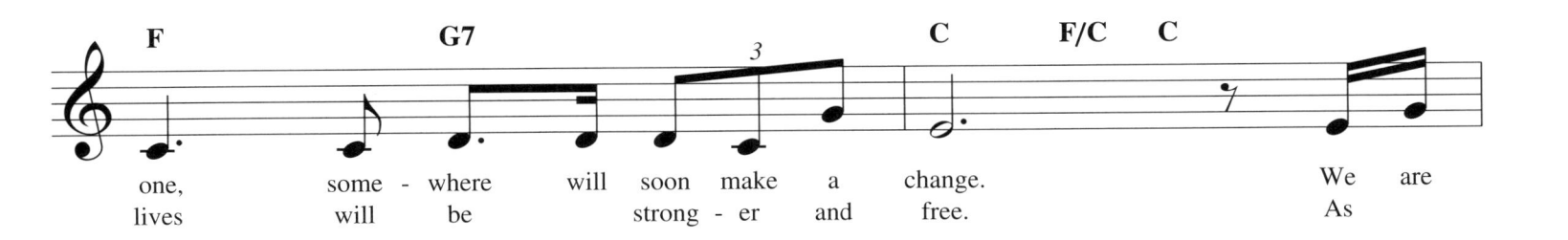

Moderately slow

There comes a time when we heed a cer-tain call, when the world must come to-geth-er as one. There are peo-ple dy-ing and it's time to lend a hand to life, the great-est gift of all.

We can't go on pre-tend-ing day by day that some one, some-where will soon make a change. We are
Send them your heart so they'll know that some-one cares and their lives will be strong-er and free. As

242

all a part of God's great big fam-i-ly and the
God has shown us by turn-ing stone to bread, so we

truth, you know, love is all we need.
all must lend a help-ing hand.
We are the world,

we are the chil-dren, we are the ones

to make a bright-er day, so let's start giv-ing. There's a

choice we're mak-ing, we're sav-ing our own lives, it's true;

we make bet-ter days just you and me.

When you're down and out, there seems no hope at all,

C F/C C Ab Bb
but if you just be - lieve, there's no way we can fall.
C Am
Let us re - al - ize that a
Em Dm
change will on - ly come when we stand to - geth - er as
G F G C
one. We are the world we are the chil - dren, we are the ones
F G C
to make a bright - er day, so let's start giv - ing. There's a
Am Em
choice we're mak - ing, we're sav - ing our own lives, it's true;
Repeat and Fade
Dm F/G C C/E
we make bet - ter days, just you and me. We are the world,

WHAT I LIKE ABOUT YOU

© 1979 EMI APRIL MUSIC INC.

Words and Music by MICHAEL SKILL, WALLY PALAMARCHUK and JAMES MARINOS

Bright Rock

What I like a-bout you, you hold me tight.
What I like a-bout you, you keep me warm at night.

Tell me I'm the on-ly one,
Nev-er wan-na let you go,

wan-na come o-ver to-night. Yeah!
know you make me feel al-right. Yeah!

Keep on whis-per-ing in my ear, tell me all the things that I

wan-na hear, 'cause it's true. That's what I like a-bout

To Coda

you.
What I like a-bout you,
That's what I like a-bout you.

you real-ly know how to dance. When you go

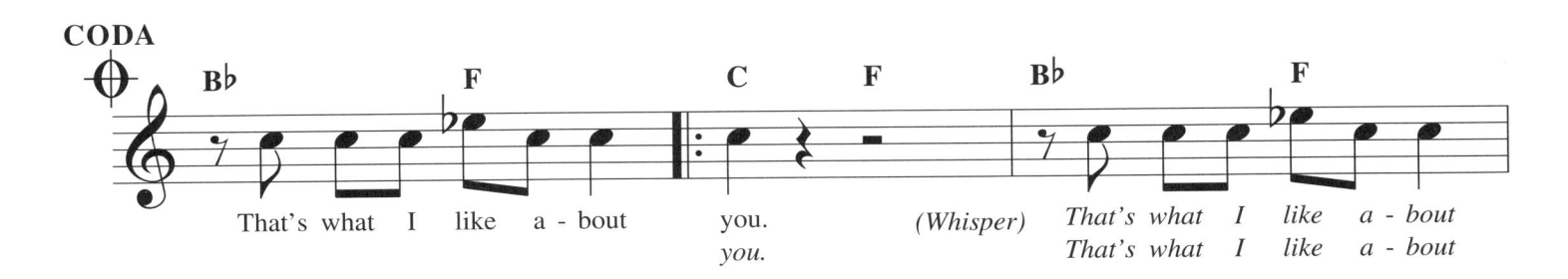

up down, jump a-round think I've found true ro-mance. Yeah!

Keep on whis-per-ing in my ear, tell me all the things that I wan-na hear, 'cause it's true.

That's what I like a-bout you. That's what I like a-bout you.

D.C. al Coda

That's what I like a-bout you.

CODA

That's what I like a-bout you. *(Whisper)* *That's what I like a-bout*
you. *That's what I like a-bout*

you. *That's what I like a-bout*
you. *That's what I like a-bout you.*

When I Think of You

Words and Music by JAMES HARRIS III,
TERRY LEWIS and JANET JACKSON

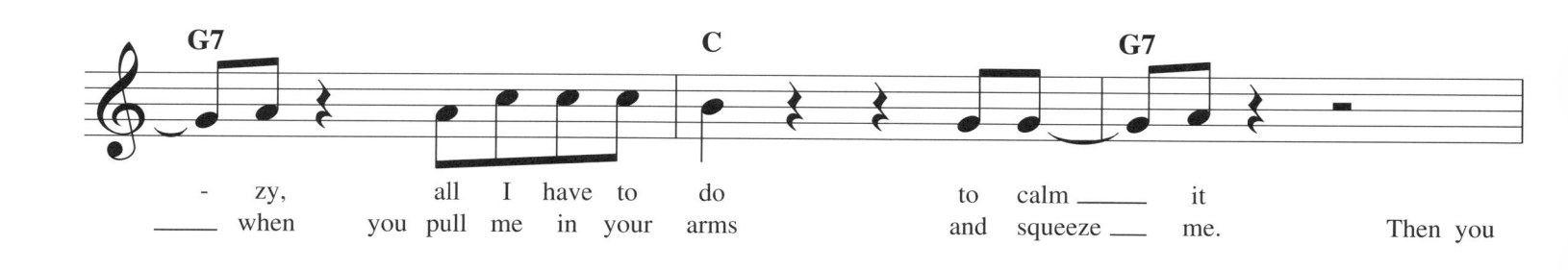

Moderately fast

Ooh, baby, any time my world gets cra-
I just get more attached to you

-zy, all I have to do to calm it
when you pull me in your arms and squeeze me. Then you

is just think of you. 'Cause when I think of you, ba-
leave me, makin' me blue. 'Cause then I think of you, ba-

-by,
-by, } nothing else seems to matter, 'cause when I think of

you, baby, all I think about is our love.

2
C G C G7
think a-bout is our love. So in love. So in love, So in love.
1, 2 3
C G7 G7
So in love. So in love. When I think of
C G7 C
you. I'm so in love.
G7 C G7
I just think of you, if you're not a-round,
C G Am Bm C
oh. When I think of you, so in love.
G7 C
So in love. So in love. So in love.

WHO CAN IT BE NOW?
featured in the Motion Picture VALLEY GIRL

© 1982 EMI SONGS AUSTRALIA PTY. LTD.
All Rights Controlled and Administered by EMI BLACKWOOD MUSIC INC.

Words and Music by
COLIN HAY

Moderate beat

1. Who can it be knock-ing at my door?
2. Who can it be knock-ing at my door?
3. *Instrumental*

Go a-way, don't come 'round here no more.
Make no sound, tip-toe a-cross the floor.

Can't you see that it's late at night?
If he hears, he'll knock all day.

I'm ver-y tired, and I'm not feel-ing right.
I'll be trapped and here I'll have to stay.

All I wish is to be a-lone,
I've done no harm, I keep to my-self.

Stay a-way, don't you in-vade my home.
There's noth-ing wrong with my state of men-tal health.

Best off if you hang out-side, don't come in,
I like it here with my child-hood friend. Here they come,

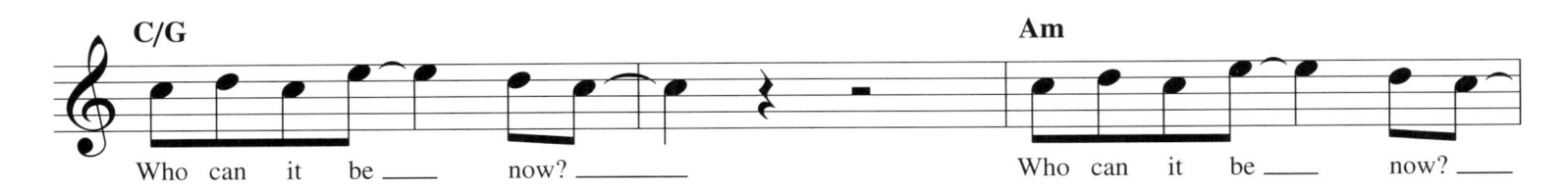

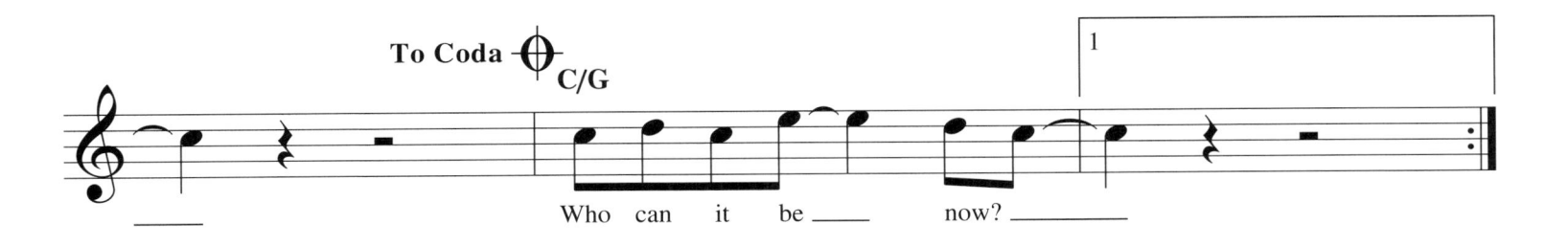

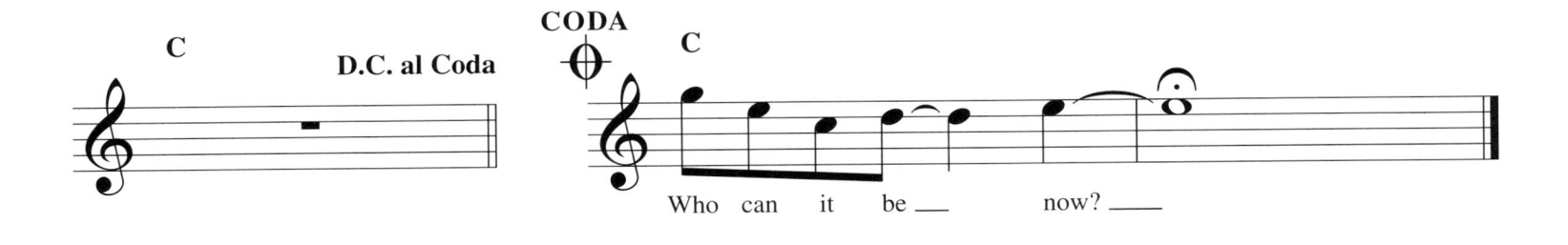

I'll only run and hide.
those feel-ings a-gain.
Instrumental ends

Who can it be now? Who can it be now? Who can it be now? Who can it be now?

Is it the man come to take me a-way? Why do they fol-low me? It's not the fu-ture that I can see, It's just my fan-ta-sy.

D.C. al Coda

CODA

Who can it be now?

YOU GIVE LOVE A BAD NAME

Words and Music by BON JOVI,
DESMOND CHILD and RICHIE SAMBORA

Copyright © 1986 UNIVERSAL - POLYGRAM INTERNATIONAL PUBLISHING, INC.,
BON JOVI PUBLISHING, SONY/ATV MUSIC PUBLISHING LLC and AGGRESSIVE MUSIC
All Rights for BON JOVI PUBLISHING Controlled and Administered by
UNIVERSAL - POLYGRAM INTERNATIONAL PUBLISHING, INC.
All Rights for SONY/ATV MUSIC PUBLISHING LLC, and AGGRESSIVE MUSIC
Administered by SONY/ATV MUSIC PUBLISHING LLC, 8 Music Square West, Nashville, TN 37203

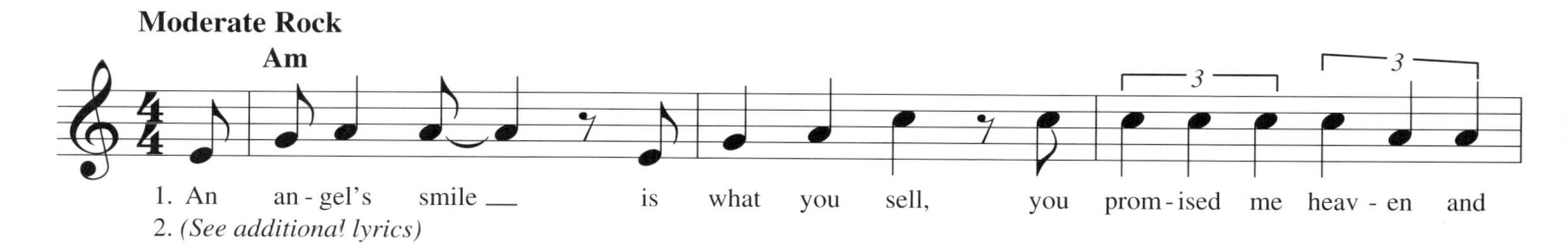

Moderate Rock

1. An angel's smile is what you sell, you promised me heaven and
2. (See additional lyrics)

put me through hell. Chains of love got a hold on me, when

passion's a prison you can't break free. Whoa, you're a

loaded gun, yeah. Oh, there's

nowhere to run, no one could save me, the damage is done.

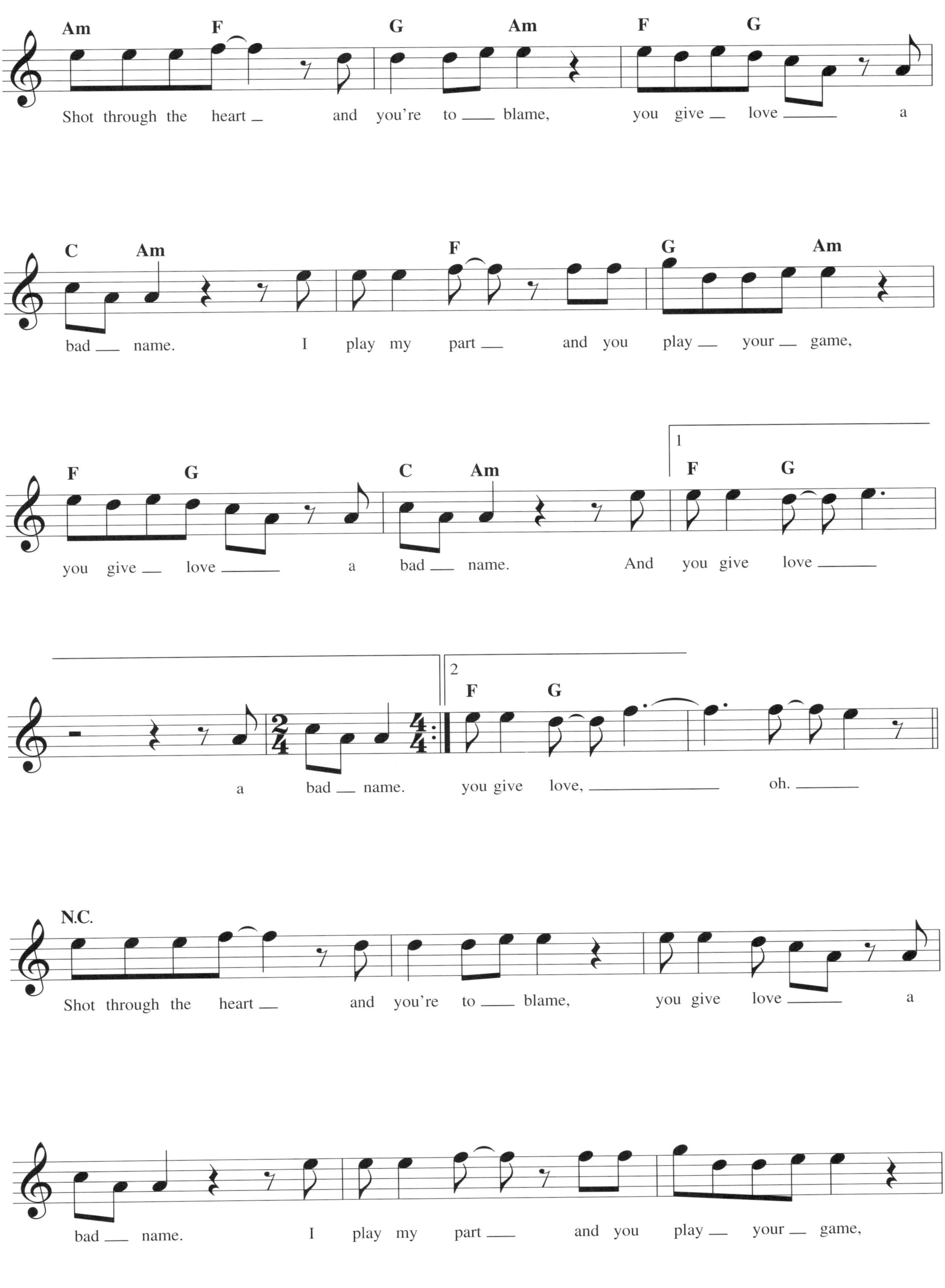
Am F G Am F G
Shot through the heart and you're to blame, you give love a
C Am F G Am
bad name. I play my part and you play your game,
F G C Am 1 F G
you give love a bad name. And you give love
2 F G
a bad name. you give love, oh.
N.C.
Shot through the heart and you're to blame, you give love a
bad name. I play my part and you play your game,

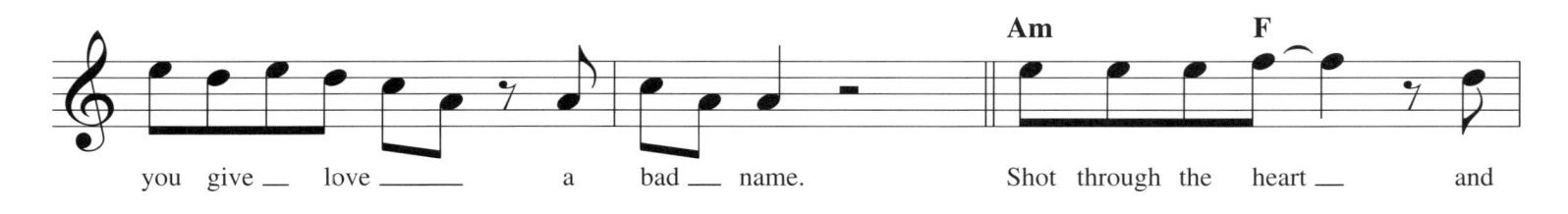

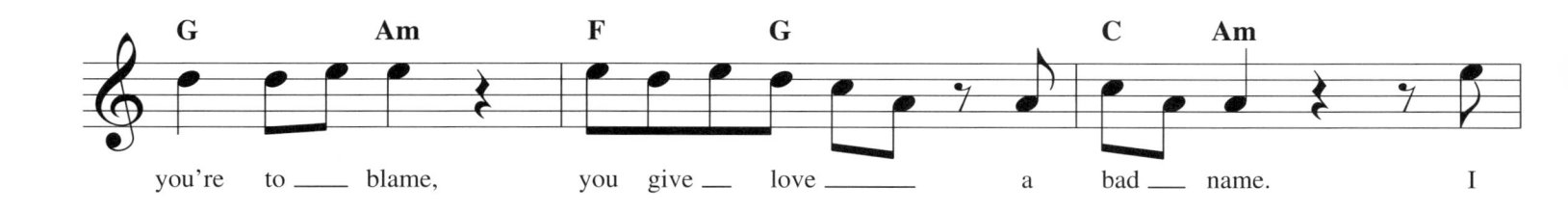

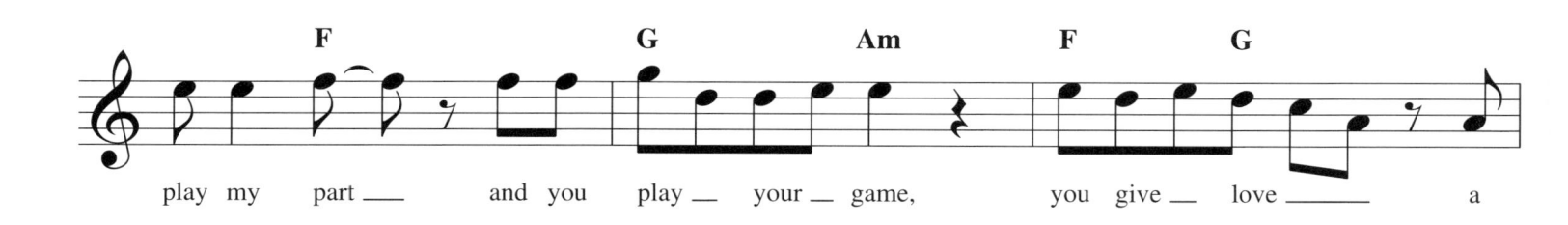

Additional Lyrics

2. You paint your smile on your lips.
   Blood-red nails on your fingertips.
   A school boy's dream, you act so shy.
   Your very first kiss was your first kiss goodbye.

CHORD SPELLER

C chords		C♯ or D♭ chords		D chords	
C	C–E–G	C♯	C♯–F–G♯	D	D–F♯–A
Cm	C–E♭–G	C♯m	C♯–E–G♯	Dm	D–F–A
C7	C–E–G–B♭	C♯7	C♯–F–G♯–B	D7	D–F♯–A–C
Cdim	C–E♭–G♭	C♯dim	C♯–E–G	Ddim	D–F–A♭
C+	C–E–G♯	C♯+	C♯–F–A	D+	D–F♯–A♯

E♭ chords		E chords		F chords	
E♭	E♭–G–B♭	E	E–G♯–B	F	F–A–C
E♭m	E♭–G♭–B♭	Em	E–G–B	Fm	F–A♭–C
E♭7	E♭–G–B♭–D♭	E7	E–G♯–B–D	F7	F–A–C–E♭
E♭dim	E♭–G♭–A	Edim	E–G–B♭	Fdim	F–A♭–B
E♭+	E♭–G–B	E+	E–G♯–C	F+	F–A–C♯

F♯ or G♭ chords		G chords		G♯ or A♭ chords	
F♯	F♯–A♯–C♯	G	G–B–D	A♭	A♭–C–E♭
F♯m	F♯–A–C♯	Gm	G–B♭–D	A♭m	A♭–B–E♭
F♯7	F♯–A♯–C♯–E	G7	G–B–D–F	A♭7	A♭–C–E♭–G♭
F♯dim	F♯–A–C	Gdim	G–B♭–D♭	A♭dim	A♭–B–D
F♯+	F♯–A♯–D	G+	G–B–D♯	A♭+	A♭–C–E

A chords		B♭ chords		B chords	
A	A–C♯–E	B♭	B♭–D–F	B	B–D♯–F♯
Am	A–C–E	B♭m	B♭–D♭–F	Bm	B–D–F♯
A7	A–C♯–E–G	B♭7	B♭–D–F–A♭	B7	B–D♯–F♯–A
Adim	A–C–E♭	B♭dim	B♭–D♭–E	Bdim	B–D–F
A+	A–C♯–F	B♭+	B♭–D–F♯	B+	B–D♯–G

Important Note: A slash chord (C/E, G/B) tells you that a certain bass note is to be played under a particular harmony. In the case of C/E, the chord is C and the bass note is E.

HAL LEONARD PRESENTS
FAKE BOOKS FOR BEGINNERS!

Entry-level fake books! These books feature larger-than-most fake book notation with simplified harmonies and melodies – and all songs are in the key of C. An introduction addresses basic instruction in playing from a fake book.

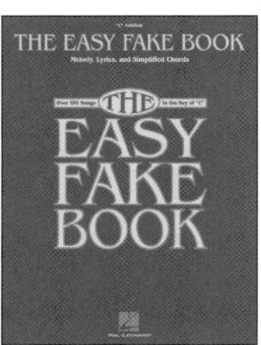

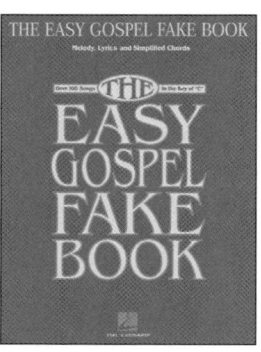

YOUR FIRST FAKE BOOK
00240112...$19.95

THE EASY FAKE BOOK
00240144...$19.95

THE SIMPLIFIED FAKE BOOK
00240168...$19.95

THE BEATLES EASY FAKE BOOK
00240309...$21.99

THE EASY BROADWAY FAKE BOOK
0C240180...$19.95

THE EASY CHRISTMAS FAKE BOOK – 2ND EDITION
00240209...$19.95

THE EASY CLASSICAL FAKE BOOK
00240262...$19.95

THE EASY CONTEMPORARY CHRISTIAN FAKE BOOK
00240328...$19.99

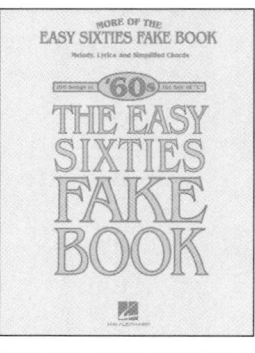

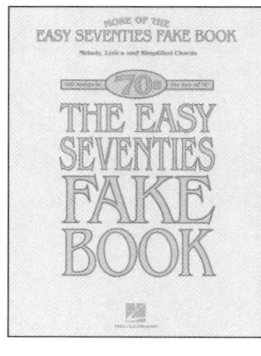

THE EASY COUNTRY FAKE BOOK
00240319...$19.95

THE EASY GOSPEL FAKE BOOK
00240169...$19.95

THE EASY HYMN FAKE BOOK
00240207...$19.95

THE EASY LATIN FAKE BOOK
00240333...$19.99

THE EASY MOVIE FAKE BOOK
00240295...$19.95

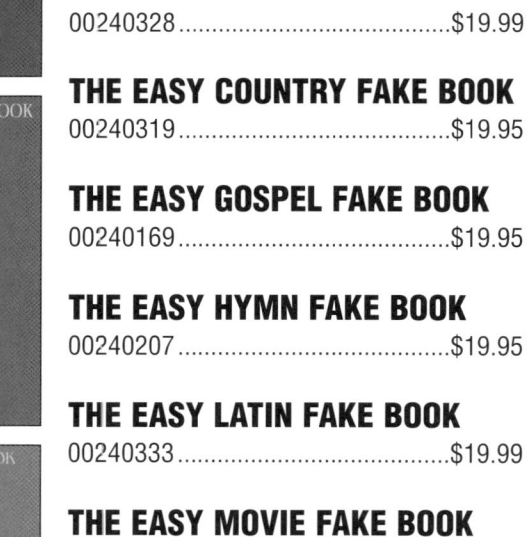

THE EASY SHOW TUNES FAKE BOOK
00240297...$19.95

THE EASY STANDARDS FAKE BOOK
00240294...$19.95

THE EASY WORSHIP FAKE BOOK
00240265...$19.95

THE EASY 1920S AND BEFORE FAKE BOOK
00240336 ....$19.99

THE EASY FORTIES FAKE BOOK
00240252...$19.95

MORE OF THE EASY FORTIES FAKE BOOK
00240287...$19.95

THE EASY FIFTIES FAKE BOOK
00240255...$19.95

MORE OF THE EASY FIFTIES FAKE BOOK
00240288...$19.95

THE EASY SIXTIES FAKE BOOK
00240253...$19.95

MORE OF THE EASY SIXTIES FAKE BOOK
00240289...$19.95

THE EASY SEVENTIES FAKE BOOK
00240256...$19.95

MORE OF THE EASY SEVENTIES FAKE BOOK
00240290...$19.95

Prices, contents and availability subject to change without notice.

FOR MORE INFORMATION, SEE YOUR LOCAL MUSIC DEALER, OR WRITE TO:

HAL•LEONARD® CORPORATION
7777 W. BLUEMOUND RD. P.O. BOX 13819 MILWAUKEE, WI 53213

www.halleonard.com

THE ULTIMATE COLLECTION OF FAKE BOOKS

The Real Book – Sixth Edition
Hal Leonard proudly presents the first legitimate and legal editions of these books ever produced. These bestselling titles are mandatory for anyone who plays jazz! Over 400 songs, including: All By Myself • Dream a Little Dream of Me • God Bless the Child • Like Someone in Love • When I Fall in Love • and more.

00240221	Volume 1, C Edition	$29.95
00240224	Volume 1, B♭ Edition	$29.95
00240225	Volume 1, E♭ Edition	$29.95
00240226	Volume 1, BC Edition	$29.95
00240222	Volume 2, C Edition	$29.95
00240227	Volume 2, B♭ Edition	$29.95
00240228	Volume 2, E♭ Edition	$29.95

Best Fake Book Ever – 3rd Edition
More than 1,000 songs from all styles of music, including: All My Loving • At the Hop • Cabaret • Dust in the Wind • Fever • From a Distance • Hello, Dolly! • Hey Jude • King of the Road • Longer • Misty • Route 66 • Sentimental Journey • Somebody • Song Sung Blue • Spinning Wheel • Unchained Melody • We Will Rock You • What a Wonderful World • Wooly Bully • Y.M.C.A. • and more.

00290239	C Edition	$49.95
00240083	B♭ Edition	$49.95
00240084	E♭ Edition	$49.95

Classic Rock Fake Book – 2nd Edition
This fake book is a great compilation of more than 250 terrific songs of the rock era, arranged for piano, voice, guitar and all C instruments. Includes: All Right Now • American Woman • Birthday • Honesty • I Shot the Sheriff • I Want You to Want Me • Imagine • It's Still Rock and Roll to Me • Lay Down Sally • Layla • My Generation • Rock and Roll All Nite • Spinning Wheel • White Room • We Will Rock You • lots more!
00240108 $29.95

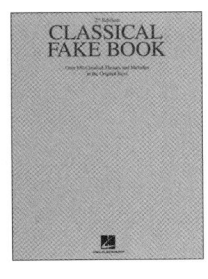

Classical Fake Book – 2nd Edition
This unprecedented, amazingly comprehensive reference includes over 850 classical themes and melodies for all classical music lovers. Includes everything from Renaissance music to Vivaldi and Mozart to Mendelssohn. Lyrics in the original language are included when appropriate.
00240044 $34.95

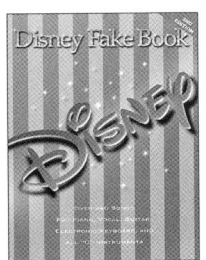

The Disney Fake Book – 2nd Edition
Over 200 of the most beloved songs of all time, including: Be Our Guest • Can You Feel the Love Tonight • Colors of the Wind • Cruella De Vil • Friend Like Me • Heigh-Ho • It's a Small World • Mickey Mouse March • Supercalifragilisticexpialidocious • Under the Sea • When You Wish upon a Star • A Whole New World • Zip-A-Dee-Doo-Dah • and more!
00240039 $27.95

(Disney characters and artwork © Disney Enterprises, Inc.)

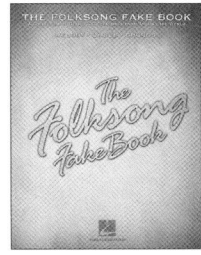

The Folksong Fake Book
Over 1,000 folksongs perfect for performers, school teachers, and hobbyists. Includes: Bury Me Not on the Lone Prairie • Clementine • Danny Boy • The Erie Canal • Go, Tell It on the Mountain • Home on the Range • Kumbaya • Michael Row the Boat Ashore • Shenandoah • Simple Gifts • Swing Low, Sweet Chariot • When Johnny Comes Marching Home • Yankee Doodle • and many more.
00240151 $24.95

The Hymn Fake Book
Nearly 1,000 multi-denominational hymns perfect for church musicians or hobbyists: Amazing Grace • Christ the Lord Is Risen Today • For the Beauty of the Earth • It Is Well with My Soul • A Mighty Fortress Is Our God • O for a Thousand Tongues to Sing • Praise to the Lord, the Almighty • Take My Life and Let It Be • What a Friend We Have in Jesus • and hundreds more!
00240145 $24.95

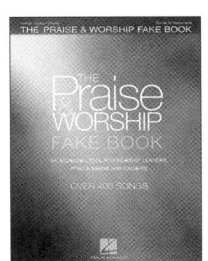

The Praise & Worship Fake Book
400 songs: As the Deer • Better Is One Day • Come, Now Is the Time to Worship • Firm Foundation • Glorify Thy Name • Here I Am to Worship • I Could Sing of Your Love Forever • Lord, I Lift Your Name on High • More Precious Than Silver • Open the Eyes of My Heart • The Power of Your Love • Shine, Jesus, Shine • Trading My Sorrows • We Fall Down • You Are My All in All • and more.
00240234 $34.95

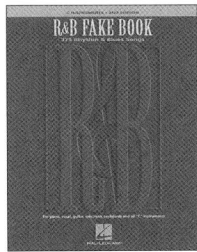

The R&B Fake Book – 2nd Edition
This terrific fake book features 375 classic R&B hits: Baby Love • Best of My Love • Dancing in the Street • Easy • Get Ready • Heatwave • Here and Now • Just Once • Let's Get It On • The Loco-Motion • (You Make Me Feel Like) A Natural Woman • One Sweet Day • Papa Was a Rollin' Stone • Save the Best for Last • September • Sexual Healing • Shop Around • Still • Tell It Like It Is • Up on the Roof • Walk on By • What's Going On • more!
00240107 C Edition $29.95

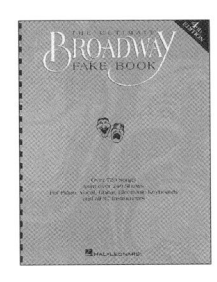

Ultimate Broadway Fake Book – 4th Edition
More than 700 show-stoppers from over 200 shows! Includes: Ain't Misbehavin' • All I Ask of You • Bewitched • Camelot • Don't Cry for Me Argentina • Edelweiss • I Dreamed a Dream • If I Were a Rich Man • Memory • Oklahoma • Send in the Clowns • What I Did for Love • more.
00240046 $47.50

FOR MORE INFORMATION, SEE YOUR LOCAL MUSIC DEALER, OR WRITE TO:

HAL•LEONARD® CORPORATION
7777 W. BLUEMOUND RD. P.O. BOX 13819 MILWAUKEE, WI 53213

Complete songlists available online at
www.halleonard.com

Prices, contents and availabilty subject to change without notice.

The Ultimate Christmas Fake Book – 5th Edition
This updated edition includes 275 traditional and contemporary Christmas songs: Away in a Manger • The Christmas Song • Deck the Hall • Frosty the Snow Man • A Holly Jolly Christmas • I Heard the Bells on Christmas Day • Jingle Bells • Little Saint Nick • Merry Christmas, Darling • Nuttin' for Christmas • Rudolph the Red-Nosed Reindeer • Silent Night • What Child Is This? • more.
00240045 $24.95

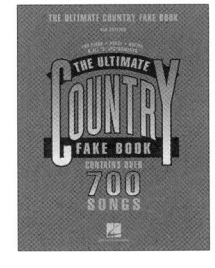

The Ultimate Country Fake Book – 5th Edition
This book includes over 700 of your favorite country hits: Always on My Mind • Boot Scootin' Boogie • Crazy • Down at the Twist and Shout • Forever and Ever, Amen • Friends in Low Places • The Gambler • Jambalaya • King of the Road • Sixteen Tons • There's a Tear in My Beer • Your Cheatin' Heart • and hundreds more.
00240049 $39.95

The Ultimate Fake Book – 4th Edition
Includes over 1,200 hits: Blue Skies • Body and Soul • Endless Love • A Foggy Day • Isn't It Romantic? • Memory • Mona Lisa • Moon River • Operator • Piano Man • Roxanne • Satin Doll • Shout • Small World • Speak Softly, Love • Strawberry Fields Forever • Tears in Heaven • Unforgettable • hundreds more!

00240024	C Edition	$49.95
00240026	B♭ Edition	$49.95
00240025	E♭ Edition	$49.95

The Ultimate Pop/Rock Fake Book – 4th Edition
Over 600 pop standards and contemporary hits, including: All Shook Up • Another One Bites the Dust • Crying • Don't Know Much • Dust in the Wind • Earth Angel • Every Breath You Take • Hero • Hey Jude • Hold My Hand • Imagine • Layla • The Loco-Motion • Oh, Pretty Woman • On Broadway • Spinning Wheel • Stand by Me • Stayin' Alive • Tears in Heaven • True Colors • The Twist • Vision of Love • A Whole New World • Wild Thing • Wooly Bully • Yesterday • more!
00240099 $39.95

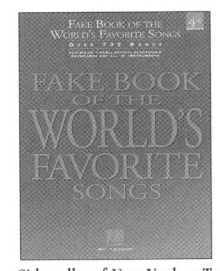

Fake Book of the World's Favorite Songs – 4th Edition
Over 700 favorites, including: America the Beautiful • Anchors Aweigh • Battle Hymn of the Republic • Bill Bailey, Won't You Please Come Home • Chopsticks • Für Elise • His Eye Is on the Sparrow • I Wonder Who's Kissing Her Now • Jesu, Joy of Man's Desiring • My Old Kentucky Home • Sidewalks of New York • Take Me Out to the Ball Game • When the Saints Go Marching In • and hundreds more!
00240072 $22.95

0409